DISEASE AND EMP[

D0077968

Before the nineteenth century, European soldiers serving in the tropics died from disease at a rate several times higher than that of soldiers serving at home. Then, from about 1815 to 1914, the death rates of European soldiers, both those serving at home and abroad, dropped nearly 90 percent. But this drop applied mainly to soldiers in barracks. Soldiers on campaign, especially in the tropics, continued to die from disease at rates as high as ever, in sharp contrast to the drop in barracks death rates.

This book examines the practice of military medicine during the conquest of Africa, especially during the 1880s and 1890s. Curtin examines what was done, what was not done, and the impact of doctors' successes and failures on the willingness of Europeans to embark on imperial adventures.

DISEASE AND EMPIRE

THE HEALTH OF EUROPEAN TROOPS IN THE CONQUEST OF AFRICA

PHILIP D. CURTIN

CAMBRIDGE
UNIVERSITY PRESS

PUBLISHED BY THE PRESS SYNDICATE OF THE UNIVERSITY OF CAMBRIDGE
The Pitt Building, Trumpington Street, Cambridge CB2 1RP, United Kingdom

CAMBRIDGE UNIVERSITY PRESS
The Edinburgh Building, Cambridge CB2 1RP, United Kingdom
http://www.cup.cam.ac.uk
40 West 20th Street, New York, NY 10011-4211, USA
http://www.cup.org
10 Stamford Road, Oakleigh, Melbourne 3166, Australia

First published 1998

Printed in the United States of America

Typeset in Palatino inQuark XPress™ [JH]

Library of Congress Cataloguing-in-Publication Data is available.

*A catalog record for this book is available from
the British Library*

ISBN 0-521-59169-4   hardback
ISBN 0-521-59835-4   paperback

CONTENTS

A picture gallery falls between pages 174 and 175.

v

TABLES, FIGURES, AND MAPS

Tables

Appendix Tables

PREFACE

Books tend to grow and change in mysterious ways. This one began as an exploration of a hypothesis about a possible relationship between the European drive for the conquest of Africa and the remarkable nineteenth-century success of European medicine in keeping soldiers alive in tropical conditions.

In the tropical world before that time, European soldiers had died from disease at much higher rates than they did on home service – typically four or five times the death rate in Europe. Then, military death rates began a spectacular decline that continued through the First World War and beyond. The drop in death rates overseas was especially sharp from the 1840s to the beginning of the First World War. The first major decline took place between the 1840s and the 1860s, and the trend was clear by the 1870s (Figure 0.1 and Appendix Table A0.1).

The two largest European overseas armies were the French in Algeria and the British in India. Over these two decades, the French military death rate in Algeria dropped by 60 per thousand; the rate for British troops in India dropped by 22 per thousand; and the change was equally impressive in other tropical territories, such as the British West Indies or the Dutch East Indies.[1] These changes suggested the hypothesis that because of lower mortality of soldiers overseas, tropical warfare was cheaper in lives and money than ever before, and if that were the case, it might well have made Europeans more willing than ever before to undertake such imperial adventures as the conquest of Africa.[2]

The timing is significant. The conventional Age of Imperialism began with the 1870s, and the conquest of Africa began in the 1880s. But the link between imperialism and the achievements of tropical medicine turns out,

[1] Philip D. Curtin, *Death by Migration: Europe's Encounter with the Tropical World in the Nineteenth Century* (New York: Cambridge University Press, 1989), pp. 7–10, 36, 194–95, 199–202.
[2] Daniel R. Headrick, *The Tools of Empire: Technology and European Imperialism in the Nineteenth Century* (New York: Oxford University Press, 1981). I have argued this case myself in an early edition of P. D. Curtin and others, *African History* (London: Longman, 1978), pp. 445–48.

Figure 0.1. *Disease Mortality of European Troops Serving Overseas – Change Between the 1840s and the 1860s*

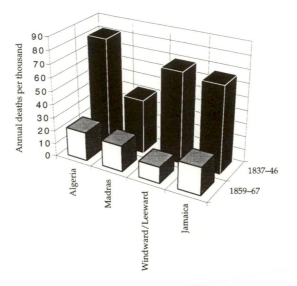

on examination, to be quite different from the original hypothesis. A causal link is far from certain. The desire for tropical empire may well have been independent of the advance in tropical medicine, or it, indeed, may been the principal incentive for research and discoveries in tropical hygiene.

As the simplistic implications of the original hypothesis faded, this book began to turn to the problems in tropical medicine itself – to the relationship between what was known in the best informed scientific circles and the practical applications of that knowledge in the field. The question then became a sequence: What was known? What was done? What was the measurable result in mortality from disease in tropical armies? This sequence turned out to have political ramifications at many levels, often having nothing to do with medicine.

Decision-makers and the public evaluated death by disease in tropical armies in curious and unexpected ways, by present-day standards. The medical achievements illustrated by Figure 1 were officially reported, but they reflect what was possible when treating soldiers only in barracks during peacetime. There, the constraints on medical initiatives were hardly different from those faced by civilian medical practice. By the early twentieth century the medical care of soldiers in peacetime Europe was better than that available to ordinary civilians.[3] Many of the important advances in preventive medicine were pioneered by military doctors, and tropical medicine as specialized field in European medicine began with military doctors serving overseas.

[3] Curtin, *Death by Migration*, pp. 157–58.

What happened on campaign was different. The disease toll for soldiers on campaign was inevitably higher than it was in peacetime, but the constraints on military doctors differed from those of garrison duty. In wartime, military doctors were part of a fighting organization which took it for granted that death in combat and increased death from disease were part of the price victory. Military doctors were also part of a military organization acting under the command of non-medical personnel. Even in peacetime, armies were trained and orgnized to gain military objectives as the first priority. Military medicine as specialized branch of medical practice was formed to achieve this objective.

The performance of military doctors can be judged by at least three different standards. One is from the retrospective standpoint of present-day preventive medicine, where the main constraints are material costs and the state of medical knowledge. A second is the common public appreciation of medicine in the nineteenth century, which viewed the doctors' duty to be that of caring for the sick and curing them if possible, with little concern for the possibility of prevention as a function of medical practice. Finally, there is the perspective of military medicine, where medical practice, both preventive and clinical, is exercised under military command, and for the primary objective of military victory.

This book will touch on all three of these standards of judgment, but it will not attempt a history of military medicine in the European conquest of Africa. That history would require a far more thorough treatment of the British and French armies as military organizations, as well as the stature of the medical departments in each country's army. Those with a primary interest in the history of military medicine should turn to other authorities.[4]

Nor will this book attempt a military history of the European conquest of Africa, which has already been covered by an enormous literature. Even the campaigns dealt with here are examined strictly in terms of the military and political causes and consequences of disease mortality, not as military history. Readers in search of a more balanced military history should also turn elsewhere.[5]

In the last analysis, I have tried to limit myself to the relation between disease and imperialism in the European conquest of Africa. The disease cost of that conquest, and the way policy-makers reacted to it was so vari-

---

[4] See for example, Neil Cantlie, *A History of the Army Medical Department*, 2 vols. (London and Edinburgh, 1974); Albert Fabre (ed.), *Histoire de la médicine aux armées*. 2 vols. (Paris: Lavauzelle, 1984); Lloyd, Christopher, and Jack L. S.. Coulter, *Medicine and the Navy, 1200–1900*, 4 vols. (Edinburgh: Livingstone, 1957–1963); Pierre Pluchon, *Histoire des médecins et pharmaciens de marine et des colonies* (Paris: Privat, 1985).

[5] Thomas Pakenham, *The Scramble for Africa: The White Man's Conquest of the Dark Continent from 1876 to 1912* (New York : Random House, 1991), a recent popular account from the European side only is neverless a place to begin. Brian Bond (ed.), *Victorian Military Campaigns* (London: Brian Hutchinson, 1967) contains chapters on several of the campaigns treated here.

able – and so different from what I had expected at the beginning and this research – that it seemed worth exploring, even through it constitutes only a single aspect of the military history of the conquest, of the history of military medicine, and of the history of African-European interaction at the period of the conquest.

An author accumulates debt of gratitude far wider than he can ever acknowledge, but I am especially grateful to the staff of History of Medicine Division at the National Library of Medicine in Bethesda and to the staff of Interlibrary Loan and the Express departments at the Milton E. Eisenhower Memorial Library at the Johns Hopkins University in Baltimore. Among the many friends and colleagues who have given advice and counsel, I am especially grateful to those who took time to read and comment on major sections of the manuscript. I alone am responsible for the instances where I have failed to pay adequate attention to their good advice. They are: William Cohen, Anne G. Curtin, Steven Feierman, Dale C. Smith, Robert J.T. Joy, and Alexander Sydney Kanya-Forstner.

ABBREVIATIONS

AHMC	*Annales d'hygiène et de médecine coloniale*
AHPML	*Annales d'hygiène publique et de médecine légale*
AHR	*American Historical Review*
AMN	*Archives de médecine navale*
AMPH	*Archives de la médicine et pharmacie militaire*
AMPC	*Archives de médicine et de pharmacie coloniale*
AMSR	*Report* of the British Army Medical Service (later Army Medical Department, still later Royal Army Medical Corps)
BHM	*Bulletin of the History of Medicine*
BMJ	*British Medical Journal*
CO	Great Britain, Colonial Office
DESM	*Dictionaire encyclopédique des sciences médicales*
GMA	*Gazette médicale de l'Algérie*
HM	*History of Medicine*
ICHD	*International Congress of Hygiene and Demography*
JAH	*Journal of African History*
JIH	*Journal of Interdiscipliary History*
JO	France, *Journal Officiel*
JRAMC	*Journal of the Royal Army Medical Corps*
JSSL	*Journal of the Statistical Society of London*
JTMH	*Journal of Tropical Medicine and Hygiene*
MH	*Medical History*
MTG	*Medical Times and Gazette*
PP	Great Britain, *Parliamentary Sessional Papers*
RC	*Revue coloniale*
RGCMSM	*Revista general de ciencias médicas y de sanidad militar*
RHPS	*Revue d'hygiène et de police sanitaire*
RMMM	*Recueil de mémoires de médecine militaire*
RTC	*Revue des troupes coloniales*
TMCSE	*Transactions of the Medico-Chirurgical Society of Edinburgh*
TSICHD	*Transactions of the Seventh International Congress of Hygiene and Demography* (London, 1891)
WHO	World Health Organization
WO	Great Britain, War Office

DISEASE AND EMPIRE

CHAPTER 1

THE WEST AFRICAN DISEASE BACKGROUND

This book is mostly about the changing politics and practice of military medicine in Africa after the 1860s, changes that grew out of older patterns of experience in tropical Africa. Before the 1860s, the European presence in tropical Africa was limited almost entirely to West Africa, with the French and British as the main players; Dutch, Danes, and Portuguese sat on the sidelines. At that time, the disease mortality of newly arrived Europeans was higher than it was anywhere else in the world. It was so high, in fact, that one historical problem is to discover why people were willing to go to a place where the probability of death was about 50 percent in the first year and 25 percent a year thereafter.

The European Presence

By the 1780s, the principal French posts in West Africa were the islands of Saint Louis, at the mouth of the Senegal River, and Gorée, off the Cape Verde peninsula, a few miles from the future city of Dakar. The British post at James Island, within the mouth of the Gambia River, had been abandoned, though some private British traders worked the river trade from privately owned trading posts upstream.

For Britain, the Gold Coast forts were the most substantial establishment in West Africa, though they were not even sovereign British territory, merely rented from African authorities who allowed the British officials *ad hoc* jurisdiction within the forts themselves. Along the Gold Coast, British forts and trading posts were interspersed with Danish and Dutch establishments over a stretch of 300 miles – a shifting group of twenty-five to fifty in all, some fortified, some not. Sometimes, as at Accra, the three European powers had forts within sight of one another; the main British fort at Cape Coast was only eight miles from the main Dutch fort at Elmina. Fortified or not, all were lightly manned, largely because half of any group of the newly arrived Europeans could be expected to die within the year. The survivors died in later years at rates almost as high.[1] All trade with the interior was left to African merchants, many of whom lived in an African town in the shadow of the forts and were the Afro-European descendants of earlier generations of European traders.[2] Some had their own commercial contacts in the interior, while others depended on merchants from the interior to bring trade goods down to the coast.

Nor were the British Gold Coast forts under direct royal authority. In the last decades of the slave trade, they were administered by an organization called the Company of Merchants Trading to Africa. It was not a trading company, but a chartered company in the business of running the forts and trading posts. All merchants trading to Africa were required to join and contribute to the cost, while the company received a royal subsidy as well. Once the legal slave trade had ended in 1809, the forts lost their importance; but the merchants trading on the Gold Coast still had a commercial interest in what trade was left – mostly gold and tropical forest products.

From the 1780s, the Atlantic slave trade came under attack in Europe. In 1794, France briefly abolished both the trade and Caribbean slavery. In 1808, Britain abolished its own slave trade and began a diplomatic campaign urging others to do the same. It was a long struggle, but, by the 1860s, significant slave exports had ceased. The gradual end of this trade forced the former slave-trading powers to reconsider what they could do, or should do, in West Africa.

Beginning in the 1780s, several currents in European thought directed attention to new possibilities for imperial activity. An occasional suggestion through the eighteenth century was that the Atlantic slave trade was inherently inefficient. Why take labor to the tropical Americas, when land of equivalent fertility was available in West Africa, where the labor came from?

With the slave trade likely to end, France and Britain alike began to reconsider the fortunes of their American plantations. For Britain, the loss of the American mainland colonies in 1783 suggested that something might be done in Africa to redress the balance. For France, the impetus

---

[1] Philip D. Curtin, *The Image of Africa* (Madison: University of Wisconsin Press, 1964), pp. 58–87, 483–87; "The White Man's Grave: Image and Reality, 1780–1850," *Journal of British Studies*, 1:94–110 (1961); *Death by Migration: Europe's Encounter with the Tropical World in the Nineteenth Century*, esp. 7–8; K. G. Davies, "The Living and the Dead: White Mortality in West Africa, 1684–1732," in Stanley L. Engerman and Eugene D. Genovese, *Race and Slavery in the Western Hemisphere: Quantitative Studies* (Princeton, 1975), pp. 83–98; H. M. Feinberg, "New Data On European Mortality in West Africa; The Dutch On The Gold Coast, 1719–1760," *Journal of African History*, 15: 362–67 (1974); Jean-Bernard Lacroix, *Les français au Sénégal au temps de la Compagnie des Indes de 1719 à 1758* (Vincennes: Service historique de la marine, 1986), pp. 6–9.

[2] Margaret Priestley, *West African Trade and Coast Society; a Family Study* (London, Oxford University Press, 1969); Philip D. Curtin, *Economic Change in Precolonial Africa: Senegambia in the Era of the Slave Trade*, 2 vols. (Madison: University of Wisconsin Press, 1975). esp. 1:104–121.

came a generation later in 1803, with the loss of Haiti, the most valuable America colony. No new departures were possible during the Napoleonic Wars, but the return of peace after 1815 opened up new possibilities.

For Britain, one problem that followed from the loss of American colonies was that convicts sentenced to transportation could no longer be sent to North America. A plan to divert them to West Africa was proposed, suggesting MacCarthy's Island in the Gambia as the settlement site. The government went so far as to buy the island from the African authorities, but Parliament was impressed by evidence that exile to the Gambia was equivalent to the death sentence. In this instance, the disease environment of West Africa halted a forward move, and the convicts were sent to New South Wales instead.[3]

Humanitarian currents in British thought nevertheless suggested that new colonies in Africa might well help European settlers create a good society and redress the damage done to Africa by the slave trade. These utopian projects merged with a belief that "legitimate trade" could replace the slave trade, to the betterment of Africa and the profit of the traders. Dozens of projects emerged, and several were actually attempted, but the main outcome was the foundation of Sierra Leone. It was first intended as a center for the spread of legitimate trade and as a place of settlement for elements of the "black poor" resident in London. It then became a place of settlement for African Americans who had taken the British side in the War of the American Revolution and found themselves settled for a time in Nova Scotia. They were joined later by Maroons from Jamaica, who had fought unsuccessfully against the colonial government there. Finally, after the Napoleonic Wars, it became a base for the British attempt to suppress the slave trade with a naval blockade, and a place for the resettlement in Africa of slaves captured at sea.[4]

The publicity surrounding slave trade abolition and these new activities in West Africa gave the European public more information about African problems than ever before – including a sharpened knowledge of those posed by the African "climate."

The West African Disease Environment

For many decades, Europeans recognized that tropical Africa was not a healthy place, but statistical measures of deaths per thousand at risk per year were not yet in common use. Death rates were expressed as the number of people sent West Africa against the number who died of disease over an imprecise period of time, sometimes a year, sometimes more. Published records from the period show that, in the first year of the settlement of Sierra Leone, 46 percent of the white settlers died. When the

[3] Curtin, *Image of Africa*, pp. 93–94.
[4] Curtin, *Image of Africa*, pp. 88–139.

Sierra Leone Company took over the settlement in 1792–93, 49 percent died in the first year. Over the years 1804–1825, the Church Missionary Society lost 54 out of the 89 Europeans it sent to West Africa. Exploring expeditions reported similar spectacular losses, but the losses among the survivors were usually lower after the first year or so.[5]

Reports of military mortality came closer to a statistical picture of deaths per year among a measured population at risk. The earliest viable samples of this kind came with the Napoleonic Wars, when both Britain and France sent government troops to West Africa, as they had not done in the era of the slave trade. They both kept garrisons – at different times – on the island of Saint Louis in the Senegal River and on the island of Gorée offshore. Britain kept about 200 men at each post from 1810 until it returned the posts to France in 1816. Over that period, the annual military disease mortality per thousand was reported at 220 in Saint Louis and 179 in Gorée. In 1819 to 1831, after the French took over the two islands, the disease death rate was 191 per thousand. The annual variation was considerable; in 1830, during the yellow-fever epidemic the death rate was 573 per thousand, falling to 146 per thousand in 1832–87, when the epidemic was over.[6]

Over the period from 1819 to 36, British troops of the Sierra Leone command also died at a high annual rate, 483 per thousand, with yellow fever again a major cause. Major Alexander Tulloch, who supervised much of the early British statistical work with military mortality, believed, from a variety of evidence, that the expected disease mortality of foreign visitors in West Africa would be lower, at about 250 per thousand each year.[7]

The principle at work in producing these high death rates was the fact that an individual's pattern of immunity is largely established in childhood. In the nineteenth century, and even today, a person moving to a different disease environment can expect to suffer an increased danger of infection. Childhood diseases, such as measles, kill some, but in Europe or North America measles immunizes for life the great majority of each generation. Other immunities are only partial, but the childhood environment builds a substantial pattern of protection. No human population could sustain itself with annual losses of more than 50 per thousand among young adults.

One measure of the disease cost of movement from one environment to another is called "relocation cost," expressed as a percentage increase in

---

[5] Curtin, *Image of Africa*, pp. 483–87 reports a selection of data of this kind.

[6] "Statistiques coloniale. Mortalité des troupes," *Revue coloniale*, 10(2nd ser.):473–81 (1853); Jean Pierre Ferdinand Thévenot, *Traité des maladies des Européens dans les pays chaud, et specialement au Sénégal, ou essai statistique, médicale et hygiènique sur le sol, le climat et les maladies de cette partie de l'Afrique* (Paris, 1840).

[7] ([Tulloch],), *Statistical Reports on the Sickness, Mortality, & Invaliding, Among the Troops in Western Africa, St. Helena, The Cape of Good Hope, and Mauritius* (London, 1840), p. 7. Also found in British Parliamentary Papers (cited hereafter as PP) 1840, xxx [C. 228], p. 8); Claude Faure, "La garnison européene du Sénégal et la recrutement des premières troupes noires," *Revue de l'histoire des colonies*, 5:5–108 (1920), pp. 48–55.

the death rate, or in some other measure of health. Almost any movement from Europe to the tropical world in the nineteenth century (and earlier) exacted a price in increased deaths. In the early nineteenth century it was around 200 to 300 percent for movement to India, and it rose to 600 percent for movement to West Africa, even under the best of circumstances.[8] As the death rates of Europeans fell over the past two centuries or so, they fell in Europe and Africa alike. In spite of medical science, relocation costs continue. No precise studies have been made for the most recent past, but the relocation cost from Europe to West Africa in the 1990s may well be 100 to 200 percent, though measured from such a low base that it is not a serious threat to the individual traveler.[9]

For Europeans in West Africa the disease threat came mainly from three disease groups: malaria, yellow fever, and gastrointestinal infection. These three disease groups alone accounted for nearly 94 percent of all deaths. They remained the dominant cause of death throughout the nineteenth century, even through the death rate of Europeans in West Africa was to drop by more than 90 percent. From 1819 to 36, the earliest and most carefully documented cause-of-death records available for West Africa cover British troops stationed in Sierra Leone. Deaths from "fevers" (combining malaria and yellow fever, among others) were 84.93 percent of all deaths. Those from gastrointestinal infections were another 8.55 percent.[10] For 1909–13, the best cause-of-death sample available is for French troops stationed in French West Africa. At that time, 56.1 percent of all deaths were from malaria, 2.64 percent from yellow fever, and 21.71 percent from gastrointestinal infections. Those three disease groups still accounted for more than 80 percent of all deaths.[11]

Malaria

The most important killer throughout was malaria, and still is today. Tropical Africa was and remains the most dangerous malarial region in the world. The malarial parasite is a protozoan, of which three groupings are present in tropical Africa. The most common is the *Plasmodium falciparum* group, once thought to be a single species, but now known to be at least five separate but similar species. *Falciparum* probably originated in West Africa, but it is widely distributed through the tropical world today. It is by far the most fatal of malarial parasites. *P. malariae* is also present in tropical Africa. Less fatal than *falciparum*, it is noted for its slow development and long persistence in the human host. The even milder

[8] Curtin, *Death by Migration*, pp. 1–7.
[9] Philip D. Curtin, "The End of the 'White Man's Grave,'? Nineteenth-Century Mortality in West Africa," *Journal of Interdisciplinary History*, 21:63–88 (1990).
[10] [Tulloch], *Statistical Reports*, p. 7.
[11] Curtin, "The End of 'White Man's Grave?' Nineteenth-Century Mortality in West Africa."

P. vivax, a species of Mediterranean origin, is notably rare in West Africa, though somewhat more common in central and east Africa. Vivax malaria is rarely fatal, but it is debilitating and the victim is subject to frequent relapses.[12]

The outstanding aspect of malaria in tropical Africa is the unique combination of mosquito vectors – the most effective transmitters of malaria anywhere in the world. Two members of the *Anopheles gambiae* complex – *An. gambiae strictu sensu.* and *An. arabiensis* – along with *An. funestus,* are responsible for more than 95 percent of infective bites in tropical Africa. All three are intensely anthropophilic, which means that they tend to live around and, if possible, within places of human habitation. *An. gambiae* larvae will grow in any small collection of water (as small as an animal or human footprint) as long as it is in sunlight. *An. gambiae* flourishes best during the rainy season, but much of coastal West Africa has enough rain to keep this mosquito active during most of the year.[13]

A. funestus is the other important vector in tropical Africa. It, too, is intensely anthropophilic but is sufficiently different from the *An. gambiae* to make the two together an effective team. *A. funestus* prefers shaded and still water, often in larger quantities than foot-print size. While *An. gambiae* flourishes in the heart of the rainy season, the eggs and larvae of *An. funestus* can be washed away by heavy downpours. In the West African savanna country, *An. funestus* is found in greatest quantity in the first half of the dry season, after the number of *An. gambiae* has already declined. Together, the two can maintain the transmission of malaria through most of the year, even in the savanna country with a dry season that can last from four to six months. Where stagnant pools are left in a stream-bed by falling water, even *An gambiae* can be a significant vector through the dry season. Europeans associate malaria with rainfall, dampness, and swamps, but malaria can be more dangerous in the savanna country of West Africa than in the forest itself.[14]

In the West African savanna, the annual number of infective mosquito bites per person can run as high as several hundred. It is safe to assume than no one living in the West African forest or savanna for as long as year can escape an infective bite. The governing factors are the availability of plasmodium-infected humans and the density of the anopheline vectors. In the savanna in particular, the density of vectors will vary

---

[12] Leonard Jan Bruce-Chwatt, *Essential Malariology* (London, 1980), pp. 22–30.

[13] Mario Coluzzi, "Advances in the Study of Afrotropical Malaria Vectors," *Parassitologia,* 35(Suppl.):23–29 (1993) and "Malaria and the Afrotropical Ecosystems: Impact of Manmade Environmental Changes," *Parassitologia* 36:1223–27 (1994).

[14] L. J. Bruce-Chwatt, "Malaria in Nigeria," *Bulletin of the World Health Organization,* 4:301–27 (1951), pp. 317–320; Jean Delmont, "Paludisme et variations climatiques saisonnière en savanne soudanienne d'Afrique de l'Ouest," *Cahiers d'études africaines,* 22:117–34 (1983); J. Hamon and J. Cos, "Épidémiologie générale du paludisme humain en Afrique occidentale. Répartition et fréquence des parasites et des vecteurs," *Bulletin de la société de pathologie éxotique,* 59:466–83 (1966), pp. 467–469; M. J. Colbourne and F. N. Wright, "Malaria in the Gold Coast," *West African Medical Journal,* 4:3–17, 161–174 (1955), p. 167.

Figure 1.1.   *Monthly Malaria Morbidity in Tivaouane, Senegal – Data from 1961–62*

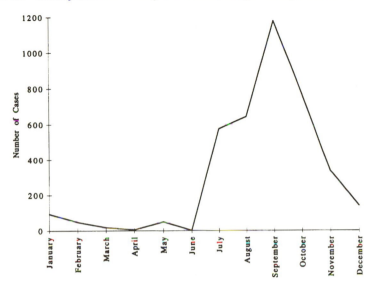

greatly with rainfall, humidity, and temperature and with topographical features that make for standing water.

In the savanna, patterns of vectoral distribution through the year were significant historically, both for Africans and for visitors from the outside. In general, the number of malaria cases will increase greatly within a week to a month after the beginning of the rainy season, typically in June, and will continue to rise throughout the rains, which end about early October. The long dry season till the following June can be divided into a relatively cool dry season lasting into January or early February, followed by a very hot dry season from March into June. In the savanna, the majority of infective bites in a year will fall in the wet season, but as many as a third of the total can fall in the cool dry season that follows, though few will continue in the hot dry period of March to June.[15] In spite of local variation, Figure 1.1, based on data from Tivaouane in western Senegal can illustrate a typical pattern of malarial morbidity by month, based in this case on data from 1961.

The cases reported for Tivaouane would have been mainly among children. Tivaouane had annual rainfall of about 600 mm at that period, which would put it in the savanna zone, as opposed to the sahel or desert-edge farther north. Children in West Africa, south of the desert-edge would be infected with malaria parasites shortly after birth and were frequently reinfected afterwards; if they lived beyond the age of

[15] Delmont, "Paludisme," pp. 122–125.

Table 1.1. *Causes of Death among British and African Troops Serving in the Sierra Leone Command, 1816–37*

	Africans in the Sierra Leone Command			Europeans in the Sierra Leone Command	
Disease Group	Deaths per Thousand	Percentage of All Deaths from Disease	Disease Group	Deaths per Thousand	Percentage of All Deaths from Disease
Eruptive fevers	6.9	26.04	Continued fevers	3.3	0.68
Other fevers	2.4	9.06	Other fevers	406.9	85.13
Diseases of the Lungs	6.3	23.77	Diseases of the Lungs	4.9	1.02
Diseases of the Liver	1.1	4.15	Diseases of the Liver	6.0	1.25
Stomach and Bowels	5.3	20.00	Stomach and Bowels	41.2	8.63
Diseases of the Brain	1.6	6.04	Diseases of the Brain	4.3	0.91
Dropsies	0.3	1.13	Dropsies	4.3	0.91
Other Diseases	2.6	9.81	Other Diseases	7.1	1.48
Total Disease	26.5	100.00	Total Disease	478.0	100.00

Note:
The published data had categories only for "continuous," "intermittent," and "remittent" fevers.
The Sierra Leone Command at this period included the Gambia and the Isles de Los, located off the coast of present-day Guinea-Conakry.
Eruptive fevers at this time would have been almost entirely smallpox.
Continued fevers would have been mainly typhoid fever, with perhaps some typhus.
Other fevers would have included both malaria and yellow fever.

Source: PP, 1840, xxx [C.288], pp. 8–9,16, 31.

about five, they acquired an apparent immunity. The parasite remained with them, normally in the liver, but clinical symptoms were rare so long as they continued to be reinfected with the same species of *P. falciparum*. A low rate of reinfection may bring on light symptoms, and the apparent immunity can be partially lost if a person lives outside the infectious region for several years.[16]

The most common measure of malaria in a population is the spleen rate, the percentage of people in a significant sample who have enlarged spleens, detected by palpitation of the upper abdomen. The World Health Organization's classification of malaria endemnicity is based on spleen rates. The lowest level of endemnicity is called hypoendemic, where the spleen rate in children between two and nine years of age is less than 10 percent. Mesoendemic malaria is indicated when the child spleen rate lies between 11 and 50 percent. Hyperendemnicity is indicated by a child spleen rate of more than 50 percent, and an adult rate of more than 25 percent. Finally, a holoendemic region is defined as one where the child spleen rate rises higher than 75 percent and the adult spleen rate is lower than 25 percent. This pattern of high rates in children and low rates in adults shows the apparent immunity of adults, an immunity developed from childhood.[17]

Yellow Fever

The other important insect-borne disease of tropical Africa is yellow fever, with an epidemiology vastly different from malaria. It is a virus transmitted by the mosquito *Aëdes aegypti*, sometimes called a domestic mosquito because it tends to stay near human habitation, breeding in open containers of water around houses. *A. aegypti* is long-lived, up to four months, but its flight is short – less than a hundred yards – so that urban epidemics tend to spread slowly, often house by house and street by street. In the longer run, *A. aegypti* was as easy to control as the *A. gambiae* group was difficult, and yellow fever ceased to be a serious problem after the first decade of this century.

Yellow fever is hard to diagnose. Many cases, especially in children, show small and variable clinical symptoms, and sometimes none at all. In the nineteenth century, serious adult cases tended to be diagnosed by the characteristic yellow skin color and black vomit, but these signs were by no means universal. Yellow fever was easily mistaken for jaundice, malaria, or influenza.

Yellow fever left its victim with a life-long and complete immunity, which accounts for its epidemic pattern. In order to survive, the virus needed a number of non-immunes collected together within the vector's

---

[16] Bruce-Chwatt, *Essential Malariology*, pp. 58–61.
[17] Bruce-Chwatt, *Essential Malariology*, pp.140–47.

flight range. Once a substantial majority of the people in a town has been infected, the virus can no longer find human hosts and dies out, or transfers to primates in the forest canopy, where it can still circulate, carried by other species of aëdes mosquitos. This fact did not necessarily mean that yellow fever was confined to forest environments. *Aëdes aegypti's* domesticity and long life made it possible for it to travel, especially by ship. Outbreaks of ship-borne yellow fever occurred several times in North America and northern Europe, and in West Africa it could spread north into the savanna as far as the desert edge.[18]

Because most Africans had passed through a light case early in life, yellow fever in West Africa was a strangers' disease, attacking those who grew up elsewhere. Soldiers from overseas were an ideal target – a large group of non-immunes concentrated in one place. The experience of the French in Saint Domingue was a famous case in point. Out of a force of 59,000 sent to suppress the slave revolt between 1791 and 1803, only 10,000 returned to France. The rest died, mainly of yellow fever.[19]

Table 1.1 illustrates the contrasting epidemiology of foreigners and Africans in West Africa over the period 1816–37.[20] The Africans died at a rate barely higher than the normal military mortality for soldiers on peacetime duty in Europe. About a quarter of all deaths were from smallpox. Another quarter came from pneumonia and tuberculosis, diseases for which Africans had only a weak immune response. Gastrointestinal infections came third, accounting for 18 percent of deaths from disease. Malaria was significant, but in fourth place, while yellow fever hardly counted.

The European mortality represented in the chart was not the normal West African experience, but only typical of what could happen during a yellow fever epidemic. Several urban epidemics of the nineteenth century carried away more than half of a particular European community. The epidemic that struck these soldiers on the Gambia in 1825 killed so many that the statistician who wrote it up had to add a special note explaining why it was possible to have a death rate of more than a thousand per thousand mean strength. In this case, between May 1825 and December 1826, fevers killed 279 British soldiers out of a force that was seldom more than 120 and often as low as 40.[21]

---

[18] William Coleman, *Yellow Fever in the North: The Methods of Early Epidemiology* (Madison: University of Wisconsin Press, 1987).

[19] Pluchon, *Histoire des médecins et pharmaciens de marine et des colonies* (Paris: Privat, 1985), p. 366.

[20] The data in this table are the only serious statistical survey of cause of death in West Africa in the early nineteenth century. The numbers of black troops were statistically significant, in the range of 200 to 750 per year through the 18-year period. The European troops, however, were 10 or less in most years, except for the height of a yellow fever epidemic in 1825–29. The total N for the entire period was only 1,843. The reader is warned, but the data are printed here because they are consonant with mortality levels during yellow fever epidemics later in the century. See PP, 1840, xxx [288], esp. pp. 8–9 and 31.

[21] Tulloch, *Statistical Report*, p.13; G. M. Findlay and T.H. Davey, "Yellow Fever in the Gambia," *Transactions of the Royal Society of Tropical Medicine and Hygiene*, 29:667–678 (1936).

Nineteenth-century Europeans believed that most West Africans had a innate, racial immunity. Recent evidence is that all races are equally suscep- tible, with the possibility that some resistance inherited from an infected ancestor could be passed on for a few generations, probably combined with some cross-immunity from previous infection by flaviviruses, such as dengue fever or Japanese encephalitis.[22] In nineteenth-century West Africa, immunity from childhood infection seems to have protected most Africans most of the time, but not always. In the Senegal epidemic of 1830, Africans on Gorée died in at least the same proportion as the Europeans.[23]

Gastrointestinal Infections

"Disease of the stomach and bowels," "dysentery," and "diarrhea" were the common nineteenth-century designations for a variety of diseases that in retrospect are virtually impossible to identify. Military doctors tended to label sickness of any origin marked by loose stool as diarrhea. Loose stools with blood was called dysentery. "Liver abscesses" were most likely to indicate amebic dysentery. Among the water-borne disease groups, French and British doctors of the nineteenth century could usu- ally identify cholera on one hand and typhoid or enteric fever on the other. What is left is a non-specific set of other water-borne infections of the gastrointestinal tract.

Most of the time, these gastrointestinal infections lagged well behind the more serious killers. From 1819 to 36, for example, they killed only about one-tenth the number of British soldiers killed by "fevers." (Table 1.1) For African soldiers in British service, however, they were far more significant, especially in Senegal. There, over the period 1852–73, they were the most important cause of death for African soldiers serving France and French soldiers alike.[24] This tendency to high mortality from dysentery continued in French West Africa. In 1909–13, when sanitary engineering was far advanced in Europe, French soldiers in West Africa died of these infections at more than 5 times the rate for soldiers in France; death from gastroin- testinal infection in West Africa was many times higher than in India, Algeria, the British West Indies, or British West Africa.[25]

Disease Expectations

Given the risk of death in West Africa, it is hard to explain why European governments and firms were willing to risk the lives of their servants and

[22] Thomas P. Monath, "Yellow Fever, " in G. Thomas Strickland (ed.), *Hunter's Tropical Medicine*, 6th ed. (Philadelphia: Saunders, 1984), pp. 176–81;

[23] Thevenot, *Traité des maladies des Européens*, p. 154.

[24] Alfred Borius, "Topographie médicale du Sénégal," AMN, 37:401 (1882).

[25] P. D. Curtin, "Nineteenth-Century Mortality in West Africa," p. 83; Curtin, *Death by Migration*, Appendix tables A16, A30, A44. AMSR for 1914, pp. 144–57.

soldiers. Even harder to explain is why people would voluntarily risk their own lives in West Africa. The probable answer is a combination of ignorance, coercion, and conditions of life in Europe that seemed to be intolerable. Most of the European soldiers who manned the slave-trade forts were recruited by allowing them to substitute service in Africa for punishment in Britain. On the side of ignorance, Europeans knew that West Africa was unhealthy, but not how unhealthy it was. There were no published health statistics, and the investigations of "medical topography" were just beginning. Some may have known better than others, but the fact that the West African disease environment was roughly twice as fatal to Europeans as that of the Caribbean was not a matter of public knowledge in Europe until the 1820s and later.

Psychological defenses against the fear of death were also important. The habit of blaming the victim for his disease was already old in European thought about disease and death. At the deepest level, it drew on the need to believe that we live in a world that tends at least toward some measure of justice. If death from disease were simply random, the world is unjust indeed; and what about the supposed role of an omniscient and just God? Christianity held out the afterlife as consolation, but many believers still held onto a hope for some measure of justice in this world as well.

In medicine, the humoral theory promised some measure of control. If, as ancient Greek cosmology suggested, the world was made up of the four basic elements – earth, air, fire, and water – these elements were represented in the human body as four humors: blood, phlegm, black bile, and yellow bile. Some measure of human control was therefore available by manipulating the basic qualities – hot and cold, wet and dry – that affected the humors.

These concepts had many ramifications in medical thought. One way to deal with the special perils of the tropical world was to elaborate a set of hygiene rules for self-protection. Most of them stressed the importance of careful attention to perspiration, diet, liquid intake, heat, and cold – with emphasis on moderation and regularity. Specific injunctions varied from one authority to another. With so little agreement, it was easy to assume that any victim of a tropical illness had somehow broken one rule or another. He might have acted unknowingly, but his own actions were the cause of his illness, making it in some degree his own fault; the lists of hygiene rules were so long that it was easy to blunder.[26]

Neither the general public nor the medical profession understood clearly that certain disease environments would exact a measurable price in death from disease, a price that could be predicted. A few astute observers on "the Coast" did, however, recognize the psychological need

---

[26] Philip D. Curtin, *The Image of Africa*. pp. 77–80, 190–93. For representative samples see J. O. M'William, *Medical History of the Expedition to the Niger River in 1841* (London, 1843), pp. 16–24, or, for Senegal, Thévenot, *Traité des maladies des Européens*, pp. 256–83.

to account for mortality ". . . by reference to some exposure to the weather, to some defect in the constitution, or some imprudence in the mode of life, of those who have perished."[27]

With the winding down of the slave trade and the opening of new prospects for West Africa, information about high death rates began to spread, in the face of continued optimistic counter currents. A new arrival on the coast would expect a "seasoning sickness." If he recovered, as all hoped to do, he would remain relatively healthy. In much the same way, settlement in a new place was thought to exact a price in disease and death, which in time could be offset by clearing and cultivating the land. Even as the dangers of the unhealthy coast became established, the unknown interior held out the promise of being drier, and therefore healthier.

New Moves in West Africa

With the end of the Napoleonic Wars and the beginning campaign against the slave trade at sea, Sierra Leone improved in British opinion, while the Gold Coast forts declined. Many in government regarded the subsidy for their upkeep as an unwarranted gift to some inconsiderable merchants in a dangerous part of the world. In 1821, the Company of Merchants was abolished, and the forts were transferred to the government of Sierra Leone. That move gave them a marginal role in the campaign against the slave trade and may have saved them from abandonment.[28]

Other and newer schemes grew out of the expectation that the interior of Africa, virtually unknown to Europe in the era of the slave trade, would offer new sources of wealth. The interior was a known source of gold and promised a healthier life for Europeans than the humid coast. The Swedenborgian religious sect added the promise that the inhabitants of the interior were a spiritually superior people. This unrealistic optimism gave mild support to exploration. In 1788, enthusiasts in Britain had founded the Association for Promoting the Discovery of the Interior Parts of Africa, commonly called the African Association. This group actually did send out explorers, who, in 1799, brought back the first direct account of the region between the Gambia and the upper Niger.[29]

The sponsors of the African Association were after knowledge and wealth, but the directors of the Sierra Leone Company were imbued with the same evangelical Christianity that led the fight against the slave

---

[27] R. R. Madden, Commissioner's Report, PP, 1842, xii (551), p. 434. See also "Reminiscences of the Gold Coast, Being Extracts from Notes Taken during a Tour of Service in 1847–48," *Colburn's United Service Magazine*, 3:587 (1850); Curtin, *Image of Africa*, pp. 177–97.

[28] Eveline C. Martin, *The British West African Settlements 1750–1821* (London: Longmans, Green and Co., 1927); Curtin, *Image of Africa*, pp. 151–55, 175.

[29] Mungo Park, *Travels in the Interior Districts of Africa* (London, 1799).

trade. They were dismayed at the mortality of the early settlers, but they trusted that agricultural cultivation would improve the "climate." They also held that the moral purpose of ending the slave trade should not count the cost. Others in Britain meanwhile opposed the Company as a futile effort to suppress the slave trade at too great a cost in lives and money.

In France, new post-war activity lacked those humanitarian overtones. The French at the mouth of the Senegal had been fascinated for decades by the promise of gold in the interior. Occasional governors had been active on the upper river, and orders to build a new fort on the Falémé were issued in 1808. It had to be postponed when the British captured Saint Louis in 1809, but plans were renewed when France regained the Saint Louis and Gorée in 1818, part of French efforts to control commerce on the Senegal, using steamboats in 1819 for the first time in tropical Africa. The French aspired to construct some form of commercial empire in the far interior. The 1819 scheme included grandiose plans for a thousand colonists from Europe and for extensive plantations on the lower Senegal river. As early as 1820, however, it was clear that plantations were impractical. The good land in the neighboring kingdom of Waalo was in use and could not be purchased for the price the government wanted to pay, and labor was very scarce. The plantation segment limped along until it was officially abolished in 1831.[30]

The renewed drive into the interior continued, with special emphasis on the existing gum trade and a hoped-for trade in gold. The Senegalese government backed the river strategy with new forts in African territory and built with the permission of African rulers, beginning with a fort at Bakel. The steamboats also made it possible to bring military pressure to bear on the riverine kingdoms, since the streamers carried light artillery and could bombard riverside villages with impunity. Territorial annexation, however, was postponed until the 1850s.

The French commercial push paralleled that of the British from the Gambia. In 1818, Gaspard Mollien explored to the sources of the Senegal and Gambia Rivers. In 1827, René Caillié reached Timbuktu itself, that ancient symbol of the mysterious heart of the western Sudan. In the 1840s, Anne Raffenel explored widely throughout the hinterland of Senegambia. A few caravans organized in Saint Louis pushed inland as far as the Niger, though African merchants from the interior controlled most of the trade east of the Senegal navigation.[31]

On the Gambia, the British had abandoned their fort at James Island some decades earlier, but in 1807 they founded a new post at Banjul (which they renamed Bathurst) to serve as their own enclave, equivalent to Saint Louis on the Senegal. They matched the French post at Bakel by

[30] Boubacar Barry, *Le royaume du Waalo: le Senegal avant la conquête*, new ed. (Paris: Karthala, 1985).
[31] Curtin, *Economic Change*, pp. 127–36.

reannexing MacCarthy's island, 125 miles to the east. Afro-British merchants from Banjul began to extend their trade into the interior, just as the Afro-French were doing from Saint Louis.[32]

The Disease Factor

However ignorant and overly optimistic European planners had been in the 1780s, by the 1820s they had better information. With the outbreak of yellow fever at Sierra Leone in 1825 and again in 1826, 86 percent of the European garrison died in the first year and another 73 percent of the reinforced garrison died in the second, and the garrison on the Gambia suffered even more severely.[33] In 1826, the British government appointed James Wellington and Herbert Rowan as a Royal Commission to look into the situation on the ground. Their report of 1827 was negative and unequivocal. They could find no evidence that high mortality was related to hygienic misconduct on the part of individuals. Nor was there evidence that clearing, or cultivation, or sanitary regulations in the decades since the foundation of Sierra Leone had made any difference. Nor was any part of the coast deemed especially healthy; in Wellington and Rowan's estimation it was all unhealthy, though mortality varied with the periodic yellow fever epidemics. The only remaining hope was that the interior might be healthier than the coast, and on that point the Commissioners found the evidence insufficient.[34]

The Commissioners also threw doubt on the old belief that black people were immune to the fevers that killed Europeans. They called attention to early mortality figures for the Sierra Leone settlement, data which had been published as early as 1795. During the very first year, 46 percent of the European settlers had died, but 39 percent of the "black poor" they brought from London also died. When the colony was resettled by the Sierra Leone Company in 1792–93, 49 percent of the Europeans died in the first year, but at least 17 percent of the black loyalists from the American colonies also died. Even the immigrant population from Jamaica declined at first before it stabilized and began to rise again.[35]

At the time the Commissioners could not explain these differences, though they are clearer in retrospect. The "black poor" in London had been away from Africa long enough to lose whatever immunity they or their ancestors may have had. Many of the "Nova Scotians" had spent

---

[32] Curtin, *Econmic Change*, pp. 136–52.

[33] [Tulloch], *Statistical Reports*, p. 7.

[34] Report of the Commissioners, PP, 1826–27, vii (312), pp. 12–13, 20, and 104–09.

[35] As of 1826, out of 18,000 slaves recaptured at sea and landed at Sierra Leone, only 11,000 (including childen born to this community) were still alive. Of the 1,100 African-American loyalists landed in 1792, only 578 (including descendents) were still alive. Of the 550 maroons from Jamaica landed in 1800, the maroon community in 1826 had grown to 636. ([Tulloch], *Statistical Reports*, p. 16.)

their childhood in Maryland and Virginia and other then-malarious colonies farther south, but malaria there was probably not even hyperendemic and was certainly not holoendemic. Even the Jamaicans had only a limited immunity, despite their tropical background. The Africans recaptured from the slave ships had come from an African disease environment, but one that was some thousand miles to the east, hence not identical with that of Sierra Leone; they, too, were slow to develop a self-sustaining population. Up to 1840, 63,000 recaptives were landed in Sierra Leone, but their population as of 1842 was estimated at only 50,000, though much of the loss could have been emigration, not disease.[36]

In 1830, a Select Committee of the House of Commons reviewed the Commissioners' report and its main recommendations, largely on account of the disease problem. It decided to reduce the European population of Sierra Leone to the bare minimum while retaining the colony as a British possession. Were it not for the various groups of black settlers, Sierra Leone would have been evacuated. The main base for the anti-slavery patrols and the court to adjudicate the captured slavers was to be moved to the high island of Bioko (then Fernando Po), where the peak, at more than 3,000 meters, promised safety from fever. European soldiers were to be evacuated, and the defense of all settlements was to be entrusted to troops of African origin, serving under British officers.[37]

Not all of these actions were undertaken, though the intention to withdraw was clear. The government did withdraw from the Gold Coast, but it turned over the forts to a new committee of merchants with a government subsidy of only £4,000 a year. In 1830, the committee appointed George Maclean as governor, giving him command of a combined military and police force barely over a hundred men.[38] All in all, these moves were finally a rational response to the problem of disease, and the reaction was international. The decision of the British parliamentary committee in 1830 was nearly simultaneous with the French liquidation of the Waalo plantations in 1831. Some British and some French, however, still hoped for great things from the exploration and penetration of the interior.

African Soldiers

The general retreat of the early 1830s included a shift from European to African soldiers wherever possible, for France and Britain alike. Their long-established practice had been to recruit much of the local defense force by purchase as "castle slaves." They were often brought from a distance on

[36] MacGregor Laird, "Memoranum to the West Africa Committee, 11 July 1842," PP, 1842, xi (551), p. 570.

[37] Report of the Committee, PP, 1830, x (661), pp. 1–5.

[38] John D. Fage, *Ghana: A Historical Interpretation* (Madison, Wis.: University of Wisconsin Press, 1959), p. 73; George E. Metcalfe, *Maclean of the Gold Coast: The Life and Times of George Maclean, 1801–47* (London: Oxford University Press, 1962).

purpose, so that they would have no loyalty to the local population. The British sometimes sent Senegambian slaves to serve as soldiers on the Gold Coast, and Gold Coasters to the Gambia. In Senegal, the French slave soldiers were often called "Bambara," after the ethnic group in the far interior, although many were not actual Bambara.

The mixture of soldiers from Europe and Africa on the Gold Coast varied greatly over time, but the garrisons were small. In 1771, the European troops in all the Gold Coast forts together were about 100 men, company soldiers not royal troops, plus the "castle slaves," who were often more numerous because they died off more slowly. By the early nineteenth century, the local force was about 120 Africans, recruited by purchase, serving under part-time European officers who also served as factors.[39]

In the Caribbean, both France and Britain used government troops, and both tried to increase the proportion of Africans. In the British West Indies, slaves had served as soldiers all through the eighteenth century, usually as a local militia with varying organization. In 1795, the military pressure of the struggle with France seemed to call for a more formal organization under metropolitan, not colonial, control. The result was the foundation of the West India Regiments, organized from the beginning as a regular part of the British army with equipment and status identical to other units recruited in Britain. In this case, however, soldiers were recruited by purchase, often bought directly from arriving slave ships, though the officers and many non-commissioned officers were European.[40]

With the end of the legal slave trade in 1809, the old source of recruits was cut off, but the British navy began to capture slavers at sea. Many recaptives were landed in Sierra Leone, where, with a degree of coercion, they could be persuaded to enlist in the West India Regiments. Between 1808 and the peace of 1815, more than 2,000 of these recaptives had enlisted in the British service – over half of all the men landed from captured slave ships in that period. Some joined local African units, but most were sent off to serve in the West Indies. Until the supply of recaptives began to slacken in the 1850s, the West India Regiments were recruited in this way.

In the mid-1840s, the British began to merge the local corps of African troops with the West India Regiments. Each of the three West India Regiments provided two companies for service in West Africa, in rotation for four to five years at a time, though their European officers and non-coms served in Africa for only a one-year tour.[41]

[39] Martin, *West Africa Settlements*, p. 36–37; PP, 1840, xxx [C. 228], *Statistical Reports on Sickness, Mortality, and Invaliding among Troops in Western Africa, St. Helena, Cape of Good Hope, and Mauritius*, pp. 18–19.

[40] Roger Norman Buckley, *Slaves in Red Coats: The British West India Regiments, 1795–1815* (New Haven, 1979), esp. pp. 68, 130–44.

[41] S. C. Ukpabi, "West Indian Troops and the Defense of British West Africa in the Nineteenth Century," *African Studies Review*, 18:33–50 (1974), pp. 137, 140; Paul Mmegna Ubaeyi, *British Military and Naval Forces in West African History, 1807–1874* (New York: Nok, 1978), pp. 88–112.

In 1819, the British withdrew all European units from West Africa, and the West India Regiments were to take over the defense of the posts. In 1824, however, Britain became involved in a Gold Coast war between the kingdom of Asante and an alliance of coastal kingdoms. European troops returned with predictable results. In the years 1824–26, their annual death rate was 668 per thousand mean strength. Of these deaths, 382 per thousand were from "fevers." Another 221 per thousand died from gastrointestinal diseases. These troops were not on campaign during the whole four years, but their death rate from disease can be taken to be a campaign, rather than a barracks, death rate.[42] After 1829, the West India Regiments took over once more, and in smaller numbers than before, usually five hundred to a thousand for all British possessions in West Africa.[43]

The French lacked the convenience of the Sierra Leone recruiting ground, but they continued their old practice of recruitment by purchase through most of the nineteenth century. The former slave became a soldier for ten to fourteen years, a more limited time than he might have served under another master. Some French officials believed that the purchased soldiers should have been assigned to separate and segregated units, on the model of the West India Regiments, but they were actually added to existing European military units, where the proportion of Africans and Europeans shifted with purchases of new Africans and the death of the Europeans. The proportion of Africans increased through the 1830s and 1840s; the change can be seen in the mortality record of the Senegalese garrison, which dropped from 171 per thousand in 1819, when few black soldiers were present, to 44 per thousand in 1850, when the force consisted of 45 Europeans and 450 Africans.[44]

The Advance up the Senegal and the Niger

The European hesitancy in the face of a dangerous "climate" lasted only about a decade. During the 1830s, the number of British Europeans on the West African coast was lower than it had been for at least a century – a slightly fluctuating total of about two hundred or a bit less, including the military, government officials, and merchants. That number was also less than it would ever be again.[45] In this same period, from 1830 to 1836, Sierra Leone began to recover its reputation for comparative safety from disease. But then, in 1836 and 1837, yellow fever returned – in the dry season, as it often does in West Africa because *Aëdes aegypti* is more indepen-

---

[42] PP, 1840, xxx [C. 228], pp. 6, 19–20.
[43] Ubaeyi, *British Military*, pp. 218–33 contains a year-by-year survey for the period from 1810 to 1873.
[44] Faure, *Garnison européene, passim.*
[45] W. Walton Claridge, *A History of the Gold Coast and Ashanti*, 2 vols. (London, 1964), 1:331. First Published 1915. Robert R. Kuczynski, *Demographic Survey of the British Colonial Empire*, 5 vols. (London, 1948–), 1:187, 318.

dent of rainfall than the malarial vectors are.[46] Again it carried off a substantial majority of the European population, just as, in 1830, it had already killed more than half the Europeans in the garrison of Senegal

In the late 1830s, both Britain and France began to plan forward moves in West Africa, without any medical justification for changing the policy of retrenchment established at the beginning of the decade. The only possible cause for optimism, or for a change of policy, was the lure of the interior, with its twin promises, however false, of wealth and a relatively healthful "climate." Both based their plans on the possibility of exploiting a river route to the interior. For the French, it was the eastward drive up the Senegal, to be extended overland to the upper Niger. The British, meanwhile, would move upstream from the Niger delta, which had been confirmed in 1831 to be the true mouth of that river. Several explorers from Senegambia or from across the Sahara had reached upper Niger, but the river's outlet had been unknown up to that time.

In Britain, the political climate changed in 1832, following the passage of the Parliamentary Reform Act. Middle-class evangelical humanitarians had been a force in African policy since the foundation of Sierra Leone, but in the 1830s and '40s they had more power in Parliament and exercised far more influence in the Colonial Office than ever before, or ever again.[47]

It was they, not commercial interests, who urged the advance up the Niger. They were the main force behind slave emancipation in 1833, and they supported the naval anti-slavery blockade of the African coast. In the late 1830s, it was recognized that the navy, operating largely at sea, was not able to capture more than about 10 percent of the slavers leaving Africa. Beginning in 1837, Thomas Fowell Buxton, principal leader of the anti-slavery group, put forward a new plan to suppress the slave trade, supported by the kind of political agitation that had led to slave emancipation.

The Buxton plan had four principal points, published in detail in two fat volumes. The naval blockade was to be strengthened and moved closer to the coast. It was to be reinforced by new treaties with the African authorities, who would receive financial subsidies from the British government in return for suppressing the slave trade in their own territory. The government was also to encourage the non-slave trade all along the coast, and, finally, it was to urge the African authorities to produce more goods for export, especially cotton. A new supply of African cotton would reduce Britain's dependence on slave-grown cotton from the United States.[48]

The showpiece to implement these policies was a government-sponsored expedition up the Niger river using iron steamboats of the latest design. With light artillery for protection and persuasion, the expedition

---

[46] [Tulloch]. *Statistical Reports*, pp. 9–10.

[47] Curtin, *Image of Africa*, pp. 289–91.

[48] It was first presented informally to the government, but in 1839–1840 Buxton published *The African Slave Trade* (London: 1839) and *The Remedy, Being a Sequel to The African Slave Trade* (London: 1840).

would steam up the river, encourage legitimate trade, sign anti-slave-trade treaties with riverside kingdoms, and set up a model plantation near the confluence of the Niger and the Benue Rivers.[49]

Given the Commissioners' report and the conclusions of the Parliamentary committee of 1830, it is surprising that such a plan could get a hearing. The Niger's record for disease was worse than ever. In 1832–33, the first steamboat expedition on the river had lost 40 of the 49 participating Europeans to disease. A further expedition in 1835 had lost 16 percent of its European staff. Buxton certainly knew about these dangers, though he said nothing on the subject in his book. He did, however, step in to prevent a nephew and two other protégés, who had volunteered for the expedition, from going.

Others found various reasons to play down the danger from disease. Some expected, as missionaries commonly did during this period, that God would save from harm any who went to Africa to do His work. Still others expected dangerous miasmas in the swampy delta region. The expedition, however, planned to pass rapidly through the forest belt and into the drier savanna country. It was common knowledge that tropical mountains were healthier than the low country, and the map Buxton included in his book showed the Kong mountains running across Africa at about the latitude the expedition was expected to reach. Buxton himself believed that people would be safe from malarial miasma once they reached an altitude of 400 feet or higher, though in fact safety from *An. gambiae* rarely begins below 2,000 feet.[50]

In the savanna destination, which the expedition reached toward the end of the rainy season, the combination of *An. gambiae* and *An. funestus* assured as effective a network of malarial vectors as could found anywhere in the world.

Steamers also promised some protection from disease, as well as rapid transportation. The record of the naval anti-slave-trade patrols seemed to show that open water, unlike swampy ground, threw off little or no miasma. The Royal Navy on the African Station had higher disease mortality than elsewhere, but far lower than that of troops on shore. It could be hoped that the protection of surrounding water would extend up the river, as well as along the coast.

Dependence on the rivers, however, posed a special problem. The Senegal was navigable only at high water, from August to November, occasionally into December. On the Niger, water high enough to reach the confluence with the Benue could be depended on only in these same months. In savanna country these months came after the heaviest rains,

[49] Howard Temperley, *White Dreams, Black Africa: The Antislavery Expedition to the River Niger 1841–1842* (New Haven: Yale University Press, 1991), pp. 20–65; Curtin, *Image of Africa*, pp. 298–303.
[50] Temperley, *White Dreams, Black Africa*, pp. 52–53; T. Fowell Buxton, *The Remedy: Being a Sequel to The African Slave Trade* (London, 1840), p. 67.

but they were also the season for *An. funestus*. In the savanna belt, the lowest malaria morbidity tends to occur between February and June, precisely when steamers were most useless. (See Figure 1.1)

The safest part of the voyage was probably in the regions of mangrove swamps in the Niger delta, which the leadership most feared. *An. gambiae, s.s.* is not a swamp dweller, though *An. melas*, another member of the gambiae group, does breed in salt water, and would in all probability have been present in the Niger delta at that time. Recent studies of similar settings, however, indicate that *An. melas*, as a vector for human malaria, is only about one-tenth as effective as *An. gambiae, s. s.*[51]

In 1841, three steamers entered the river in August, the height of the rainy season, with a total of 159 Europeans on board. The longest time any of the steamers spent in the river that year was just over two months, but even for this brief period the death rate was 350 per thousand. Eighty-two percent of the crews came down with malaria, and the case-fatality rate was 30 percent. The standard statistical measure of annual deaths per thousand at risk is obviously impossible to determine. Unlike Tulloch's problem with a high death rate on the Gambia, no reinforcements were involved. The death rate per month gives a measure more nearly comparable with similar expeditions, and the overall monthly death rate in this case, based on the number of days each man was at risk on a steamer in the Niger, comes to 162 per thousand, *per month*.[52] Even so, a statistical problem remains, because we have no information about the mean strength, only the number that set out. As they died, the number at risk was lower, so that to divide the gross death rate by the number of days will slightly underreport the death rates later in the campaign. For such a short period, however, the error from this source should not be significant.

After such a spectacular disaster, one might expect another withdrawal, like that of the early 1830s, or the later French retreat from their effort to build a Panama canal in the face of yellow fever and malaria. The Niger failure was as widely publicized as the plan itself, but withdrawal is not what happened – though the Government did take away the steamers. Even before the expedition sailed, the Government had sent a medical man, Dr. R.R. Madden, to report on British affairs in the Gambia, Sierra Leone, and the Gold Coast. His primary concern was the suppression of the slave trade, but he was instructed to report as well on the mortality of Europeans on the coast.[53]

In 1842, a new Parliamentary Committee met to consider what to do about West Africa. In spite of the Niger disaster, it went ahead with a modified extension of the original anti-slave-trade project, calling for more activity in West Africa, not less. It moved the focus west, recommending new fortified posts on the Gambia and near Sierra Leone. It wanted the Gold

[51] Coluzzi, "Afrotropical malaria vectors," pp. 25–26.
[52] M'William, *Medical History*, p. 126–28.
[53] Lord John Russell to R.R. Madden, 26 November 1840, CO 267 / 170.

Coast forts (then under the merchants' committee) returned to government control, and in wanted several posts abandoned in the past to be reoccupied, including the British fort at Ouidah (now in the Bénin Republic).

The Government took back the forts but found an anomalous situation. The merchants' government under George Maclean had begun to arbitrate disputes between the microstates of the hinterland. From that beginning, Maclean began to sit on certain African courts trying cases in African law, and he then began trying to change the law. By 1840, his drive to abolish human sacrifice was largely successful, and he had built up what amounted to an informal judicial protectorate. In 1844, the new royal government took over where Maclean had left off. It began signing treaties, called "bonds," with each of its neighbors, turning Maclean's informal influence into a formal, if limited protectorate. In effect, only two years after the final failure of the Niger expedition, the British on the Gold Coast had moved on from control of the forts alone to a kind of territorial jurisdiction beyond anything Buxton had proposed.

Regardless of whatever lesson the Niger failure of 1841–42 ought to have taught, the British followed it up with the reoccupation of the Gold Coast forts in 1843, the signing of the bonds formalizing Maclean's protectorate in 1844, the purchase of the Danish Gold Coast forts in 1850, and the occupation of Lagos in 1851, as a base for anti-slave-trade patrols.

Nearly simultaneously, the French also became more active on the Senegal and along the coast, partly a response to the British forward movement, partly a response to the problem of the continued slave trade, and partly a response of merchants from Bordeaux, who saw the advantage Marseille derived from the new colony in Algeria and hoped for some similar advantage in West Africa. In 1838–39, Edouard Bouët-Willaumez was given command of an expedition to evaluate the commercial and strategic positions along the coast, from Gorée south and to the east as far as Gabon. In 1840–42, he proposed three new fortified strong points, and he began signing treaties with African authorities even before the plan had approval from Paris.

In 1843, the project was finally approved, and the fortified *points d'appui* were established at Grand Basam and Assinie, in what was to become Côte d'Ivoire, and at Gabon.[54] In due course, Bouët became Governor of Senegal, where he sought to further French trade from new posts in the "southern rivers," thus laying the basis for the later colony of French Guinea. Most were simple trading posts, protected by a modest fortified blockhouse; in Gabon, however, Libreville was founded on the model of Freetown in Sierra Leone, as a place of settlement for slaves captured at sea by French anti-slave-trade patrols.[55]

---

[54] Bernard Schnapper, *La politique et le commerce francais dans le golfe de Guinee, de 1838 a 1871* (Paris: Mouton, 1961), pp. 51–73.

[55] Hubert Deschamps, *Quinze ans de Gabon: les débuts de l'établissement français,1839–1853*, (Paris, Société française d'histoire d'outre-mer, 1965).

Quinine and Quinine Prophylaxis

Just when the French and British began their advances in the face of a hostile disease environment, medical discoveries began to set the stage for genuine reductions of European death rates in tropical Africa. The process was slow, however, and measurable results for armies on shore were not to appear until the 1860s, and often not until much later.

The changes in medical practice came in two parts. One was the chemical manipulation of natural substances that attacked specific sources of infection. Ipecacuanha roots from South America had been used for some time against dysentery. In 1817, the French chemist Joseph Pelletier isolated emetine, which was widely used in the nineteenth century as an emetic and a specific against amoebic dysentery.

In much the same way, cinchona bark from the Andes had been used as a specific against malaria since the seventeenth century, but the quality of the bark varied, and it had an unpleasant, bitter taste. In 1820, Pelletier and Joseph Caventou isolated quinine and the other antimalaria alkaloids in the bark. It could be used not only to help cure malaria; it could also be used as a prophylactic to prevent some malaria and otherwise reduce its seriousness. The use of quinine spread rapidly in the United States during the 1820s and in Algeria during the 1830s, though its general use in the tropical world was delayed. Prophylactic use lagged behind its use as a cure. It was most effective in a sufficient prophylactic dose, taken daily; but its unpleasant taste discouraged people from taking it either regularly enough or in sufficient dosage, so that acceptance was uneven to the end of the century and beyond.

In British West Africa, prophylactic quinine spread first in naval circles. Since at least 1814, the British navy's printed *Instructions to Surgeons* ordered ships's surgeons to give all men going ashore in the tropics "a drachm of bark in half a gill of sound wine" both morning and evening.[56] Quinine was produced commercially in Britain from 1827 onward and was used occasionally in the 1830s as a substitute for bark. The proper dosage was still uncertain, but the Niger expedition turned up some helpful evidence. The expedition carried bark, but some quinine as well. One of the surgeons, T.R.H. Thomson, experimented with the dosage. The official recommendation had been 2 or 3 grains daily (13 to 19 centigrams), but Thomson suspected this dosage was too small and switched his own intake to 6 to 10 grains (38 to 65 centigrams), or about the same dosage as later came to be recommended. At that rate, he had no clinical symptoms of fever the whole time he was in Africa, but he came down with malaria after he had returned to England and stopped taking the medication.[57]

---

[56] Great Britain. Admiralty, *Instruction for Surgeons of the Royal Navy* ([London], 1814), and the instruction was reprinted in the later editions of 1825, 1835, and 1844.

[57] T.R.H. Thomson, "On the Value of Quinine in African Remittant Fever," *Lancet,* 1846, 1, pp. 244–45 (28 February).

One reason for the Royal Navy's interest in tropical medicine was the size of the force it kept off shore, with occasional landings as part of its fight against the slave trade. Dr. Alexander Bryson studied the medical records of ships on the African station and reports of other doctors practicing on the coast, and, in 1847, published the results, which were transmitted through official channels to the commanders of the squadron.[58] He was able to establish the incubation period for falciparum malaria, the ordinary range of the principal vectors, and to show that the incidence of the fever could be systematically related to the place of infection. This made it possible to order ships to anchor at least a mile from shore and to restrict detached shore service. Any commander who sent boats on shore overnight had to justify the action in writing to the Commander-in-Chief of the African Station.

Before Bryson's investigation, sailors going ashore received an issue of wine and bark only on the days of actual shore service. The new recommendation called for a daily dose of one ounce of wine containing 4 grains of quinine (26 centigrams) not merely on the day of shore service, but to be continued for at least fourteen days thereafter. Three to 5 grains a day was to become standard in British service.[59] It was largely Bryson's influence that led the Director-General of the army Medical Department to send a circular to West African Governors, advising the general use of quinine prophylaxis.

The second important change in West African medical practice over the 1830s and 1840s was the slow battle against dangerous forms of treatment. In France, tropical medicine in the first half of the early nineteenth century was dominated by François Broussais, professor at the Val-de-Grâce hospital in Paris, where most French army doctors were trained. He believed that all fevers were caused by inflammation, arising from some irritation. The proper response was debilitation, to be achieved by a light diet, heavy bloodletting, and heroic doses of mercurial preparations and opium.[60]

British medicine, too, was dominated by variants of the ancient humoral pathology, with its emphasis on the impurity or imbalance of the bodily fluids. Treatment was often an effort to readjust the balance by bleeding and purging. In the eighteenth century, James Brown had popularized a form of treatment that came to be known as the Brunonian System, and it still had followers into the early nineteenth. It held that the problem was one of balance or "tone" of the nervous system. The treatment of disease was therefore designed to stimulate or relax tensions, as required. The

---

[58] Alexander Bryson, *Report on the Climate and Principal Diseases of the African Station* (London, 1847).

[59] Alexander Bryson, "On the Prophylactic Influence of Quinine," *Medical Times and Gazette*, 8(n.s.):6–7 (January 7, 1854); Patrick Manson, *Tropical Diseases: A Manual of the Diseases of Warm Climates*, (London, 1898). p. 125.

[60] Erwin H. Ackerknecht,, "Broussais and a Forgotten Medical Revolution," *Bulletin of the History of Medicine*, 27; 320–43 (1957).

means to that end were the usual assortment of bleeding and purging, stimulants, tonics, and dietary rules.[61]

In the early nineteenth century, the medical practice of blood-letting reached one of its periodic peaks.[62] The human body is generally accounted to contain about 180 ounces of blood. The ordinary blood donation is about 20 ounces. The usual practice in West Africa was to take 20 to 50 ounces at the outset of a fever, and more thereafter to reach a total that could be more than 100 ounces over a few days – more than half the blood the patient had to begin with. Malaria causes serious anemia, and its victims need all the blood they can get.

Malaria also causes serious dehydration. Mercurial preparations like calomel are purgatives, which increase the dehydration, but the usual dosage went beyond a simple purge. Calomel was commonly given to bring on a profuse salivation, which could mean a dosage of 50 to 60 grains a day for four or five days, sometimes reaching as much as 500 grains.[63] At the most extreme, this combination of bleeding and calomel might well cause the death of a healthy person. For patients suffering from dehydration and anemia, these treatments certainly killed many who would otherwise have survived.

These ideas dominated medical practice in Britain into the 1850s and beyond. On the African coast, however, a shift away from heavy bleeding and mercury began as early as the 1830s. In 1831, James Boyle, a naval surgeon who served as colonial surgeon for Sierra Leone, published a new study based on African conditions.[64] Among other things, he gave African fevers new names based on their geographical location, which helped to free him from the authority of medicine as practiced in Britain. For African conditions bleeding and mercury were not recommended, and these practices began to decline. By 1841, only one doctor in eight on the African coast still practiced heavy bleeding, but seven out of eight still used heavy doses of mercury. On the Niger expedition, only light bleeding was used, but calomel was prescribed to the point of salivation. The expedition's case-fatality rate for malaria was 31 percent, which is probably higher than it would have been with no treatment at all. Only a year earlier, boat companies consisting of 130 men on detached anti-slavery service in the Gallinas River had a case-fatality rate of only 15 percent.[65]

[61] R.H. Shryock, "Nineteenth-Century Medicine: Scientific Aspects," *Journal of World History*, 3:881–908 (1957); Wiliam F. Bynum and Roy Porter, *Companion Encyclopedia of the History of Medicine*, 2 vols. (London: Routledge, 1993), 1:335–56; Thomas Trotter, *Medica Nautica*, 3 vols. (London, 1797–1803), 1:334–44.

[62] Bynum and Porter, *Encyclopedia of the History of Medicine*, 2:948–51.

[63] E. Doughty, *Observations and Inquiries into the Nature of Yellow Fever* (London, 1816), pp. 11–12; Nodes Dickinson, *Observations on the Inflamatory Endemic . . . Commonly Called Yellow Fever* (London, 1819), pp. 121–68; Bryson, *Principal Diseases*, pp. 240–47.

[64] James Boyle, *A Practical Medico-Historical Account of the Western Coast of Africa* (London: 1831)

[65] R.R. Madden, Commissioner's Report, PP, 1842, xii (551), pp. 226, 424–25; J. O. M'William, *Medical History of the Expedition to the Niger River*, pp. 126, 294–98.

The opposition to both bleeding and mercury continued to grow. Bryson opposed both, and the popularity of mercury declined through the 1840s. Civilian practitioners in West Africa then took up reforms that had begun with the navy.[66]

In France, a similar shift away from dangerous forms of treatment began in the early 1830s. The circle of Broussais considered quinine an irritant and used it sparingly and only in the later stages of a malaria attack. François Maillot, an army doctor working in Algeria, greatly reduced the use of bleeding. He ignored the prophylactic use of quinine, but he used it to cure malaria with a dosage at approximately the present recommendation. Maillot's discoveries spread through the French army in Algeria, and some authorities believe that the French conquest of Algeria would not have been possible otherwise.

Between the 1840s and the 1860s, the military death rate for malaria in Algeria dropped by more than 60 percent.[67] In Senegal, Thévenot's estimate of troops mortality in the early 1830s was still around 200 per thousand By the period 1857–72, malaria deaths among the European garrison of Senegal were down to 18 per thousand, and total deaths from disease were down to 72 per thousand.[68]

The timing of this major change seems to fit the introduction of prophylactic quinine. The fit is even closer for the Royal Navy on the African station, and it corresponds to the period of Bryson's reforms. Over two decades from 1825 to 1845, annual mortality per thousand was 65, and it remained as high as 58 during the three years 1840–42. Then, in 1846–48, it dropped sharply to 27 per thousand; it was still at 27 for the period 1858–67.[69]

In 1854, the British public learned that some dangers of the African "climate" could now be remedied. MacGregor Laird, whose steamboats had pioneered on the Niger in the 1830s, renewed his former interest in the river with a specially designed steamboat and a subsidy from the Admiralty. The original commander died before the expedition could sail, so that the actual command fell to a naval doctor, W.B. Baikie, with medical arrangements dictated by Bryson himself. The expedition used careful quinine prophylaxis, and, for the first time on a Niger expedition, no one died. The contrast with the expedition of 1841 was so strong that the Niger now seemed at last to promise an open road to the interior. Some authorities even gave Baikie credit for inventing quinine prophylaxis.[70]

For British troops on land in West Africa, however, the change was more modest. For the British non-commissioned officers serving with the

---

[66] Bryson, *Principal Diseases*, pp. xi–xii, 232–34.
[67] Curtin, *Death by Migration*, pp. 36,
[68] Borius, *Topographie médicale*, p. 401; Thévenot, *Maladies des Européens*, p. 195.
[69] Bryson, *Principal Diseases*, pp. 177–78; PP, 1850, xxiv (35), appendix, p. 211; PP, 1867–68, lxiv (158), p. 7.
[70] Curtin, *Image of Africa*, pp. 311, 357.

West India Regiments in West Africa, the mortality remained at 151 per thousand over the whole period from 1859 to 1875. (Refer to table 3.2.) It was not enough for advanced medical circles to know what had to be done; someone in command had to make sure that it *was* done.

Conclusion

In West Africa over the period from the 1780s into the 1850s, a number of contrary trends appear in the correlation of imperial activity and disease. In the first period, before the abolition of the slave trade in 1809, the British rushed forward with both the Sierra Leone project and attempts to explore the continent, full of ignorance and optimism about the cost in death from disease, and about the possible benefits from commerce or settlement. The loss of life was disastrous and disappointing.

The campaign against the slave trade changed the picture for an important class of people in Britain. The humanitarians, who had backed abolition, now had a calling to follow through in West Africa, both to suppress the remaining slave trade and to obtain a settlement place for slaves recaptured at sea. In their view, continued military and naval activity would be justified, even at a price now recognized to be higher than people had reckoned a few decades earlier. The French in Senegal also joined in, though less out of humanitarian sentiments than out of hope for the discovery of gold and the development of commerce in the interior.

By the early 1830s, the representatives of France and Britain on the African coast were forced once more to acknowledge a cost in mortality, from their West African activities, that was still higher than they had realized. They might have withdrawn at this point, but the actual course taken by France and Britain alike was to reduce the scale of imperial activity and to substitute African for European soldiers.

By the late 1830s, renewed and misplaced confidence in their technical capacity to handle the disease problem, combined with renewed and equally unjustified confidence in the promise of the interior, spurred a new appetite for exploration in both the British and the French, with the Niger expedition as its centerpiece. Its failure led to a brief pause, not withdrawal.

By the 1840s, the implicit question had changed dramatically. During the disease crises of the late 1820s and early 1830s, the questions had been: How can we limit our activities to reduce the cost in European deaths? How much empire-building would this disease environment allow? By the 1840s the question now became: How can we protect ourselves in order to carry out the imperial activities we believe to be in our personal and national interest? This change in the phrasing of the central issue was significant. The spread of prophylactic quinine and other empirical reforms actually did reduce by more than half the mortality cost of keeping garrisons in the African tropics and operating ships off African shores.

The disease problem in the second half of the century was to be significantly different, partly because of the medical reforms brought forth by the drive for empire in the first half. But over-optimism was far from dead; it could be built in part on the disease record of two British campaigns in Africa – the Ethiopian campaign of 1868 and the Asante campaign of 1874. Through a combination of luck and good management, each handled its disease problem well enough to make it plausible claim to victory over disease in tropical Africa. In each case, the well-publicized victory was deceptive, but the reputation of these two campaigns lived on to the end of the century and beyond as examples of what should be possible.

CHAPTER 2

THE MARCH TO MAGDALA

". . . to exercize the troops . . ."

Even before the European conquest of Africa began in earnest, two British campaigns in Africa were important in forming European opinion about the disease cost of small wars for empire. One of these was the 1867–68 Anglo-Indian march from the Red Sea coast to the fortress of Magdala in the heart of highland Ethiopia.[1] The other was a shorter march by a smaller force from the Gulf of Guinea to the Asante capital at Kumasi in 1873–74.

Both were hailed at the time as brilliant military achievements under extraordinary leadership, in the first case that of Sir Robert Napier (later Lord Napier of Magdala), in the second, that of Sir Garnet Wolseley (later Lord Wolseley). Both were punitive expeditions, designed to punish the enemy by seizing and destroying a particular objective, with no intention to occupy territory or expand the empire. Both seized and destroyed that objective, then withdrew.

Both were, more clearly than most expeditions, "campaigns to exercise the troops" – elaborate military maneuvers against a real enemy. Each had, of course, a stated political objective, but the training function was more important to the army, if not to all the politicians involved. The new European industrial power was only beginning to be applied to warfare; military planners had only limited knowledge of how the new military and medical technology might work out in field conditions. Such expeditions also had important training functions for junior officers and the rank and file.

These two campaigns fit chronologically on either side of the important army reforms under Edward T. Cardwell, Secretary of State for War in the Gladstone government of 1868 to 1874. Gladstone and Cardwell took

---

[1] The more acceptable transliteration is Meqdela, but Amharic words are especially diffi-cult to transliterate and styles of transliteration are still changing. I will therefore use the form used by the British army at the time, with apologies to speakers and scholars of Amharic.

office in 1868, just after the Magdala campaign ended and left office mid-way through the Asante campaign. The first campaign, mainly waged by the Indian army, showed what a series of recent Indian military reforms had made possible. Hence it provided helpful impetus toward Cardwell's reforms. The Asante campaign was the earliest demonstration of what Cardwell's reforms had accomplished.

The popular press hailed each of these as a model military expedition, though the press was far from unanimous before the fact. The Earl of Derby was to hail the Asante expedition, in advance, as "an engineer's war, a doctor's war." In fact, the Magdala campaign *was* the engineer's war. It was commanded by an engineering officer and hailed by obervers as a triumph of logistical planning. The Asante campaign was the doctors' war, perceived as the first evidence that modern medicine made it possible for European troops to act safely in the tropical world. Taken together, these campaigns seemed to indicate that European armies could be mobilized on short notice and sent, with reasonable expectations of safety, almost anywhere in Africa. They implied, in effect, that the mortality cost of the conquest of Africa would be low, if the European powers ever wanted to undertake it – a verdict that contrasted sharply with the European experience in West Africa in the first half of the nineteenth century. Other than that, these campaigns had a negligible direct influence on the course of African history, though their influence on military doctrine and the practice of imperial wars was to be crucial.

The Military Background

All through the early nineteenth century, the British army had been a gentleman's preserve. Professional training for officers was rudimentary. Commissions and promotion were awarded by purchase. The more technical branches of the service, like artillery, engineering, or the medical department, had lower social prestige than the line regiments, especially the cavalry. Even with the technological progress of the industrial age, the army paid little attention to the development of new weapons; though it was willing to use them, if private firms undertook their development.

Some voices demanded reform of the army in many different areas – from weapons to military organization to military medicine – and others stoutly resisted these demands. In the 1830s, for example, the East India Company developed its own iron-clad steamers for service in south and east Asia, but it did so largely in secret. The secrecy was not to protect against foreign enemies; it was to protect against opposition from the Royal Navy, with its attachment to wooden sailing ships.[2]

[2] See Daniel R. Headrick, *The Tools of Empire: Technology and European Imperialism in the Nineteenth Century* (New York: Oxford University Press, 1981).

Other reforms originated within the central command itself. Beginning in the 1830s, military doctors in France and Britain began systematic programs of medical reform. The changes included the more systematic use of quinine against malaria, statistical studies of the health of the armies, and a serious concern for sanitation, ventilation, and medical topography. In the 1850s, nevertheless, both the British and French high commands were shaken by public criticism of hospital conditions and high death rates from disease in the Crimean War. With the Indian rebellion of 1857, the ill-health of the army in India added another scandal, and the British government appointed a Royal Commission to investigate.

Even though the real foundation of scientific medicine came only in the 1880s and later, with the devlopment of germ theory, army medical departments began to respond to their domestic and overseas health crises with a series of empirical steps, such as ventilation, cleanliness, and quinine that cut the mortality rates of British and French soldiers serving at home and abroad by 50 to 75 percent between the 1840s and the 1860s. (See preface, Figure 0.1 and Appendix Table A0.1)

In the 1860s, demands for military modernization in all fields became still more strident.[3] The American Civil War had been a testing ground for new tactics and new weapons. In Europe itself, the Austro-Prussian War of 1866 was even more impressive, given the easy victory of the Prussian infantry armed with breech-loading rifles. The Prussian victory over France in 1871 underlined the lessons of the past decade, and the sum of these lessons was the realization that industrialization was changing the nature of warfare. The victorious armies of the future would be those with a professional officer corps, capable of using the new weapons and developing still newer ones for the future.

For European forces in Africa, the crucial new weapon was the breech-loading rifle. The British had used some muzzle-loading rifles as early as the 1850s. They were more accurate than the standard musket of the time, but their loading time was long – a weakness shared with their successor, the Enfield rifle. Breech-loading rifles became common late in the American Civil War, and the British army decided as early as 1864 to begin introducing them on a larger scale. In 1866, alarm over the Prussian victory against Austria and the possible American threat to Canada spurred an emergency reequipment with the breach-loading Snider rifles.

The Snider was the first British rifle to have the powder packed with the projectile as part of a single cartridge. In Africa, the Sniders were first used in the Magdala campaign. By 1869, they were issued to all regular troops, and even to some of the militia in Britain.[4] The Sniders had at least

---

[3] For the background of these military reforms see John William Fortescue, *A History of the British Army*, 12 vols. (London: Macmillan, 1930), 12: 520–60. For their influence on the late Victorian British Army see Edward M. Spiers, *The Late Victorian Army 1868–1902* (Manchester: Manchester University Press, 1992).

[4] Fortescue, *British Army*, 12:547–9.

four times the rate of fire of a muzzle-loader, and the rifling in the barrel meant that they could be as accurate at 400 yards as a smooth-bore musket was at 50 – at a time when the Ethiopians, the Asante, and all other armies in tropical Africa were still equipped with smooth-bore muzzle-loaders. In 1869, the hammerless Martini-Henry rifle was distributed to British units on a trial basis. It had a smaller bore, greater range, and greater accuracy than the Snider, and it became the standard weapon in the small wars for empire in the final quarter of the century.

The army in British India had been reformed after the unsuccessful rebellion of 1857. Up to that time, the East India Company had its own armed forces, with 238,000 Indian soldiers and 45,000 Europeans. The Company's European soldiers were recruited in Britain, but they were not part of the Royal Army and they served only the Company's sphere east of the Cape of Good Hope. When Britain abolished the Company's government over India in 1858, it took the company's army and coordinated it more closely with the with the Royal Army. This major reorganization was completed only in 1863.

The Company army had been organized as three semi-separate armies, one for each of the Presidencies of Bengal, Bombay, and Madras. In 1857, the Indian troops of the Bengal Army had been the heart of the rebellion. As a result, the Bengal army was treated with caution and completely reformed. The Indian troops in the other two armies had been mainly loyal, which induced reformers to keep them separate even under Royal command. Separate armies for Bombay, Bengal, and Madras were retained until 1895.

By 1863, the new Indian Army emerged, theoretically reformed, smaller than the Company's army, but more European, with 140,000 Indian troops and 65,000 Europeans. The central command was now in the British War Office, but the cost of the Indian Army was borne by the Indian governments – ultimately by the Indian taxpayers. Many officers of this reformed Indian Army hoped for an opportunity to test its strength, and especially its logistical capabilities, since, in the Crimean War and the suppression of the Indian rebellion, the failure to move troops and supply them efficiently had been almost as notable as the medical scandals.

The East African Background

In Africa, Britain had long-standing relations with West Africa, beginning in the seventeenth century and evolving alongside British participation in the slave trade. Britain also had a strategic concern with South Africa, on account of its position on the route to India. By contrast, East Africa was of no particular consequence, either commercial or strategic. Before the era of steamships, the Red Sea was not an effective channel for navigation. Over the northern half of the sea the winds blew from the north in

Map 2.1.   The Arabian Sea and Vicinity

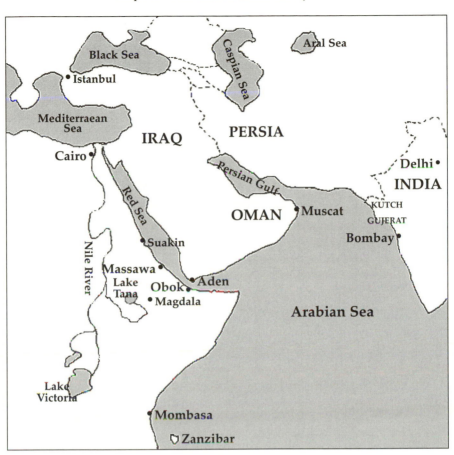

all months of the year. The usual commercial practice in earlier centuries had been to unload in a port like Jiddah, halfway from Aden to Suez, and let camel caravans continue the journey, either to the Nile on the west, or north across the desert to the fertile crescent. Commercially and strategically, as far as Britain was concerned, the Arabian Sea was like a great cul-de-sac, stretching north and west from India and the well-traveled routes to Europe.

Toward the end of the eighteenth century, European interest in the Arabian Sea and the Persian Gulf began to grow. The French invasion of Egypt in 1798 posed the threat of a push eastward along the overland route to India. When the French removed their army from Egypt in 1802, the immediate threat disappeared, but the East India Company, acting through the Bombay Presidency became conscious of possible future danger and began to increase diplomatic activity to add informal influence to the west.

For the Bombay authorities, one possibility was to seek local allies west of the Arabian Sea, allies that could be bound to Britain by mutual interest. One such opportunity appeared in Oman, where in 1749 the Busa'idi, a commercial family, had replaced an older dynasty that ruled through claims to religious prestige and command over the agricultural riches of the Omani highlands. For the British, the Busa'idi emphasized their new concerns by moving the capital from the better-watered interior to Muscat on the coast. The Busa'idi Sultan of Muscat, Seyyid Sa'id bin Sultan, who ruled Oman from 1804 to 1856, seemed the most desirable ally.

The Busa'idi interest in commerce coincided with Bombay's interest in finding clients to the west. With British assistance, Oman sought technological modernization, especially in maritime affairs, copying European ship types and styles of fighting at sea. In earlier centuries, mariners from Oman had sailed down the African coast following a South-Arabian pattern of mainly peaceful trade diasporas. The Muscat government now turned to the European model of an armed trade diaspora, a trading-post empire, with naval and military control over selected port towns in Africa.

Imperial expansion with European weapons brought Oman into a pattern that historians of Africa often call secondary empire, referring to territorial expansion of an African power based on access to European weapons, usually establishing its control over other people who lacked such weapons. It was secondary in that it was based on technology that came from somewhere else, and it was to become all-important as the nineteenth century advanced.[5]

The Omani secondary empire extended the militarized trade diaspora by seizing the Afro-Arabian trading cities on the East African coast, ruling

---

[5] For the Omani and Zanzibari background, see Abdul Sheriff, *Slaves, Spices, and Ivory in Zanzibar: Integration of an East African Commercial Empire into the World Economy, 1770–1873* (London: James Currey, 1987), pp. 1–32.

over them from an advanced base on the island of Zanzibar. These moves were undertaken with the tacit consent, and sometimes the support, of the British officials in Bombay. Oman, in short, was allowed and helped to build its secondary empire because it was simultaneously part of Bombay's informal empire in the west. By 1835, the Omanis had a 74-gun ship of Western design, three frigates, two corvettes, and a brig, in addition to armed dhows – in all, the most powerful non-European fleet between Europe and Japan.

With his other ties to India, Seyyid Sa'id welcomed a new generation of Indian merchants and bankers. He himself was an Ibadi, a descendent of the Kharijite sect that broke off from sunni Islam after the first conquests of the fertile crescent, but he invited Hindus and Muslims of other sects to come to Muscat and Zanzibar. They came in numbers, bringing entrepreneurial talent, some capital of their own, and access to Indian capital. Some looked back to an Indian base in Bombay, but others came from Gujerat and Kutch, further north. By the 1840s, the Zanzibari of Indian origin were a major source of entrepreneurship all along the African coast. They financed shipping, caravans into the interior, and plantations on the islands and the nearby African mainland.

By the 1830s, Seyyid Sa'id's East African interests had grown to overshadow Muscat itself, and he moved his capital to Zanzibar. With that, Arabian-based traders lost some influence, while the newly arrived Indian traders gained. As Zanzibar moved ahead, so did Bombay. In 1837, Zanzibar conquered Mombasa, which had the best harbor on the East African mainland, while, in 1839, Company troops of the Bombay Army occupied Aden at the entrance to the Red Sea.

Until the 1860s, these moves had greater significance to the British officials in Bombay than in London. Once work began on the Suez Canal, the strategic importance of the Arabian Sea shifted abruptly. The canal was not actually open to traffic until 1869, but the implications of its opening were easily foreseen. Once open, and with steamships now in common use, it would transform the Red Sea from a cul-de-sac into a strategic waterway. Various powers reacted to the prospect. In 1862, France established control over the port of Obock (in the future Djibouti). Egypt planned its own moves to the south and in 1865 established military posts at the Red Sea port of Suakin. Egypt also took over the former Turkish post at Massawa (in future Eritrea) and threatened to move overland from the Nilotic Sudan into the Ethiopian highlands and even further down the coast into northern Somalia.

The Ethiopian Background

During the eighteenth and early nineteenth centuries, the Ethiopian highlands had passed through a phase of political division and quasi-anarchy, known in Ethiopian history as the *Zamana Mesafent* – the "Era of the Princes." Political primacy had shifted back and forth between various Christian princes bearing the title of *ras,* or provincial governor, passing occasionally into the hands of one of the Muslim rulers who controlled the foothills and some sections of the Ethiopian highlands.[6]

That era began to come to an end with the rise of a new centralizing military power from the borderlands against the Sudan. As a young man in the 1850s, Ras Kassa began the military reunification of what had been Christian Ethiopia, taking the title of Emperor under the name Tewodros in 1854. He knew about the power of European arms from his frontier experience against the Egyptian secondary empire in the Sudan, but he had trouble getting weapons. The Turkish garrison at Massawa was a possible but unreliable source. From the 1850s into the 1860s, Tewodros tried to force Western missionaries to manufacture weapons and teach Ethiopians to do the same; he also began a road-construction program to give his army the mobility necessary to control the highlands. In fact, he succeeded quite well for a time, raising an army of 70,000 to 80,000 men, a large army for Ethiopia at that time; but, by the mid-1860s, his kingdom began to come apart. He lost control of Tigray in the north and of Showa in the south, where Menelik, the future emperor, had already proclaimed his independence. The territory under Tewodros' actual control was reduced to about a fifth of what he had claimed at earlier moments of triumph, and the ranks of his army had dropped to about 10,000 men.[7]

In the longer run, it was Menelik who was to unite Ethiopia and establish the empire that was to last until 1974. Tewodros' problems in the early 1860s were a result of his own unstable personality. In his desperation to obtain guns from Britain or France, or both, he tried diplomatic initiatives, but the Europeans simply refused to answer his letters. Then, in 1864, he seized the British Consul posted to Massawa, who happened to be in the highlands at the time. Tewodros had already seized some missionaries for other reasons, and he hoped to use the hostages as bargaining chips to pay for weapons.

After 1864, Tewodros' control was slipping fast and his army disintegrating. In the winter dry season of 1867–68, just as the British were planning their expedition, he burned his capital at Debre Tabor and marched the remains of his army to the fortified heights at Magdala, arriving only a few weeks before the Anglo-Indian army. Whatever else the British

---

[6] Sven Rubensen, "Ethiopia and the Horn," in John E. Flint (ed.), *Cambridge History of Africa.* Volume 5 (Cambridge: Cambridge University Press, 1976), pp. 51–98; Mordechai Abir, *Ethiopia in the Era of the Princes: The Challenge of Islam and the Re-unification of the Christian Empire 1769–1855* (London: Longman, 1968).

[7] Rubensen, "Ethiopia and the Horn," pp. 74–75; Richard Pankhurst, "Ethiopia and Somalia," UNESCO, *General History of Africa: Africa in the Nineteenth Century until the 1880s* (London, Heinemann, 1989), 6:376–411; Donald Crummey, "Tewodros as Reformer and Modernizer," *Journal of African History,* 10:457–469 (1968).

expedition might done, it did not drive Tewodros from power. He had
already lost power on his own.[8]

The British Decision to Invade

One might well ask why, in these circumstances, the British cabinet
thought it worth while to send an elaborate expedition against Ethiopia.
Tewodros held some British officials and Continental European missionaries hostage, but diplomacy or a small payoff in guns might well have
secured their release. Though the British military were anxious to try out
the new equipment and organization, the main initiative at the cabinet
level came from the Foreign Office, not the War Office, in a mixed bag of
separate concerns. Egypt was crucial, and the British Government was
still impressed by Egypt's role in easing the cotton famine during the
American Civil War. Egyptian cotton seemed essential to prevent a similar event in the future. No one in the Foreign Office knew or cared about
what was happening in Ethiopia, but the India Office and the Foreign
Office both feared French intervention if Britain failed to act. In most dis-
cussions within the British government, the captives receded far into the
background. The danger the government sensed was a threat, however
remote, to the Red Sea route to India[9]

The need to uphold "white man's prestige" was also important in
London and Bombay. The faith that white men actually had prestige to be
upheld was partly a reflection of the growing pseudo-scientific racism,
but concern about "white man's prestige" was more than that. An important European military and imperial doctrine of the period held that non-
Western states on the fringes of European empires would be quiet and
obedient only if they recognized that disobedience or disrespect brought
sure and rapid punishment. One offshoot of this belief was the doctrine of
"paramountcy" in India, which stated in effect that Britain was para-
mount on the sub-continent and, as such, had a right to intervene where
and when it saw fit. Most Indian states had little choice but to accept; they
knew that the failure to do so might well bring swift military retribution,
and the authorities in Bombay acted on the belief that an occasional
extravagant intervention saved the cost of many smaller conflicts.

Another source of the doctrine was recent European experience with
guerrilla warfare, going back to the Napoleonic experience in Spain.
Then, as always, the advantage of guerrillas or terrorists alike was to
strike with surprise at chosen targets, forcing their enemies into the

---

[8] Darrell Bates, *The Abyssinian Difficulty: The Emperor Theodorus and the Magdala Campaign 1867–68* (Oxford: Oxford University Press, 1979), pp. 41–55, 60–85; Sven Rubensen, *King of Kings: Tewodros of Ethiopia* (Addis Ababa and Nairobi: Oxford University Press, 1966), pp. 80–89.

[9] J.R. Hooker, "The Foreign Office and the Abyssinian Captives," *Journal of African History*, 2:259–71 (1961).

expensive simultaneous defense of all important strategic points. The French solution in the Peninsular War was to abandon fixed fortified positions and take the offensive, not only against the guerrillas but against the civilian population at large. Goya's painting of a French firing squad has helped to fix the Spanish experience in historical memory.

After 1841, General Bugeaud adapted the doctrine for the French conquest of Algeria. He abandoned fixed defenses in favor of mobile columns that could attack not merely guerrillas themselves, but the peasant community that gave the guerrillas essential support. The doctrine led to a form of scorched-earth policy but with a corollary of making punishment as spectacular as possible – not nearly enough to win the campaign, but as an example to those who might be imprudent enough to consider defying French authority in future.[10] Terrorism is often thought of as a appropriate tactic for the weak; this doctrine translated into terrorism by the strong.

Britain had no reason to want territorial control over the Ethiopian highlands, but the exemplary march to Magdala might be worth the expense, if others in Asia and Africa were shown what Britain could and would do if it chose. Thus, even though Tewodros' empire had already collapsed before the expedition sailed; it could be justified in Britain and Bombay alike as a useful lesson for others, and an opportunity to exercise the troops.

Planning for the March

The projected campaign attracted considerable public attention, not all of it favorable, at first. The Liberal Parliamentary opposition was somewhat more favorable than the ruling Tories, so that Disraeli, as Chancellor of the Exchequer, managed to get Parliamentary approval for an expenditure of £2,000,000, even though this would mean a 25 percent increase in the income tax for one year, and even though the Government conceded that it might cost twice that much in the end. It fact, it cost the British government alone more than £9,000,000, and the government of India paid the cost of the Indian forces, whether Indian or European in origin.[11]

The press coverage was intense. The *Daily Telegraph*, the *Times of London*, the *Standard*, the *Morning Post*, and the *Times of India* all sent correspondents. Both the *Lancet* and the *British Medical Journal* published reports by Army doctors who were members of the force. The *Illustrated London News* sent an artist and published his sketches throughout the campaign. Among the corespondents were G.A. Henty, who was to be a major publicist in the cause of empire through the rest of the century.

---

[10] Henri L. Wesselling, "Les guerres coloniales et la paix armée, 1871–1914: esquisse pour une étude comparative, " in *Etudes en l'honneur de Jean-Louis Miège* (Aix-en-Provence: Publications de l'universitée de Provence, 1992), 1:105–126., esp. 113–15.

[11] Bates, *Ethiopian Difficulty*, pp. 85–92.

Henry Morton Stanley, back from America as correspondent for the *New York Herald*, also went along, thus undertaking the first of his many visits to Africa.

Continental powers were also represented. Austria, France, the Netherlands, Italy, Prussia, and Spain all sent at least one military attaché to accompany the force. France sent a member of its diplomatic service as well. The scientific observers included a meteorologist, a zoologist, a geologist from the Indian Geological Survey, a civilian doctor from the Bombay Medical Service, an archaeologist from the British Museum, and Clements Markham from the Royal Geographical Society.[12]

Preparations favored the latest technology, but the invasion ultimately took shape as an Indian Army operation, commanded by Robert Napier, an old-line officer of the Indian Army, chosen mainly because he was the commander of the Bombay army. He had risen through the Royal Engineers, which implied a lower social status than that of the line officers, but his background qualified him for the task of moving a large force through unknown country.[13]

At first, official thinking suggested a small force of perhaps 6,000 men, but Napier asked for double that number and ended with 13,164 soldiers – 4,114 Europeans of the Indian Army and 9,050 Indians – but the soldiers were supported by 49,000 civilian workers, almost all from India. In British military terminology, they were called "followers," and they had many different occupations: servants of the officers, cooks, stretcher bearers, laborers, muleteers, bheesties to carry water for the soldiers on march or in battle, and mahouts to control the elephants.[14]

This was an enormous force for the time. Only 97,800 British troops had been engaged in the Crimean War,[15] but steamships were now readily available to move the force from India to the African coast. In all, the government chartered 688 ships to move this force and its equipment between December 1867 and April of 1868, when the final assault took place.

The army first constructed a pier at Zula, on a deep bay it called Annesley Bay (now Zula Bahir) south of the port of Massawa, then under Egyptian control. It then built a railway to carry the force ten miles to the

---

[12] Henry Morton Stanley, *Coomassie and Magdala: The Story of Two British Campaigns in Africa* (London, 1874), p 355; Bates, *Ethiopian Difficulty*, pp. 102–03; C.B. Currie,"Medical History of the Abyssinian Expedition," AMSR, 9:277–99 (1867), 282. The events of the campagn were also discussed byA. F. Shepherd, *The Campaign in Abyssinia* (Bombay: Times of India Office, 1868); Clements R. Markham, *A History of the Abyssinian Expedition* (London: Prideux, 1869), and in many later works, of which the most recent are Bates, *Ethiopian Difficulty*, and Frederick Myatt, *The March to Magdala* (London, 1970).

[13] Bates, *Ethiopian Difficulty*, pp. 93 ff.

[14] PP, 1868–69, vi, pp. 142–43. Other accounts give different totals. Dr. Currie, the Principal Medical Officer gave the number of followers as 19,000, (Currie,"Medical History," p. 280), but no one was responsible for keeping careful records of the followers and other civilians.

[15] A.G. Mackenzie, "War Mortality in Recent Campaigns with Special Reference to the German Experience in the War of 1870–71, *Transactions of the Actuarial Society of Edinburgh*, pp. 137–54 (1881), pp. 140–41.

foot of the mountains. Tewodros' road system was far from complete, so that further advance into the interior was made with pack animals, rather than the wagons that moved armies in Europe or India. To start with, the army landed at Zula 44 elephants, 16,000 mules, 1,650 ponies, 5,700 camels, and 1,800 donkeys, but their later landings and purchases in neighboring countries brought the total to 44,723 head of animals of all sorts, including 17,000 camels and nearly 18,000 mules.[16] For communications, the army built a telegraph line, carried forward as the troops advanced. In the end, only 3,500 soldiers participated in the assault on Magdala, but to move them so far in these few months was a striking achievement.

The medical preparations were equally careful; preventive medicine in the Indian Army had improved greatly since the Royal Commission of 1863. Improved sanitation, water purification, ventilation, and flight from epidemic cholera had made it possible to reduce the death rate of European soldiers in India from 42.7 per thousand over the years 1859–61 to 23.7 per thousand over the years 1866–68.[17] Europeans knew next to nothing about the possible risk from disease in the Ethiopian highlands, but the image of a "white man's grave" had traditionally centered on the humid tropics of West Africa. Dr. A.F. Shepherd, who covered the expedition for the *Times of India*, highlighted some of the problems:

Fever, dysentery, ague, and a long train of diseases besides, were to meet the army at every turn; ugly flies with ugly names were to be the scourge of all and sundry; water was always to be scarce, and often poisonous. No wonder that Lord Stanley and the Government pondered long before committing the country to an expedition so beset with horrors behind and before.[18]

Even before the expeditionary force had arrived on the Red Sea coast, the *Lancet* answered concerns of this kind with an editorial maintaining:

that Abyssinia proper is not an insalubrious climate, that the dangers to health have been exaggerated to a ridiculous extent, and that there is nothing so formidable that the Bombay Government and the Medical Department may not overcome it by the exercise of vigilance, foresight, and by the expenditure of money.[19]

---

[16] Currie, "Medical History," p. 283; Stanley, *Coomassie and Magdala*, pp. 507–510; E. Taverna, "Un detail des expéditions coloniales: le service du train dans la campagne des Anglais en Abyssinie (1867–68)," *Journal des sciences militaires*, 63 (9th series):185–210 (1896), p. 210.

[17] Curtin, *Death by Migration: Europe's Encounter with the Tropics in the Nineteenth Century*, pp. 198 and *passim*.

[18] A.F. Shepherd, *The Campaign in Abyssinia* (Bombay: Times of India Office, 1868), pp. xi–xii.

[19] *Lancet*, 1867 (2), p. 367–68, Sept. 21, 1867; and the *Lancet* returned to this theme from time to time in the months to come.

The *British Medical Journal* printed fewer reports of the campaign, but it, too, insisted that the problems of the expeditionary force were logistical, not medical.[20]

Pure water was a principal concern. Most steamers could distill fresh water from sea water, and they could supply the troops at Zula itself. Of the 50,000 tons of fresh water supplied to the troops on shore at Annesley Bay, two-thirds was condensed from sea water and one-third was brought from Bombay and elsewhere in the transports.[21]

Large water filters were provided for the advance into the interior, but they were too heavy to take beyond the end of the railway. This failure probably made little difference; the British army at that time used charcoal filters to improve the smell, with sand or other filter matter to strain out impurities. Neither would have made any difference to the bacterial content of the water, nor would the pocket filters that were issued to each soldier – but probably not used most of the time. The Indian army normally used alum to precipitate foreign matter in the water, but that too was left on the coast; it would have made no difference to the bacteria in any case. At a few points in the interior it was possible to use a device called Norton's American pump, which was designed to bring up underground water through tubes driven into the earth. This device might have made some difference, but not enough to counter the fact that the bheesties who carried water for the troops used whatever surface water they could find.[22]

Evacuation of the sick and wounded was another logistical problem. Hospital ships – redesigned and rebuilt as such, as opposed to troop ships designated to carry sick and wounded – were a recent innovation, first used in the British expeditionary force against China in 1859. Three steamers specially fitted for the European troops were stationed in Annesley Bay. Two sailing ships were held offshore to evacuate sick and wounded Indian troops, while sick or wounded followers were held on shore at two base hospitals, one at the foot of the mountains and the other in Zula.[23]

The another problem was to transport the sick and wounded soldiers to these facilities. Carts and horse-drawn ambulances were impractical in the Ethiopian terrain. The Indian army used a kind of heavy-duty stretcher, called a dhooley, that could be carried by porters. The top and sides were covered, a little like a sedan chair with the passenger lying down, and it could be entered through a small door on either side. An unloaded dhooley weighed between 90 to 120 pounds, and each one required ten dhooley bearers. Lighter stretchers, called dandies, were also available, but even they required six porters. For the advance beyond the

[20] BMJ, 1868, 1, 173 (Feb. 22, 1868).
[21] PP, 1868–69, VI, p. 142.
[22] Currie, "Medical History," p. 294.
[23] Currie, "Medical History," p. 286.

railhead, one dhooley and two mules were assigned to every 100 soldiers
– either Indian or European, plus 15 dhoolies for each field hospital. Sick
or wounded followers apparently had to make their way back as best
they could.[24]

This inequality of treatment for each different category of participant
extended to rations as well. In India, it was expected that Indian soldiers and civilian employees would add to their official rations by
spending some of their pay for food. The commissariat evaluated the
cost of rations for a European soldier at eight times the cost for an
Indian soldier; civilian followers in India normally got half that much.
In Ethiopia, it was impossible to buy food along the line of march, so
larger rations were issued. Followers and Indian soldiers began with the
same food allotment, but a disparity developed as the expedition
moved inland. By the end of February 1868, European troops had 24
ounces of meat, Indian troops 16 ounces, followers 16. European troops
had 16 ounces of flour, Indian troops had 14 ounces, followers, 12
ounces. Everybody got 2 ounces of ghee, but the Europeans alone got
vegetables, tea, and sugar.

The March to Magdala

In early December 1867, the first British and Indian troops began to land
at Zula. In January, General Napier arrived, and the force began its 400-
mile trek to Magdala. On April 10, 1868, as the vanguard approached
Magdala, Tewodros attacked with the small force he still controlled – an
army estimated at somewhere between 3,400 and 7,000 men. A few hundred men with artillery and Snider rifles easily stood off this attack with
no loss of life and only 20 wounded.

That was enough for Tewodros, who agreed to meet the British
demands and release his prisoners. He turned over the captive British
officials and all the other Europeans he had been holding, including
German missionaries and European artisans, a total of 67 people including families and servants. The official objective of the expedition was
thus attained after this first firefight, but Tewodros and a small force
remained in control of his mesa-top fortress. On April 13, Napier ordered
an assault on Magdala, and the fort fell with very little opposition to a
force of 3,500 troops, half Indian and half British. Tewodros committed
suicide; the British discovered his body inside the fortress. They
removed everything they could find that seemed to be valuable and
destroyed as much as possible of the fort and village. On April 18, they
began their return march to the coast. The first evacuations from Zula
began on May 25, even before the withdrawal from the highlands was
complete.

---

[24] Currie, "Medical History," p. 285.

Medical Aspects

It was a great victory, and the Army Medical Department claimed that mortality cost fell within reasonable limits. Dr. C.B. Currie, the Chief Medical Officer, reported the death rate of European troops for the 25-week campaign of only 13 per thousand and a rate of repatriation for illness of only 125 per thousand. In comparison with military disease mortality elsewhere, however, the triumph was less then spectacular. It was about three times the death rate of British troops in Britain, and double the disease death rate of British troops in India. (See Table 2.1.) Troops on campaign were, of course, expected to sustain higher disease deaths rates than those in barracks – often three to ten times higher. (Refer to Tables 4.3 and 7.2).

But self-congratulation in this case could have been more moderate. The line of march offered a combination of desert and highland disease environments. Magdala was a far cry from the British or French experience in West Africa. Malaria was negligible; the only cases were infections acquired in India. Cholera and yellow fever were completely absent. Typhoid fever, which was to be the most important cause of death in later African campaigns, was then classified with other "continued fevers," but that whole group was responsible for less than 2 percent of deaths from disease.

Gastrointestinal infections were the chief cause of death, as one might expect from the fact that effective water purification disappeared once the force began to advance into the mountains. But Dr. C. B. Currie concluded that Ethiopia, unlike most tropical countries, must be considered a "healthy country for Europeans," and, according to him, the mortality that *did* occur was entirely caused by fatigue, cold and wet, bad food, and the bad water that plagued campaigning anywhere.[25] Gastrointestinal infections and heat stroke together accounted for more than half the excess death rates over those to be expected in Britain. Ethiopia, indeed, offered a substantial advantage in decreased deaths from tuberculosis.[26] (See Table 2.1.)

Nineteenth-century European experience of infectious disease was altogether different from that of developed societies in recent decades. In the 1830s, a healthy man of twenty could expect 10 to 20 percent of his age cohort to die of disease before he reached the age of thirty. In the 1860s, the equivalent figure was still more than 8 percent; in the late twentieth century, it had fallen to less than 1 percent.[27] That experience lurked in the background of any medical officer assessing the losses in a particular campaign.

[25] Currie, "Medical History," p. 293.
[26] Currie, "Medical History," pp. 298–99.
[27] Approximations based on military statistics for peacetime Britain, drawn on P. D. Curtin, *Death by Migration*, pp. 165, 166, 172; AMSR for 1943, p. 19.

Table 2.1. *British Military Mortality on the Magdala Campaign, 1867–68*

Mortality per Thousand Mean Strength per Month

	British Troops in Britain 1860-77	British Troops in Ethiopia 1867-68	Added Mortality For Service on Campaign
Zymotic diseases			
Eruptive fevers	0.02	0.00	-0.02
Paroxysmal fevers	0.00	0.11	0.11
Continued fevers	0.03	0.06	0.02
Rheumatism	0.01	0.00	-0.01
Enthetic diseases	0.01	0.00	-0.01
Class II – Constitutional Diseases			
Tubercular	0.24	0.00	-0.24
Class III – Local diasesses of the. . .			
Nervous system	0.05	0.06	0.00
Circulatory system	0.10	0.06	-0.04
Respiratory system	0.11	0.00	-0.11
Digestive system	0.06	1.28	1.23
Urinary system	0.02	0.11	0.09
Locomotive system	0.00	0.00	0.00
Integumentary system	0.00	0.00	0.00
Heat stroke	0.00	0.67	0.67
Other or not specified	0.02		-0.02
Total Disease	0.67	2.18	1.51
Accidents	0.06	0.78	0.72
Battle	0.00	0.00	0.00
Homicide	0.00	0.00	0.00
Suicide	0.03	0.06	0.03
Punishment	0.00	0.00	0.00
Grand Total	0.74	3.01	2.27

Note:
The monthly average mortality for British troops in India over the years 1864–73 was 1.18 per thousand. (Curtin, *Death by Migration*, p. 195.)
Dysentery and diarrhea, when classified separately are included here as "diseases of the digestive system."

Source: The first column is the unweighted mean of monthly mortality of British in the United Kingdom in the periods 1860–67 and 1869–77. (Curtin, *Death by Migration*, appendix tables.) For British troops in Ethiopia, AMSR for 1868, pp. 205–08. These data are based on the published annualizaed data for a campaign of 25 weeks only.

The nineteenth-century military commanders, and the informed public, also thought about death on several different planes. Death in combat or from enemy action was different from other kinds of death. It was a professional risk that soldiers ran – "the fortunes of war" – but it was also a mark of honor. It was well known that far more soldiers died of disease on campaign than in barracks; but death from disease, even on campaign and in wartime, was evaluated differently from death in action. It was somehow less honorable, perhaps because no show of bravery was required. Bravery or cowardice made no difference. Disease struck in war or peace, among civilians as well as soldiers. Many accounts of military campaigns said nothing at all about deaths from disease, only those from enemy action.

In the official and the public mind, the deaths of some participants weighed more heavily than others. The deaths of officers counted for more than the deaths of other ranks. Enemy deaths were measured on a different scale; they could even be a measure of victory, like the body-count figures that were compiled during the Vietnam War. "Native troops" in European service counted for less than European troops, but they counted much more heavily than "native" civilians. In the Indian Army, British troops counted most; regular Indian soldiers counted a little less, though far more than irregular auxiliary troops serving under their own commanders. Indian civilians, whether "coolies," porters, servants, or laborers for the army on campaign counted for little or nothing. These weightings were very important for the kind of assessment ruling-class Europeans would make once they had added up the costs and benefits of a particular military action.

Dr. Currie's report, consequently, told little about the health of the Indian soldiers and nothing at all about the health of the followers. It was there that the triumph of medicine was less than complete. The followers' troubles began on some of the troop ships that brought them from Bombay to Zula. One ship, the steamer *India*, left Bombay with 417 Indian workers identified as "coolies," some of whom were infected with typhoid fever. One hundred and thirty-one, 31 percent, died on board or on landing in Zula, where they were placed in a special quarantined camp to prevent the disease from spreading to the rest of the force. Of the survivors, 251 were shipped back to India as invalids, and only 8 percent were left in Africa and certified as fit to work.[28] After the experience of the passengers on the *India*, someone deserves credit for preventing the typhoid epidemic from spreading to the rest of the force, though the fact that the only water available in Zula was the distilled water from the ships may have been all that was required.

The fate of the other followers is hard to trace in detail. They were separately recruited by many different authorities, often for particular tasks,

[28] Shepherd, *Campaign in Abyssinia*, pp. 24–25; T.J. Holland and H.M. Hozier, *Records of the Expedition to Abyssinia Compiled by Order of the Secretary of State for War* (London, HMSO, 1870). pp. 438–39.

sometimes by government, sometimes by military officers or the civilians who went along, as their private employees. One unit, called the Bengal Coolie Corps, was planned to muster 3,000 men, promised pay at 8 rupees a month (equivalent to 15 British shillings) plus daily rations at about 1 pound of rice or other grain, 2 ounces of dhall, 1 ounce of ghee, and a third of an ounce of salt. In fact, only 2,041 sailed, including the unfortunates on board the *India*. Of those who left Bombay 12 percent died, and 27 percent were invalided back to Bombay, where more may have died.[29] More men died in this single unit than in all European formations covered by Dr. Currie's report.

Another similar unit was the Army Works Corps, recruited partly from Bombay and partly in China for transport work in the lowlands between Zula and the road into the mountains.[30] These men were given rations on two different scales – the Chinese received the European scale, while the Indians were on the "followers" scale. Whether because of different rations or home disease environment, only 73 per thousand of the Chinese were declared unfit for service and sent home, while 312 per thousand of the Indians were invalided back to India.[31]

It is impossible to know what happened to the rest of the followers; numbers reported differ from one authority to another. Many certainly died. Many others deserted in Ethiopia and simply disappeared from the record. The most comprehensive official figures suggest that of the total of 41,056 followers landed in Zula, only 24,706 reembarked for the voyage back to Bombay. This suggests that as many as 40 percent either died or deserted – more people missing or dead than the number in the entire fighting force they were meant to serve.[32]

These were the officially published figures, but those who commented on the campaign at the time and in retrospect paid no attention, presumably because – in their minds – Indians simply did not count. Sir Clements Markham, one of the scientific observers wrote:

From most points of view this Abyssinian expedition may be looked upon by Englishmen with unmixed satisfaction. The cause of quarrel was absolutely just, the main objects for which the expedition was undertaken were secured, and public opinion was still sufficiently alive to the honour of England to approve the addition of a penny to the Income-tax to maintain it. The experience acquired during active service by many young officers is a clear gain to the country; and, in traversing a very interesting and remarkable region, some additional knowledge has been collected, by those who were specially sent out for the purpose, in several branches of science.[33]

---

[29] Holland and Hozier, *Expedition to Abyssinia*, pp. 435–39.
[30] Shepherd, *Campaign in Abyssinia*, pp. 24–25; T.J. Holland and H.M. Hozier, *Expedition to Abysinia*, pp. 438–39.
[31] Holland and Hozier, *Expedition to Abyssinia*, pp. 428–33.
[32] PP, 1868–69, vi, pp. 142–43.
[33] Markham, *Abyssinian Expediton*, p. 389.

The *Times of London*, which had opposed the expedition beforehand, changed its mind afterward and greeted it as a marvelous adaptation of science to warfare. Its editorial published on May 1, 1868 reflected the tone of other press commentary as well:

We have really proved ourselves adepts in the art of war. We have done something more than march on and on, encounter foes, kill or be killed, survive gloriously, or retreat without loss of honour. The arrangements have been made with skill, and executed with precision. An impregnable fortress has been taken, not with mere flesh and blood, but with perfect marvels of ordnance admirably adapted to the purpose and excellently handled. A few wounds on our side against a great slaughter on the other duly represents the difference between civilized and semi-barbarous warriors. . . . Certainly, we are all aware that without science it would be impossible to overcome the peculiar difficulties of the Expedition.[34]

Subsequent editorials pursued the same vein, with a recurrent emphasis on the use of science, on the fact that Napier was an officer of Engineers, and on the need for still more emphasis on professional training, as opposed to Britain's older tradition of officers as gentlemen who could depend on bravery in combat without need of other skills.[35] The *Times'* use of the campaign foreshadowed its support for the kinds of reform Edward Cardwell was about to propose.

On the medical side, *The Lancet* was not so overwhelmed. It recognized that there was more sickness on the retreat than on the advance, and that the followers and Indians soldiers had suffered more than the Europeans, but the tone was still one of congratulation that the losses from disease had been kept so low.[36]

The foreign press was not so enthusiastic, but the *Revue des deux mondes* ran a long article analyzing the campaign in the setting of African affairs, with the conclusion that it was probably essential, since rule over so many in India with so few troops depended on European prestige – on the threat of force more than force itself. The author thought, however, that the cost of so many millions of pounds sterling to rescue so few people was exorbitant, especially when Ethiopia badly needed foreign help to prevent the country from falling back into anarchy. Britain had been in a position to provide such help but had failed to use its advantage. The article mentioned nothing about the cost of the war in terms of death from disease.[37]

Some unfavorable reaction did follow in Britain, but it concentrated on the financial cost. A Select Committee of the House of Commons considered the matter, with criticism centering on the cost of chartering ships to carry the expedition to Zula, an expense that amounted more than a third

---

[34] The *Times*, May 1, 1868, p. 6.
[35] See, for example, the editorials of May 19, p. 9 and September 17, p. 8.
[36] *Lancet*, 1868 (1), p. 732. (June 6), p. 792 (June 20).
[37] H. Blerzy, "La guerre d'Abyssinie," *Revue des deux mondes*, 74:449 (1868).

of the whole cost of the expedition. Aside from a few complaints about the flogging of muleteers, the Indian side of the expedition got very little attention, nor was the loss of life from disease seriously considered.[38]

Retrospective mention of the expedition was much the same. A French analyst of military medicine in the tropics over the last third of the century saw it as a great success, writing that "les maladies furent peu nombreuses, et occasionnées surtout par la dysenterie et des rechutes de fièvre palustre contractée dans l'Inde." In summary, "l'expédition fut conduite à bonne fin, en temps voulu, et avec une perte d'hommes très minime." Fortescue's massive *History of the Army* also looked back on the campaign as a landmark in the introduction of new mechanical and scientific practices into warfare.[39] At the time, this impression was overwhelming. The losses of Indian soldiers and followers were simply ignored, and they remained ignored. The real cost in lives was not counted because the dead were not European.

[38] *Report of the Select Committee on the Abyssinian War*, PP, 1868–69, VI, [380] [380–I], p. 223; Bates, *Abyssinian Difficulty*, esp. p. 214; Myatt, *March on Magdala*, pp. 177–80.

[39] Gustave A. Reynaud, *Considerations sanitaires sur l'expédition de Madagascar et quelques autres expéditions coloniales, françaises et anglaises* (Paris, 1898), pp. 34–35; Fortescue, *History of the Army*, 13:474.

CHAPTER 3

THE MARCH TO KUMASI

"... an engineer's war, a doctor's war ..."

The second British campaign to exercise the troops and test military reforms was the march on Kumasi in 1874. The setting altogether was different from that of Magdala. It was West African tropical forest, considered at the time the most dangerous disease-environment anywhere in the world for Europeans. The most recent all-European units fighting there, in the Anglo-Asante war of 1824–26, had lost 638 per thousand annually from disease alone, before they were withdrawn to safer "climates."[1]

Even more than Magdala, the Asante campaign formed European opinion about what was militarily possible in tropical Africa, and the publicity was even more intense. Henry Morton Stanley was back once more for the *New York Herald*. Winwood Reade wrote for the *Times of London*, and that paper ran 209 articles on the Asante affairs in the second half of 1873, and another 206 in the first half of 1874. During the most intense period of preparation and fighting in the last quarter of 1873 and the first of 1874, they ran a total of 300 pieces, or more than one a day. Three other London dailies also sent reporters, while other papers published despatches from military officers or merchants already on the coast. The *Lancet,* the *Medical Times and Gazette,* and the *British Medical Journal* published regular reports from medical officers on the campaign.[2] Seven books on the campaign appeared in London before the end of 1874.[3]

[1] PP, 1840, xxx [C. 228], pp. 6, 19–20.

[2] Alan Lloyd, *The Drums of Kumasi* (London: Longmans, 1948); Winwood Reade, *The Story of the Ashantee Campaign* (London, 1874), p. 332.

[3] *The Times, Palmer's Index,* 1873 and 1874; Frederick Boyle, *Through Fanteeland to Coomassie* (London, 1874); Henry Brackenbury, *The Ashanti War: A Narrative Prepared from the Official Documents by Permission of Major-General Sir Garnet Wolsely. . . ,* 2 vols. (London, 1874); John Dalrymple Hay, *Ashanti and the Gold Coast and What We Know of It* (London, 1874); J. F. Maurice, *The Ashantee War: A Popular Narrative* (London, 1874); Winwood Reade, *The Story of the Ashantee Campaign;* E. Rogers, *Campaigning in West Africa: The Ashantee Invasion* (London, 1874); Henry Morton Stanley, *Coomassie and Magdala: The Story of Two British Campaigns in Africa* (London, 1874).

Britain and the Gold Coast

It was remarkable that the Gold Coast could arouse such interest. In the second half of the nineteenth century, Britain's West African interests were even more diminished than they had been at the height of the anti-slave-trade campaign. As of 1860, the three colonies of Sierra Leone, Gambia, and the Gold Coast had a total European population of just over 500 people, of whom 70 lived in the Gold Coast. The value of British trade with Jamaica was two and half times the value of trade with all three together. The trade of the Gold Coast amounted to about a fifth of Britain's West African trade, or less than its annual trade with British Honduras.[4]

Other Europeans had already begun to pull out. In 1850, Denmark decided that the cost of its Gold Coast forts was too great in money and lives and sold them to Great Britain. In 1871, France evacuated its officials and troops from Assinie and Grand Bassam on the Ivory Coast, though it kept a shadowy legal claim by paying African rulers to fly the French flag. In 1872, the Dutch also sold their posts on the Gold Coast to Britain, for the time being the only European power claiming a serious strategic interest in that part of Africa, though others still came for trade.[5]

In the hinterland, the most important political and military power was Asante. Most people on the Gold Coast and its hinterland were Akan in language and culture, but they had been organized as a series of micro-states until the late seventeenth century. From that time, Asante, with its capital at Kumasi some 130 miles inland from Cape Coast, began to incorporate some of its Akan neighbors and to conquer some of the non-Akan peoples further north. (See Map 4.2.)

These mostly Fante micro-states closer to the coast were a tempting prospect for Asante expansion. They were a source of disorder, and Asante trade would be more secure and more profitable under their own control. The Europeans were divided, and the congeries of mostly Fante micro-states between Asante and the sea appeared to be an easy mark. In 1806–07, 1809–11, and 1814–16, Asante had invaded and broken Fante military power in the neighborhood of the European forts. This Asante threat posed two alternatives for the coastal Europeans – either to remain neutral and deal with the victor in the local struggle, or to support their immediate neighbors. In 1824, Governor Sir Charles MacCarthy joined militarily in support of the coastal Fante states to roll back the Asante threat. He was killed in a skirmish near Accra; but the coastal alliance managed to hold out and established peace with Asante in 1831.[6]

---

[4] PP, 1860–61, xxxviii (147), pp. 4–5.

[5] Curtin, *Image of Africa*, pp. 305–7; Albert Numa Cabasse, *Notes sur une campagne au Gabon, à bord de l'hôpital flottant, La Cordeliere, en 1873 et 1874* (Commercy, 1876), pp. 33–37; David Kimble, *A Political History of Ghana, 1850–1928* (Oxford: Clarendon Press, 1963), p. 170.

[6] Curtin, *Image of Africa*, pp. 152–55, 170.

From then onward through the middle third of the century, several decisions hung fire. On the Asante side, opinions differed as to whether to drive through to the coast; a war party favored occupation and rule over the coastal zone, while a peace party favored the status quo and the peaceful expansion of Asante trade.[7] European opinion on the coast was also divided between Dutch, Danish, and British authorities; each had a choice between neutrality or entering the local balance of power, which usually implied joining an alliance of coastal states. For Britain, the value of Gold Coast trade hardly justified expensive military action. Through the middle decades of the century, a serious military crisis with Asante appeared imminent from time to time, but the worst was always postponed.

Disease and the Military

Both Britain and Asante faced military problems with disease, but their problems were different. From the Asante side, assembling a large army – and an army of 20,000 to 50,000 men was not unusual – brought together in close quarters people of diverse origins. Most Africans were already protected against yellow fever by childhood infection and were already infested with malaria, so malaria was not an obvious problem; hunger, wounds, or severe fatigue, however, could bring out malarial symptoms. The Asante armies were therefore well protected against the two diseases that most frequently killed European soldiers. For Asante armies on the march, the serious threats were dysentery and smallpox – dysentery for the same reason it plagued all armies, smallpox because of its epidemiology in much of tropical Africa.

Smallpox is like yellow fever in that its victims acquire a non-infective lifetime immunity against another attack. In Europe, and many other societies with dense population and endemic smallpox, infection in childhood was so common that smallpox was virtually a childhood disease and the adult population was largely immune. In Africa, however, as in many less developed regions of the world, sparse populations and less intense intercommunication often made it possible for largely non-immune populations to grow to adulthood. When this happened, the population risked a smallpox epidemic that could reach almost all the non-immune population, with a case-fatality rate that could be as high as 25 to 35 percent. Wartime dislocations, calling in men for service, and military campaigns were ideal situations to set off an epidemic.[8]

Dysentery and smallpox placed a recurrent strategic limitation on Asante military action. The longer an army was in the field, the greater its

[7] Ivor Wilks, *Asante in the Nineteenth Century* (Cambridge: Cambridge University Press, 1975), pp. 166–93.

[8] Donald R. Hopkins, *Princes and Peasants: Smallpox in History* (Chicago: Chicago University Press, 1983), pp. 164–94.

losses, whether it fought or not. In 1824, an Asante army beseiging Cape Coast had been forced to withdraw on account of smallpox. Again in the 1860s, at least one Asante army withdrew under the impact of smallpox and dysentery working together.[9]

For the British, the problems of malaria, yellow fever, and gastrointestinal infection were little changed. With a gradual end of slave trade from West Africa, the West India Regiments were recruited in the West Indies, rather than Africa. The 1860s were a transitional decade, with some West India units still mainly African, others almost entirely West Indian in origin. West Indian recruits therefore had the immunities appropriate to their West Indian childhood, not those their ancestors had brought from Africa. The death rate for non-Europeans in British service in West Africa rose from 29 per thousand per annum in the years 1816–37 (virtually all of African origin), to 32 per thousand in 1859–63 (partly West Indian),[10] and 38 per thousand for West Indians in 1869–73.[11]

From the mid–1860s onward, British officials began to complain about the sickliness and lack of energy of the West Indian soldiers. Their death rate was nevertheless lower than that of their European non-commissioned officers. Over the period 1859–75, European non-coms assigned to West India Regiments in West African service died at 151 per thousand.[12] These men were normally sent to West Africa for a one-year tour. Their higher death rate may be accountable to lack of time to acquire effective immunities. The lower West Indian death rate may be accountable to their longer tour of several years on the coast, plus some possible carry-over of their ancestors' African immunities.

Wavering British Policies

Through the 1830s, 1840s, and 1850s, the British force on the Gold Coast remained small, and British policy toward their African neighbors remained uncertain. The Asante crossed the Pra river, the conventional frontier of Maclean's protectorate, on two significant occasions, in 1853–54 and again in 1863–64, but these campaigns were directed against Britain's African allies, not at the forts themselves. The British countered both with a combined force of West Indian Regiment and allied African troops, but neither led to extensive military operations.

On the second of these occasions, Governor Pine of the Gold Coast asked for enough troops to undertake a full-scale invasion of Asante and

---

[9] Wilks, *Asante in the Nineteenth Century*, p. 180; James Africanus Beale Horton, *Letters on the Political Condition of the Gold Coast* (London, 1870), p. 65.

[10] AMSR for 1859, pp. 150–51; for 1860, pp. 172–73; for 1861, pp. 172–073; for 1862, pp. 196–97; for 1863, pp. 216–17; for 1864, pp. 14–15.

[11] AMSR for 1869, p. 324; for 1871, pp. 385; for 1872, pp. 492–93; for 1873, pp. 88–89; for 1874, pp. 77–78.

[12] Refer to Table 1.1 and Tables 3.2 and 3.3.

an attack on Kumasi.[13] He assembled a mainly West Indian force of some 1,700 men, but used it mostly in defensive positions at the Pra through the wet season of 1864. The West Indians on the Gold Coast that year lost 83 dead from disease per thousand, in a purely defensive operation – more than three times the rate of loss of British forces elsewhere in West Africa that year. In the face of such a heavy loss from disease alone, the home government ordered a withdrawal to the coastal forts.[14]

Past losses had been higher, but this cost of defense against Asante was high enough to call into question once more the value of keeping the Gold Coast forts. A Special Commissioner reported in favor of keeping the forts, once again placing them under the Governor of Sierra Leone, but Parliamentary opinion in favor of evacuation remained strong. A Select Committee of the House of Commons recommended the evacuation of all posts except Sierra Leone, and the Colonial Office tried to guide local governments in that direction. The long-term objective was to encourage the coastal people to run their own affairs and protect their own interests.[15]

Race as a Military Issue

The Anglo-Asante War of 1863–64 helped to shift medical opinion about the problems of stationing troops in West Africa. The dominant medical opinion up to this time – and for some time afterward – was that people of African descent were racially endowed with a certain immunity to fevers; but a counter-current of information suggested that this was not always the case. Back in the 1840s, Captain Trotter of the Niger expedition noted that the African-Americans under his command had lost any immunity their ancestors may once have had. The African-American settlers in Liberia had a mortality rate in the range of 60 to 90 per thousand per year,[16] and their children died in great numbers before they had again acquired an apparent immunity.

In 1864, Staff Assistant-Surgeon W.A. Gardiner published a new sanitary report on the West Indians' expedition to the Asante frontier. He concluded, correctly, that the West Indians were not immune to the disease environment of West Africa. He also found that newly arrived recruits from Barbados and Jamaica died at higher rates than those who had

---

[13] Paul Mmenga Mbaeyi, *British Military and Naval Forces in West African History, 1807–1874* (New York: Nok, 1978), pp. 138–44; E.W.D. Ward, "To Kumassi and Back with the Ashanti Expeditionary Force 1895–96," *Journal of the Royal Service Institution*, 40:1021–30 (August 1896); Claridge, *A History of the Gold Coast and Ashanti*, 2 vols. (London, 1964),1:501–30.

[14] AMSR for 1864, p. 81.

[15] W. Walton Claridge, *Gold Coast and Aahanti*, 1:533–35; David Kimble, *Political History of Ghana*, pp. 205–9.

[16] Tom W. Shick, "A Quantitative Analysis of Liberian Colonization from 1820 to 1843 with Special Reference to Mortality," *Journal of African History*, 12:45–59 (1971).

served for some time in West Africa, apparently "seasoned" to the "climate."[17]

Gardiner might well have concluded that future troops for West African service should be recruited in West Africa, as the French were doing, but he believed that black troops of any origin "have none of the hardihood and spirited endurance of the white man."[18] The prevalent racism of the era, in short, suggested that European troops ought to be used, in spite of their high mortality from the "climate."

Line officers took up the argument. Captain (later Lieutenant-General) Andrew Clarke, who had served on the Gold Coast in 1863 and reported on military conditions there, gave his own opinion that West Indian soldiers lacked the "moral qualities" of Europeans. He argued that it cost as much man for man to keep West Indians on the coast, as compared with Europeans, but the alleged racial superiority of a European force meant that it could be smaller. He thought that 200 Europeans could replace 1,600 West Indians at no loss of security and great overall savings.[19] Such opinions were not yet dominant, but they reopened the possibility of again assigning European troops to West Africa, in spite of their mortality.

British Background of the Asante War

The Asante campaign had one set of origins in Britain and another in Africa, and the two were largely independent. In the years since Magdala, the British army had embarked on the reforms associated with the name of Edward Cardwell, head of the War Office in the Gladstone administration that took office in 1868. Among the changes he introduced was a new distribution of the British army between the colonies, India, and home service; he introduced a new short-service enlistment policy that made the army less than a lifetime career; and he sought to abolish the purchase of commissions. These changes aroused heated opposition from officers of the old school. The abolition of purchase passed the House of Commons in 1871, but it failed in the House of Lords; Gladstone finally pushed it through by royal decree in spite of the Lords.

These reforms were not the thoroughgoing reorganization some had hoped for, but they contained significant changes. They greatly strengthened the Army Medical Department and the authority of medical personnel. Before 1873, medical officers were regular regimental officers under the sole command of their regimental authorities. The only units controlled by medical officers were the two army hospitals at Netley and Woolich. After 1873, the Army Medical Department was reorganized and given a hierarchy of its own, from the Director-General through a number

---

[17] W.A. Gardiner, "Sanitary Report of the Gold Coast, Including Likewise a Short Account of the Expedition against Ashanti," AMSR, 5:323–38 (1863). pp. 335–37.

[18] Gardiner, "Sanitary Report," p. 337.

[19] Ukpabi, "West Indian Troops," pp. 143–44; Mbaeyi, British Forces, pp. 160–4.

of Surgeons-General, down to ordinary Surgeons. Medical officers continued under the immediate command of their regimental commanders, but they also belonged to a larger medical entity which supervised hospitals and came to include non-medical officers and enlisted men.[20]

Cardwell meanwhile sought allies among the serving officers. In 1868, Major-General Sir Garnet Wolseley attracted his attention by publishing *The Soldier's Pocketbook for Field Service*, in which he criticized the existing relations between officers and their men, the aristocratic tradition of the service, and the purchase of commissions. He favored instead a professional, educated officer corps. Cardwell brought Wolseley into the War Office in 1871 as his principal professional advisor on army reform. It was partly in return for this service that Wolseley gained command of the Asante expedition in 1873, and it was partly Wolseley's influence at the War Office that made people look for an opportunity to show what a modernized, professionally led army could accomplish in the field. Lord Derby hailed the expedition in advance as "an engineer's war, a doctor's war."[21]

The African Background

The more immediate origins of the Anglo-Asante War of 1873–74, however, lay in Africa. Asante politics still revolved around a struggle between a war party, interested in making good the Asante claims to the south, and a peace party content with the status quo. Kofi Karikari was about thirty years of age in 1867, when he became Asantehene, as the somewhat reluctant candidate of the war party. Up to 1872, he managed to avoid outright hostilities, but then the Anglo-Dutch treaty, transferring the Dutch posts to Britain, reopened old problems. The Dutch claimed Elmina as sovereign Dutch territory, but Asante claimed it, too, and insisted that the annual Dutch subvention was a kind of rent. Asante also claimed sovereignty over a number of African states in the southwest Gold Coast, including Akyem, Assin, Denkyira, and Wassa.[22]

Late in 1872, power in Kumasi shifted to the more extreme faction of the war party, and in January of 1873, Asante armies crossed the Pra River north of Cape Coast and began to occupy much of the territory Britain considered to be in its protectorate sending starving Fante refugees fleeing toward the coast for protection under the guns of the British forts.

[20] PP, 1883, xvi [C. 3607], *Report*, pp. vii–xii; Edward M. Spiers, *The Late Victorian Army, 1868–1902* (Manchester: Manchester University Press, 1992).

[21] Joseph H. Lehmann, *All Sir Garnet* (London, 1964), pp. 156–65, 180.

[22] Ivor Wilks, *Asante in the Nineteenth Century: The Structure and Evolution of a Political Order* (Cambridge: Cambridge University Press, 1975), pp. 235–36, 497–503; W.E.F. Ward, *A History of the Gold Coast* (London: Allen and Unwin, 1948), pp. 239–67. For an account of the diplomatic and military affairs, in addition to the contemporaneous accounts, see Claridge, *The Gold Coast and Ashanti*, 2:3–193. See also a Colonial Office confidential memorandum dated October 1, 1873 in CO 879/5, African 37c, pp. 1–42.

Meanwhile a smallpox epidemic broke out in Cape Coast and in the Asante armies. In June, the Asante defeated an army of coastal allies at Jukwa, only 17 miles north of Cape Coast.

Up to this time, the Gold Coast government had not entered the war. It could hardly be otherwise: the available force of mainly West Indian troops was divided among five different forts, and the central garrison at Cape Coast Castle had only 95 men, in the face of an Asante army estimated at more than 20,000. In early June of 1873, Royal Marine detachments began to arrive. On June 13 and 14, they marched from Cape Coast to Elmina to help stand off a substantial Asante attack on the town and the fort. They helped save the town, but their losses from disease were so heavy they had to be withdrawn. Other Marines arrived from time to time, along with new contingents of African troops from Lagos, and reinforcements of West Indians.[23]

Even before the situation on the Gold Coast began to stabilize, London was already alarmed. Lord Kimberly at the Colonial Office became convinced that the only way to handle the Asante problem was to launch a punitive offensive – to deliver such a telling blow that the Asante would never again threaten the protectorate. This strategy had been suggested again and again earlier in the century, but without wholesale support from London.[24] Even in 1873, the press was largely negative. Kimberly, however, saw it as the best way to assert British power. Cardwell saw it as a way to demonstrate how a professional war might be waged. Both joined in pressing Sir Garnet Wolseley to take military command and to act as Governor of the Gold Coast for the duration of the campaign. Wolseley saw it as an opportunity to demonstrate the "moral value" of European troops, even in the tropics.

At the beginning of October, Wolseley arrived at Cape Coast to take command of the motley assortment of troops already in place. The government remained fearful of risking European troops in West Africa, but Wolseley had arranged for certain European troops to be held in readiness in Britain, in case the situation in Africa demanded. Only ten days after his arrival, Wolseley called up these reinforcements, though only 1,450 were ready at that time.

His arguments had obviously been prepared well in advance to meet the expected opposition on grounds of health to the use of European troops. He began with the proposition that: "It is well-known here that Europeans suffer from the climate less than black men from other localities."[25] (On this point he was quite wrong and was contradicted by the Army Medical Department's published figures.) He complained about

---

[23] Anthony D. Home, "Medical History of the War in the Gold Coast Protectorate in 1873," AMSR, 15:217–59 (1873); Great Britain, Admiralty, *Statistical Reports of the Health of the Navy,* volume for 1873, pp. 204–5, 215.

[24] Wolseley to War Office, October 13, 1873, PP, 1874, xlvi [893], pp. 234–5.

[25] Wolseley to War Office, 13 October 1873, PP, 1874, xlvi [893], p. 235.

the cowardice of the Fante and the ill-health of the West Indians.[26] He turned back in time to the reports of Andrew Clarke and W.A. Gardiner on the Anglo-Asante War of 1863, and to the recent opinion of Dr. Anthony D. Home, C.B., V.C., then the Principal Medical Officer on the Gold Coast. And he promised to bring in the European troops only for the dry season – confining their operations to the months of December through March and for "no more than six weeks, or at most two months."[27]

The claimed military superiority of European troops was supported by the exuberant racism of the period; Wolseley's first-hand reports of the fighting on the Gold Coast were full of racial slurs against the West Indians and all African troops and African carriers.[28] But Wolseley's distrust of "native" troops intersected with another quarrel in British military politics. Wolseley and his supporters stood for strategic emphasis on home and colonial defense, while a group of opponents saw India as the strategic source of the Empire's power and influence in the world. Wolseley's contempt for the British commanders of the Indian Army spread to include a contempt for the Indian troops under their command – hence for all non-European troops.[29]

Wolseley was not only convinced of European superiority, he was convinced that the Asante were equally convinced. His "notes" for the guidance of soldiers on the advance into Asante were quite explicit:

It must never be forgotten by our soldiers that Providence has implanted in the heart of every native of Africa a superstitious dread of the white man and that prevents the negro from daring to meet us face to face in combat. A steady advance or a charge, no matter how partial, if made with determination, always means the retreat of the enemy.[30]

Lord Kimberly's response to Wolseley's project was somewhat guarded. He promised the European troops, but only with reluctance on the part of the Government; their use was to be strictly limited in time, and they must be withdrawn by February or March 1874, at the latest. Although a march to Kumasi was a possibility, Kimberly advised that something less than total victory would be preferable, and that Asante should be given every assurance of future freedom to trade to the coast at

---

[26] Wolseley to War Office, 58/73, 24 October 1873; Wolsely to War Office, 39/73, 31 October 1873; Wolsely to War Office, 72/73, 9 November 1873, WO 32/7638.

[27] Wolseley to War Office, 13 October 1873, p. 235.

[28] For the common tone see especially Percy P. Luxmoore, "Ashantee: Extracts from the Journal of a Naval Officer Addressed to His Wife," *Blackwood's Edinburgh Magazine*, 115:518–524 (April 1874), who despised the "niggers" working on his own side and espoused a kind of racial hierarchy in which the Asante were superior to Britain's Fante allies.

[29] Adrian Preston, "Wolseley, the Khartoum Relief Expedition and the Defence of India, 1885–1900," *Journal of Imperial and Commonwealth History*, 6:254–80 (1979), p. 261.

[30] "Note" dated Cape Coast Castle, December 20, 1973, signed by Col. G.R. Greaves, Chief of Staff, quoted in the *Times*, January 21, 1874.

Elmina or elsewhere. In short, he recommended a negotiated peace, not a victory march.[31]

In mid-October, 1873, Wolseley began an advance toward the Pra River, using non-Europeans troops to prepare a road for the main invasion when that action might finally take place. The Asante armies in the protectorate continued to hold their own against the available British and allied forces, though the British did well at the battle of Abakrampa on November 6.

The anti-war party in Kumasi, however, had been gaining strength during the fall months. Especially in September and October 1873, the Asante army was short of food and the losses from dysentery and smallpox were serious. On the evidence of a Basal missionary detained in Kumasi, the Asante losses from all causes had been enormous. Of the 40,000 men who had invaded the coastal zone at the end of 1872, only 20,000 were alive to retreat across the Pra toward the end of 1873.[32] In early November, the Asante decided to withdraw, and messengers ordering the retreat reached the Asante army on the very day of the battle of Abakrampa. It was ironic that the victory of the war party in London was so nearly simultaneous with the victory of the peace party in Kumasi.[33]

From the middle of December, various units of the promised European troops began to arrive off Cape Coast. The troop ships anchored well offshore or cruised out to sea, where the troops awaited the time to embark and march inland. The plan of campaign called for the invading forces to assemble at four different points just short of the Asante frontier, with a simultaneous advance on Kumasi from different directions beginning on January 15, 1874. On the right was a column of so-called Hausa troops, recruited in Lagos and vicinity and led by Captain J.H. Glover, R.N. On the left were two separate columns of allied African troops under British commanders, while the central attack due north from Cape Coast was under General Wolseley himself along with the European units Wolseley thought so well of.

The weapons of the different columns also varied. The Europeans and West India Regiments were regular British units, equipped with the new Snider rifles. The "Hausas" from Lagos served under British officers, and they too had Sniders. The Fante "allied" troops served under their own commanders and fought with whatever weapons they happened to have, which meant the smooth-bore, muzzle-loading muskets the Asante used as well, though Asante had a very few Enfields in action in 1874.[34]

[31] Earl of Kimberley to Sir Garnet Wolseley, November 24, 1873, CO 879/5, Gold Cost no. 36, pp, 376–78
[32] Home, "Medical History," pp. 229, 141; Winwood Reade, *The Story of the Ashantee Campaign*, pp. 107, 223.
[33] Wilks, *Asante in the Nineteenth Century*, pp. 237–38.
[34] Great Britain. Admiralty. *Statistical Reports of the Health of the Navy*, volume for 1874, p. 176.

Some of the "Hausa" were artillery units, using portable seven-pounders and rockets that could be fired from portable launching tubes. Heavier guns would have been difficult to use without traction or pack animals, and such animals could not be used in the tropical forest with the prevalence of trypanosomiasis. The expeditionary force also took two Gatling guns, an early machine gun of American design, manufactured in England by Armstrong. The Gatlings proved hard to move and maintain. One was abandoned about halfway to the Pra. The other made it as far as the Pra, but it was left there during the advance to Kumasi.

By December 1873, the Asante army that had served in the south was in full retreat and partly demobilized, but Kofi Karikari ordered remobilization to defend the capital, and the Asante army fought hard in the last five days of Wolseley's advance on Kumasi, in spite of its inferior weapons. Wolseley nevertheless reached the emptied capital on February 4. At this point he had so many sick and wounded to be carried back to the coast that he had to limit himself to burning the capital and ordering a retreat two days later.[35] Of the other columns, only Captain Glover's Hausas managed to reach Kumasi; but they arrived only after Wolseley's force had left, and they had followed the main column back down the road to Cape Coast.

It was only during Wolseley's return that Asante emissaries reached him with an offer to make peace. In the resulting Treaty of Fomena, the British got little more than they might have done if the force had never set out, but it made the victory claim plausible. The Asantehene promised to deliver 10,000 ounces of gold and to renounce his claims to Elmina and the other recalcitrant territories to the southwest. Both parties promised to keep the trade routes open, and the Asantehene promised to do all he could to end human sacrifice. Meanwhile in Asante, the opposition to Kofi Karikari grew in strength. In October 1874, his opponents deposed him and forced him and his closest followers into exile.[36]

By that time, the British expeditionary force was gone. Wolseley had continued down the paths to Cape Coast and began reembarkation, as promised, before the end of February. He stayed on only briefly; he gave up his civil command over the Gold Coast and sailed away on March 4.

It was a curiously inconclusive war. Asante was defeated, but its relations with Britain hardly changed in fundamental ways. Once the British troops were safely on their way home, military pressure was no longer available; and Asante had no reason to pay the promised gold. The British let their former enemies live in peace, but they took out their resentment on their former allies. Late in 1874, the British government unilaterally annexed the "protectorate" to create the Gold Coast Colony, with its governor ruling Lagos, as well.[37]

[35] Wilks, *Asante in the Nineteenth Century*, pp. 497–516

[36] Ward, *Gold Coast*, p. 279; Wilks, *Asante in the Nineteenth Century*, pp. 497–516.

[37] Claridge, *Gold Coast and Ashanti*, 2:170–182.

Like Magdala, the campaign's most important consequence was its apparent demonstration of what a modern European army could do, even in tropical climate. Up to the end of May 1874, out of 2,587 European officers and men of army units and the naval brigade that also fought its way to Kumasi, only 71 had died – 27 per thousand, mostly from disease.[38] Some of this achievement could be attributed to sheer luck, but a lot of it depended on careful planning by the medical staff.

Medical Planning: Evacuation by Sea

Every precaution known to medical science at that time was used, beginning with the selection of the dry season for the attack and the limitation on the time European troops could stay on the coast. Surgeon-General Sir William Muir, the head of the Sanitary Branch of the Army Medical Department was the chief medical planner. He drew up a list of Sanitary Instructions, based on past studies of medical topography and information from medical officers recently on the Coast.[39]

The chief medical officer for the expedition itself was Deputy Surgeon-General Sir Anthony D. Home, C.B., V.C., a distinguished military doctor who had played a significant role in civilian public health in Britain. On the march to Kumasi, 73 of the of 270 officers were medical officers – more than a quarter of the total.[40]

As with Magdala, the evacuation of the sick and wounded formed an important aspect of medical planning. Ships designed, or redesigned, as hospital ships had been used for some time on the African coast. The Royal Navy had learned from anti-slavery patrols that a ship lying a mile or two offshore was safe from the "miasma" that brought on fevers. Beginning in 1859, the French had stationed a small troop transport, the *Caravane*, in the Gabon estuary as a semi-permanent hospital for the naval forces in that part of Africa. It had a complement of four surgeons, a pharmacist, and almost 200 men, half African and half European. The Gold Coast had no such secure anchorage, but a trip at sea was a recommended way of clearing out the miasma of shore duty. In the crisis of 1863, Governor Pine of the Gold Coast had ordered himself taken for a cruise to improve his health.[41]

For the Asante expedition, the key hospital ship was *Victor Emmanuel*. She was a steamer of 5,157 tons and 79 guns, launched in 1855 as *Repulse*.

---

[38] Albert A. Gore, *A Contribution to the Medical History of Our West African Campaigns* (London, 1876), p 138.

[39] "Sanitary Instructions for the Guidance of the Principal Medical Officer on the Gold Coast," signed Surgeon-General W.M. Muir, AMSR for 1873, pp. 212–15.

[40] Home, Medical History," p. 258; *Medical Times and Gazette* (London), cited hereafter as MTG, February 21, 1874, 1:218.

[41] Griffon du Bellay, "Rapport médical sur le service de l'hôpital flottant la Caravane mouillé au rade du Gabon, comprenant une period de deux années (du 1er novembre 1861 au 1er novembre 1863), AMN, 1:14–80 (1864); Cabasse, *Notes sur une campagne au Gabon*, pp. 33–37; PP, 1864, xli [C.3364].

In the summer of 1873, she was completely refitted as a hospital ship, including changes to reduce roll while anchored in the open sea off the West Africa coast. Among other things, she was equipped with 18 latrines for enlisted men and four for officers, and like the sleeping quarters for 240 sick and wounded, all were served by forced-air ventilation. She also had special lighting and heating, as well as steel boilers for disinfecting used linen and cooking utensils. Her equipment included surf boats, which could towed by steam launches to the outer edge of the surf, for bringing off the sick and wounded in reasonable comfort (though in fact, the surf boats did not steer well in the surf or under tow, and they had to be abandoned in favor of the ordinary African surf boats paddled by African crews). But the vessel's crowning glory was an ice machine capable of producing 200 pounds of ice a day, using 300 pounds of coal.[42]

The plan was to use *Victor Emmanuel* as the key depot in an elaborate evacuation plan. Three additional steamers that had carried the European troops to the Gold Coast were then kept on, anchored off Cape Coast as auxiliary hospitals in case of need. Their principal role was to evacuate all casualties fit to travel, carrying them to São Vicente in the Cape Verde Islands. There, H.M.S. *Simoom*, a troopship, was stationed to receive sick and wounded and pass them on, as required. Previous experience with dysentery patients from India had suggested that arrival in Britain during the winter months was dangerous. The medical planners had originally hoped to use to use Madeira as a sanitorium, but the Portuguese government turned down the plan for fear of infecting the local population with yellow fever. Gibraltar was the chosen alternative.

Commercial vessels were also assigned a role. Steamers passing São Vicente toward Britain were expected pick up as many of the sick and wounded as they could carry, and the British and African Line ran steamers from Luanda, stopping here and there along the coast, including Cape Coast itself. Other steamers regularly passed São Vicente on their way from South America or South Africa. The Royal Mail Brazilian Line passed twice each month, and steamers from Cape Town, three times a month.[43]

Evacuation by Land

On land, the transportation problem was more difficult. The central Gold Coast was infested with tsetse fly, the carrier of human sleeping sickness, but even more dangerous for animals. No pack or traction animals could live there for long. The whole of the 130 miles from Cape Coast to Kumasi

---

[42] Home, "Medical History," pp. 245–46; MTG, March 14, 1874, 1:296; Léon Colin, "L'expédition anglaise de la côte d'or: étude d'hygiène militaire et de géographie médicale," GHMC, 11(2nd ser.):37–40, 52–54 (1894) p. 53

[43] Commodore W.N.W. Hewett to Sec. Admiralty, 2 February 1874, Africa no. 45, CO 879/6, p. 141–2; Home, "Medical History," 245–46; *Lancet*, Feb. 14 1874, 1:249; MTG, February 21, 1874, 1:218.

was also deep rain forest, except where villagers had cut down the trees or underplanted them with food crops. The main roads were hardly more than trails. To move troops single file along such trails invited ambush.

African workers under the direction of Royal Engineers began building a road wide enough for a carriage from Cape Coast to the Pra River. Early in the planning phase, Sir Garnet Wolseley had hoped to build a light rail tramway along the route to the Pra, modeled on the tramway from Annesley Bay to the foot of the mountains. Equipment for nine miles of track actually arrived in Cape Coast on an experimental basis, along with two light steam "sappers" that could serve as traction vehicles on rails or on a road.

The trail had to cross too many deep gullies to make a tramway practical, but some British planners set great store by it. The *Lancet* in particular kept returning to it in editorials:

This Ashantee expedition is an altogether peculiar one. The military dangers are utterly insignificant compared to those arising from a deadly climate, and we must be prepared to apply the achievements of modern science to the task.[44]

It saw in the rail line not only a way to victory in campaign but also a way to ensure that a friendly government would remain in power in Kumasi once the war was over.[45]

For the advance to the Pra, Wolseley ordered the construction of seven camps – eight counting a major site at Prasu on the river bank. They were spaced about ten miles apart, reckoned to represent a day's march and a distance appropriate to the climate. Each camp had a series of huts sufficient to accommodate 400 men, with split bamboo walls and palm thatch roofing sometimes reinforced by used canvas supplied by the navy. The plan was to move the men forward in units of 400, each new unit taking the place of the one that moved on, until they were all at at the Pra, where the prepared camp for European troops could accommodate 2,000.[46] West Indians and Africans had to make do with tents they carried or other shelter they could find. Once beyond the Pra, the expedition had to set up tented camps each evening. Wolseley himself traveled along the road in an open carriage pulled by a eight Africans in front, with four pushing from behind.

The soldiers for the main push of January and February were also equipped with tropical uniforms designed and manufactured especially for the occasion, made of grayish-brown woolen homespun, for the hot days and cool nights. The tunic was loose with an open neck. Each man carried a waterproof ground sheet, a blanket, a flannel undershirt, a pocket water filter, and a wooden water bottle copied from the one used

[44] *Lancet*, 1873, 2:344 (September 6.)
[45] *Lancet*, 1873, 2:497 (October 4). See also Cardwell to Wolseley, Sept. 23, 1873, CO 879/5, No. 35.
[46] Home, "Medical History," 246–47; MTG, 1874 1:129 (January 31, 1874).

by the Italian army.[47] African porters carried the food, additional water, and equipment – some of it, like cots for the camps, carried forward before the troops actually arrived. As at Magdala, this required far more porters than fighting men.

The main constraint, indeed, was transport, and the reason seems clear enough. Wolseley expected thousands of local laborers to volunteer, where only hundreds turned up. He blamed the Africans for "their natural laziness and their habits of self-indulgence lead them to run away, rather than remain and work, although they are well paid." If the illustrations by the artist for *Illustrated London News* are correct, the British officers were liberal with the use of the lash on porters, and the pay and rations were less than generous. The British offered 4-1/2 pence a day, plus rations of a quarter-pound of salt meat and a pound of rice per person. Wolseley thought that would be enough to maintain Africans in "health and efficiency"[48] – repeating the error of underfeeding that had been so disastrous on the Magdala campaign.

Nor was the pay generous by Gold Coast standards. Men of the ill-fated Gold Coast Corps of the 1850s were paid seven pence a day, even though they were recruited by purchase, not voluntary enlistment. In 1874, the Kru sailors the Navy recruited on the Liberian coast were paid one shilling, six pence plus normal Navy rations; "Hausa" recruited in the hinterland of Lagos received a shilling, plus three pence in lieu of rations.[49]

On the 1874 expedition, the allied African soldiers received a half-pound of meat per day, while the West Indian Regiments had one pound of meat (either fresh or salt), one pound of bread or rice, some tea and sugar, and a half-gill of rum. European troops did even better. Their daily ration was one and a half pounds of bread, one and a half pounds of salt meat, plus rice or peas, potatoes, tea, sugar, sausage, cheese, chocolate, a half-gill of rum, and an ounce of lime juice.[50]

With the passage of time, the problem of recruiting carriers became increasingly difficult, and it was especially serious on the retreat. At first, Wolseley had hoped to get by with only lightly coerced or "volunteer" laborers, but, from January on, he changed to a policy of forced labor for every able-bodied man he could catch south of the Pra. A few of the "Hausas" recruited in Lagos were also slaves recruited by purchase for £5 each, though home authorities frowned on that practice.[51]

[47] Home, "Medical History," 245. The regulations for the naval brigade of 310 marines and sailors were similar, though issued by their own officers. Great Britain, Admiralty, *Statistical Reports of the Health of the Navy*, volume for 1874, p. 170.

[48] Wolseley to Secretary of State for War, No. 135/73 m.s., 15 December 1873, WO 32/7639; *Illustrated London News*, March 6, 1874, p. 12; Wolseley to Secretary of State for War, No. 101/73, 17 November 1873, WO 32/7638.

[49] Gore, "Leaves from my Diary During the Ashantee War," BMJ, 1, 1874, pp. 377, 572.

[50] A.G. Delmerge, GB, Admiralty, Statistical returns for 1873, p. 206.

[51] Wolseley to Secretary of State for War, No. 23/74 m.s., 25 January 1874, WO 32/7639; Glover to Wolseley, Accra, 8 November 1873 and Kimberley to Sir G. Wolseley, 17 December 1873, PP, 1874, xlvi, part 2, [C. 893], pp. 19, 21.

Aside from walking, the usual means of transportation on the Gold Coast was a hammock slung from a long pole carried by four men. To remove each wounded or sick man from the interior to the coast required the labor of four porters for up to two weeks. For the advance beyond the Pra, 150 bearers were stationed at the Prasu, ready to rush forward and bring back any men who fell sick or were wounded on the final advance into Asante. Since the army was surrounded on all sides most of the way the Pra to Kumasi, the sick and wounded had to be carried forward and then back again with the retreat.[52]

For the return to the coast, each of the camps was outfitted with a small hospital of 35 beds, with enough bearers stationed at each to carry these men on canvas cots down the road to the next camp. There, the bearers dropped off the invalids and returned for a new roundtrip the next day. In emergencies, it was expected that they might make two roundtrips a day.[53] The Europeans, in short, were expected to travel only ten miles a day with light packs, but the African bearers had to carry heavy loads twice that far routinely – and up to fifty miles a day in emergencies.

Not all of the camp hospitals were finished in time for the advance, but space for the sick and wounded could be found in the regular huts. Nor were hospitals fully provided on the coast or at the Pra, but enough hospital equipment was forwarded to accommodate 45 percent of the European troops if necessary, plus 20 percent of the West Indians, and with a reserve equal to 7 percent of the whole force.

Fevers

The most important single fear was "fevers." On the Gold Coast this meant the continuous threat of falciparum malaria, and the background threat of a yellow fever epidemic; which would have been the most serious threat of all, if an epidemic had occurred during the expedition. In the 1870s, medical opinion about the cause of yellow fever was still divided. Many still thought it was caused by miasma or others local conditions in much the same way as malaria. Others considered it to be infectious, carried from one person to another in some unknown way. Whether miasma or contagion, the standard defense against the disease in the West Indies had been flight from wherever the outbreak occurred. This stratagem was sometimes successful, and it generally worked whether the flight was to escape miasma or contagion.

The medical officers in charge of this expedition considered yellow fever to be contagious. They set up a strict quarantine of all ships arriving at Cape Coast from African ports. As a precaution against the possible contagion reaching the sick on board *Victor Emmanuel*, they bought *Ilione*,

---

[52] Surgeon-Major Mackinnon quoted in Home, "Medical History," p. 254.
[53] AMSR for 1873, p. 214; Home, "Medical History," p. 249.

a transport then on the coast, and fitted her out as an isolation hospital for any yellow fever cases that might occur. If the disease did begin to spread aboard *Victor Emmanuel*, she had orders to proceed immediately to a cold climate. Because Africans were supposed to be immune, the emergency plan was to replace *Ilione's* European crew with African sailors, Krumen recruited in Liberia.[54]

Yellow fever was thought to appear less frequently on the Gold Coast than elsewhere in West Africa, but it had appeared in 1852, 1857, 1859, and 1862. In February 1873, a yellow fever epidemic struck Sierra Leone. In April and May, another hit the Bonny River in the Niger delta, killing two-thirds of the small group of European residents. A close call for the Gold Coast came in November 1873, when the African Mail Company's steamer *Ambriz*, sailing from Luanda, lost 13 dead to yellow fever before it reached Cape Coast. It was quarantined, but the mail it carried was transferred to another ship, presumably along with at least one infected passenger, because the yellow fever outbreak continued on the second ship between Cape Coast and Liverpool.[55] If the infection had appeared on shore at Cape Coast during the expedition itself, the result could have been the medical and military disaster so many had predicted. Past West African experience would indicate a probable loss of life in the range of 30 to 70 percent.

Malaria was less fatal but more predictable. Dr. Albert Gore, one of the principal medical planners, believed in quinine prophylaxis; he may be the source of the order to give 5 grains (32.4 centigrams) a day for all European troops. In July 1873, the Admiralty made arrangements to send 70 pounds of quinine to Cape Coast. The navy still gave men daily quinine on shore duty, but not on board ship. The naval medical officer in charge of the men at Cape Coast and Elmina in June 1873 had followed a variant of that policy, giving the men quinine when they left the fort but not while on barracks duty. But even he was forced to give daily quinine from late June onward, when the orders for the expedition came down from London.[56]

Anthony Home, the chief army medical officer who brought those orders was not himself a believer in quinine – either as a preventive or to mitigate the seriousness of the fever. He was convinced, like most other medical men of his time, that malarial fevers were caused by miasma, especially gasses rising from damp ground or swamps. He saw protection against damp and cold as the first line of defense against fever. In his view, everyone on the Gold Coast breathed in miasma and was harboring the disease after only a short period of residence. To make the latent disease actual requires an exciting cause, of which cold is the most common,

[54] MTG, February 21, 1874, 1:219; Home, "Medical History," pp. 245–46.
[55] Home, "Medical History," p. 233; MTG, December 13, 1873, 2:667.
[56] A.G. Delmerge in Great Britain, Admiralty, *Statistical Reports of the Health of the Navy*, volume for 1873, p. 206.

and this was why he took such pains to keep the troops on march to the interior as dry and warm as was humanly possible. The special clothing and the prepared camps were partly anti-malarial precautions.[57]

Water and Sewage

Pure water was not well understood. After the losses of the Marines in the summer of 1873, naval authorities were especially concerned. They believed that water could absorb gases: bad water therefore not only caused dysentery, but could also cause fevers, due to the malarial miasma dissolved in it.[58] No one at the time understood purity as the absence of bacteria; pure water meant water that was chemically pure and had as little organic content as possible. Anthony Home had his own interpretation. For him, malaria and dysentery were simply two different manifestations of poisoning by malarial gas, an illness which sometimes took the form of "bilious remittent fever," sometimes dysentery, and sometimes both.[59]

Drinking the water wasn't the only dangerous thing a soldier could do: walking in it could also cause sickness. Some of the British medical men believed that Guinea worm (*Dracunculus medinensis*) could be acquired through the skin, by stepping in pools of water. In fact, as the Gold Coast Africans had long understood, the worm enters the body in drinking water and passes through the walls of the stomach into the blood. Pools of water, however, posed still another kind of threat from chilled feet. Albert Gore believed streams along the route could be a "fertile source of colic and diarrhea," and he thought this and Guinea worm were so serious that he arranged for guards to be placed at each pool and stream along the way, in order to prevent the men from stepping in the water or using it in any way.[60]

As in the Magdala campaign, medical authorities called on the steamers' ability to distill drinking water, which they knew was safe. But what if steamers were not available in every circumstance? The naval medical officer in charge of the marines at Cape Coast in the summer of 1873, for example, thought that all drinking water should be boiled, but accommodation at the cook house was too limited to make that possible. He retreated to putting drip-stones outside the barracks and ordering the men not to drink water until it had dripped through the stones, though he suspected that many men would drink the water before filtration rather than wait.[61]

---

[57] Lushington to Colonial Office, July 21, 1873, in Africa No. 35, CO 879/5; Gore, *West African Campaigns*, p. 164; Home, "Medical History," pp. 219–22, 229.

[58] Richard Eustace to Sir Alexander Armstrong, August 26, 1873, PP, 1874, xlvii [C. 891], pp. 98–99.

[59] Home, "Medical History," p. 222

[60] Gore, *West African Campaigns*, p. 36; Muir, "Sanitary Instructions," p. 215.

[61] Great Britain, Admiralty, *Statistical Reports of the Health of the Navy* for 1873, pp. 205, 209.

As the departure of the main expedition approached, naval medical authorities installed two distilling devices on shore in Cape Coast, capable of delivering 2,000 gallons a day. To carry distilled water was impractical once the march inland had begun. Muir's recommendations for the road included chemical testing, and suitable test kits were sent along. He also recommended "Norton's tubular pumps," which could draw water from four to six feet deep in sandy soil during rainy periods, as well as general filtration and pocket filters for officers.[62]

Home's more detailed instructions were based on a War Office circular on the treatment of water. First of all, alum should be added to precipitate foreign matter. Water was then to be passed through three filter layers of sponge, sand, and charcoal. Ironically, this process alone would have strained out large impurities and improved the taste, but left the bacteria untouched. But then the water was to be boiled and, finally, "to complete oxidization" a few drops of potassium permanganate were to be added.[63]

The recommendations to boil and to add potassium permanganate were both new, both introduced since the march to Magdala; sufficient boiling and potassium permanganate would have made the water safe for drinking. Home conceded, however, that the entire procedure would be impossible to follow under field conditions, but he ordered the medical officers to do as much as they could under the circumstances. He also ordered them never to make camp where the retreating Asante army had camped before them, which may well have made as much difference as all other forms of advice.[64]

Whatever the cause, the European deaths from gastrointestinal infection were substantially lower than they had been in the Magdala campaign – down from more than 20 to less than 7 per thousand. For the West Indians, deaths from this cause were still less than 8 per thousand – a very creditable rate for that period.

The Medical Results

It is hard to fight a war and keep records at the same time. The statistical picture of health on the Asante campaign is inevitably less accurate than peacetime records. It is also confused by the fact that the British Army and the Navy kept separate records, each following its own procedures, and the European officers and non-coms of the West India Regiments were omitted from the army records for European units. The army records nevertheless cover 2,300 of the 2,587 European troops

[62] "Sanitary Instructions," AMSR for 1873, pp. 212–15; Leveson to Colonial Office, September 4, 1873, CO 879/5, African no. 35.
[63] Richard Eustace to Sir Alexander Armstrong, August 26, 1873, PP, 1874, xlvii [C. 891], pp. 98–99; Home, "Medical History," p. 223.
[64] Colin, *Expédition anglaise*, 4:53; MTG, December 20, 1873, 2:695.

Table 3.1. *Morbidity and Mortality on the Gold Coast Campaign, 1874*

Gold Coast Campaign - Morbidity and Mortality of European Troops

Cause of Death	Number		Proportion per Thousand per Month		Percentage of Total	
	Admitted	Died	Admitted	Died	Admitted	Died
Fevers and sunstroke	739	21	161	4.57	54.9	52.5
Dysentery and diarrhea	153	15	33	3.26	11.4	37.5
Other or unknown	453	4	98	0.87	33.7	10.0
Total disease	1345	40	292	8.70	100.0	100.0
Enemy action	158	13	34	2.83		
Total	1503	53	327	11.52		

Note:
Included admissions in the Gold Coast from January 1, 1874, to February 28, 1874, plus deaths occasioned by tropical duty down to May 31, 1874. Deaths and admissions classified as sunstroke and apoplexy have been included with fevers. Strength was 2,300. Proportions are based on numbers at January 1, not average mean strength, but no new strength was added during the campaign. Data are for enlisted men only.
All columns may not add on account of rounding.

Morbidity and Mortality of West Indian Troops

Cause of Death	Number		Proportion per Thousand per Month		Percentage of Total	
	Admitted	Died	Admitted	Died	Admitted	Died
Fevers and sunstroke	258	9	56	1.96	26.1	26.5
Dysentery and diarrhea	134	17	29	3.70	13.5	50.0
Other and unknown	598	8	130	1.74	60.4	23.5
Total disease	990	34	215	7.39	100.0	100.0
Enemy action	22	1	5	0.22		
Total	1012	35	220	7.61		

Mortality of "Irregular Native Troops"

All Causes	22		8.65	

Note:
Total Strength was 1,271 of men enlisted and serving under British officers. This does not include allied Fante and other troops serving under their own commander. Deaths from disease were not reported.

Source:
A.D. Home, "Medical History of the War," pp. 258–59.

that made the advance on Kumasi. The results are summarized in Table 3.1.[65]

For a short campaign of this kind, another statistical problem comes from the habitual ways of collecting and presenting records about the health of the army. One tradition, going back to Tulloch and Balfour in the late 1830s, was to produce annual figures, based on hospital admissions and deaths per thousand average mean strength, an appropriate measure for troops in barracks in peacetime.

A second kind of measure is the cost of casualties to attain a particular objective, in addition to the cost of keeping troops in field or barracks for a particular time. Records for short campaigns in Africa, like M'Williams' report in the Niger expedition, or Anthony Home's medical report on the march to Kumasi, cover too short a period to be annualized. For comparison to other, similar, campaigns their figures have to be translated into rates of death or morbidity per month.

The overall mortality for European troops on the Asante expedition was usually given as 27 per thousand *for the two-month campaign,* from all causes. The sample used in Table 3.1, at 23 per thousand, is therefore somewhat lower. In fact, deaths from enemy action came to nearly 6 per thousand per month, leaving deaths from disease at 8.7 per thousand per month.

The losses of the West Indians and Africans who fought on the British side were less carefully recorded, which creates the large category of "other" on Table 3.1 and throws doubt on the accuracy of the West Indian part of the table as a whole. Even so, West Indian deaths from disease as reported came to 7.39 per thousand per month. African troops fighting in British units – as opposed to the Fante and other allies who fought under their own commanders – suffered deaths from all causes at 8.65 per thousand per month, more than the West Indians but less than the Europeans. Thus, while losses could vary greatly from one unit to another, the soldiers' varied origin in Europe, the Caribbean, or West Africa made far less difference on this campaign than it had done earlier in the century, and would do when the conquest of tropical African began in the 1880s. (See Table 1.1, Tables for chapter 4.) The losses to disease of Indian and European soldiers had also been similar on the Magdala expedition.

Seasonal differences in the disease death rate were higher. A detachment of 104 Royal Marines enlisted men and six officers landed on the Gold Coast on June 6, 1873, and they reembarked in late July and early August after about two months on shore, roughly the same duration as the main expedition in the next dry season, but this was the wet season.

---

[65] Home, "Medical History," p. 258. The figures he presents are a little hard to interpret because he listed seven deaths from sunstroke and apoplexy. The temperatures during the march on Kumase were mainly in the low 80s F., far too low to produce genuine heat stroke. The most probable explanation is that cases listed as "sunstroke" were actually cerebral malaria.

Table 3.2. *British Military Mortality in West Africa, 1859–75*

Year	Deaths per Thousand	Year	Deaths per Thousand
1859	666.00	1867	133.33
1860	400.00	1868	66.67
1861	181.80	1869	0.00
1862	0.00	1870	ND
1863	69.00	1871	250.00
1864	115.00	1872	0.00
1865	66.67	1873	145.45
1866	66.67	1874	ND
		1875	111.11
Average 1859–75 (omitting years without data)			151.45

Note:

The number present in any year was about 10 non-coms assigned to the West India regiments, except for 1874, when a substantial force was landed; though it remained on shore for only two months. There is no statistically meaningful way to include its losses as an annual rate.

Of the enlisted men, 18 died – a loss of 173 per thousand, or 87 per thousand per month – ten times the death rate of European troops on the march to Kumasi the following year.[66] The sample is small but suggests what might have happened if the army had no choice of season for its main thrust. The navy also sent a naval brigade and a marine battalion, totaling 310 men altogether on the march to Kumasi. Their losses were higher than those of army units, both from enemy action and from disease: 16.13 per thousand per month from all causes; and 11.40 per month from disease alone.[67]

The large sample of army casualties used in Table 3.1 is the best we have for cause of death. Fevers had been most feared, and malaria was indeed responsible for more than half of all deaths from disease among European troops in this sample, while gastrointestinal infections accounted for 38 percent. For the West Indian troops, these proportions were nearly reversed. The gastrointestinal group was responsible for half of their mortality, as against only 27 percent from fevers. The malaria case-fatality rate of 2.84 percent for the European troops was a truly remarkable achievement for that time and place. It was likely the result of the disciplined administration of prophylactic quinine. The case-fatality rate for gastrointestinal infection was higher – but still only 9.8 percent.

[66] Richard Eustace to Sir Alexander Armstrong, August 26, 1873, PP, 1874, xlvii [C. 891], pp. 98–99; Home, "Medical History," p. 225.
[67] Great Britain, Admiralty, *Statistical Reports of the Health of the Navy* volume for 1874, p. 207.

Table 3.3. *Mortality of European Officers in West Africa, 1876–90*

Rates per thousand mean strength

	Deaths	Deaths plus Repatriated on Account of Health
1876	0.00	111.11
1877	0.00	181.82
1878	0.00	33.33
1879	83.33	250.00
1880	0.00	250.00
1881	0.00	933.33
1882	111.11	333.00
1883	0.00	400.00
1884	0.00	250.00
1885	181.11	818.17
1886	76.92	153.84
1887	0.00	500.00
1888	0.00	500.00
1889	29.41	176.47
1890	0.00	0.00
Average 1876–90	32.13	326.07

Source:
AMSR, annual series.

It was a common assumption of military medicine in the nineteenth century that death from disease would be considerably higher on campaign than in barracks. Since no European troops were on the Gold Coast in the 1870s, it is hard to make a direct comparison. It is possible, however, to compare the losses on this campaign with the usual barracks death rate of European non-commissioned officers serving with African or West Indian troops. Men in this service were too few for a single year's mortality to have any meaning, but the death rate of these troops over the period 1859–75 presented an annual average of 151 per thousand (12.6 per month). It was thus significantly higher than the death rate on the march to Kumasi, underlining once more the extent to which that campaign was atypical of West African health conditions.

Perhaps as a result of lessons learned on that expedition, their annual average loss from 1876 onward to 1890 dropped to 32.1 per thousand (2.68 per month), but the repatriation rate of nearly 300 per thousand per year (25 per month) was so high, one is forced to conclude that it is statistically so weak that it may be meaningless. It was hardly higher than the disease death rate of "seasoned" West Indians, and lower than the death rate of Europeans in West Africa, both before and after.

Remarkable as the medical achievements of the march to Kumasi were, British authorities reported them in a way that exaggerated them still more. The expedition was hailed as final proof that European soldiers could now be sent safely to fight in any part of the world. Lord Carnarvon, who succeeded Kimberly at the Colonial Office in the middle of the campaign, gave the death rate as 23 per thousand and claimed that this was "about the same as the death rate in the metropolis, and lower than the death rate in some other English towns."[68] This is a statement that suggests Mark Twain on lies, damned lies, and statistics. Carnarvon was comparing two-month losses on the Gold Coast with an entire year in London, and those of young men at the prime of life with civilians of all ages. In fact, the annual average disease death rate of British troops serving in Britain over the years 1869–77 was 7.68 (0.64 per month); their death rate on the march to Kumasi was thus twelve times what it would have been if they could have stayed at home.[69]

Professional military reactions were also favorable, if less exaggerated. The director of the Hôpital de Val-de-Grâce, the training hospital for French military doctors, recognized that the Gold Coast represented to worst "climate" on earth for European troops; a success there was all the more outstanding, and other French medical authorities held up the example as a lesson on what could be done in the tropics.[70] Both the *Lancet* and the *Medical Times and Gazette* hailed the achievements of modern medical science. As an editorial in the *Medical Times and Gazette* put it:

One fact the present campaign has conclusively established, and that is the possibility of sending British troops to fight in any part of the known world without incurring exceptionally heavy loss from climate, if – as in this case – the medical department is allowed to make its own preparations and provisions. It would be difficult to point to a spot in any country more deadly to the Europeans than the West Coast of Africa . . . and this can be readily understood when it is remembered that even to the natives themselves it proved deadly.[71]

Other public figures were not so quick to give the credit to medical science. Both Gladstone, who had been Prime Minister at the beginning of the war, and Disraeli, who was Prime Minister at its end, rose in the House of Commons to heap praise on the commanders of the expedition – especially on Sir Garnet Wolseley and the naval leaders. The habit of blaming or praising the commander, whatever his actual role, was common enough, but this time it was noted in medical circle. The *Lancet* called

---

[68] Quoted in Claridge, *Gold Coast and Ashanti*, 2:166.
[69] Curtin, *Death by Migration*, Table A.4, p. 168.
[70] Colin, *Expédition anglaise*, 3:36 ff.; E. Rochefort, "Étude médicale sur l'expédition anglaise contre les ashantis," AMN 21:321–46 (1874); P. C. V. Huas, *Considerations sur l'hygiène des troupes en campagne dans les pays intertropicaux* (Bordeaux, thesis no. 17, 1886).
[71] MTG, 1874, 1;240 (Feb. 18, 1874). See also *Lancet*, March 21, 1874, 1:421; MTG, March 14, 1874, 1:293; *Lancet*, June 10, 1874, 1:889.

attention edtorially to this neglect, and a few members of Parliament rose to complain that the doctors' contribution was slighted.[72]

The medical reputation of the campaign grew over the years, though Wolseley usually got most of the credit. It was generally taken as the landmark campaign proving that Europeans could fight in the tropics, though some critics pointed out that losses were still high, unless European troops were used as Wolseley used them – in emergency situations only, and on shore for the shortest possible periods of time.[73]

Whether success was based on skill or luck, it was hard to duplicate. Down to 1900, no French expedition in the tropical world had such a low rate of loss from disease alone, though the Asante expedition of 1874 was often cited as example what was possible. For the British, only the Asante expedition of 1895–96, which did no fighting at all, was a notable improvement over the record set in 1874.[74] More than a century later, the Magdala campaign and the march on Kumasi were still held up by military historians as the model campaigns of their time.[75]

[72] *Hansard*, 218(3rd ser.):412–31 (March 30, 1874).
[73] Gustave A. Reynaud, *Considerations sanitaires sur l'expédition de Madagascar et quelques autres expéditions coloniales, françaises et anglaises* (Paris, 1898), pp. 247.
[74] Anon., "Army Medical Efficiency: Mortality of French and British Military Expeditions," *British Medical Journal*, 1898, ii, 991–92.
[75] Hew Strachan, *European Armies and the Conduct of War* (London: Allen and Unwin, 1983), p. 78.

CHAPTER 4

TROPICAL CONQUEST IN
WEST AFRICA

"... the tax in blood ..."

It was five years after the exemplary march of Kumasi that the conquest of tropical Africa began, the beginning conventionally dated from the resumption of the French advance up the Senegal Valley in 1879. The European conquest was confined, to the decades of the 1880s and the 1890s, with a few exploratory thrusts before that period, and several forays in the early decades of this century to clean up lingering pockets of resistance. European control was clearly established by 1900, even though the Anglo–Boer War was to drag on till 1902.

It was a conquest of one continent by people from another, but it was also part of the worldwide and final phase of European imperialism. Some aspects of the conquest of West Africa had closer parallels to events in the Amazon forest or Southeast Asia than they did to those in Egypt or South Africa.

West Africa was a comparatively unimportant region to Europe at this time. Algeria, and later Tunisia and Morocco, were far more important to France. Egypt, and later South Africa, were to be much more important to Britain. An exploration of relations between disease and empire in Africa nevertheless begins logically with West Africa where the European confrontation with disease was longer, and the disease problem was more serious than anywhere else in the tropical world. The disease cost of empire building was perhaps highlighted in West Africa more than elsewhere. The fact that European interest in tropical Africa, commercial or strategic, was marginal at best sharpens the contrast between the costs in death from disease and potential gains from territorial acquisition.

As military operations, these conquests were a myriad of small campaigns by tiny "European" armies that were, in fact, mostly African. They were armed with the latest military technology, and sought to use the best of modern medicine as well; though they killed the enemy more effectively than they protected their own troops from disease. Rather than attempting to deal with so many small campaigns, the complexity of the relationship between disease and empire can be illuminated by dealing with the two segments of the conquest of West Africa that are best known: the French push eastward from Senegal into the Western Sudan; and the European advance northward from the Gulf of Guinea. That second advance can be investigated in turn through the sample of two French expeditions against Dahomey and two British expeditions against Asante.

Political Background in France

The conquest of tropical Africa began in Senegal where the French expansion inland had stopped in the 1850s. In the late 1870s, the idea of a forward move into the Western Sudan received new support from a reconfiguration of French schemes, in the wake of defeat in the Franco–Prussian war. Algeria had been by far the most important French interest in Africa, and elements of the Algeria lobby in Paris suggested a trans-Saharan railway to expand that colony and tap the mythical commercial wealth south of the desert. On reexamination, the trans-Saharan link did not appear as feasible, technically or politically, as it had first seemed, but in 1879, Admiral Jauréguiberry, the Minister of the Navy, seizing the impetus of the Algerian scheme, pushed for a separate railroad eastward from Senegal to the Niger, beginning at Kayes, the head of navigation on the Senegal. In due course, the Chambre des Députés passed an initial appropriation for the railway, and for six new forts along the projected railway line.

It might seem curious that the French navy should be concerned about a region so far from the ocean, but it had a long-standing concern with the colonies. Before 1894, France had no colonial ministry, so that colonial affairs fell under the preview of the navy, or sometimes under the Minister of Commerce. Because of this naval connection, most colonial land warfare outside North Africa fell to the *infantrie de marine* and the *artillerie de marine*. In Algeria, as in France itself, the Minister of War held the chief responsibility, and under Napoleon III, the War Department had become the effective ruler of Algeria. Elsewhere, colonial governors were often naval officers, either shipboard officers or from the marine infantry or artillery. Thus the French *forces armées* were divided between the rival ministries of *guerre* and *marine*, each with its own conventional authority over a part of the overseas world. The rivalry had its own setting in French political life, but it paralleled aspects of the conflict in Britain between "Wolseley's Ring" and the Indian Army in those same decades.

The French marine infantry and artillery were usually made up of voluntary recruits, occasionally filled out with men from the annual calls for national service. It was generally known that tropical service was dangerous, but not precisely how dangerous. Annual reports on the health of troops stationed in France and Algeria had been published since the 1860s, but the parallel series for soldiers under the naval ministry began only in 1897. Some said that the navy had withheld this information, because its losses from disease were so great.[1] In any event, service with the marines was intentionally voluntary, partly to protect draftees from the recognized health hazards, partly because of the prevalent belief that soldiers under about 22 years of age had weaker immunities to a tropical "climate."

By the 1870s, the navy recognized a kind of hierarchy of danger from disease, with service in Senegal, Madagascar, or later on, the French Sudan, seen as more dangerous than service in the Antilles, Réunion, or Oceania. This scale of danger had several consequences. Marines served only a two-year tour of duty on Madagascar or in Senegal. In Senegal, soldiers were screened each year for physical condition, and those who failed were sent home before the first of May, to save them from the dangers of the fever season that arrived with the summer rains. For similar reasons, reinforcements were sent out so as to arrive in October, in time for the usual dry-season campaigning beyond the upper Senegal.

Planning for service in Madagascar was even more elaborate. Troops on a two-year tour spent the first year on the island of Réunion, which was malarial but less lethal than coastal Madagascar, where they spent their second year at Diego-Suarez (now Antsiranana) near the northern end of that island. In Senegal, in a less systematic project, new troops were stationed for the first six months at Gorée or Saint Louis, where the malaria death rate was far lower than it was in the interior (refer to Table 4.3); in any event, as many European soldiers as possible were pulled back to the coast during the rainy season.[2] By the 1880s, marine infantry units stationed in France were paired with an equivalent unit stationed overseas, but – unlike the similar British practice – they did not change places. Instead, personnel from the units in France were called overseas as needed.

In Senegal and its hinterland, where the War Ministry had no role at all, the Naval Ministry was especially strong, and even the Ministry of Foreign Affairs had little say in the absence of a rival colonial power in the neighborhood. The governor was usually a former naval officer, and the military officers who led the conquest of the French Sudan were either from the *infantrie de marine* (like Louis-Alexandre Brière de l'Isle or Joseph Galliéni) or from the *artillerie de marine* (like Gustave Borgnis-Desborde or Louis Archinard). The Haut-Sénégal-Niger, as the interior was called, was so isolated from other political currents that officers there could often act on their own.

---

[1] *Revue des troupes coloniales*, 3:14–15, 399–420; Bonnafy, "L'armée coloniale," *Bulletin de la société de géographie commericale du Havre*, 1900–01:13–26, 91–110 (1900–01); Bonnafy, "Statistique Médicale de la Cochinchine (1861–1888)," *Archives de médicine navale*, 67:161–96 (1897).

[2] A. Legrand, *L'hygiène des troupes européenes aux colonies et dans les expéditions coloniales* (Paris, 1895)., pp. 392–404; Charles De Singly, *L'infantrie de marine* (Paris, 1890); Edouard François Plouzané, *Contribution à l'étude d'hygiène pratique des troupes européenes dans les pays intertropicaux: Haut Sénégal et Haut Niger* (Bordeaux, Thesis no., 89, 1887), pp. 12–14.

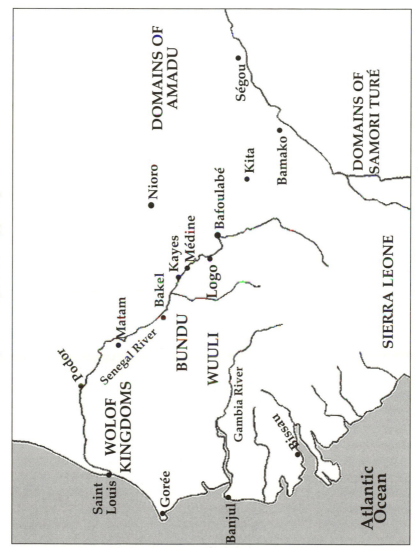

Map 4.1. Senegal and the Upper Niger

French opinion about the overseas world was sometimes concerned that empire building might weaken France in Europe, especially in the face of a continued German threat. Marine officers on the upper Senegal were largely free of that problem because most of the troops under their command were African. Even taking the Europeans into account, a total force of five hundred to a thousand men in Haut-Sénégal-Niger could hardly weigh heavily in the European balance. Yet the force was large enough for the military conquest of the Sudan, and the marine officers who led it often did so without authorization from Paris, sometimes in the face of orders from Paris. The most flagrant disobedience of orders occurred under the command of Louis Archinard from 1888 to 1893, after which the navy recalled him and replaced him with a civilian governor. In 1894, his opponents became the principal officials of the newly founded Ministry of Colonies.[3]

In Senegal, those who contemplated French expansion to the east had several possible reasons for supposing that the fearful mortality of the early century had finally subsided. They had the example of the Asante expedition of 1874, with its widely advertised low death rate. They could point to the reduction of garrison mortality in Senegal; over the two decades from 1852 to 1873 the death rate of the Senegal garrison troops fell to 70 per thousand – less than half the loss of 151 per thousand among British troops on West African duty over the years 1849–75.[4] (Refer to Table 3.2.)

But the comparatively low mortality for Senegal could be deceptive. Steamers between Saint Louis and France were now regular and frequent; sick soldiers could easily be repatriated, and some of those repatriates certainly died. In some ways, an index of dead plus repatriated is a more accurate indicator of the cost of disease, and this index for Senegal over the period 1852–73 was 228 per thousand. The expected death rate on campaign would have been substantially higher, but French advocates of a drive east toward the Niger could fall back on the fact that the *tirailleurs sénégalais* were by now an effective force serving under French marine officers. It was the tirailleurs who would do most of the fighting.

The Yellow Fever Epidemics

Whatever the French expected as they prepared to move toward the Niger, the disease reality was far worse than anyone predicted. Yellow fever epidemics reached the French posts in 1878 and again in 1881, killing half or more of the European population each time. Yellow fever had been a periodic visitor in the past, but the time between epidemics

---

[3] Alexander Sydney Kanya-Forstner, "The French Marines and the Conquest of the Western Sudan, 1880–1899," in J. H. De Moor and H.L. Weselling, *Imperialism and War* (Leiden: Brill, 1989), pp. 121–45.; Kanya-Forstner, *The Conquest of the Western Sudan: A Study in French Military Imperialism* (Cambridge, 1969), esp. 55–83, 174–214.

[4] Alfred Borius,"Topographie médicale du Sénégal," AMN, 33:114– , 270– , 321– , 416– ; 34:1278– ,330–,340– ; 35:114– ,280– ,473– ; 36:117– ,321– ; 37:140– ,230– , 297– ,367– ,456– (1879–82), 33: 438.

Table 4.1. *Death Rate of European Civilians in Senegal Yellow Fever Epidemics*

Year	Place	European Mortality Percent	Case Fatality Percent
1778	Saint Louis	70	
1830	Gorée	57	59
	Saint Louis	50	66
1836	Saint Louis	51	
1837	Gorée	23	58
1859	Gorée		70
1866–67	Gorée	33	47
1878	Gorée and Dakar	64	85
	Saint Louis	20	34
1881		81	

Sources:
Le Jemble, *Epidémiologie de la fièvre jaune au Sénégal*, pp. 16-23, 90.
C. Baril, "Rapport médicale sur l'expédition du Logo," p. 241.
P.-E. Duval, *Gorée comme foyer de fièvre jaune au Sénégal*.
Chevé, *Fièvre jaune*, pp. 46–48.

had been variable, as long as fifty years, or less than a decade (Table 4.1). In a crowded urban setting, like that of the island towns of Gorée and Saint Louis, almost all of the non-immune population would be infected, and 50 to 70 percent of those infected would die.

French naval doctors had a good deal of experience with yellow fever in the Caribbean and during the Mexican expedition of the 1860s. They knew that it came as an epidemic that usually lasted less than a year and then disappeared. They knew that it was in some sense contagious, but opinion was divided as to whether it passed from one person to his neighbor through contact or proximity, in the manner of smallpox, or whether it simply affected many people in the same town because of miasma or some other conditions that came to be associated with that place.

They also understood the disease could not travel fast, unless it was associated with the movement of an individual. The usual steps taken against the disease were quarantine to prevent the import of the fever and flight once it arrived. Plague and cholera were treated in much the same way. When yellow fever appeared, military doctors usually acted as rapidly as possible to disperse their troops to new barracks at a distance, or under tents at a new location. Given the short range of *Aëdes aegypti*,

this tactic sometimes worked remarkably well. The problem was to identify yellow fever, which was not always marked by the tell-tale yellow
skin color and black vomit. An epidemic could be well advanced before
being recognized. Delay in recognition meant that one or more of the dis-
persed soldiers might have carried the infection with them.[5]

Disinfection was another common precaution. Wherever a victim
died, the place of his death and everything he had touched were thoroughly disinfected by every known means, from burning sulfur to
washing the walls with chemical disinfectants, but, where flight sometimes worked, disinfection was either ineffective or worse. It distracted
effort and attention from quarantine measures that might have helped,
and it attracted people to a place where an infected mosquito had
recently been active.

The Senegal epidemic of 1878 began on Gorée in July. The garrison was
immediately evacuated to the mainland – apparently free of fever at first
– but the epidemic reached them in due course and most of them died.
Gorée was somewhat removed from the Senegal River and the projected
military moves into the interior, but the disease followed an intricate pattern that devastated the military effort that year. It moved slowly at first –
not to Saint Louis at the mouth of the river, but jumping to Bakel, far
upstream – carried there by a naval doctor transferred from Gorée.
Between mid-August and mid-September, seven of the eight Europeans
in the Bakel garrison had died.

While the government in Saint Louis tried to seal off the capital from
the infection, the government in Paris nevertheless ordered an expedition
to the upper river, in opposition to the kingdom of Logo. The problem
was that Logo, just above the highest French post at Médine, was at war
with France's ally, Sambala of Khasso, whose territory included Médine.
Paris believed that a sharp military lesson would help clear the way for
future advances, and Logo at the moment blocked passage to the interior.
This expedition was ordered before the epidemic had reached Saint Louis
or Bakel, but it had already reached Gorée and there was danger that the
expedtion might pick up yellow fever somewhere on the road to its destination in Logo.

The expedition left Saint Louis by river just before yellow fever was recognized there. It was a small force, 317 European marines and 225
tirailleurs sénégalais, plus 28 French officers and 89 Europeans as crew on
the steamers that carried them. It moved relatively fast: ten days by
steamer for the 490 miles from Saint Louis to Médine. From there it was
only a ten-mile march to Sabourciré, the capital of Logo. Speed was essential, because deaths later identified as yellow fever began on one of the
steamers even before the fleet reached Bakel.

[5] P.D. Curtin, *Death by Migration: Europe's Encounter with the Tropics in the Nineteenth Century*
(New York: Cambridge University Press, 1989) esp. pp. 68–70.

The expedition nevertheless arrived at Saboucifé with only nine dead or left behind at Bakel or Médine. Up to that point, the medical staff still lacked a positive identification of the disease as yellow fever, and the relatively healthy force was able to bombard, capture, and destroy its objective in one day, leaving it free to return to the coast.

The usual incubation period of yellow fever is three to six days, and more fever cases began to appear even on the return march to Médine. Still more followed as the survivors embarked on the steamers for the coast. At that point, the epidemic was identified as yellow fever, and Saint Louis had a full-scale epidemic of its own. For the safety of themselves and others, the survivors of the force were put on shore at various fortified posts on the lower river.[6] In all, the Logo expeditionary force lost from disease about 49 percent of its European strength in a period of less than two months – roughly 245 per thousand per month.[7]

That ratio pushes it off the scale of losses from disease in West African conquest. With a group of non-immunes in close contact, virtually all would have been infected within two months or so. After that they were either immune or dead. Thus the annual rate and the rate of loss over two months would have been about the same.

The losses were high, however measured, but they never became a political issue. For one thing, the numbers were small, and the losses were equally large among other troops who simply sat in isolation barracks with the yellow fever they had brought with them. It was even more lethal for the European civilian population of Gorée, 64 percent of which died of yellow fever between July and September that year, though the equivalent at Saint Louis was only 17 percent. With civilian losses at this level, the military losses attracted much less attention.

Normally yellow fever epidemics do not recur without the passage of time or the influx of non-immunes. They are limited by their own immunizing action. The 1878 epidemic, for example, killed 99 out of a population

---

[6] Claude Baril, *Souvenirs d'une expédition au Sénégal, pendant l'épidémie de la fièvre jaune, en 1878* (Paris, 1883, thesis no. 200); Alexandre Le Jemble, *Epidémiologie de la fièvre jaune au Sénégal pendant l'année 1878* (Paris: Alphonse Derenne, 1882, thesis no. 91), pp. 28–30. The reporting on the yellow fever epidemics of 1878 and 1881 was extremely rich on account of the number of young naval doctors who turned their experience into doctoral theses. In addition to Baril and Le Jemble, see Pierre-Emmaneul Duval, *Gorée considéré comme foyer de fièvre jaune au Sénégal; imminence de l'importation en France* (Bordeaux: Imprimerie nouvelle A. Bellier, 1883, thesis no. 24), Jean Genebrias de Boisse, *Étude sur une épidémie de fièvre jaune à bord des bâtiments de l'état (Sénégal 1881)* (Paris, Ollier-Henry, 1884, thesis no. 52); Jacques Vincent, *La fièvre jaune (épidémies de 1878 et de 1881 au Sénégal)* (Montpellier, Grollier et Fios, 1883, thesis no. 47). Later writers have also dealt with with these epidemics. See especially Claude Pulvenis, "Une épidemie de fièvre jaune (Saint-Louis du Sénégal, 1881)" Bulletin de l'IFAN, 30 B:1353–73 (1968) and J. Malcolm Thompson, "Dissemination Camps and Disease Foyers: Military Quarantine and the 'Contaminated' African in Colonial Senegal, 1878–1883," (Unpublished paper presented at the African Studies Association, Toronto, November 1994).

[7] Claude Baril, "Une page d'histoire médicale. Rapport sur l'expédition militaire au Logo (Soudan, 1878) et l'épidémie de fièvre jaune qui la termina," AMPC, 33:241–301 (1935), p. 241.

of 275 Europeans in Gorée and Saint Louis together, but it also left 81 individuals who had been attacked and survived – plus 94 who had somehow escaped.[8] In a more stable population, the epidemic of 1878 would have left some level of "herd immunity," but, by the time yellow fever returned in 1881, all the common soldiers had been rotated home, the survivors taking their hard-earned immunities with them. They were replaced by fresh non-immune contingents. Many of the civilians had also gone home, and hundreds of Moroccan railway workers had newly arrived. The railway building and preparations for the Sudan campaigns, in short, may have created the conditions that made the new epidemic possible. They certainly increased its severity.

The Conquest of the French Sudan

The style of warfare in the conquest of what was to become the French Sudan was in the tradition of the punitive expedition on the model of the British in Ethiopia in 1868 or Asante in 1874. The object was to march a body of soldiers through enemy country to a set objective without seeking to occupy the territory itself. The *politique du fleuve* in mid-century Senegal had been similar. The new push up the river was based on a series of strongpoints, each fortified and occupied by a French garrison and linked together by small steam gunboats which the French called *cannonières*. The objective was not territorial rule, but the extension of French trade into the interior and protection of Senegalese traders.

The French operation on the Senegal harked back to an even older European tradition of the "trading-post empire," a system of fortified port cities with no substantial control over the hinterland. In the sixteenth-century Indian Ocean, the Portuguese established an empire of this type based on Mozambique, Goa, Melaka, and Macau. Other trading-post empires extended overland, like those of the seventeenth-century fur traders in North America or Siberia.

The French push into the African interior in the 1850s had carried them as far as Médine, and up the Faleme River as far as Senoudébou in the Almamate of Bundu. The new advance that began in 1879 was to extend overland along the projected rail line from Kayes (just downstream from Médine) to a fortified post at Bamako on the Niger.

Each dry season, moving columns would fan out through the Western Sudan. Some were sent to provision or reinforce the line of posts, others to demonstrate the force of French arms, to punish enemies, or to sign treaties putting African authorities under French "protection." The French sometimes replaced one African ruler with another more favorable to their interests, but most of the African rulers continued ruling as they had done in the past. The main force was the tirailleurs, a thoroughly

---

[8] A. Le Jemble, *Epidémiologie de la fièvre jaune au Sénégal,* pp. 16–23, 90.

African institution of slave soldiers, recruited by purchase, and allowed to capture slaves of their own on campaign.

The first advance projected for 1879 was 79 miles from Kayes to Bafoulabé, where the junction of the Bafing and Bakoy Rivers formed the Senegal. Yellow fever slowed the advance; but the expedition of the 1879–80 dry season did establish a fort at Bafoulabé. In 1880–81, a typhoid epidemic struck the expeditionary force around Médine before it could push inland, with a death rate of around 20 per thousand from that alone, as well as the usual malaria. In the wet seasons of 1881, yellow fever returned to Saint Louis, with death rates so high that the very presence of the French at the mouth of the Senegal was threatened.

In 1881–82, in spite of yellow fever, Paris decided to send a small expedition, only 349 men, to resupply the isolated garrisons at Bafoulabé and Kita, the next important post toward the Niger. Colonel Borgnis-Desbord, the commander that season, managed to move his troops from France upriver past the yellow fever in Saint Louis. He not only supplied the posts as ordered; some of his column advanced to the Niger and made the first military contact with Samori Turé, whose empire was expanding from the south, just as the French were expanding from the west. In the campaign season of 1882–83, the French troops reached Bamako, where they built their first fortification on the Niger; they soon had gunboats operating there as well.[9]

Throughout this advance, only two real powers stood in the way. One of these was Amadu, son and successor of Sheikh Umar Tal, who, beginning in the 1850s had led a Muslim jihad and founded an empire that stretched at one point from the vicinity of Kayes to Timbuktu on the Niger bend. The French line of advance lay just to the south of Amadu's center of power, and his strength was not that of his father. In the 1860s, Umar had been able to field armies as large as 30,000, consisting of cavalry and musketeers, but the number available in the 1880s was more on the order of 10,000.[10]

The second major player was Samori Turé, who began to assemble an important secondary empire in what is now Guinée-Conakry. Unlike Amadu, he was able to buy European rifles through traders in Sierra Leone. His army was smaller than Amadu's, but was better trained and equipped. Samori was advancing down the Niger valley just as the French reached it in 1883, and they fought briefly in 1882 and 1883; but the French strategy at that time was to recognize Samori's conquests and encourage him to make further advances to the east, into the present central and northern Côte d'Ivoire. Meanwhile, from 1883 to 1890, the French

---

[9] Pulvenis, "Epidémie," pp. 1366–71; Kanya-Forstner, *Conquest*, pp. 106–12; France, Ministère de la Marine et des Colonies, *Sénégal et Niger. La France dans l'Afrique occidentale 1879–83*, 2 vols. (Paris, 1884), 1:158–61; Yves Person, *Samori: Une révolution Dyula*, 3 vols. (Dakar: Ifan-Dakar, 1968–75), 1:377–387.

[10] Kanya-Forstner, *Conquest*, pp. 139–41.

columns moved back and forth consolidating their paper protectorate and laying claim to any territory not already claimed by Portugal or Britain. This included, in 1891, the remains of Amadu's empire and much of the territory Samori brought under his control in this first phase of his conquests. Samori's forces meanwhile kept moving across the Côte d'Ivoire and into present-day northern Ghana.[11]

The number of French troops involved was tiny compared to the Magdala campaign, or even to the 2,000 Europeans and West Indians that marched to Kumasi in 1874. The fortified posts were defended by as few as 20 or up to 150 men. Through the 1880s, the total annual force of tirailleurs and marines in any campaign season varied between 400 and 700, though it nearly doubled during the final stages in the early 1890s. Such small numbers were possible because of the superiority of their weapons. All the French infantry, including the tirailleurs, were equipped with Kropatscheck magazine rifles, just then being introduced to French troops at home. Each rifle company had, in addition, three machine guns, and the columns marched with light artillery units, important for breaching timber stockades or the walls of African towns, which were mainly adobe but occasionally stone.

Disease in the French Sudan

Table 4.2 indicates the marked improvement in disease mortality between the campaign of 1883–84 and that of 1887–88, a decline of 59 percent, achieved largely through an adjustment in French military activity. The developed pattern was to remove most European troops to the coast during the rainy season, usually from May to November, leaving only the small garrisons of tirailleurs and their French officers. The commander and many French officers would take the steamer to France for a holiday or for other assignment till the end of the rains and the beginning of the next campaign.

The annual deaths reported for most years in the 1880s are therefore a combination of garrison rates for four to six months, plus campaign rates for six to eight months in the dry season. Only Dr. Laffont's detailed study of the campaign of 1887–88 clearly separates out the monthly death rate on campaign – 13.22 per thousand – for the six-month period between November 1, 1887 and May 1, 1888. Because that was a relatively healthy year, the monthly rate reported is probably lower than that of most campaigns in this period. The overall annual figure for 1880–83 was unusually high because it included the deaths from yellow fever of soldiers who stayed in Saint Louis. So, too, was the figure for 1891–92, again owing to a new yellow fever epidemic on the upper river, though not in lower Senegal at that time.[12]

[11] Person, Samori, 1:489–512.
[12] Primet, "Rapport sur l'épidémie de fièvre jaune au Soudan," AMN, 59:241–56, 357–77, 443–67; 60:16–42 (1893).

Table 4.2. *Disease Mortality of French Troops in Haut-Sénégal-Niger, 1880–92*

Years	Mean Strength	Deaths per Thousand	Campaign Deaths per Month
1880-83		400	
1883–84	443	282	
1884–85	471	225	
1885–86	677	201	
1886–87	546	222	
1887–88	380	117	13.22
1888–89	280	210	
1889–90	287	204	
1891–92		300	

Note:
Data for 1887–88 and 1889–90 are suspicious because the arithmetic does not agree with the conclusion.

Sources:
1880–1887
Laffont, "Rapport médical sur la campagne de 1887–1888 dans le Soudan français," AMN, 51:292, 348-53 (1889).

1887–88 to 1889–90
Durand, *Campagne du Soudan*, p. 10.

1891–92
Primet. "Rapport sur l'épidémie de fièvre jaune au Soudan," AMN, 59:376 (1893.)

Joseph Galliéni, who commanded in the Haut-Sénégal-Niger in the two campaigns of 1886–87 and 1887–88, took pride in his attention to the health and creature comforts of his men. In 1887–88, each European soldier had a mule to ride, so that the European units were effectively mounted infantry. The mounts were introduced to spare the men physical effort in such a difficult climate, and, since fatigue was thought to be an important cause of malaria, they were a form of anti-malarial. In the earlier campaigns, it was hard to supply wine to the men in the columns, though some got through to the base camps like Kayes. In the earlier 1880s, rum or millet beer was often substituted, and what wine did arrive up-river came in 25-liter wooden barrels that were not properly airtight, with the result that the wine was often vinegar by the time it arrived. By 1887–88, wine of good quality was delivered in glass bottles, and each man was entitled to a half liter a day, even in the moving columns, and as far inland as Bamako, 310 miles beyond Kayes; and the soldiers' ordinary ration was supplemented with fresh eggs, meat, chicken, and vegetables purchased locally.[13]

Whether the low point for mortality in 1887–88 was owing to Galliéni and Laffont, his medical officer, can only be speculation. Louis Archinard's general reputation as a far more aggressive commander suggests that he may also have been less concerned about the health of the troops, hence the rise in the disease death rate of the early 1890s.

Laffont also reported on the causes of death by disease, and his data for the years 1883–88 make possible a comparison with the mortality of troops in barracks in western Senegal over the period 1852–73. It was clearly hard to gather data of this kind on campaign in the Haut-Sénégal-Niger, but the contrast between the two sets is so striking that it stands out, even allowing a considerable margin for error (see Table 4.3). Some differences are easily explained. Yellow fever was present in Gorée in 1866–67, while it was absent from the interior during the sample period. Cholera was unusual in sub-Saharan Africa, but the fourth pandemic of 1863–75 penetrated the interior of East Africa and reached as far as Madagascar. In the west, it was especially serious for the Gambia and Senegal, though more so for Africans than for Europeans. In Senegal, it killed 50 per thousand annually among the tirailleurs over the years 1868–70, but it then disappeared from that part of Africa.[14]

It is harder to explain why the death rate from malaria should be four times higher in the interior than on the coast. Campaign conditions would be a partial explanation. Soldiers on campaign, and their officers, were likely to be careless about regular prophylactic quinine. At this time, ten centigrams of quinine a day was ordered to be taken under medical supervision, though it was always hard to enforce. Sometimes, quinine was in the form of pills, but sometimes dissolved in 6 centiliters of wine.[15] The dosage was only about half of the 3 grains (19.4 centigrams) a day used for the march to Kumasi in 1874, and the recommended dosage toward the end of the century was 32.4 centigrams (5 grains). The lower dosage may explain part of the malaria death rate in the French Sudan.

In Senegal, climatic difference between the coast and the interior were also important. From December to May, the climate at Gorée and Saint

[13] Joseph Galliéni, *Deux campagnes au Soudan français, 1886–1888* (Paris: Hachette, 1891); Laffont, "Rapport médical sur la campagne de 1887–1888 dans le Soudan français," AMN, 51:164–74, 259–93, 338–54, 426–43(1889); AMN, 52:35–54, 122–43, 225–37 (1890).
[14] P.F.A.T. Carbonnel, *De la mortalité actuelle au Sénégal et particulièrement à Saint-Louis* (Paris, thesis no. 10, 1873).
[15] Laffont, "Rapport médical," AMN, 51:167–68, 174–75 (1889).

Table 4.3. *Senegal and French Sudan – Barracks and Campaign*

Disease	Annual Mortality of French Troops in Barracks Saint Louis and Gorée, 1852–73		Annual Mortality of French Troops on Campaign in the French Sudan,1883–88	
	Deaths per Thousand	Percentage of All Deaths from Disease	Deaths per Thousand	Percentage of All Deaths from Disease
Malaria	18	25.00	97.74	48.81
Yellow fever	17	23.61	0	0.00
Typhoid fever	0	0.00	24.24	12.11
Gastrointestinal infections	19	26.39	60.79	30.36
Cholera	3	4.17	0	0.00
Diseases of the liver	3	4.17	3.18	1.59
Tuberculosis	2	2.78	4.77	2.38
Heat stroke	1	1.39	3.58	1.79
Other	9	12.50	5.94	2.97
Total mortality from disease	72	100.00	200.24	100.00

Note:
Includes deaths in the hospitals in Gorée and Saint Louis only of soldiers from units whose strength was known.
Disease listed as typho-malaria in the original is listed here as typhoid fever.

Source:
"Borius, Topographie médicale du Sénégal," p. 401.
Laffont, "Rapport médical," 51: 292–93, 353.

Louis is delightful, with temperatures rarely higher than 80 degrees Fahrenheit. In the interior, however, temperatures begin to rise from March onward, with readings often more than 100 degrees Fahrenheit until the rains begin in June. The temperature alone would account for the fourfold increase in heat stroke in the interior. Cerebral malaria probably accounts for the single death from that cause reported on the coast.

The climatic variation also suggests probable differences in vectoral efficiency. Both *An. gambiae, strictu sensu*, and *An. arabiensis* can continue as important vectors in the dry season, if they can find still water in open sunlight. That opportunity would be weak at either Gorée, surrounded as it is by sea water, or at Saint Louis in the tidal lower Senegal. Upriver, however, the dry season brings an end to the swift flow of the river, leaving frequent pools as the Senegal and its tributaries dry up. Because the railroad, and hence the armies, followed the water courses it may well be that they were subject to fairly intense vectoral activity well into the dry season.[16]

As far back as the 1820s, Bakel, the farthest inland of the French posts at that time, was reputed to be far more unhealthy than the coastal towns, so much so that the military tried to use only African troops for its garrison. It was a recurrent opinion on the coast that Africans suffered from movement within Africa. Those recruited on the upper river and beyond were less healthy on the coast, while those from the coast were less healthy upriver.[17] Cross-immunities between species in the *Plasmodium falciparum* group are often weak, so that an immunity acquired in one region might not be as valid elsewhere.

The shift in reported typhoid fever deaths – from none in barracks during the 1850s and 1860s, to 24 per thousand on campaign in 1883–80 – is a puzzle. Borius's failure to report typhoid fever before 1872 was no doubt part of a continuing confusion in the classification of continued fevers like typhus and typhoid, though the characteristic signs of typhoid on postmortem examination had been known since mid-century. The first recognized case of typhoid fever appeared in Senegambia with the epidemic of 1881, quite possibly brought by troops newly arrived from France. In the French army in France and Algeria alike, typhoid had been comparatively unimportant in the 1860s, but typhoid deaths in the French army in France had doubled by the mid-1880s, with nearly the same increase in Algeria as well.[18] Serious typhoid outbreaks, which will be discussed in chapter 6, occurred in 1881 in southwestern Algeria and among the French forces invading Tunisia.

Laffont promoted some further confusion by labeling the typhoid cases upriver as typhomalaria. This category was common usage in America during the Civil War, and it continued in France more than in Britain into the 1870s and 1880s. By 1880, however, C.J. Erberth had published his discovery of the typhoid bacillus, and Laveran had made a microscopic identification of plasmodium in the blood of a malaria victim.[19] The occasional diagnosis nevertheless lived on. Patrick Manson, writing near the end of the century, believed that malaria-like symptoms appeared as a result of latent infection when the body was weakened by typhoid attack.[20] As for Laffont's classification in the 1880s, in the absence or brucellosis, or Malta

---

[16] I am indebted to Dr. Keneth Vernick, Department of Embryology, Carnegie Institution of Washington, for this suggestion.

[17] Claude Faure,"La garnison européene du Sénégal et la recrutement des primières troupes noires," *Revue d'histoire des colonies*, 5:5–108 (1920), pp. 34–35; 84; Prosper Léonard Keisser, *Souvenirs médicaux de quatre campagnes du transport a la côte occidentale d'Afrique (Sénégal et Gabon), Seudre et Arièges* (Bordeaux, thesis no. 31, 1885), pp. 37–38; Laffont, "Rapport médical, AMN, 51:170 (1889).

[18] Curtin, *Death by Migration*, appendix tables.

[19] Dale C. Smith, "The Rise and Fall of Typhomalarial Fever," *Journal of the History of Medicine*, 37:182–220, 287–321 (1982).

[20] Primet,"Fièvre jaune au Soudan," AMN, 59:367–77 (1893); Patrick Manson, *Tropical Diseases: A Manual of the Diseases of Warm Climates*, 2nd ed. (London, 1900), pp. 225–26.

fever (which was comparatively rare in the Western Sudan), the vast majority of these cases were probably ordinary typhoid fever.[21]

By the campaign of 1888–89, the French in the Sudan had developed the tactic of dispersing both men and animals, partly against typhoid and partly against epizootic infections, even though such measures made it difficult to reconcentrate the forces when the military situation called for it.[22]

The typhoid death rate of 24 per thousand per year that Laffont reported for the Sudan was less than the 54 per thousand that died of typhoid in the Tunisian campaign of 1881 (refer to Table 6.4); Laffont, who paid a great deal of attention to the quality of food and wine, paid no attention at all to the purity of the water supply. He nowhere mentioned the possible connection between pure water and dysentery and diarrhea; nor did his list of recommended sanitary improvements include the water supply.[23] This may help to account for the fact that the death rate from gastrointestinal infections on the Gold Coast ten years earlier had been 3.08 per thousand, as against 5.07 per thousand in the French Sudan.

Ironically, it was precisely in the mid-1880s that the Pasteur-Chamberland porcelain filters were introduced in France itself. The filter consisted of a porcelain cylinder, about an inch and a half in diameter and one or two feet long, called a candle or bougie because of its shape. Filtration took place when water was allowed to drip through the tube from one end to the other. The material was extremely dense, so dense that most microorganisms could not pass through. For the filter to yield an appreciable supply of pure water required a battery of candles and a force pump to speed the filtration. The whole apparatus was heavy and hard to clean, which made these filters difficult to use on campaign; but in barracks they were remarkably effective. The French war ministry ordered more than 200,000 of these new filters for military installations in France and Algeria, and, between 1886 and 1891, hospital admissions in the French army dropped by more than half, and total mortality dropped by 38 percent.[24]

Lessons Learned

The most curious aspect of the campaigns in the French Sudan was the combination of high mortality and low public concern. The monthly morality for Europeans on the Niger expedition of 1841 had been 167 per thousand and had raised such a public furor that the advance up the Niger was temporarily abandoned. The monthly death rate from disease on the Logo expedition was 245 per thousand and hardly caused a ripple. The rate of disease mortality in West African barracks earlier in the century

[21] Personal communication from Dale C. Smith.
[22] Louis Archinard, *Soudan français en 1888–89* (Paris, 1889), p. 9.
[23] Laffont, "Rapport médical," 51:429–30, 433–36. 52:35–54.
[24] Legrand, *Hygiène des troupes*, pp. 207–35.

had been in the 200s per thousand and had led to periodic retrenchment and occasional withdrawal. Among French troops in the Haut-Sénégal-Niger in the 1880s, disease mortality at that same level no doubt caused some concern, but without withdrawal and without extensive public complaint against the marine officers who were ostensibly in charge.

Yellow fever was perceived differently from the combination of malaria and water-borne disease on campaign. The deaths in Saint Louis and Gorée were not seen as the result of military action – more nearly an act of God for which no one could be held responsible. It provoked horror in the French medical press, but without political overtones. Then, and in retrospect, people complained of mismanagement, especially in the timing of the dispersal of troops and their care in the bush camps; but the planned advance into the interior went on.[25]

Nor was yellow fever quite so exclusively a tropical disease as, say, falciparum malaria. Some sensed a danger to France itself;[26] in 1878, the disease had swept through the American South. One investigator of the Senegal epidemics reminded his readers that America had 125,000 cases and 12,000 deaths in that year, and that yellow fever had reduced the population of Memphis by half. (In fact, his numbers were off; recent authorities believe that the Memphis population loss was about 10 percent.) In fact, yellow fever in the American south was far less lethal than it was among non-immunes in West Africa, but that fact did not necessarily penetrate French opinion.[27]

The factor of race entered the assessment, as it had done all through the nineteenth century. Africans had been recruited to fight for the French cause precisely because of their superior immunity. The French medical press was overwhelmingly convinced that the Africans were absolutely immune to yellow fever, but believed that they could nevertheless carry the disease and infect others, largely on account of their "filthy habits."[28]

Alexandre Le Jemble, on the other hand, made a careful epidemiological study of Saint Louis during the epidemic of 1878. For civilians, the cause of death was not recorded, but Le Jemble was able to reconstruct the pattern of the epidemic for different groups distinguished by race and place of origin. For each group, he compared the overall death rate at the peak of the epidemic with the similar rate in the same months, a year before and a year after. His study showed a negligible increase in deaths among native-born Saint-Louisians regardless of race, but a significant increase in the death rate among Africans visitors, especially the Trarza

---

[25] For a survey of contemporaneous opinion see Claude Pulvenis, "Une épidemie de fièvre jaune" esp. pp. 1370–73.

[26] Pierre-Emmanuel Duval, *Gorée comme foyer de fièvre jaune.*

[27] A. Le Jemble, *Epidémiologie de la fièvre jaune*, p. 111; T.H. Baker, "Yellow-Jack. The Yellow Fever Epidemic of 1878 in Memphis, Tennessee," *Bulletin of the History of Medicine*, 42:241–64 (1968); for yellow fever in American South see especiallly Margaret Humphreys, *Yellow Fever in the South* (New Brunswick: Rutgers University Press, 1992).

[28] Malcolm Thompson, "Dissemination camps," pp. 39–46.

Moors from the desert edge whose home territory was out of the normal endemic range of yellow fever. By taking into account the apparent immunity of Europeans born and brought up in the tropics, or who had previously had yellow fever, he came to this conclusion:

Experience demonstrates two categories of people enjoying an absolute immunity, and that this immunity is independent of all conditions of race or color, that it is not limited, and that it is not lost under the influence of any modification in the conditions of residence or climate. For those who possess it, it is irrevocable.

The first category consists of people native to a country where yellow fever is endemic: the fact of being born in such a country confers an immunity that we call native.

The second consists of those who have survived a first attack of the disease. They have an acquired immunity.[29]

At that time, he could not have known the cause of either immunity, but the statement about who was and who was not immune would still be accurate in a textbook on tropical medicine a hundred years later.

None of these medical writers hinted at the possibility that French activities in Africa should be curtailed. The furthest move in that direction was to use the apparent immunity of the Africans to argue once again that African, not European, soldiers should be used wherever possible.

Within the French military, moreover, service in the Sudan became more popular, not less so. In the past, marine infantry officers held a low status within the French military, but in the 1880s, the marine infantry began to attract some of the most able and ambitious graduates of French military institutes. It seemed to offer adventure, rapid promotion, and the ability to act on one's own authority – much as service in Algeria had done under the Second Empire – and all of this in spite of the known danger from disease.[30]

For French officers volunteering for the marine infantry or artillery, two factors were in the balance – the danger of death from disease and the rapidity of promotion. That so many took up the challenge is probably simply another indicator of the ancient belief of each individual that he can beat the odds.

Military writers tended not to make much of the disease problem, though they recognized its existence. Galliéni, for example, spent a page or two (out of 500 or more) recognizing its existence but treating it as one of the many hurdles that lay between the advance of a French column and its ultimate victory.[31] Nor was the medical press seriously critical of health conditions in the French Sudan; the threat of disease was an

---

[29] Le Jemble, *Epidémiologie de la fièvre jaune*, p. 68.
[30] Kanya-Forstner, "French Marines," 143–45; *Conquest of the Western Sudan*, p. 14.
[31] The French press in general showed a notable lack of serious concern about the mortality of these campaigns, or for those in Bénin and Dahomey in the 1890s. The contrast with the outcry over the Madagascar exepedition of 1895 is especially striking. Personal communication from Sydney Kanya-Forstner and William Cohen.

accepted fact of life. Precautions were necessary and expected, but the losses were accepted with little complaint, even when precautions were not as successful as they should have been. There was no outcry in the 1880s, for example, at the contrast between the high French mortality in the Sudan and the lower British mortality in the march of Asante ten years earlier.

Several factors helped to damp down the potential protest against French disease losses in the western Sudan. The officers and common soldiers alike were volunteers, and most of the actual fighting was done by Africans. Though death *rates* were high, the absolute number of casualties was small. The Colonial Ministry's review of the campaigns from 1880 to 1883 recognized that "sanitary conditions" (a euphemism for the high death rate) had been criticized, but it answered that long marches were necessary and fatigue brought on illness. It would have been the same in France itself. The final defense was that those three victorious campaigns took the lives of only 194 Europeans and 35 Africans.[32]

Medical commentators or the statistically inclined might have been shocked by annual deaths from disease at more than 250 per thousand, but the public was apparently unconcerned as long as the actual number seemed small and the national gain seemed large. The ministry's summary of the Sudan campaign of 1882–83 pointed out that the expedition that year had fielded a total of 542 combatants. It attacked and captured two fortified towns, fought four other engagements, marched 3,620 kilometers, and added new territory a third the size of metropolitan France – all at a cost of less than a hundred French lives. Presented that way, it could look like a bargain.[33]

At a time when French pride was beginning to recover from the defeat of 1871, some in France still resented any diversion from the central goal of revenge against Germany, but cheap victories in Africa could seem worth the price. That had been the attitude of military commanders like Galliéni.[34]

Medical men like Laffont had a similar view. He was proud of his role in reducing the disease mortality of his command to 117 per thousand per year, but he added:

While this figure may seem a little high to make it possible to consider the Soudan as a healthful country, one must not conclude too rapidly that it is not occupiable by Europeans; pessimism is not to be taken into account when it comes to colonial expansion, and when the goal appears clear and profitable, one must march toward it without swerving.[35]

---

[32] France, Ministère de la Marine et des Colonies, *Sénégal et Niger. La France dans l'Afrique occidentale 1879–83*, 2 vols. (Paris, 1884).

[33] France, Ministère de la Marine et des Colonies, *Sénégal et Niger*, 1:230–36.

[34] Joseph Galliéni, *Voyage au Soudan français (Haut-Sénégal et pays de Ségou), 1879–1881* (Paris: Hachette, 1883), pp. 573–75; *Deux campaignes*, pp. 26–27.

[35] Laffont, *Rapport médical*, p. 352.

And, beyond the call of duty, was the fact that all valued prizes had a price:

Every new country is unhealthy, and this axiom, proved by past experience, has lost none of its power. It seems that hot climates do not pardon our intrusion, do not deliver up their products, do not become merciful toward us until hundreds of victims offered to the holocaust have satisfied the tax in blood.[36]

The "Imperialism of Free Trade" on the Guinea Coast

John Gallagher and Ronald Robinson pointed out some decades ago that the British objective overseas in the mid-nineteenth century was not to acquire territory but to achieve influence, especially over commercial policy; that influence could qualify as "informal" rather than formal empire. Gallagher and Robinson called this policy "the imperialism of free trade." Formal rule was expensive, but influence was cheap and was preferred so long as it worked to the British advantage. Maclean's judicial protectorate on the Gold Coast in the middle decades of the century, or the British patronage of Oman in the early century would be examples of informal empire and the imperialism of free trade.[37]

But the imperialism of free trade was inherently unstable. If a non-Western country became strong, it was likely to favor its own commercial interests over those of the British. If it became weak, civil war and anarchy were likely, and they were also bad for trade. On the Gold and Slave Coasts of the 1890s, both of these things happened. Dahomey was to became uncomfortably strong for French interests. Asante was to became uncomfortably weak for the British – as we will see as political and military relations played out over the two decades after 1880.[38]

The geographical setting was different from that of the harborless Gold Coast. To the east of the Volta River mouth the series of rocky headlands backed by tropical forest gave way to the tropical savanna country of the Benin gap in the forest belt. The coast itself was often a sand spit only a few miles wide, separated from the mainland by a lagoon.

Three points along this coast had special importance for the Europeans. From west to east the first of these was Ouidah, called Whydah or Ajuda as well. The town had been the principal port for the extensive slave trade of the kingdom of Dahomey, with its capital at Abomey, about 65 miles to the north. Ouidah itself was on the mainland, across a narrow lagoon from the beach on the sand spit where goods were ferried out to ships anchored off shore. At various times in the past, Dahomean authorities had allowed Portugal, France, and Great Britain to maintain fortified

---

[36] Laffont, *Rapport médical*, p. 354.
[37] "The Imperialism of Free Trade," *Economic History Review*, 6(2nd ser):1–15 (1953).
[38] A similar arguement about the partition of Africa in general is made by P.J. Cain and A.G. Hopkins, *British Imperialism: Innovation and Expansion 1688–1919* (London: Longman, 1993), pp. 394–96.

trading houses in the town. In the 1880s, only the Portuguese post was actually occupied, and the principal foreign traders were Afro-Brazilian returnees from the New World.

Thirty miles farther east was Cotonou, which was important because the shifting sand bar often made it possible for small craft to enter the lagoon at that point. Cotonou, to the west of the lagoon opening, was Dahomean territory, but to the east was the kingdom of Porto Novo, centered north of the lagoon and including the mouth of the Ouémé River, a principal route for canoe traffic into the interior. The Ouémé was increasingly important from the 1860s onward because developing palm oil plantations used this water route to get the oil to the coast for export. This advantage was crucial in a region where trypanosomiasis prevented the easy use of pack or draft animals. The shift from slaves toward palm oil as the principal export gave Cotonou a new importance. Slaves could walk from Abomey to Ouidah; palm products needed a navigable river.

About 75 miles to the east, another opening through the barrier island at Lagos made it possible for ocean shipping to enter the lagoon. Great Britain had seized Lagos in 1851, principally to support the naval campaign against the slave trade. The opening at Lagos not only gave shelter to the Royal Navy, it also controlled the passage of local vessels from the sea to the lagoon; which the Lagos administration was quick to turn this into a source of customs revenue.[39]

French merchants had long traded with Dahomey, and some entered the palm oil trade through Porto Novo. Sodji, the king of Porto Novo was under pressure from Lagos to the east and Abomey to the west. He needed friends, and France became his ally in 1863.[40] In 1883, the alliance had led to a formal protectorate with a small garrison and a French resident. At times in the past, Porto Novo had been a vassal state to Abomey, and Abomey claimed a good deal of its hinterland. Dahomey also claimed Cotonou and actually exercised authority there. This meant, in effect, that the French garrison in Porto Novo could only be reached conveniently through British Lagos or Dahomean Cotonou.[41]

---

[39] For the slave coast in this period see Colin W. Newbury, *The Western Slave Coast and its Rulers* (Oxford: Clarnedon Press, 1961), pp. 49–76; John Hargreaves, *West Africa Partitioned*, 2 vols. (Madison: University of Wisconsin Press, 1985); David Ross, "Dahomey," in Michael Crowder (ed.), *West African Resistance. The Military Response to Colonial Occupation* (London: Hutchinson, 1971), pp. 144–69.

[40] Bernard Schnapper, *La politique dans le Golfe de Guinee*, pp. 194–200.

[41] Dahomey and Benin are confusing toponyms. Dahomey began as the Fon kingdom centered on Abomey. After the French conquest, it became the name of the far larger French colony. Benin was originally the name of a kingdom in what is now west-central Nigeria, and it still maintains its identity within the Nigerian state. In the seventeenth century, however, Europeans applied the name to the body of water off shore, the Bight of Benin in English or the Golfe du Bénin in French. When the French established their protectorate at Porto Novo, they called it Bénin, after the gulf. After the independence of the colony of Dahomey, the new republic chose to become the République du Bénin, which was more neutral politically than to keep the name of one former kingdom for the whole country.

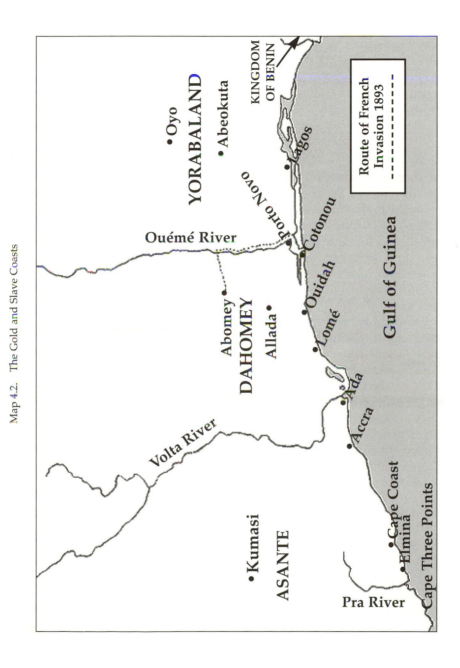

Map 4.2.   The Gold and Slave Coasts

Asante and Dahomey in the 1880s

One consequence of the kingdom of Asante's campaign in the Gold Coast in 1872–74 had been a fundamental weakening of the Asante state structure. The British punitive expedition was only part of the problem. In 1872–73, the material costs of the unsuccessful attacks on its southern neighbors had already forced the Asante armies to withdraw, even before the British had prepared their counterattack. A new Asantehene, Osei Mensa Bonsu was nevertheless enstooled early in 1875 and managed, until his death in 1881, to maintain some of the old strength of his office.

At that point, the state began to come apart in the face of complex stresses and strains in Asante society. One set of conflicts involved the relationships between the central authority and the regional leadership at various levels. Another and crucial problem was finding a viable response to the threat of European power – and that problem was posed differently in different fields of activity. What military response was possible? How to respond to the increase in Christian missions? How to meet foreign criticism of human sacrifice? Or, in commercial policy, how or whether to use the remaining power of the state to organize foreign trade – as the state had done in the past – or to move to a greater degree of private enterprise?[42]

Conflicts over the policy, combined with more personal issues, led to civil war in 1887 and, in 1888, to the choice of Agyeman Prempeh as the new Asantehene, perhaps with support from British officials in the Gold Coast Colony. By the early 1890s, the British were not the only danger. To the east, the Germans were moving north from coastal Togo; to the west, the French were moving inland from Côte d'Ivoire; to the north, Samori Turé was advancing into a former sphere of Asante influence. For the British in Accra and in London, Asante weakness was a threat to the future of British influence. If Asante were truly able to withstand these threats, all might be well from the British point of view. A friendly but weak Asante, however, was a real danger, since it blocked the British in Gold Coast Colony from carrying out annexations that might secure the northern hinterland before a rival power could do the same.

The position of Dahomey was decidedly different in the late 1880s and early 1890s. A revival of the slave trade brought in foreign exchange for the purchase of modern weapons. Kondo, the crown prince who, at the end of 1889, was to become King Behanzin was a leading advocate of this policy, selling slaves to the Congo Independent State for work on the new railway from Matadi to the present-day Kinshasa. The Portuguese also bought workers for their plantations on São Tomé and Principe, as the

---

[42] For Asante developments from an Asante perspective, see Ivor Wilks, *Asante in the Nineteenth Century: The Structure and Evolution of a Political Order* (Cambridge: Cambridge University Press, 1975) and Thomas J. Lewin, *Asante Before the British: The Prempean Years, 1875–1900* (Lawrence: The Regents Press of Kansas, 1978).

Germans did for plantations in Cameroon. The Dahomean army therefore captured slaves and sold them on the coast to the Europeans, who exported them as "indentured laborers." With the proceeds, Dahomey bought arms, mostly from Germany – and not the usual muskets of the old arms trade, but the best European weapons of the time, including rapid-fire rifles, machine guns, and light artillery.[43]

Given the French commitments to Porto Novo, the arms shipments posed a problem for France not unlike that of the British on the Gold Coast in the early 1870s. Real French interests here were only marginal, and one possibility was simply to abandon Porto Novo; to stay, risked an expensive war. Dahomean armies in search of slaves were raiding into territory claimed by Porto Novo in the Ouémé valley, and still farther east into Yorubaland. Given the rate of Dahomean rearmament, some French observers thought that war would be preferable sooner rather than later.

Toward the end of the 1880s, the Naval Ministry in Paris preferred a pacific approach, but Jean Bayol, its representative on the ground, thought that a war with Dahomey was inevitable. He was a former naval surgeon, now Lt.-Governor of Senegal in charge of coastal points like Porto Novo, where he arrived in 1889. His first act was forceful diplomatic representation to Dahomey in favor of Porto Novo, but his threats backfired, and Behanzin once more attacked territory claimed by Porto Novo.

The French garrison was too small to defend the threatened territory, so that, in February 1890, Bayol called in 1,200 reinforcements from Senegal and Gabon. He hoped to take over the whole of coastal Dahomey, but Paris was unwilling to risk a major war at that point and recalled him. The force he had assembled occupied Cotonou, held off a Dahomean attack, and fought a another skirmish north of Porto Novo. Otherwise, it sat in barracks, while diplomats negotiated. In October, Behanzin signed a treaty recognizing the French protectorate over Porto Novo and giving the French the right to occupy Cotonou for an annual payment of 20,000 francs.[44]

Dahomey, 1892–93

The Franco-Dahomean settlement of 1890 could hardly be other than temporary. The Dahomean arms build-up continued, and so did their slave raiding. In 1891 and up to August of 1892, Dahomey imported 1,700 magazine rifles, 6 Krupp cannon, 5 machine guns, and 400,000 rounds of rifle ammunition. Yet the Dahomean army was still untrained to fight using

---

[43] Hargreaves, *Partition*, 1:265–67; Jules Poirier, *Campagne du Dahomey, 1892–1894* (Paris, 1895), pp. 267–69.

[44] Poirier, *Campagne du Dahomey*, pp. 62–97; Hargreaves, *Partition*, 2:140–63; Colin Newbury, *The Western Slave Coast and its Rulers*, pp. 127–30; Ross, "Dahomey," pp. 156–58.

the disciplined infantry tactics of the *tirailleurs sénégalais,* and it had trouble using the new weapons to best effect. The slave raiding alienated Britain and helped clear away international objections to a French invasion of Dahomey. The arms build-up also moved French parliamentary opinion, and, in April 1892, the Chambre des Députés authorized the funds for an invasion of Dahomey to bring down Behanzin's government.

The naval ministry in charge of the operation gave the command to Col. Alfred Amedée Dodds of the marine infantry. Col. Dodds had been born in Senegal of African and European ancestry. His military career, however, was in the usual French tradition, beginning with education at Saint Cyr, moving on to the marine infantry, with service in Réunion, the Franco-Prussian War, and Indo-China, as well as in Africa.

The Dahomey campaign of 1892–93 looks on the surface like a replay of the march on Kumasi in 1874. In each case, a European army of about 2,000 men marched rapidly inland to capture an African capital and the war was over. The differences, however, were significant. Southern Asante was forest country, and the Europeans had to march inland along narrow paths. The region between Cotonou and Abomey was part of the Bénin gap where savanna and light woodland extended right down to the Gulf of Guinea. Trypanosomiasis was still a risk to animals, but the French were able to use donkeys and mules to pull the *voiture Lefebvre,* a light two-wheeled cart that had proved useful in Algeria.

Where the Asante, in 1874, had to depend entirely on muzzle-loading smooth-barreled guns, at least half of the Dahomean army of 1892 had new weapons. Where the British force of 1874 had to fight its way from the Pra River to Kumasi, a distance of about 75 miles, the French in Dahomey were able to use the Ouémé River for the first part of their advance, moving inland with a fleet of *cannonières.* The steam gunboats towed barges loaded with troops and supplies, while providing artillery cover of the banks. From the Ouémé to Abomey was about forty miles, though the French had to fight all the way.[45]

The Dahomeans opposed the advance with a variety of tactics, and with battles every few days, seventeen in all by French count. The French left the Ouémé on October 3 and, by November 5, they were in Cana, just short of Abomey, where they halted for negotiations. The negotiations failed, but the Dahomean army had been destroyed, and the French marched into a deserted Abomey. Behanzin fled to the north where he was captured in 1894 and exiled to Martinique. The French treated Dahomey as a protectorate for a few years, but they later put it under direct administration. By contrast, Tofa of Porto Novo remained king under French protection, though with diminished powers, until his death in 1908.

---

[45] For secondary accounts of this campaign, see Ross, "Dahomey," pp. 158–62; Poirier, *Dahomey, passim;* Hargreaves, *Partition,* 1:140–89.

Asante, 1895–96 and 1900

Asante weakness continued through the early 1890s, as the forward movement of France or Germany on either side of the Gold Coast increased the pressure on Britain. Finally, in 1895, the British decided once more to send an expedition up the paths to Kumasi, this time to demand that the Asantehene place himself under British protection. The expedition was prepared with great care. Lord Wolseley himself presided over a planning conference that included several officers who had participated in 1874. The commander hoped to provoke a fight, but Asante offered no forceful opposition. The expedition marched into Kumasi, declared the British protectorate, and arrested and exiled Agyeman Prempeh together with some other high officials. The British then built a fort in Kumasi to protect their garrison and sent up a "Resident" to be de facto ruler of the new protectorate.

Prempeh may not have been a popular Asantehene, but his removal rallied many and diverse Asante factions to his support. On Prempeh's arrest, people had hidden the Golden Stool, the symbol of Asante unity. Most Asante thought their country had not been defeated, only tricked into surrender. The cultural chauvinism of the British administration soon deepened the resentment. Some factions within Asante began to accumulate weapons in anticipation of the time when they could try to restore independence.[46]

In 1899, Governor Sir Frederick Hodgson sent out a small and unsuccessful expedition to try to recover the Golden Stool. Once that failed, he made a personal visit to Kumasi in March 1900, convened a meeting of all the important Asante leaders, and demanded the surrender of the Stool so that he, as Victoria's representative, might sit on it. The Golden Stool of Asante was not simply a throne in the European sense, but a symbol sent by the Gods some two centuries earlier. The demand for the Stool touched off the rebellion already in preparation. The Asante forces surrounded the Governor and his party and confined them to Kumasi Fort. In April, an Asante surprise attack near Kumasi turned back a small force sent to reinforce the fort, but other reinforcements from the Northern Territories arrived in May, bringing the garrison up to 750 regular soldiers, plus friendly African irregulars, and a good supply of artillery. The fort nevertheless began to run low on supplies. On June 24, the governor and part of the garrison broke through the Asante lines and reached the coast with the assistance of African allies.

None of these events, nor the maneuvers and the confused fighting through the first half of 1900, left a medical record, but they brought on the third and final expedition to march with a flourish from the coast to

---

[46] For shifts in Asante opinion over these years, see Lewin, *Asante Before the British*, pp. 206–22.

Kumasi. The popular press called it "the relief of Kumasi," but it was actually the final stage of the unsuccessful war for independence that began with the rebellion of the Golden Stool and ended with the British conquest of Asante.

The Anglo–Boer War was then in progress, so that no all-European military units could be spared. The attacking force consisted of 2,800 African soldiers under 152 British officers and NCOs, hastily assembled from up and down the West African coast, and from East Africa. This time, the advance began in the middle of the rainy season, and the casualties, both from disease and from enemy action, were far higher than they had been on either of the earlier expeditions to Kumasi. A tentative advance began in May, but the real advance waited until early July. By mid-September, the relief force had entered Kumasi, though the Asante army remained undefeated. The final important engagement took place on September 30, at Aboasa near Kumasi. The British command arrested the rebel leaders, executed some, and sent others to join Prempeh in the Seychelles. In October, it offered amnesty to those who would put down their arms, and on October 14 the main force began its return march from Kumasi to the coast.

The Health Record of Four Campaigns

Although these four campaigns were superficially similar, the role of disease was quite different in each. The Dahomey campaign of 1890 was not an expedition into African territory. It was largely static and defensive. The health problems were therefore closer to those of caring for troops in barracks. The natural vegetation of the region of the Bénin and Dahomean campaigns was the savanna of the Bénin gap, a region where the double rainy season left two dry seasons that are too long and too dry to support a dense forest with a high canopy. This not only influenced the kind of tactics an army might employ, it also changed the vectoral pattern of malaria from that of the forest to that of the savanna, making it more like the Western Sudan and less like the Gold Coast.

Table 4.4 summarizes the mortality statistics of these four campaigns. No health statistics of an army on campaign are as accurate as those of a peacetime army. Direct comparison of the four campaigns is also a problem. Only the Dahomey campaign of 1892 received reinforcements. The others had the strength they began with, minus losses. The longer the campaign and the greater the losses, the lower the mean strength late in the campaign. The Bénin campaign of 1890 and the two Gold Coast campaigns had no significant reinforcements. The Gold Coast campaign of 1896 spent only 55 days in the field, but it did no fighting and remains a special case.

The data in Table 4.4 are presented in two ways – for the entire campaign, which measures the cost in disease mortality of achieving its objective, and again in deaths from disease per month, which measures the

Table 4.4. *Campaign Mortality – Dahomey and Gold Coast, 1890–1900*

All rates are per thousand mean strength

Bénin 1890	Europeans			Africans		
	Number	Rate for Campaign	Rate per Month	Number	Rate for Campaign	Rate per Month
Total	582			671		
Killed in action	6	10	1.15	18	27	2.98
Died of disease	23	40	4.39	12	18	1.99

Note: A nine-month campaign.
Source: Giraud, "Pays du Bénin," pp. 421–22

Dahomey 1892	Europeans			Africans		
	Number	Rate for Campaign	Rate per Month	Number	Rate for Campaign	Rate per Month
Total	1,423			2,176		
Killed in action	47	33.03	6.61	27	12.41	2.48
Died of wounds	15	10.54	2.11	19	8.73	1.75
Died of disease	158	111.03	22.21	33	15.17	3.03
Repatriated	752	528.46	105.69			

Note: A five-month campaign. Data are for all ranks.
Source: Rangé, "Rapport médicale," pp. 177–85. Legrand, *L'hygiène des troupes*, pp. 412–13.

Gold Coast 1895–96	Europeans			Africans		
	Number	Rate for Campaign	Rate per Month	Number	Rate for Campaign	Rate per Month
Total	999			375		
Admitted to hospital	401	401	222	320	853	123
Died of disease	7	7.01	3.88	1	2.67	1.47

Note: A fifty-five-day campaign. Data for all ranks.
Source: Taylor, "Report of the Medical Transactions of the Ashanti Expeditionary Force," pp. 311-12.

Gold Coast 1900	Europeans			Africans		
	Number	Rate for Campaign	Rate per Month	Number	Rate for Campaign	Rate per Month
Total	152			2,804		
Killed in action	9	59.21	9.87	113	40.30	6.72
Died of disease	7	46.05	7.68	102	36.38	6.06
Wounded	52	342.11	57.02	680	242.51	40.42
Repatriated	54	355.26	59.21			
Hopital admission	360	2368.42	394.74	4963	1769.97	295.00

Note: Campaign lasted approximately six months.
Source: Biss, *The Relief of Kumasi.* pp. 313–14.

success of the medical services in keeping the men alive during a campaign in the tropics. In one respect, the Asante campaign of 1900 was unique for tropical Africa and rare elsewhere in nineteenth-century warfare. For European and Africans alike, the number of deaths from enemy action was greater than the number of deaths from disease.

Table 4.4 shows that the disease death rate of Europeans was higher than that for African troops, though the two rates rose or fell together with particular campaigns. The narrowing distance between the two rates is also a measure of the success of military doctors in dealing better with the health problems of European troops. It is also significant that the British samples show a smaller spread between the two rates than did the French campaigns. Finally, even though the march to Kumasi in 1896 was not a battle against an enemy, the performance of the Royal Army Medical Corps, measured by the monthly death rates for African and European troops alike, was probably the lowest in any European campaign for the conquest of tropical Africa. The medical problems of the achievements of the four campaigns are so nearly unique that they are better explained one by one.

Health in the Franco-Dahomean Wars

The medical record of the nine-month occupation of Cotonou and vicinity is interesting chiefly as an indication of what naval doctors were now able to do to protect the health of their men on the Guinea coast. The sample is reasonably large at about 1,200 men, and the period covered, February to November, includes the whole of the rainy season, when malaria deaths were likely to be most numerous. Losses from accident and enemy action were significant, but the period of campaign conditions was short. The whole record is better taken as comparable to that of soldiers in barracks.

Data collected on the expedition provide a comparatively rare look at the mortality of European and African troops, distinguished by cause of death; the pattern is probably nearly typical of West Africa in the nineteenth century. The European death rate from malaria was many times that of the Africans – in this case, 18 times. Europeans and African suffered at much the same rate from gastrointestinal infections, while the African death rate from diseases of the lungs (grippe plus pulmonary gangrene, in Table 4.5) was nearly four times the European rate.

The same data make it possible to compare barracks-like death rates for European troops with those of French troops in Senegal in 1852–73. Table 4.6 shows an over-all drop in mortality, but one that is not very impressive for a thirty-year period: from 6 per thousand per month to 4.39 per thousand. The size of the change in total death rates, however, disguises more important changes in particular diseases, like the doubling of the death rate from malaria, balanced by the improvements in water supply with the

Table 4.5. *Mortality by Cause of Death of French Troops Serving in Bénin February to November 1890*

All rates in deaths per thousand

	European Troops			African Troops		
Mean Strength	582			671		
	Number	Rate for Campaign	Rate per Month	Number	Rate for Campaign	Rate per Month
Malaria	16	27.49	3.05	1	1.49	0.17
Dysentery	4	6.87	0.76	4	5.96	0.66
Tetanus	1	1.72	0.19	3	4.47	0.50
Grippe	1	1.72	0.19	3	4.47	0.50
Peritonitis	1	1.72	0.19	0	0.00	0.00
Pulmonary gangrene				1	1.49	0.17
Total disease	23	39.52	4.39	12	17.88	1.99
Enemy action	6	10.31	1.15	18	26.83	2.98
Accident (drowned)	6	10.31	1.15	3	4.47	0.50
			0.00			
Grand total	35	60.14	6.68	45	67.06	7.45

Note:
Deaths listed as heat stroke are assumed to have been cerebral malaria.

Source:
Giraud, "Le pays du Bénin," AMN, 55:376-89, 401-23 (1891).

new Pasteur-Chamberland filters. Deaths from gastrointestinal infections dropped by half. Boiled drinking water would also have saved lives in Senegal of the 1860s, but there is no evidence that it was even tried, and the death rate from water-borne infections supports the inference that it was not. By the 1890s, however, Senegal was far healthier than Dahomey. By 1891–95, the barracks death rate from all causes had dropped to 19 per thousand per year or 1.58 per thousand per month.[47] The relatively high Bénin death rate of 1890 may have been the result of conditions at a new installation with fighting still on the fringes.

The second Dahomey campaign had the worst mortality record of the four, from disease and combat alike. The intensity of the fighting meant that general reporting on cause of death was impossible, though some doctors reported on total mortality or cause of morbidity of the sample of

[47] Fernand Burot and Maximilien Albert Legrand, *Les troupes colonialiaux. Statistiques de la mortalité. Maladies du soldat aux pays chauds. Hygiène du soldat sous les tropiques*, 3 vols. (Paris, 1897–89), 1:26–29.

Table 4.6. *Changing Death Rates from Disease for European Soldiers in Senegal,*
1852–73, and Bénin, 1890

Deaths per Thousand per Month

Disease Group	Senegal	Bénin
Malaria	1.50	3.05
Gastrointestinal	1.58	0.76
Yellow fever	1.42	0.00
Cholera	0.25	0.00
Hepatitis	0.25	0.00
Other	1.00	0.58
Total disease	6.00	4.39

Source:
Tables 4.1 and 4.5.

soldiers that came under their care.[48] As usual, the principal causes of death from disease were malaria and dysentery.

The initial orders on hygienic matters were standard for the time: ten centigrams of quinine daily; all water to be either boiled or filtered; men to start the days with a canteen full of a boiled infusion of coffee or tea and forbidden to drink water from any other source.[49] The disease mortality figures suggest that these orders were rarely followed. Several different types of Pasteur-Chamberland filter were supplied. One was so cumbersome it took four men to carry it. The filters worked well enough in Cotonou and on board the boats moving up the Ouémé, but the water of the Ouémé was also swift and clear, and could go directly into the porcelain filters without danger of sediment blocking the filter. Beyond the river, however, the water was often muddy. It could have been pre-filtered or precipitated with alum, but that was rarely done. The men also had pocket filters, which would not have stopped bacteria and may have built a false confidence.[50]

The low dosage of quinine is one probable cause of the high death rate from malaria, but carelessness in its use must have been more important still. Dr. Barthélemy, a medical officer in charge of a roughly equal number

---

[48] P. Barthélemy, "La guerre de Dahomey: histoire médicale du 1re groupe de la colonne expéditionnaire de Dahomey, 1892," AMN, 609:161–206 (1893); M. L. C. Rangé, "Rapport médical sur le service de santé du corps expéditionnaire d'occupation du Bénin," AMN, 61:26–62, 90–109, 174–92, 262–84 (1894).

[49] Barthélemy, "Guerre de Dahomey," 172–74

[50] Rangé, Rapport Médical, pp. 31–32; M. Molinier, "Quelques remarques sur les filtres Chamberland en usage dans la colonne expéditionnaire du Dahomey (1892)," AMN, 62:460–66 (1894); Barthélemy, "Guerre de Dahomey," pp. 174–80.

of European and African troops, reported that none of the experienced non-commissioned officers serving with the tirailleurs came down with malaria. He believed this was because they were faithful in their use of quinine. He himself remained free of malaria during eleven months on the coast.[51]

If malaria and dysentery worked against the French, smallpox worked against the Dahomeans. European soldiers and the tirailleurs alike were vaccinated routinely on entering the service. They were then revaccinated in preparation for this expedition. Some French naval doctors had advocated vaccination programs for civilians living near French posts, not just for humanitarian reasons but as a way of protecting the lives of those who might sometime serve them as soldiers and workers. Once the Dahomey expedition came within the range of the epidemic, smallpox began to attack the carriers. Some medical officers immediately began to vaccinate all local carriers they could find, and, although some slipped through the net, the epidemic was not serious on the French side. Those who did come down with the disease also had a relatively light case, suggesting that the ancient African practice of variolation may still have been popular. The smallpox death rate among the Dahomeans was large but unreported in detail, even though smallpox was a known disease in this part of Africa, and Sakpata, the god of smallpox, was one of the most important in the Fon pantheon.[52]

One reason this expedition's medical record-keeping was so bad was that its logistics were relatively good. Field hospitals could systematically evacuate sick and wounded back to the Ouémé River and down to the coast for repatriation to France. More than half of the total number of Europeans who began the expedition were repatriated, though the repatriation rate, like the disease death rates, was different for different units. The infantrie de marine was mainly made up of relatively young recent recruits newly arrived from France. Eighty percent of those units were repatriated, many so early in the campaign that the marine infantry was effectively out of action during the final push toward Abomey. The foreign legion, normally stationed in Algeria, however, only suffered a 45 percent repatriation, and that late in the campaign.[53] One possible reason was a degree of immunity from service in Algeria, but they were disciplined veterans who may have known the importance of hygienic orders.

Health in the Asante Campaigns of 1896 and 1900

The march to Kumasi in 1896, even more than the expedition of 1874, deserved to be the showpiece of British tropical campaigns. The force itself was chosen with great care and placed under Sir Francis Scott, a

[51] Barthélemy, "Guerre de Dahomey," pp. 72–74.
[52] Laffont, "Rapport Médical" 51:458; Barthélemy, "Guerre de Dahomey," 272–74.
[53] Rangé, Rapport Médical" esp. p. 182.

retired Lieutenant-Colonel then serving as commander of the Gold Coast police. In order to begin with the healthiest possible force, the authorities asked for volunteers from units serving in the United Kingdom and then gave them a rigorous medical inspection. Those who passed were formed into a "Composite Service Battalion." Another part of the force, the West Yorkshire Regiment was chosen because it was already "acclimated" to a tropical climate by its current service in Aden. Finally the force was filled out with units from the West Indian Regiments, and "Hausas" recruited in Nigeria.[54] The whole force came to just under a thousand Europeans, 375 West Indians, and a variable number of carriers that reached a peak of 13,800 in January 1896.[55]

This expedition fell considerably short of the publicity given its predecessor in 1874, a unique news event in its time. The expedition of 1895–96 competed for headlines with the Jameson raid in the Transvaal, the French invasion of Madagascar, the Italian defeat at Adwa, and the beginning of the British advance up the Nile against the Mahdi's successor. The *British Medical Journal* and the *Lancet* nevertheless had correspondents present. Robert Baden-Powell was an active officer with the force who also wrote for several papers and later published a book on the campaign. Still another active participant, E.D.W. Ward, published an account in a military journal.[56] The only full-time reporters were Bennett Burleigh for the *Daily Telegraph* and J. Rowley for the *Liverpool Daily Post*. [57] Surgeon-Major-General W. Taylor, the principal medical officer, provided the usual report on the medical transactions of the expedition. Press publicity, in short, was organized for an expedition whose victories were expected to be military, rather than hygienic – in spite of the elaborate sanitary precautions.

The preparation was thorough, beginning with the logistics. The Gold Coast government passed a Labor Ordinance, which legalized forced labor from all adult males at the rate of one shilling per day, a 43 percent increase over the pay for porters in 1874, but still a third less than the voluntary Krumen were paid. Additional "followers" were recruited in Sierra Leone and Nigeria. This brought the number of carriers to nearly 100 for each combat soldier at the peak of the campaign, which must have been close to the record for the African campaigns of this period.[58]

Water was both boiled and filtered. The porters not only carried forward the Pasteur-Chamberland water filters, they often carried purified water as well so that each stop was prepared with pure water when the bulk of the troops arrived. Even ice, manufactured on shipboard was supplied as

---

[54] *Lancet*, 1896, 1:956 (April 4, 1896).

[55] E.W.D. Ward, "To Kumassi and Back with the Ashanti Expeditionary Force, 1895–96," *Royal United Services Institute*, 20:1021–30 (1896), pp. 1021–23.

[56] R.S.S. Baden-Powell, *The Downfall of Prempeh: A Diary of Life with the Native Levy in Ashanti, 1895–96* (London, 1900); Ward, "To Kumasi and Back."

[57] Joseph Chamberlain to Maxwell, Nov. 29 and Dec. 23, 1895, CO 879/44, pp. 8, 22.

[58] Ward, "To Kumasi and Back," 1021–23.

far as Prahsu, carried by runners so as to arrive before it had melted in the heat. Taylor, the medical officer, was so concerned with the water supply that his hygienic instructions warned the troops not even to walk or wade in water along the way on account of the danger of Guinea worm (*Draculculus medinensis*). In fact, Guinea worm, a major cause of lameness among the carriers, comes from drinking infected water, not bathing in it. Taylor knew better, but allowed himself this "excusable fraud" to discourage the men from playing in the water and perhaps drinking some by accident. Partly as a result, the force had only two deaths from gastrointestinal infections.[59]

Quinine was ordered at the rate of two grains (13 centigrams) per person per day, to be taken under the supervision of an officer, but Taylor (like his predecessor on the expedition of 1874) doubted that it did much good. He believed that the best prophylaxis against malaria was personal hygiene, including care about drinking nothing but pure water.[60] The correspondent for the *Lancet* was even more firmly convinced that impure water caused malaria through the presence of "decomposed organic animal and vegetable matter and general impurity."[61]

The labor supply also made it possible to prepare as never before for the evacuation of sick and wounded. In all, 156 hammocks were available, with 11 porters assigned to each, so that they could move the sick and wounded smoothly through to the coast. Hammocks were so plentiful, indeed, that officers had hammocks and bearers to carry them forward, on grounds that in Europe they would have been entitled to horses.[62]

Even creature comforts were better supplied than usual. By this time, tinned rations were reported to be appetizing as well as healthful. The emergency rations came in a "blue tin" and a "brown tin" each containing cocoa and soup. In addition, "Maconochie's ration," an ancestor to the C-ration of the Second World War, was a tin can weighing a pound and a half, containing 12 ounces of meat along with gravy, carrots, onions, and potatoes. The expedition also carried with it thousands of sick-comfort diets, each consisting of a bottle of brandy, a bottle of whisky, a half bottle of champagne, plus arrowroot, pearl barley, tins of meat extract, Bovril, condensed milk, tea, sugar, candles, condiments, and coffee, along with a knife, fork, corkscrew, and can opener.[63]

The data in Table 4.7 are not detailed, but they reflect the medical leadership's emphasis on pure water and lack of interest in quinine prophylaxis. Malaria alone accounted for 77 percent of all European deaths – a

---

[59] *Lancet*, 1896, 1:1171–74 (April 25); W. Taylor, "Report of the Medical Transactions of the Ashanti Expeditionary Force During the Period from 14th December 1895 to 7th February 1896," AMSR, 38:300–15 (1896), p. 305.
[60] Taylor, "Medical Transactions," pp. 305, 309.
[61] *Lancet*, 1896, 1:1171–74 (April 25).
[62] Ward, "To Kumasi and Back," pp. 1024–26.
[63] *Lancet*, 1896, 1:1252 (May 2).

Table 4.7. *Mortality among British Troops in the Asante Campaign of 1895–96*

All rates per thousand mean strength

Disease Group	Rate for the Campaign				Rate Per Month			
	Europeans		West Indians		Europeans		West Indians	
	Admitted	Died	Admitted	Died	Admitted	Died	Admitted	Died
Malaria	342	5.01	248	2.67	189	2.77	137	1.47
Dysentery	22	2.00	16	0.00	12	1.11	9	0.00
Other	37	0	0	0.00	20	0.00	0	0.00
Total	401	7.01	264	2.67	222	3.88	146	1.47

Note:
Period 12/14/1895 to 2/7/1896
Deaths attributed to sunstroke and apoplexy are assumed to have been cerebral malaria.

Source:
Taylor, "Report of the Medical Transactions of the Ashanti Expeditionary Force," pp. 311–12.

proportion similar to that of the Bénin expedition of 1890, where water supply was also good and quinine prophylaxis was also irregular (refer to Table 4.5). For the West Indian troops, the relatively high death rate from malaria was no doubt because they *were* West Indian, lacking the immunizing consequence of an African childhood.[64]

The final British advance to Kumasi in 1900 attracted little publicity. Overshadowed as it was by the Anglo–Boer War, no correspondents covered the campaign for any of the British dailies. The Royal Army Medical Corps published no report on the medical transactions, nor were there any "special correspondents" of the medical press, though three books on military aspects appeared within five years.[65]

This news blackout went back in part to events on the Asante expedition of 1896. Bennett Burleigh and other full-time correspondents at that time resented the fact that serving officers, such as Robert Baden-Powell, were competing with them in filing copy with the British press. Burleigh accused Baden-Powell and Charles Cunningham, the anonymous correspondent for the *Lancet*, of using their official positions to cover parts of the operation other reporters were not allowed to see.[66] Whether on account of Burleigh's complaints, or for some other reason, the army

[64] See P.D. Curtin, "Malarial Immunities in Nineteenth-Century West Africa and the Caribbean," *Parassitologia*, 36:69–82 (1994).

[65] Harold C.J. Biss, *The Relief of Kumasi* (London, 1904); C.H. Armitage and A.F. Montaro, *The Ashanti Campaign of 1900* (London, 1902); James Willcocks, *From Kabul to Kumasi* (London, 1904).

[66] Bennett Burleigh, *Two Campaigns: Madagascar and Ashantee* (London, 1897), pp. 496–97, 553–95.

Table 4.8. *Comparative Mortality of European and Non-European Troops in West Africa,*
1897–1904

Disease	Annual Deaths per Thousand		Percentage of all Deaths from Disease	
	Non-European	European	Non-European	European
Smallpox	0.06	0.00	0.49	0.00
Enteric fever	0.12	1.05	0.98	4.79
Yellow fever	0.36	0.00	2.95	0.00
Malaria	3.60	11.49	29.46	52.37
Gastrointestinal	0.78	3.14	6.38	14.31
Tuberculosis	3.36	0.00	27.50	0.00
Local diseases of the . . .				
Nervous system	0.42	2.05	3.44	9.34
Circulatory system	0.78	2.09	6.38	9.53
Respiratory system	1.50	0.00	12.27	0.00
Urinary system	0.60	0.00	4.91	0.00
Other	0.70	2.12	5.73	9.66
Total disease	12.22	21.94	100.00	100.00
Injuries	0.60	1.05		
Enemy action	0.00	0.00		
Grand Total	12.82	22.99		

Note:
The non-European soldiers at this period were about half West Indian and half the West
African Regiment, recruited in the vicinity of Sierra Leone.
The West African Frontier Force was not included in these data.
Data originally labelled "dysentery" and "diseases of the digestive system" are combined as
"gastrointestinal infections."

Source:
AMSR for 1905, pp. 308–9, 312–3.

issued an order in May 1896 prohibiting "persons in official employment"
from covering military operations. We are therefore left with little more
than the statistical material Biss published (refer to Table 4.7). With a total
sample of only 152 European officers and NCOs, the data cannot have
much significance, though the fact that the African as well as the
European troops suffered more deaths from battle than from disease tells
something about the campaign.

Just as the pattern of disease for soldiers in Senegal before the wars of
conquest provides a statistical point of departure, the pattern of disease in
British West Africa over the period 1897–1904 is a comparable indicator
for troops in barracks in West Africa at the end of the century. The data in

Table 4.8 were more detailed, covered a larger sample, and were more carefully collected than any data for troops on campaign. At this period, the non-European part of the force was about half West Indian and half West African. This means that its expected immunities to malaria would be lower than those of an all West African force, and malaria accounted for nearly 30 percent of all non-European deaths from disease. The comparatively high immunity to gastrointestinal infections would also be expected of people with a childhood background in the tropics. For the Europeans, malaria and gastrointestinal infections were still the principal causes of death, but at rates that were now minuscule compared with those of the early century.

Public and Professional Reaction

The public commentary in Europe on the four expedition from Bénin and the Gold Coast was even more subdued than commentary on yellow fever in Senegal or malaria in the French Sudan. Military men like Willcocks, Armitage, Ward, and Baden-Powell mentioned disease only in passing, as one of the minor problems of a soldier's life on imperial service. What commentary they did supply could turn to veterans' advice for the newcomers to tropical life. Lt.-Col. A.F. Montaro of the 1900 Asante expedition, for example, laid down a paragraph of "golden rules of health":

They are as follows: Take 5 grains of quinine daily; but if you have to undergo any undue exertion, or get very wet, then take 10 grains a day; never touch alcohol till sundown, and then don't spare it, but never be intemperate; never take a cold bath, and always take a warm bath.[67]

His final observation was this: "If white men were only to use the above simple precautions there would be nothing like the present mortality on the Coast."

Civilian reporters were no more informative. Bennett Burleigh covered the French Madagascar expedition of 1895 as well as the march on Kumasi in 1896, in effect the worst and the best in terms military morality from disease, a situation that will be discussed in Chapter 7. But he made very little of the disease factor in either case; on Asante in 1896, he simply published the health statistics with the observation that it was about time Britain got around to annexing the place.[68]

Medical men paid far more attention to disease, as would be expected, but they were writing from within a framework of thought where high mortality in the tropical world was known and expected. They tended simply to describe what happened, paying more attention to possible

---

[67] "Lt.-Col. Montaro's Narrative" in Armitage and Montaro, pp. 158–59.
[68] Burleigh, *Two Expeditions*, pp. 355–56, 551.

improvements than to present losses, with occasional self-congratulation when they thought it was deserved.

Active medical officers were more complaisant than outside observers. They praised what they could. Giraud was disappointed by the high morbidity on the Bénin campaign of 1890, but pleased with the low mortality. Even when the losses were high, as they were in Dahomey in 1892, Rangé could find favorable comparisons with the British march on Asante in 1874 by concentrating on morbidity, not mortality, and showing that some French units had a better record than some of the best of the British units in Asante.[69]

Albert Legrand, an important French authority on military medicine and tropical hygiene, gave a more balanced view of the march on Abomey. He believed the hygienic conduct had not been what it might have been, but the full disaster that threatened was avoided. He noted the heavy losses from a well-armed enemy, but also the good survival record of the wounded – evidence of the efficiency of the surgical service and rapid evacuation to the coast. He also recognized that the quinine dosage was too low and was probably not enforced. Nor were the water regulations enforced. The men drank what they could find and depended too much on individual filters after the failure of the Pasteur-Chamberland. He emphasized once more the fact that battle increased the death rates from disease, pointing out that occupying force in the first six months of 1893 had a mortality rate from disease alone of 7.4 per thousand per month, compared with the 22.21 thousand per month during the campaign itself. His main point, however, was that the military commanders and doctors in the field were not following the best advice available – which is to say, the advice of authorities like himself.[70]

Nor was other retrospective medical opinion of the Dahomey campaign especially negative, even though it was the most lethal of these four expeditions from the Gulf of Guinea. Gustave Reynaud's comparative study of colonial expeditions devoted a chapter to the Dahomey affair of 1892–93. He conceded that the losses to disease among the marine infantry were higher than they should have been, but he added that this was one of the least healthy regions of the world, and that enemy resistance prolonged the period of military activity, which raised the campaign death rate from disease as well. One warning in early 1895, when the French Malagasy expedition was still in the planning stage, called up the Dahomean figures as an example of what the current expedition should be prepared for.[71]

[69] T. Giraud, "Le pays du Bénin," AMN, 55:376–89, 401–23 (1891), pp. 420–22; Rangé, *Rapport Médical*, p. 185–87.

[70] Legrand, *L'hygiéne des troupes européens*, pp. 405–16.

[71] Gustave A. Reynaud, *Considerations sanitaires sur l'expédition de Madagascar et quelques autres expéditions coloniales, françaises et anglaises* (Paris, 1898); V.F., "Médecine coloniale. Le service de santé de Madagascar," *Médecine moderne*, 6:27–28 (12 January 1895).

None of the commentators on these campaigns suggested that disease mortality had serious implications for further imperial activity in Africa. The publicity never approached the level of a public scandal, as it was to do elsewhere in the world in these decades, in Vietnam, Sumatra, Egypt, or Madagascar. Military medical professionals might have regretted that the triumphs of the march on Kumasi in 1874 were not reproduced on each campaign, but the numbers engaged were small, and mostly African or West Indian.

Interaction of disease and imperialism were to be somewhat different in northern and eastern Africa, but the chief enemy there was to be typhoid fever rather than malaria or yellow fever. Compared to the campaigns in Egypt, the Sudan, or Madagascar, the conquest of West Africa was a sideshow. The campaigns on the other side of the continent, even those against Africans, were closer to the rivalries of the European powers, closer to the Europeans' perceptions of their national interest. They therefore brought out a different perception of the relations of disease and empire.

CHAPTER 5

TYPHOID AND THE
EGYPTIAN GARRISON

"... water, flies, and dust ..."

In the middle decades of the nineteenth century, European medicine won major victories over tropical disease – notably against malaria, cholera, and some forms dysentery. In the 1870s, however, typhoid fever emerged as a new threat. The threat was not simply relative – a reflection of the fact that other diseases like malaria were becoming less lethal – it was an absolute increase, measured in military deaths per thousand per year (refer to Figure 5.1). At first, the rise of typhoid was nothing but a statistical blip on the charts, but it gained public attention as an unexpected and major killer in three North African campaigns of the early 1880s: Tunisia, Egypt, and southern Oran in Algeria. Nor was it merely an expeditionary problem. By the 1890s, it was the most important single cause of death in the important overseas garrisons that held Algeria, Tunisia, Egypt, and India, and many scattered posts throughout the world.[1]

Typhoid flourishes where pure drinking water is hard to find, and where human crowding makes for easy transmission through fecal contamination. At the beginning of this century, the United States had a half-million cases a year, with around 40,000 deaths. By 1980, the number of cases reported was less than 600, mostly infections that had originated elsewhere. Typhoid had become a "tropical disease" – because the tropical world is poor, not because of the climate. Mini-epidemics still occur in advanced industrial countries, but they are sporadic and are quickly controlled.

A later chapter deals with the typhoid problem on African military campaigns. This chapter deals with the disease itself, first as it is understood today, then tracing the progress of scientific knowledge, and on to the practice of British military medicine. The most advanced medical knowledge was not necessarily common practice; but the public health measures applied by the British garrison in Egypt are a convenient touchstone for

---

[1] Philip D. Curtin, *Death by Migration Europe's Encounter with the Tropical World in the Nineteenth Century* (New York: Cambridge University Press, 1989), pp. 150–4.

113

examining what was recommended, what was ordered, and what was done. This example is striking partly because the typhoid record for the Egyptian garrison of the mid-1880s was one of the worst in the British empire and became one of the best on the eve of the First World War. Egypt is also significant because of the contrast between the control of typhoid in lower Egypt and the failure to control it on military expeditions elsewhere in northeastern Africa.

Typhoid Today

In common usage, the term "typhoid fever" means an infection by one of a number of different organisms of the salmonella family. Technically, the group as a whole is called enteric fever. *Salmonella typhi* alone is called typhoid, and the other members of the group are called paratyphoids; but in common usage and for present purposes the whole enteric fever group can be called typhoid. In the nineteenth century, before the paratyphoids were discovered, the British used the term enteric fever, while French and Americans used typhoid fever.[2]

The mode of transmission is normally through contaminated food or water, more rarely through direct personal contact with the feces, urine, or other body fluids of the patient. Food can be infected by water used in its preparation, or by contact with a typhoid victim or a "carrier" who retains the ability to infect others even after his own recovery, possibly in some instances by insects. The stools of a typhoid victim carry an enormous quantity of infection. Even those of a chronic carrier are charged with 10^6 to 10^9 *S. typhi* organisms per gram. *S. typhi*, once excreted, can survive for somewhat less than a week in untreated sewage, but it can last for several weeks in water, ice, dried sewage, or on clothing. Milk is even more favorable, since milk, milk products, and shellfish can act as a culture to concentrate the bacillus without changing the appearance or taste of the food.

After being swallowed, the typhoid organisms pass through to the small intestine. If their numbers are small enough or the host's immune response is strong enough, no clinical symptoms may occur. Otherwise, after an incubation period of about 7 to 14 days, the *S. typhi* pass into the general circulation and may invade any organ, though most commonly the intestine, spleen, liver, and bone marrow. The most striking symptom after incubation is a continuous fever, rising slowly each day. In untreated cases, the fever usually lasts about three weeks, and the temperature returns to normal among those who survive into the fourth week, though the disease can continue for several months.

Many different symptoms can accompany the fever – weakness, anorexia, and headache being common. The most characteristic pathol-

[2] This discussion of typhoid as it is understood today is based principally on Stephen L. Hoffman, "Typhoid Fever," in G. Thomas Strickland, *Hunter's Tropical Medicine*, 6th ed. (Philadelphia, 1984), pp. 282–97.

ogy, however, is perforation of the intestine, causing hemorrhaging, which takes place typically in about the third week. After recovery, many typhoid patients will continue to excrete *S. typhi* with stools or urine for several months. Only those who continue to do so after a year are now considered to be carriers.

It is now believed that about 3 percent of typhoid victims become carriers for a time, but the carrier rate in different populations varies greatly. In Britain in recent times it is below 0.001 percent. In parts of Egypt, however, it reaches 3 percent of the whole population. This is a particular local circumstance; in Egypt, infection of the urinary tract by schistosomiasis or bilhartzia is extremely common, and this infection combined with typhoid makes for urinary, as opposed to fecal, typhoid carriers. In most parts of the world, fecal carriers outnumber urinary carriers by ten to one. In Egypt, the proportion is nearly reversed.

In the developed industrial world today, few carriers are created. If patients are treated with antibiotics within three days of the onset of the fever, further complications cease and the case-fatality rate is zero. Even delayed administration of antibiotics reduces the case-fatality rate in the tropical world today to less than 4 percent, down from the level of around 30 percent that was prevalent in Europe in the late nineteenth century.

The immunology of *S. typhi* is still imperfectly understood. Early in this century, most Western physicians believed that typhoid fever was mainly a disease of late adolescence and young adulthood, with declining rates of infection later in life, presumably the result of an acquired immunity. Outside of Europe in recent decades, however, the observed relationship of age to typhoid varies locally. Countries as distant as Hong Kong and Iran show a predominance of cases in early childhood rather than young adulthood.

Vaccination with dead *S. typhi* organisms began at the end of the nineteenth century, though it was not common even in Europe, America, and Japan until just before the First World War. This vaccination gives a fairly strong immunity, but it can be overridden by a strong infective dose of the organism itself. Even without immunization, the probability of developing a full case of typhoid depends on the number of infective organisms. Experiments with healthy, previously unvaccinated human volunteers showed that a dose of 10^5 *S. typhi* organisms infected only 25 percent of the volunteers, but 10^7 organisms would infect 50 percent and 10^9 organisms would infect 95 percent.[3]

What Scientists Knew

Typhoid fever was almost certainly known to the classical Greek physicians, but it is impossible to distinguish it from other "continued fevers"

---

[3] Hoffman, "Typhoid," p. 285.

for which the ancient term was "typhus." Over time it has emerged occasionally in virulent epidemics. In 1607 to 1624, for example, settlers at Jamestown in Virginia died at an annual rate of about 500 per thousand, and the principal killer may have been typhoid.[4] By the 1820s and 1830s, many investigators began trying to distinguish the various forms of fever. After 1829, the students of Pierre Louis in Paris attempted to distinguished typhoid from typhus fever by its characteristic intestinal lesion, a diagnosis which required postmortem examination. A less certain but more obvious clinical sign distinguishing typhoid from typhus was the fact that, though both diseases produced a red rash on the skin, the rashes were distinctly different. In addition, while typhus had no accompanying diarrhea, typhoid frequently did.[5]

It was Louis who popularized the term "typhoid," meaning typhus-like, though the distinction was unclear at first. In 1837, one of Louis's former students, William Gerhard of Philadelphia carried on his work in America, introducing the French term "typhoid" into American English; while the British continued to use "enteric fever" for the rest of the century. In 1862, French military records began to recognize typhoid fever as distinct from other continued fevers; British military records did the same with enteric fever only after 1879. This change in terminology may account for part of the new attention drawn to typhoid, and hence for the increasing frequency of diagnosis, but the statistical increase is far too large, measured against earlier records of death from "continued fevers," to account for a major part of the increase.

Civilian doctors in Britain began to distinguish between continued fevers somewhat earlier. By the late 1850s, William Budd of Bristol published a series of articles in which he associated enteric fever with contaminated water – an association already made for cholera. He demonstrated that typhoid was carried by sewage, not by sewage in general but only by sewage that contained the feces of recent typhoid victims.[6] The obvious conclusion he drew was that one could protect the public's health with better sewage disposal and a better water supply.

The finding was not universally accepted, but, in 1860, Dr. Edmund Alexander Parkes, of the British army medical establishment at Netley accepted Budd's discovery and added:

[T]he grand fact is clear that the occurrence of typhoid fever points unequivocally to defective removal of excreta, and that it is a disease altogether and

[4] Carville V. Earle, "Environment, Disease, and Mortality in Early Virginia," in Thad W. Tate and David L. Ammerman, *The Chesapeake in the Seventeenth Century* (Chapel Hill: University of North Carolina Press, 1979), pp. 96–125.

[5] Dale C. Smith, "Introduction," in William Budd, *On the Causes of Fevers (1839)* (Baltimore: Johns Hopkins University Press, 1984), pp. 1–39. Edited by Dale C. Smith; Bill Luckin, "Evaluating the Sanitary Revolution: Typhus and Typhoid in London, 1851–1900," in Robert Woods and John Woodward, *Urban Disease and Mortality in Nineteenth-Century England* (London and New York, 1984), pp. 103–5.

[6] William Hobson, *World Health and History* (Bristol, 1963), p. 95.

easily preventable. Typhoid fever ought soon to disappear from every return of disease.[7]

He was right, but premature. Typhoid fever was just then beginning its rise as an important killer among European civilians and in European armies – an increase both in deaths per thousand and in its percentage of all deaths.[8] These changes took place against a background of continued advance in the methods of identifying and controlling the disease. In 1863, Casimir Davaine had identified the disease-causing bacterium of the cattle disease anthrax. Robert Koch described its life cycle in 1876, and Louis Pasteur developed a form of artificial immunization for sheep. In the late 1870s, Pasteur in France and Koch in Germany were both working toward the germ theory of disease transmission, and Koch's paper on the etiology of infective disease is regarded as the first definitive statement; but, like most scientific advances, it was one that had been foreshadowed by several different biologists over then-recent decades.

In 1880, these developments helped Karl Joseph Eberth identify and describe what he called *Bacillus typhosus*. Four years later, Georg Gaffsky cultured the bacillus and stressed once more that it was transmitted by water. While this positive identification of what is now known as *Salmonella typhi* was of crucial importance in the history of bacteriology and the germ theory of disease, it made little immediate difference in the prevention or cure of the disease itself.

The characteristic intestinal lesions were a good diagnostic guide at the stage of postmortem examination, but such a diagnosis obviously came too late for remedial action. In the 1890s, however, new diagnostic tests became available. Georges Widal in France developed a serological test, known since as the Widal test. It is based on the agglutination *B. typhosus* when exposed to serum of patients who had (or had recently had) typhoid. In spite of some serious problems of interpretation, it remained the standard serological test for typhoid fever until the recent past, and it is still occasionally used, though more accurate tests are now available.[9]

Even so, an area of uncertainty remained. Not only was it easy to confuse typhoid with other "continued fevers," it was also possible to mistake it for some cases of malaria or yellow fever, where these diseases and typhoid were both endemic. Long after Eberth's time, many practitioners still believed that the symptoms of typhoid fever were in fact caused by a number of different bacteria.

---

[7] Edmund Alexander Parkes, "Review of the Progress of Hygiene During the Year 1861," AMSR for 1860, 2:362.

[8] Curtin, *Death by Migration,* p. 151.

[9] Hoffman, "Typhoid," pp. 292–93.

One variant of new disease distinguished in the United States and France, less commonly in Britain, was typhomalaria.[10] It appeared frequently in French military records from Africa, where most cases were probably typhoid. By 1900, it was supposed to be the simultaneous action of *S. typhi* and one of the plasmodia that produce the periodic fevers of malaria. In fact, the combination seemed to be a natural occurrence in places like Algeria, where malaria was endemic and typhoid was common. Malarial parasites often remain in the liver after clinical symptoms have disappeared, and any new trauma, like typhoid fever, was likely to bring them out into the blood stream for a round of renewed activity. One rough diagnostic test was to administer quinine and see how the patient responded. The 1900 edition of Patrick Manson's standard text on tropical medicine met the problem with the advice: "when in doubt, give quinine."[11]

In the next decade, genuine new enteric bacteria began to be identified. These were the paratyphoids, and they began be added to the official British army listing of diseases from 1910 onward. Two bacilli were identified at first, called *Bacillus paratyphosus* A and B. C and a possible D were added by 1924. The two most common are now known as *Salmonella paratyphi* A and *S. schottmuelleri*, after Hugo Schottmüller, who first identified it. The symptoms are similar to those of *S. typhi*, but much milder. In the British army in India in 1911, the case fatality rate of previously vaccinated typhoid victims was 11.4 percent – 17.2 percent for the unvaccinated – but only about 2 percent of the paratyphoid victims for whom no vaccine was yet available.[12] The treatment of typhoid fever, once identified, was limited to nursing and fever control until effective chemotherapy came with the antibiotics developed after the Second World War.

Meanwhile in Europe, sanitary engineers did more than bacteriologists in the immediate battle against typhoid fever. Nineteenth-century industrialization brought urban crowding. By the 1880s, the bacteriologists had made it clear that many diseases were carried by water, and urban planners began to take action on two fronts: the provision of pure water and the disposal of waste. Pure water was available in most European cities by the turn of the century – partly by bringing water from a relatively uncontaminated source, like a mountain lake or an artesian well, partly by building filtration plants. Some plants used the slow sand filter, which strained out some impurities but, even more, allowed bacterial action to kill the dangerous microbes. Other filters removed the larger impurities,

[10] For the definitive study of the American origins of this disease see Dale C. Smith, "The Rise and Fall of Typhomalarial Fever," *Journal of the History of Medicine*, 37:182–220, 287–321 (1982).

[11] Primet, "Rapport sur l'épidémie de fièvre jaune au Soudan," AMN, 59:367–77 (1893); Patrick Manson, *Tropical Diseases: A Manual of the Diseases of Warm Climates*, 2nd ed. (London, 1900), pp. 225–26.

[12] AMSR, 52:35–43 (1910); AMSR, 53:38–40 (1911); AMSR, 55:37–40 (1913); Andrew Balfour and H.H. Scott, *Health Problems of the Empire* (London, Collins, 1924), p. 207.

followed by chemical treatment of the almost-pure water that passed through. Chlorine became the most common purifying agent, though bromine was sometimes used, as it is today.[13]

Many different methods had been used to dispose of urban waste, but the principal alternatives were three. One was the cesspit, equivalent to the present-day rural backyard privy. It might serve only one household or serve several; though the size differed, the principal characteristic was that waste was deposited in the ground and removed only at considerable intervals. The disadvantages of the cesspit were its smell and the danger that it might drain into the water table to contaminate wells or streams. Its principal advantage was to let bacterial action kill many disease germs, like a slightly less efficient version of a modern septic tank.

One alternative was some variant of the ancient system of nightsoil removal. Human waste was held in a bucket or tub for a day or two, rarely more, and then removed for disposal outside the town, in a kind of out-of-town cesspit, though nightsoil could also be aged or treated in other ways to make it a valuable and only slightly dangerous fertilizer. Nineteenth-century sanitarians called variants of these practices the "dry system," and they were widely use in European cities, virtually universally with European armies at home and abroad until the early twentieth century.

The second alternative was the waterborne system based on the flush toilet and permanent drains to carry off all kinds of liquid household waste. Needless to say, this system depended on the availability of plentiful piped water. Thus the whole complex of water supply and waste disposal depended on the skill of sanitary engineers and the increased willingness of public authorities to invest capital in equipment. European cities began to sidle into the combination of piped water and piped sewage as early as the 1830s, but the steps were often partial and halting. It was only in the late 1880s and 1890s that they moved to full-scale systems of piped water reaching individual residences and piped sewage carrying off the waste, at least from the wealthier parts of the town.[14]

Typhoid fever fitted into this set of changes in several ways. *Salmonella typhi* does not survive long in raw sewage. The old-fashioned cesspit was therefore not an altogether bad form of disposal. Waterborne sewage without adequate protection of water supplies downstream was far more dangerous, since *S. typhi* could live much longer diluted in water than it could in raw sewage. In the last two decades of the nineteenth century, some American cities found their typhoid mortality rates rising markedly when they installed waterborne sewage disposal. The consequences were

---

[13] See Curtin, *Death by Migration*, pp. 111–19 for a summary account of these developments.
[14] Anne Hardy, "Water and the Search for Public Health in London in the Eighteenth and Nineteenth Centuries," MH, 28:250–82 (1984); Mary Stone, "The Plumbing Paradox," *Winterthur Portfolia*, 14:292, 284 (1979).

Figure 5.1   *The Eighteenth-Century Rise of Typhoid among European Troops at Home and Overseas*

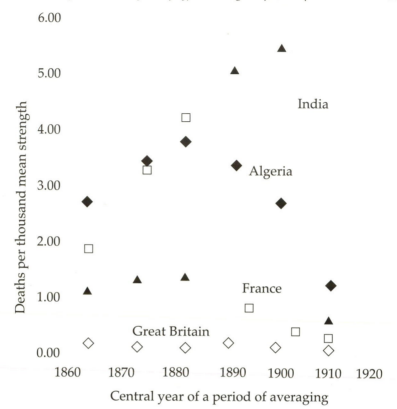

Central year of a period of averaging

even worse for other cities downstream.[15] One solution was self-protection by downstream users, who began to filter and purify their water supplies. The longer-term solution, to treat raw sewage before it was released into rivers or oceans, was slow to come; the clean-rivers movement had barely begun anywhere before the 1950s.

The rise and fall of typhoid illustrated in figure 5.1 is probably associated with these stages in sanitary engineering.[16] The increase in typhoid deaths was spectacular, roughly doubling in France and Algeria between the 1860s and the 1880s, increasing five-fold in India by 1900. It is conceivable, though hard to prove, that the upturn in typhoid deaths in all these places was brought on by the increase in waterborne sewage. Great Britain

[15] Joel A. Tarr, James McCurley, and Terry F. Yosie, "The Development and Impact of Urban Waste Technology: Changing Concepts of Water Quality Control, 1850–1930, in Marton V. Melosi (ed.), *Population and Reform in American Cities, 1870-1930* (Austin, 1980), pp. 74–78; Joel A. Tarr, James McCurley III, Francis C. McMichael, and Terry Yosie, "Water and Wastes: A Retrospective Assessment of Wastewater Technology in the United States, 1800–1932," *Technology and Culture*, 25:226–63 (1984).

[16] For numerical values of this and later figures see the appropriate appendix tables.

was the exception. There, the typhoid death rate among the military barely changed at all, but typhoid death rates in Britain were regionally variable. The civilian death rate in London reached its peak in the 1850s and 1860s, decreasing in the 1870s with an improved water supply.[17] In France and Algeria, a downturn in deaths after the 1880s had mainly the same cause, but that fact was not clearly understood at the time.

By the 1890s, military sanitarians began to run into problems. If water and water alone transmitted *Salmonella typhi,* too many cases occurred where the drinking water appeared to be demonstrably pure; and, by that time, bacterial examination of water was possible. Toward the end of the decade, American researchers, spurred on by the scandalous typhoid mortality of soldiers assembled in army camps for the war in Cuba, found that insects can also carry the typhoid bacteria from human excrement to human food. They traced the transmission from open latrines, or where the "dry earth system" left feces barely covered for a number of hours before removal to "filth trenches." Filth trenches were also left uncovered for a time; and, while they were supposed to be some distance down-wind from the camp or barracks, they might still be within the range of a housefly. The early work with flies came from Edward B. Vedder of the U.S. Army. L.O. Howard, an entomologist, followed up with more detailed studies that attracted international attention.[18]

The search for an alternate source of typhoid transmission moved on to dust and soil. Several medical reports of overseas epidemics had suggested spontaneous occurrence, without a chain of human hosts. No less an authority than Patrick Manson noted that typhoid could sometimes break out among soldiers marching through dry country with a secure water supply. He concluded that "Eberth's bacillus, under certain conditions of soil and temperature, may exist as a pure yet virulent saprophyte, for which occasional passage through the human body is by no means necessary."[19]

Manson was mistaken, but the suspicion led to examine Robert H. Firth and W.H. Horrocks of the medical center at Netley to the ability of *S. typhi* to survive in the soil. Their experiments show that the bacillus' survival time was highly variable. It could be very long in sterilized soils, but in most soils the same bacterial enemies that attacked *S. typhi* in raw sewage limited its life in the ground. It could survive in wet soil for more than two months; but it could also survive in dried soils, and it could be blown as dust. Dust and flies therefore had to be added to the possible sources of contamination. Even before 1900, the existence of typhoid carriers had

---

[17] For the atypical pattern of tyhoid in nineteenth-century Britain see Anne Hardy, *Epidemic Streets: Infectious Disease and the Rise of Preventive Medicine, 1856-1900* (Oxford: Clarendon Press, 1993), pp. 151–90, esp. p. 171.

[18] L. O. Howard, "A Contribution to the Study of the Insect Fauna of Human Excrement," *Proceedings of the Washington Academy of Science,* 2:51–604 (1900); Curtin, *Death by Migration,* pp. 152–53.

[19] Manson, *Tropical Diseases,* p. 224.

come to light, which meant that humans joined the list of dangerous agents – along with water, dust, and flies.[20]

Typhoid fever, it followed, would be far harder to get rid of in field conditions than earlier authorities had supposed, but any of the various systems of nightsoil removal was a continuing danger that could not be tolerated in barracks conditions, however unavoidable it might be for armies in the field. By about 1902 the British army began to switch to the "wet system" in one Indian post after another, and the change was followed by a sharp drop in typhoid cases and typhoid deaths.

In the early years of the new century, the multiple modes of transmission suggested new directions for preventive medicine. Rather than passively guarding the potential victim, the new aim was to seek and destroy the disease in the existing victim, "the fountain-head and chief source of infection." In hospital, this implied complete segregation of all known cases and convalescents. New drafts of troops arriving in India from Europe were segregated in a separate part of the camp for 28 days, with their own cooks and separate latrines. If any came down with typhoid, the quarantine period was increased.[21]

By 1908, the typhoid carrier became a new center of attention, and remedies now featured the segregation and continuous examination of convalescents. In British India, medical authorities set up two convalescent centers, at Naini Tal in 1908 and Wellington in the southern highlands in 1909. All convalescents diagnosed as having a fever of unknown origin, paratyphoid A or B, enteric, or Mediterranean fever (brucellosis) were to be sent to one of these centers for observation. Special laboratories at the two hill centers carried out extensive testing of their own patients and of others from all over India. The Naini Tal laboratories discovered three carriers that year. Wellington discovered one chronic and eight intermittent carriers.[22]

It was a major effort and expense, and the special concern with dust, insects, and typhoid carriers gradually died down. For barracks life, waterborne sewage reduced the fear of transmission by insects and dust. Carriers remained hard to cure until antibiotics were available after 1948, but they were comparatively few. As the experience of the First World War was to show, the combination of vaccination and pure water brought the disease under effective control, even though the cure was still far off.[23]

Immunization

Artificial immunization had a long history, stretching back for centuries. Inoculation against smallpox was an ancient practice in Asia and Africa,

[20] R.H. Firth, "Report of the Progress of Hygiene from the Year 1900–01," AMSR, 42:357–60, 382; Lancet, 1900, 1, p. 1218 (April 12).
[21] AMSR for 1904, 46:248–51.
[22] AMSR for 1913 55:41–2.
[23] Balfour and Scott, Health and Empire, p. 212

and it was popularized in Europe and North America from the early eighteenth century. The natural mode of smallpox transmission was droplets from the respiration of an infected person, but this mode of transmission carried a high case fatality rate. Variolation, or intentional transmission by introducing infected material from a smallpox sore under the skin of a healthy person, carried a much lower fatality rate, but it too gave a lifelong immunity.

In the 1790s, Edward Jenner introduced the earliest vaccination with cowpox, an associated disease in animals, which produced the same degree of immunity much more safely. After that, European medicine was conscious that infection with some diseases – even if inflicted voluntarily – could produce immunity to a future, or perhaps less serious infection. It was only natural for the early bacteriologists to think of similar possibilities for their newly discovered microbes.

In the 1880s, Pasteur began infecting animals with samples of attenuated strains of bacteria, to see whether this would produce increased immunity. Other experimenters used heat-killed bacteria to produce immunity without a serious infection. In the mid-1890s, Almroth Wright, the Professor of pathology at Netley, began experimenting with heat-killed *Salmonella typhi*, nearly simultaneously with similar work in Germany. He first inoculated himself and the professional staff at Netley. Then, in 1897, he worked with a larger sample of mental patients during a typhoid epidemic. The results were spectacular. No one died of the immunization itself, as sometimes happened with variolation, and the morbidity and mortality rates of the immunized patients were substantially lower than those of an unvaccinated control sample from the same institution.[24]

Wright was greatly encouraged and decided, in 1898, to take advantage of a trip to India as part of a plague commission to try further experiments, this time with soldiers in a tropical setting. In all, he persuaded 2,835 men to volunteer for immunization, using as a control the larger number who had been offered vaccination but refused. Of those immunized, 0.95 percent came down with fever within about a year, and 0.2 percent died. Among the non-immunized, 2.5 percent came down with fever and 0.34 percent died.[25]

---

[24] For the history of typhoid inoculation: see Harry F. Dowling, *Fighting Infection: Conquests of the Twentieth Century* (Cambridge, MA, 1977), pp. 23–27; Henry James Parish, *A History of Immunization* (London, 1965), pp. 62–69; Frederick F. Russell, "Anti-Typhoid Vaccination," *American Journal of Medical Science*, 146:803–33 (1913); William B. Leishman, "The Progress of Anti-Typhoid Inoculation in the Army," JRAMC, 8:463–71 (1907); Arnold Netter, "Les inoculations préventives contre la fièvre typhoïde," *Bulletin de l'Institut Pasteur*, 4:873–83, 921–27, 969–80, 1024–34 (1906); Zachary Cope, *Almroth Wright: Founder of Modern Vaccine-therapy* (London: Nelson, 1966), pp. 15–61; Leonard Colebrook, *Almroth Wright: Provocative Doctor and Thinker* (London: Heinemann, 1954), pp. 30–46.

[25] A.E. Wright and W.B. Leishman, "Remarks on the Results which Have Been Obtained by the Antityphoid Inoculations . . ." BMJ, 1900, 1, p. 122–29 (January 20).

It was an imperfect experiment, as Wright himself admitted. The immunized men were stationed in fourteen different places. The bacterial material had to be manufactured on shipboard or in India itself, which meant that its strength was variable. It was given as a single injection in the thigh, which caused serious soreness, often accompanied by fever, nausea, or headaches for a day or so. Wright was nevertheless so encouraged that he began to recommend general immunization in the British army, estimating that for India alone it could prevent 1,000 cases and save 250 lives each year.[26]

When Army authorities heard of Wright's activities in India, they ordered him to stop. The result was a long controversy in medical circles, the press, and Parliament. Medical people in Britain were already alarmed at the recent increase in typhoid deaths among British troops overseas, and they were especially impressed by the high typhoid mortality of American soldiers recruited for the Spanish American War. The Americans, even in camp before moving overseas, had experienced typhoid morbidity at 192 per thousand, and deaths at 14.63 per thousand – roughly eight times the typhoid morbidity and three times the mortality of British troops in India over the period 1895–1904. With the beginning of the Anglo-Boer War in South Africa late in 1899, Wright asked permission for a general vaccination of the troops being sent overseas. He had the editorial support of the *British Medical Journal*, which, early in 1900, had already predicted a typhoid epidemic in South Africa and warned that it was likely to be serious.

The opposition, however, argued that Wright's Indian data were statistically imperfect (which they were) and that caution was advisable. The typhoid immunization debate merged with the current medical controversy between contagionists and anti-contagionists. While the germ theory was well advanced in medical circles by this time, some medical opinion (and even more lay opinion) preferred to believe that disease came from atmospheric conditions or from generalized non-specific dirt and overcrowding.

Opponents of smallpox vaccination also entered the picture. In 1871, the British Parliament had passed a new Vaccination Act, which provided free vaccination for all and stiff penalties for parents who failed to have their children vaccinated. But, by the 1890s, anti-vaccinationist opposition began to build up – partly from residual anti-contageonism, partly from resentment at state interference with personal freedom. The anti-vaccinationists were so vociferous that new Vaccination Acts of 1898 and 1907 allowed parents to withhold vaccination from their children on grounds of "conscientious objection."[27]

With opposition to a proven form of immunization so strong, small wonder that Wright's relatively untested typhoid vaccination should

[26] A.E. Wright and W.B. Leishman, "Antityphoid Inoculations..." BMJ, 1900, 1, p. 122–29 (January 20) p. 124.
[27] Donald Hopkins, *Princes and Peasants: Smallpox in History* (Chicago, 1983). pp. 91–105.

meet still more opposition. The authorities allowed him to offer immunization to the troops bound for South Africa, but only on a voluntary basis; he actually succeeded in reaching some 14,000, a tiny part of the force. Even the wartime record-keeping showed a strongly favorable result for the typhoid vaccination, though many were unconvinced.[28]

Once the South African War was over, objections became louder than ever. Some complained of the statistical weakness of wartime records, others of the severity of the physical reaction to the shot itself. Wright himself weakened his case by stating that the vaccination first caused a "negative phase" of greater susceptibility to the disease shortly after the injection, which would later give way to the "positive phase" – on the evidence that the observable number of antibodies in the blood decreased slightly just after immunization. Furthermore, some soldiers among one sample group Wright inoculated in India early in 1899 came down with typhoid only 19 days after the injection. Those experimental immunizations, however, had been carried out during typhoid epidemics, making it possible that the victims had already contracted the disease. The point was unsettled at the time, but the possibility became one reason for giving a light dose of vaccine followed by a stronger one a week or so later.[29] Wright believed throughout that long-term protection far outweighed the temporary disadvantage of a "negative phase."

Statistical problems led to a prolonged controversy between Wright on one hand and the statisticians Karl Pearson and Major Greenwood on the other. The controversy was prominent enough to find a place of George Bernard Shaw's preface to *The Doctor's Dilemma*.[30] In the play itself, one charcter – a doctor – says:

I've tried these modern inoculations a bit myself. I've killed people with them and I've cured people with them; but I gave up because I never could tell which I was going to do.

Some of the early typhoid vaccines were indeed faulty; overheating during preparation could make them inert, though that simply made them ineffective, not harmful. A Subcommittee of the Advisory Board for Army Medical Services, however, looked into the production of serum and the dangers of vaccination and reported that:

There is, indeed, no doubt that public opinion would severely condemn any system of compulsory inoculation which, though it might obtain some measure of protection for the majority, was admitted to entail upon a certain number of indi-

[28] David Bruce, "Analysis of the Results of Professor Wright's Method of Anti-Typhoid Inoculation," JRAMC, 4:244–55 (1905).

[29] Frederick F. Russell, "Anti-Typhoid Vaccination," pp. 809–13.

[30] Bernard Shaw, "Preface on Doctors," *The Doctor's Dilemma, Getting Married, and the Shewing-up of Blanco Posnet* (New York: Brentano's, 1911), pp. lxxvi–lxxix; See also J. Rossen Matthews, "Major Greenwood versus Almroth Wright: Contrasting Visions of 'Scientific' Medicine in Edwardian Britain," BHM, 69:30–43 (1995).

viduals increased liability to disease, suffering, and death. Until further light is thrown upon this . . . it is from every point of view expedient that the present practice of extensive inoculations should be suspended.[31]

This was a curious piece of logic from the military mind, since all warfare increases the liability of soldiers to "disease, suffering, and death," but the army stopped immunization for a year and a half while a special Anti-Typhoid Committee at the Royal Army Medical College at Netley investigated.[32] Among other things, the committee appointed eight special typhoid officers, each attached to a particular unit bound for India. Some soldiers in each of these unit were immunized, others not. The typhoid officers followed their units for three years, investigating all typhoid cases, with attention to a possible "negative phase," and postmortem examinations at each death. One sample unit, the 17th Lancers, met a severe epidemic at Meerut in 1905. The typhoid officer's investigation showed 63 cases in all, 61 among the non-immunized, while the immunized suffered only two, and those two were men who had refused the second shot in the immunizing series.[33]

Between 1905 and 1909, William B. Leishman, Wright's successor as Professor of pathology at Netley, joined Wright himself to conduct a continuous program of research to make the vaccine more effective and less painful, with microscopic sampling of the vaccine to assume standardization. Their recommendation was pair of immunizing shots ten days apart – 500 million bacteria for the first shot, 1,000 million for the second, in a half cc and 1 cc of vaccine respectively – which reduced the patient's pain and physical reaction so much that the shots could now be given in the arm.[34] Further testing showed that the vaccine's protection weakened with the passage of time. As a result, beginning in 1910, the two shots were repeated after 30 months, later simplified to every three years. During the First World War, the vaccine was improved to include paratyphoids A and B in the single shot. With that, typhoid immunization had reached a high of clinical efficiency, though it continued to improve in the future.

Finally, in 1909, the Army Council was persuaded to make the vaccination available on a general basis, though still only voluntary, and public resistance continued. With the outbreak of the First World War, the British Parliament considered and rejected a proposal to make typhoid vaccination compulsory in the Army. Military commanders, however, achieved the same result on their own authority, and forceful persuasion led virtually all soldiers to accept vaccination "voluntarily." Some local commanders, for

[31] Great Britain, Advisory Board for the Army Medical Services, Report of Sept. 25, 1902, JRAMC, 4:244 (1905).
[32] Leishman, "Progress of Anti-typhoid," pp. 464; Netter, "Inoculations préventives," p. 974.
[33] Leishman, "Progress of Anti-typhoid," p. 464.
[34] Leishman, "Progress of Anti-typhoid," pp. 467–69.

example, ruled that typhoid fever was such a serious danger that any soldier wishing to leave the base for any reason would have to submit to voluntary vaccination.

Anti-typhoid vaccination spread only slowly to other European armies. In 1911, the French army began vaccinations on a voluntary basis, first in Morocco, where campaigning was active and the typhoid problem was most severe, then gradually elsewhere in North Africa; by 1912 and 1913, the army was vaccinating volunteers in selected garrisons in France itself. In March 1914, the Assembly passed a law making vaccination compulsory throughout the French armed forces. The actual vaccinations proceeded more slowly. Even in Morocco where the typhoid danger was considered to be most serious, only 32 percent of the force was vaccinated by 1913, rising to about 66 percent in 1914. It was only in 1916, however, that blanket vaccination was achieved for the whole French army, with a few exemptions for medical reasons.[35]

The British army therefore entered the war with more men actually vaccinated than in the French, German, or Italian armies, which entered the war with compulsory vaccination in theory. The French army suffered 12,000 typhoid deaths in the first six months of the war, while the British lost only 158 men from typhoid on the western front during the first full year. In time, all European armies followed the American lead in compulsory immunization. At the war's end, only the British lacked compulsory immunization – though only in theory, not in practice.[36]

The Egyptian Disease Environment

In the nineteenth century, the Egyptian government under Muhammad Ali had introduced a Western-style medical school and Western-style maritime quarantine service, but the targets for these early public-health measures were cholera and plague, not typhoid fever. By 1882, Egypt had a population of about 6,800,000, including about 90,000 foreigners, served by 120 European doctors and 94 Egyptians trained in Western medicine – hardly enough to take care of the Egyptian elite and the wealthier foreigners.

European armies had marched in Egypt since the Napoleonic campaigns of 1798 to 1801, when the greatest disease problem had been dysentery and plague, with trachoma as a major cause of blindness. After 1801, returning French veterans spread trachoma widely throughout Europe, though no continuous fever resembling typhoid was then recognized as a serious problem.[37]

[35] Henri Vincent and Louis Muratet, *Typhoid Fever and Paratyphoid Fevers (Symptomatology, Etiology and Prophylaxis)* (London: University of London Press, 1917). Translated from the second and revised edition and edited by J.D. Rolleston, pp. 242, 285.
[36] William B. Leishman, "Enteric Fevers in the British Expeditionary Force," JRAMC, 37:1–22 (1921); Parish, *Immunization*, pp. 68–69; Dowling, *Fighting Infection*, p. 26.
[37] W.T. Black, "Medical Notes and Statistics of the British Expedition to Egypt in 1801," TMCSE, 2(2nd ser.) :11–23 (1882–83).

Nineteenth-century economic development brought many European visitors and residents to North Africa. The Egyptian "climate" had a reputation than was neither good nor really bad; it was not in the feared category of tropical Africa or the Caribbean, but it was not considered safe in the way Canada or New Zealand were. The principal Egyptian diseases were still trachoma, dysentery, and plague – with cholera added when it appeared in the great pandemic that reached Egypt in 1829, moved on through Europe in 1830–31, reaching the United States in 1832.

Medical military planners for the British expedition that conquered Egypt in 1882 recognized the special dangers of venereal disease and trachoma and the prevalence of schistosomiasis among the peasantry, but they paid no particular attention to typhoid.[38] By the mid-1880s, however, the typhoid danger was clear. It accounted for more than half the deaths among the British garrisons in lower Egypt; gastrointestinal infections were the second most important cause of death, so that waterborne diseases accounted for more than three quarters of all deaths.

Some British authorities tended to blame the Egyptians for their "filthy habits." Others were struck by the weakness of preventive measures. Ernest Hart, a civilian doctor who visited Egypt in 1880 and again in 1885, reported:

Enteric fever and dysentery are the scourges of Egypt, and few escape light or more severe attacks according to circumstances. Both are, of course, preventable; and the most rigid orders might well be issued as to the drinking-water of our troops. Condensed [distilled] water is unpalatable, but, by the addition of about six grains of common salt to the quart, it may be greatly improved in that respect.[39]

These conditions were not entirely the Egyptians' fault, he added, because the "Capitulations" had prevented Egyptian government interference, and the Europeans could do what they liked. The Europeans, for example, had brought in water closets for their own use, which carried great quantities of infected water into the ground or the river. The sanitary condition of Cairo by 1885 was therefore worse than it had been in 1880, when human waste was removed, after treatment with dry earth, or went into simple cesspits without the water to spread it further. Hart found Cairo worse than Alexandria, with 34 percent of all civilian deaths from intestinal infection – presumably including typhoid. In Alexandria, at least, the European community had organized a more humane form of sewage disposal – unspecified, but presumably either the dry-earth system or water disposal, which flushed water into the sea.[40]

---

[38] LaVerne Kuhnke, *Lives at Risk: Public Health in Nineteenth-Century Egypt* (Berkeley: University of California Press, 1990), pp. 1–11, 26–32; AMSR for 1881, 244–48.

[39] Ernest Hart, "Letters from the East," BMJ, 1885, 1, 619–, 672–, 754–, 810–, 857–; p. 857 (April 18).

[40] Hart, "Letters from the East," BMJ, 1885, 1, pp. 754–55, 859–60 (April 11 and 18). See also E. Rochefort, "Egypte," *Dictionaire encyclopédique des sciences médicales,* 33(1st ser.):1–33 (1886), pp. 23–50.

In Egypt, virtually all water came from the Nile. The occasional rain that fell in lower Egypt made a negligible contribution to the water table. This meant that any water that reached the barracks of Cairo and Alexandria had been infected several times, though cleaned again to some degree by the natural action of other bacteria in the water. Irrigation water, used upstream, seeped underground to create a water table beneath the Nile Valley; shallow wells that could reach it were safer than the river water itself, unless they were contaminated by nearby cesspits.

Health conditions in lower Egypt were appreciably worse than those of European cities, and steadily worsening. The crude death rate in London in 1887 was 20 per thousand of the civilian population; the equivalent in Cairo had been 33 per thousand in 1801, but was 47 per thousand by 1887 – and 43 per thousand for Alexandria.[41]

The military health problem was much the same as elsewhere in the tropical and subtropical world of that period. The mission of European troops and officials was to rule over and control the local people, and therefore to occupy the cities, but the cities were also centers of disease. Cairo was a city of cesspits, which flooded and spread their filth at the time of the high Nile, or dried up and left human excrement to blow with the wind at low Nile. Clean water and adequate sanitation might be provided in barracks, but when soldiers went to town, they drank local beverages and met local women.

One possibility was to clean up the water supply and provide a sewage system for the whole town, but that was set aside as impossibly expensive. Another was to move the soldiers away from town, employing something like the Indian cantonment system, with barracks at a distance from the main centers, though not completely segregated from them.[42] The compromise solution for Egypt was to accept the cost of contact with the Egyptian population – with episodes of tight quarantine in times of special danger from cholera or plague.

Though Egypt had once been an endemic center of plague, that disease was absent from 1845 to 1899. Cholera was more common as the periodic pandemics of the nineteenth century spread out from its central focus north of the Bay of Bengal, and it was more feared than typhoid – though it killed fewer soldiers – even in India. It attracted attention for its spectacular pattern of a quick death and unlikely recovery. The case-fatality rate for British soldiers in Egypt of the 1890s was 85 percent.

One serious cholera outbreak reached Cairo in 1883. The British responded with the old tactic of flight, used in India since the early century. They evacuated part of the Cairo garrison to Suez, but those who remained suffered 183 cases and 139 deaths.[43]

[41] Black, "British in Egypt in 1801," p. 712; AMSR for 1888, p. 182.
[42] J.A. Marston, Principal Medical Officer, quoted in AMSR for 1888, p. 182.
[43] Rochefort, "Egypte," 23–50; AMSR for 1883, p. 230.

In October 1895, cholera reached Cairo once again, and, before the epidemic ended in the fall of 1896, it had killed more than 15,000 civilians and had spread downstream to Alexandria and up the Nile to Aswan, and beyond. The army confined troops in the Alexandria garrison to barracks for several months. As a result, it suffered far less cholera than the Cairo garrison did, with the by-product of less venereal disease as well. In the two cities together, the army escaped with only five cases, all fatal. The armies on campaign up the Nile suffered far more.[44]

When plague reappeared in 1899, the army was prepared for tougher action. It imposed such a tight quarantine that it escaped without a single case, though the civilian population suffered 93 cases with 45 deaths.[45] When cholera returned in 1902, the army declared all civilian quarters out of bounds, banned uncooked vegetables, dismissed all Egyptian kitchen staff, and moved some units out of barracks to tenting sites. Again, it escaped with only five cases, but again all were fatal.[46]

Meanwhile, in European civilian circles, Egypt was gaining a modest reputation as a health resort. By the mid-1890s, tourists came in the winter season between December and March, about 7,000 a year from Europe and America. New hotels attracted visitors to sites like the pyramids outside Cairo, or Aswan and Luxor up the Nile. Thomas Cook and Son served the tourist trade with well-appointed Nile steamers. The Egyptian climate was valued for its sunshine, great dryness, moderate warmth, and "asepticity." Egypt was still famous for its trachoma and dysentery, but malaria was rare south of the delta and the occasional cholera epidemic reached Europe anyway. Curiously enough, those who discussed the Egyptian climate as a tourist attraction said nothing about typhoid fever, even though it was still the most important cause of death among British troops stationed there.[47]

Sanitary Engineering for the British Garrison

Municipal water works in European cities were common even before the British occupation of Egypt. Both Cairo and Alexandria had concessionary water companies that provided water to the army barracks once the British garrison was in place. The Cairo water company pumped water from the Nile into reservoirs, filtered it through beds of sand and gravel, then distributed it to subscribers through cast iron pipes. The degree of filtration, however, was modest. It was not enough to remove all of the Nile mud, much less its bacteria. The principal British barracks in Cairo refiltered the piped water through drip-stones. That procedure might

[44] AMSR for 1895, 34:162; BMJ, 1896, 1, pp. 888, 1531 (April 4; June 20).
[45] AMSR for 1899, 41: 234–5.
[46] AMSR for 1902, 44:263.
[47] C. Theodore Williams, "The Winter Climate of Egypt," BMJ, 1896, 1, pp. 669–70; Lancet, 1899, 2, p. 1250, 1703, (Nov. 4, Dec. 16).

Figure 5.2. *Cairo and Alexandria: Military Deaths from Typhoid Fever, 1888–1905*

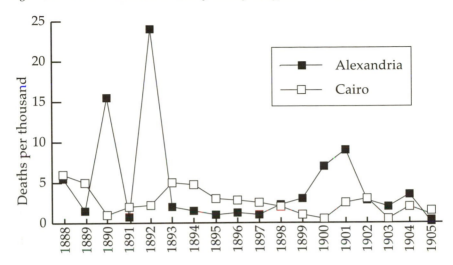

well have removed the sediment, but not the bacteria. In Alexandria, all water for the city came from the Mahmoudieh canal, tapping the western branch of the Nile midway between Cairo and the sea. There, too, the water company filtered before distribution. The Ramleh barracks filtered the water once more, but boiled it only in time of cholera.[48] The British army did not yet have porcelain filters, like the Pasteur-Chamberland; most other filtration would have merely made the water palatable without removing bacteria.

British medical opinion about the quality of this water supply differed. From 1888 to 1905, the army published separate statistics on admissions and deaths from typhoid for the two principal posts at Cairo and Alexandria (see Figure 5.2). The typhoid death rate differed substantially from one to the other, though with no consistent pattern; and opinions differed as to the cause. In 1884, the principal medical officer in Alexandria thought the water supply was adequate; the problem, he thought, was the soil under the barracks, infected with seepage from the cesspits of the neighborhood. Others, however, believed that all Nile water, especially in Alexandria, was unsafe until it was boiled and filtered. In retrospect, the cesspits were smelly but probably relatively safe; the unboiled water was not.[49]

Meanwhile, the Cairo Waterworks Company installed a new filtration system, with a slow sand filter that could theoretically produce pure water. It never did so with any consistency, though any bacterial filtration

[48] AMSR for 1883, 23:119.
[49] AMSR for 1884, 24:119–21; BMJ, 1884, 2, p. 1158. (Dec. 6).

should have been better than none. Alexandrian city filtration was still worse, having only a quarter of the Cairo filter surface and processing twice the output.[50]

By 1895, the army, conscious of Alexandria's special problems, installed Pasteur-Chamberland filters in the barracks there – ten years after the French had begun using them in France and Algeria. This porcelain filtration should have yielded safe water – and safety for the men, if they drank nothing else. Alexandria experienced a 45 percent drop in its typhoid death rate in that year. Cairo, which trusted the filtration system of the Cairo Water Company and turned down Pasteur-Chamberland as an unnecessary expense, had a typhoid death rate nearly four times higher (see Figure 5.2 and Appendix Table A5.2).[51]

By 1897, the Cairo typhoid death rate was still two and a half times Alexandria's, though it was dropping slowly. The army tried drilling for water under the barracks and began a gradual installation of Pasteur-Chamberland filters, but these measures were far from foolproof, even for use in barracks. Unless the water was under pressure, porcelain filters were very slow; the water pressure supplied by the Cairo Water Company was too low, and the army lacked supplementary pumps – a problem that remained into the new century, though additional water could be boiled. The medical authorities were still working in the dark in any case. Until 1898, they had not yet begun to test the water with bacterial cultures, so that decisions about water supply were based only on guesswork, and on trial and error.[52]

The Cairo Waterworks Company began sinking wells to replace the Nile as its principal source of water. By 1904, it had six wells in all, drilled back from the river. Each well was shielded for the first 100 feet in depth by impervious pipe, and continued with a perforated tube, surrounded by sand and mesh, for another 200 feet. This was thought to be an improvement, but the barracks still boiled and filtered water. Finally, in 1909, all the barracks were supplied with Berkeland filters, the British-made equivalent of the Pasteur-Chamberland, but these had to be equipped with a pre-filtration system to remove Nile sediment – an indication that the water company had not solved all its problems.

In the period 1897–1901, the positions of Alexandria and Cairo were reversed; the typhoid death rate at the Alexandria barracks reached three times the Cairo rate. The apparent explanation was simple carelessness, which took the cholera epidemic of 1902 to cure. Up to that time, the Alexandria barracks had depended on filtration alone, but the spectacular number of cholera deaths underlined the need to boil all drinking water, as well. The typhoid rate then dropped to rough equality with Cairo's.

---

[50] J.B. Piot Bey, "L'eau d'alimentation dans les villes du Caire et d'Alexandre," AMPM, 33(3rd ser):487–96 (1895), pp. 489–92.
[51] AMSR for 1895, 34:158.
[52] AMSR for 1897, 36:230–1, 235–6.

Figure 5.3.   *British Troops in Lower Egypt, Typhoid Admissions and Deaths, 1883–1913*

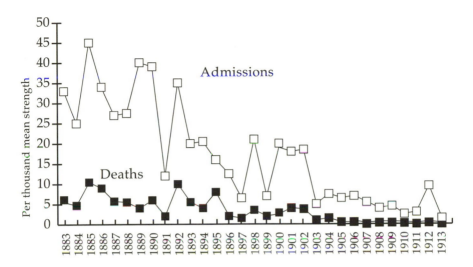

Water from the Mahmoudieh canal was still contaminated, but in 1904 the army began to install its own systematic filtration system, using settling basins and alum as a precipitant, then passing the water through Jewell filters. Drinking water was finally filtered through either Pasteur or Berkeland filters before actual use. As a result, the Alexandria garrison had no typhoid deaths at all in 1905,[53] and the typhoid death rate for the Egyptian garrison as a whole dropped below 1 per thousand in 1905 and remained there (see Figure 5.3 and Appendix Table A5.3).

Improved sewage disposal also played a role. All Egyptian barracks started out using the dry-earth system. That is, feces were deposited in buckets, with a little dry earth spread on top after each use, and at the end of the day, servants carried the buckets to cesspits away from the barracks area. They also emptied the urine tubs in a supposedly safe place. The system was never very satisfactory; the men were careless in using the dry earth, and the servants were careless in removing the tubs. The smell near the latrines was unpleasant, and later on, as the fly danger was recognized, the system was seen to be unhealthful, as well as unpleasant.[54]

In 1898, the first water closet was installed in the commanding officer's apartment at Abbasiyeh barracks in Cairo, but the general change-over to waterborne sewage was not possible because the drains from the barracks were not steep enough even to carry off ordinary waste water. Alexandria, however, was better placed for waterborne sewage disposal; sewage

[53] AMSR for 1902, 44:262, 269; AMSR for 1903, 45:295–6; AMSR for 1904, 46:344–45AMSR for 1909, 38:52.
[54] AMSR for 1883, 23:119; AMSR for 1890, 29:194.

could be dumped directly into the Mediterranean. It polluted the sea, but no one had to drink sea water, and everyone downstream had to drink from the Nile. The army nevertheless delayed waterborne sewage for the Alexandria barracks until 1904; the system was still unfeasible in Cairo because the drains were still not steep enough.[55]

By 1907, Cairo and Alexandria were nearly equal in the quality drinking water, but it became apparent that the form of sewage disposal made a real difference. Alexandria was entirely on the waterborne system, while Cairo still used dry-earth disposal. In that year, 25 of the 28 enteric fever cases occurred among troops stationed in Cairo. Still, the Cairene barracks were without the recommended water closets and septic tanks. Instead, they resorted to the half measure of adding a disinfectant, cresol, which took care of the odor and the swarms of flies, even if it was not fully efficient as a sanitary measure.[56]

Vaccination for the Egyptian Garrison

After about 1907, vaccination against typhoid fever advanced rapidly in Egypt. The first experimental immunizations had begun in 1899, when 461 men (12 percent of the force in lower Egypt) were vaccinated, but, since many men were transferred elsewhere, the results were inconclusive. In the following year, the sample rose to 720, or 21 percent of the force. The following year, the non-immunized majority had a morbidity rate of 25 per thousand and mortality of 4 per thousand. The immunized group had only one case, a death, and the timing of his admission raised the possibility that he had contracted the infection before being vaccinated.[57]

Thereafter, however, immunization in Egypt fell under the same cloud as it did elsewhere in the British army. One experimental unit, a battalion of the Coldstream Guards, under the watch of the immunization committee, arrived in Egypt. It was divided into approximately equal groups before leaving Britain – half inoculated, the other half not. Once in Egypt they were housed and fed together, and the typhoid morbidity of the non-immunized was 28 times that of the immunized group. In 1909, generalized immunization was again allowed on a voluntary basis, and, by 1911, about half of the men and their dependents were protected.[58]

After an uneven record over the years from 1905 to 1909, medical authorities saw the year 1910 as the turning point, with a sharp drop in deaths for most diseases. By that time typhoid deaths were too few to be an important indicator; typhoid cases that year were only twelve, with

[55] AMSR for 1898, 39:273: AMSR for 1904, 46:344–45; AMSR for 1905, 47:268–69.
[56] AMSR for 1907, 48:63–64; AMSR for 1908, 50:55.
[57] AMSR FOR 1899, 40:225; A.E. Wright, "Note on the Results Obtained by the Anti-Typhoid Inoculations in Egypt and Cyprus during the Year 1900," *Lancet*, 1, 1272 (May 4); also BMJ 1901, pp. 1072–73 (May 4).
[58] AMSR for 1907, 49:63.

Figure 5.4. *Typhoid Deaths as a Percentage of All Deaths, 1883–1913*

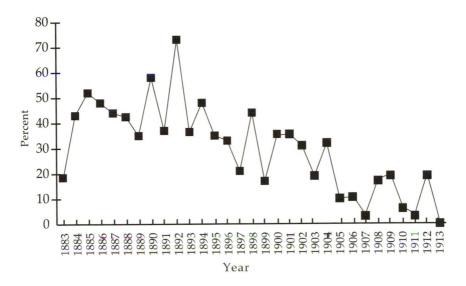

two deaths, from a garrison of 5,592. Since only half the garrison was vaccinated, the main victory was that of sanitary engineering, with only an assist from vaccination, but the case-fatality rate fell from 20 percent before 1903 to only 5.6 percent in 1912 – the probable result of vaccination.[59]

The three decades from 1883 to 1913 were a period when European preventive medicine had made great strides against all diseases, among civilian populations at home as well as armies overseas.[60] Figure 5.4 illustrates the place of typhoid in that general decline of deaths. Typhoid began in 1883 with 20 percent of all deaths, rising to more than 70 percent in 1893, but falling again to less than 20 percent of a much smaller total after 1905 – finally declining to zero in 1913.

Immunities and Seasoning

Europeans noted early in their contact with the non-European world that "natives" died out in some places while Europeans remained healthy, but Europeans died elsewhere of diseases that hardly touched the local population. One obvious question was whether these relative immunities were natural and genetic, or whether they were acquired. In the eighteenth

---

[59] AMSR for 1910, 50:30; AMSR for 1911, 51:32; AMSR for 1912, 52:63.
[60] Curtin, *Death by Migration*, esp. pp. 86–93.

Figure 5.5.   *Egypt Seasoning 1891–95 and 1901–05*

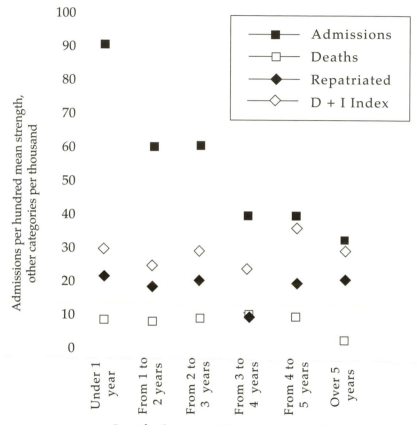

century and earlier, Europeans considered climate and disease environment as identical and talked about a "seasoning sickness" that would
"acclimatize" a new arrival in the tropical world.

In the 1890s, the nature of this seasoning process was still an open question. From 1891 through 1905, the British army tried to build a statistical
base by publishing annual data on the health indicators of soldiers by age
and by length of service in an overseas post. The indicators included hospital admissions, deaths, and repatriations ("invaliding," in the usage of
the time). Deaths plus repatriations can be combined (the D + I index) to
give a summary figure for the most seriously ill, whether they were dead
or merely sent home.

The results of the British surveys were not always conclusive. For
India, five-year surveys by length-of-service 1891–95 and for 1901–05
showed that deaths were often a little higher for first-year men and that
hospital admissions fell slightly with the passage of time, but the D + I

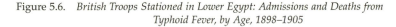

Figure 5.6. *British Troops Stationed in Lower Egypt: Admissions and Deaths from Typhoid Fever, by Age, 1898–1905*

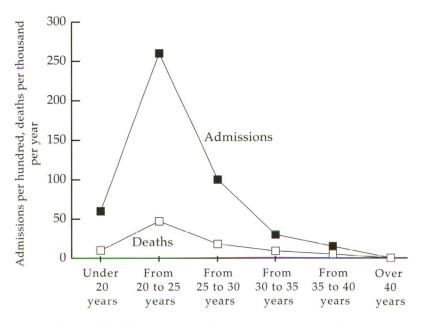

index either rose a little or remained stable regardless of the length of residence.[61]

Similar surveys for Egypt showed a clearer pattern (see Figures 5.5 and 5.6 and Appendix Table A5.4). For lower Egypt, hospital admissions fell year by year with length of residence, with a drop of more than 50 percent from the admission rate from the first-year men to the fifth. Yet the deaths and repatriations varied little with the length of residence. If acclimatization played any role, it kept men out of the hospital but gave little protection against serious illness or death. Most army doctors nevertheless continued to believe in the value of "seasoning," in spite of statistical surveys.

The age factor was especially important for typhoid. European doctors agreed that, at least in Europe, the death rates from typhoid were highest in the 20-to-25-year age range.[62] One explanation was that many older men had acquired immunity from an earlier attack of typhoid, possibly without marked clinical symptoms. What protected the under-twenties was unclear. For India, however, J. Lane Notter, the army's specialist on

---

[61] Curtin, *Death by Migration*, pp. 109–11.
[62] A sample of 5,911 cases admitted to the London Fever Hospital over the years 1848–70, showed 46 percent of all cases in the 15-to-24-year age range with similar results for both sexes. Only 13 percent of the cases occurred to people older than 30. Charles Murchison, *A Treatise on the Continued Fevers of Great Britain*, 2nd ed. (London, 1871), pp. 473–39.

military typhoid, found that increasing length-of-service correlated more closely with declining death rates than with age, leaving some role for acclimatization.[63] In Egypt, however, age played the greater statistical role. For the 20-to-25 age group, both admissions and deaths were more than twice those of any other age group (refer to Figure 5.7 and Appendix Table A5.5).

Patrick Mason's authoritative text of 1900 states:

Fortunately the liability decreases with length of residence. Apparently a sort of acclimatisation, or rather habituation, to the poison is established with time, just as tends to be the case with other organic poisons. It is not unlikely that the relative exemption of the native races is owing to a like immunising effect produced by living in constant contact with typhoid and similar toxic agents.[64]

Immune Patterns for North African Troops

The British in Egypt and the French in the Maghrib were equally concerned with the place of "native races" in the patterns of typhoid immunity. From at least the eighteenth century, the dominant medical opinion was that all races have inherited immunities or predispositions toward disease; it was part of the reason for recruiting local troops. During the conquest and colonization of Algeria, the French had debated the role of inborn biological traits.[65] By the 1880s, however, it was clear that French settlers could live in the Algerian disease environment as least as successfully as native Algerians.

As of the 1880s, Edouard Rochefort's summary of the Egyptian medical climate probably represents what was typical of French medical opinion at the time. He believed that Egyptians had a natural immunity to all gastrointestinal complaints, including typhoid, but that this immunity was countered by other factors, such as the poverty, filth, and bad food – all of which were overcompensated for by eating too much. They also had a genetic immunity to malaria, but this too was countered by the fact that most lived in the countryside, where malaria is most common. Europeans had no such immunity, but they rarely left the cities, which balanced their own lack of acclimatization. As a result, the epidemiological difference between foreigners and native Egyptians was not as great, Rochefort believed, as racial differences would suggest.[66]

In the early twentieth century, the problem of North Africans' alleged immunity to typhoid reemerged among French army doctors in Algeria.

[63] J. Lane Notter, *Spread and Distribution of Infectious Diseases; Spread of Typhoid Fever, Dysentery, and Allied Diseases among Large Communities, with Special Reference to Military Life in Tropical and Sub-Tropical Countries* (London and Manchester, 1904), pp. 11–13.
[64] Manson, *Tropical Diseases* (1900), p. 222.
[65] P.D. Curtin, *Death by Migration*, pp. 45–46.
[66] E. Rochefort, "Egypte," p. 23.

In 1901, Henri Vincent published a statistical study of the province of Algiers comparing the health of French troops from France that that of local recruits. He concluded that the typhoid morbidity of the French was more than 70 times that of the Algerians. He was uncertain whether the Algerian immunity was acquired or inherited, but he thought inheritance was more likely. In his experience, Algerian children were neither obviously nor frequently typhoid victims. He also tried Widal's test on a small number of cases, but his main argument was statistical.

In 1903, Dr. Vidal of the French army medical service gathered similar evidence from Oran province, and he also showed a comparative immunity for Algerians of military age; though the typhoid case-fatality rate of Algerians was remarkably high. His solution was to recommend the use of Algerian troops wherever typhoid control would have required expensive sanitary engineering.[67]

British record keeping for Egyptian soldiers was somewhat different. Britain had effective control over Egypt from 1882, but the Khedive remained, in theory, an autonomous provincial ruler for the Ottoman Sultan in Istanbul. Egyptian soldiers therefore continued to serve in an Egyptian army, reorganized on British lines with some British officers serving alongside Egyptians. This organization applied to the medical service as well, with British and Egyptian army doctors.

In 1884, the Egyptian army published a statistical survey of the health of the army, in the style of the annual British or French reports. The mean annual strength at that time was 6,450 men, almost exactly the same strength as the British army of occupation. Like the British, the Egyptian army was partly on garrison duty in lower Egypt and partly stationed on the fringes of the Sudan or at Suakin on the Red Sea coast, as protection against the Sudanese.

Where the overall death rate for British troops in Egypt was 11.59 per thousand that year, the Egyptian rate was 7.44 per thousand. On the other hand, where the British repatriated only 0.62 per thousand on account of illness, the Egyptian army repatriated 46.05 per thousand and discharged 22.6. Whatever the death rate, the Egyptian army was clearly far less healthy than the British. As for typhoid fever, the British death rate that year was 4.95 per thousand, while the Egyptian rate was only 1.24 per thousand, and the Egyptians had 1.71 deaths per thousand from gastrointestinal infections, compared to a British loss of only 0.93. This result, however, was hardly conclusive; similar variation in death rates occurred between the British garrisons in Cairo and Alexandria.

The Egyptian force also suffered from diseases that barely touched the British. One of these was schistosomiasis, then more commonly called

---

[67] H. Vincent, "Sur l'immunité de la race arabe à l'égard de la fièvre typhoïde," AMPM, 37:145–52 (1901); Vidal, "Contribution à l'étude de l'immunité de la race arabe à l'égard de la fièvre typhoïde," AMPM, 42:438–43 (1903); Chaudoye, "La fièvre typhoïde dans la garnison et dans la ville de Tébessa de 1890 à 1906," AMPM, 50:169–97 (1909), pp. 196–97.

Bilharzia haematobia after Theodore Bilharz who had identified the infecting agent as the worm now called *Schistosoma haematobium*. Then, as now, virtually everyone in the Egyptian countryside was infested to some degree, though not necessarily with pronounced clinical symptoms. In the Egyptian army of 1884, it was a major source of morbidity but not of deaths, and it must have been a principal source of the enormous discharge rate.[68]

The French in Algeria also paid increasing attention to the health and medical treatment of Algerian troops. Racist assumptions about health and disease had by no means disappeared, but they began to weaken. In 1910, the annual report on the health of the army pointed out that the comparative immunity of Algerian troops was lower than had once been thought. The earlier error had come from inadequate observation of disease among Algerian children, who did, in fact, have high rates of morbidity and mortality from typhoid fever. Reported typhoid cases among Algerian troops had also been rising in recent years, as French army doctors were more careful with their diagnoses; whereas in the past they had often put down typhoid as typhus or malaria. More careful testing of Algerian soldiers began to show a slightly higher immunity than that of their French colleagues, presumably from more frequent exposure in youth, but otherwise the difference was not notable.[69]

Egypt in Comparative Mortality of Europeans Overseas

Quantitative data are notorious for raising more new questions than they can answer. It is nevertheless worth a glance at the epidemiological pattern of British troops in Egypt, in order to establish a comparative context. In the late nineteenth century, French troops in Algeria and British troops in India were the largest European forces overseas. Their health records can be set alongside those for British troops in Egypt and at home at two time periods, the first in the early 1890s (1886–1894 for the British data and 1892–96 for the French) and the second encompassing the last five years before 1914 (refer to Tables 5.1 and 5.2 and Figure 5.10).

The comparative disease profiles – the comparative importance of various causes of death – is one place to begin (Table 5.1). The most striking contrast is that between European troops in Europe (represented here by British troops serving at home) and those overseas. In the earlier period, the annual disease death rate of soldiers in Britain was only 4.31 per thousand, while those who served in Algeria died at nearly twice that rate –

---

[68] *Lancet*, 1885, 2, p. 961 (Nov. 23); AMSR for 1884, p. 229; Larry W. Laughlin, "Schistosomiasis," in G. Thomas Strickland, *Hunter's Tropical Medicine*, 6th ed. (Philadelphia: Saunders, 1984), pp. 708–40, esp. pp. 708–10. See also BMJ, 1885, 2, pp. 1027, 1032–33; John Farley, *Bilharzia: A History of Imperial Tropical Medicine* (Cambridge: Cambridge Press, 1991).

[69] France. Ministère de Guerre. *Statistiques médicale de l'armée metropolitaine et de l'armée coloniale* (Paris, 1862+) volume for 1910, p. 138.

Table 5.1. *European Troops in Algeria, Egypt, India, and Great Britain:*
Changing Disease Profiles 1890s to 1913

Diseases Profiles in Percentage from Disease Owing to Each Major Disease Group

Britain	1909–13	1886–94	India	1909–13	1886–94
Typhoid	3.08	6.26	Typhoid	16.40	38.36
Gastrointestinal	15.38	8.58	Gastrointestinal	26.72	18.92
Tuberculosis	12.82	21.58	Tuberculosis	6.35	6.23
Nervous/Mental	8.21	7.89	Cholera	3.44	10.66
Circulatory	14.87	9.28	Malaria	4.76	5.56
Respiratory	21.03	30.39	Nervous/Mental	5.03	2.85
Other	24.62	16.01	Circulatory	8.73	2.85
			Respiratory	9.79	7.21
			Other	18.78	7.36
Total	100.00	100.00	Total	100.00	100.00

Algeria	1909–13	1892–96	Egypt	1909–13	1886–94
Typhoid	31.19	43.01	Typhoid	13.64	59.52
Gastrointestinal	10.40	8.34	Gastrointestinal	17.80	18.64
Malaria	7.07	8.81	Tuberculosis	10.98	3.86
Tuberculosis	15.18	10.11	Nervous/Mental	10.98	3.46
Nervous/Mental	3.12	2.70	Circulatory	5.30	2.20
Respiratory	16.01	11.87	Respiratory	16.67	6.39
Circulatory	3.74	1.53	Other	24.62	5.93
Other	17.05	15.16			
Total	100.00	100.00	Total	100.00	100.00

Note:
Where pneumonia was listed separately, it is included with respiratory diseases.
Where dysentery was listed separately, it is included with gastrointestinal disease.

Source:
Algeria, Great Britain, and India: Curtin, *Image of Africa*, Appendix Tables A.6, A.8, A.28, A.30
Egypt, AMSR for 1895, p. 227; AMSR for 1914, pp. 144–57.

Principal Cause of Death in Annual Deaths per Thousand

Britain	1909–14	1886–94	Percent Decrease	India	1909–14	1886–94	Percent Decrease
Typhoid	0.06	0.27	77.78	Typhoid	0.62	5.11	87.87
Gastrointestinal	0.30	0.37	18.92	Gastrointestinal	1.01	2.52	59.92
Tuberculosis	0.25	0.93	73.12	Tuberculosis	0.24	0.83	71.08
Nervous/Mental	0.16	0.34	52.94	Cholera	0.13	1.42	90.85
Circulatory	0.29	0.40	27.50	Malaria	0.18	0.74	75.68
Respiratory	0.41	1.31	68.70	Nervous/Mental	0.19	0.38	50.00
Other	0.48	0.69	30.43	Circulatory	0.33	0.38	13.16
				Respiratory	0.37	0.96	61.46
				Other	0.71	0.98	27.55
Total Disease	1.95	4.31	54.76	Total	3.78	13.32	71.62

Algeria	1909–14	1886–94	Percent Decrease	Egypt	1909–14	1886–94	Percent Decrease
Typhoid	1.50	3.66	59.02	Typhoid	0.36	8.94	95.97
Gastrointestinal	0.50	0.71	29.58	Gastrointestinal	0.47	2.80	83.21
Malaria	0.34	0.75	54.67	Tuberculosis	0.29	0.58	50.00
Tuberculosis	0.73	0.86	15.12	Nervous/Mental	0.29	0.52	44.23
Nervous/Mental	0.15	0.23	34.78	Circulatory	0.14	0.33	57.58
Respiratory	0.77	1.01	23.67	Respiratory	0.44	0.96	54.17
Circulatory	0.18	0.13	-38.46	Other	0.65	0.89	26.97
Other	0.82	1.29	36.43				
Total Disease	4.81	8.51	43.48	Total Disease	2.64	15.02	83.42

Note:
Where pneumonia was listed separately, it is included with respiratory diseases.
Where dysentery was listed separately, it is included with gastrointestinal disease.

Source:
Algeria, Great Britain, and India: Curtin, *Image of Africa*, Appendix Tables A.6, A.8, A.28, A.30
Egypt, AMSR for 1895, p. 227; AMSR for 1914, pp. 144–57.

and at three times that rate for those stationed in Egypt or India. Cholera and malaria were absent in Europe during this period, and death rates from typhoid and gastrointestinal infections were much lower than elsewhere, though they still accounted for 15 percent of all deaths. By this time, piped filtered water was available in many large British towns and at most army posts. Food and water consumed off post were also more likely to be safe than they were in India or Egypt. Sewage disposal left something to be desired, but that, too, was soon to be improved by the rise of sanitary engineering and the enforcement of sanitary regulations.

In this period centered in 1890, typhoid was the most important single cause of death in all three overseas regions, and the waterborne combination of typhoid and gastrointestinal infections was responsible for at least half the deaths in each – in Egypt more than three-quarters of all deaths. Egypt also had the highest overall death rate of these three territories, at 17.11 per thousand per annum. The obvious explanation is the failure to master the peculiar problems of water supply and sewage disposal in the Egyptian setting. The Egyptian data also unavoidably include some deaths contracted on campaigns up Nile.[70] (The period 1886–94, on the other hand, was one of relatively light campaigning, compared to the conquest period 1882–83 and the conquest period for the Sudan in 1896–98, which will be discussed in Chapter 7).

In the other overseas territories about 1890, India's death rate, at 13.3 per year, was nearly as high as Egypt's, even though India's typhoid death rate was more than a third less. India, however, had cholera and malaria – both missing or negligible in Egypt at the time. Algeria's lower death rate from disease, at 8.51 per thousand in the mid-1890s was mainly owing to lower rates for the waterborne typhoid and gastrointestinal infections. The obvious explanation is a better water supply, owing to porcelain filtration with the Pasteur-Chamberland filters.

Figure 5.7 shows the comparative typhoid rates of French troops in Algeria and British troops in Egypt. The more systematic use of porcelain filters probably accounts for the lower Algerian typhoid death rate until the late 1890s when the British adopted similar filters. Thereafter the Egyptian rate was usually lower. Here, the probable explanation is again a matter of water supply, as the British army in Egypt began a stricter enforcement of existing sanitary regulations. Another difference was the weaker immunization program in Algeria. The French experimented with typhoid vaccination, but the effort was much less intense than it was in Egypt.

The contrast between Algeria and France, shown in Figure 5.8, is harder to explain. In the 1860s and early 1870s, their typhoid death rates had been about the same. Both rose in the late 1870s, but the French rate then

---

[70] The data in Tables 4.1 and 4.2 represent all deaths from disease in the Egyptian command. The army reported separately for typhoid deaths in lower Egypt, but the whole range of deaths was listed only for the whole command.

Figure 5.7. *Typhoid Mortality for European Troops in Algeria/Tunisia and in Egypt, 1882–1913*

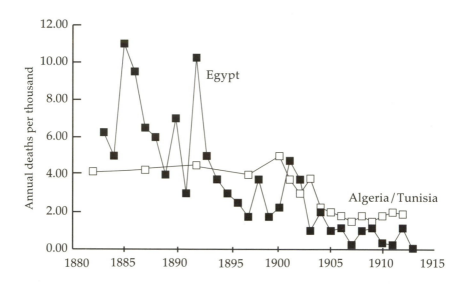

came down and the Algerian rate did not. As a result, the relocation cost in typhoid deaths for movement from France to Algeria rose from a little over 100 percent in the 1870s and early 1880s, to the range of 400 to 600 percent in the mid-1890s onward.

Algeria had malaria as well, with a death rate roughly the same as India's, but even this rate represented a triumph over past performance. In the 1860s, the malaria death rate for French troops in Algeria had been nearly four times the rate for British troops in India. By the 1890s, the Algerian rate had come down, while the Indian rate was substantially unchanged.[71]

In the period centered on 1890, the contrast between disease deaths of troops in Europe and those overseas can be separated into three disease groups. The tropical and waterborne diseases were far more fatal overseas than in Europe (refer to Figure 5.9 and Appendix Table A5.2). A second group was not notably different at home and abroad; deaths from nervous and mental disease were much the same everywhere, and deaths from heart disease were much the same everywhere except Algeria. Finally, some diseases were less fatal overseas than they were at home, like tuberculosis and pneumonia. The tropical and subtropical world had begun to earn some of its later reputation as a health resort, at least for these ailments.

By the period 1909–13, the situation had changed dramatically. The annual death rate from disease had dropped by 43 percent in Algeria; by

[71] Curtin, *Death by Migration*, p. 134.

Figure 5.8. *French Military Mortality from Typhoid in France and in Algeria/Tunisia, 1862–1912*

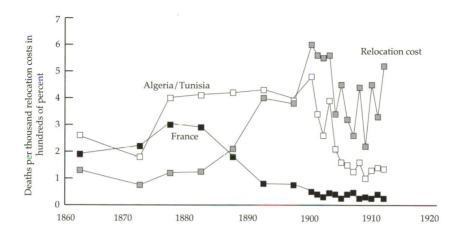

55 percent in Britain; by 72 percent in India; and by 82 percent in Egypt (refer to Table 5.2 and Figure 5.10). Egypt had the most impressive record of the four; the key was the 96 percent drop in typhoid deaths and similar improvement for other waterborne disease. Where Egypt had once had the highest overseas death rate for gastrointestinal infections, it now had the lowest. The obvious explanation is the improvement of water supply and sewage disposal. Yet the fact that typhoid and gastrointestinal infections still accounted for more than a quarter of all deaths among British forces in Egypt suggests that either the water supply was not yet perfectly safe, or that the men were not yet careful enough about what they ate or drank off post.

Typhoid fever was now lower in the other three samples as well, with a decrease of 88 percent in India, followed by 78 percent for Britain itself, and 59 percent for Algeria. It remained the principal cause of death only in Algeria. The relative position of the waterborne diseases is also significant. In the 1890s, typhoid had consistently been a more important cause of death than the gastrointestinal group; in the pre-war years, it remained so only in Algeria.

Still another significant change is the growth of the "other" category in all four samples (refer to Table 5.2). The decline of major killers, such as typhoid, dysentery, malaria, and tuberculosis, made way for new causes of death that were nearly unheard of among men of military age in the nineteenth century. Heart disease, for example, caused fewer deaths per thousand, but the decline of other causes of death increased its relative importance. Cancer also began to enter the picture, and diseases of the urinary system became a significant part of the "other" category.

Figure 5.9A. *Military Mortality in Britain and India, 1886–1914*

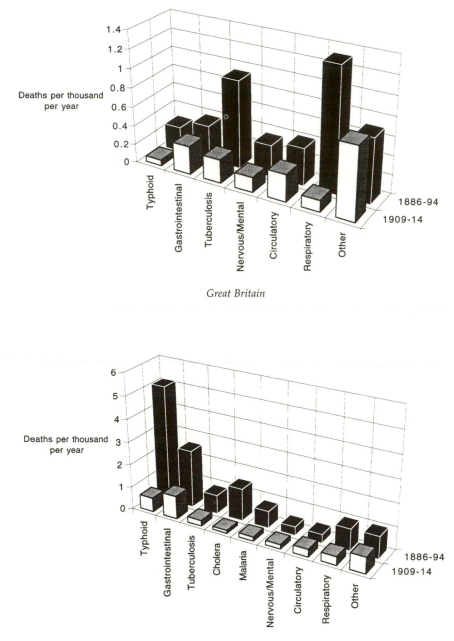

Great Britain

India

146

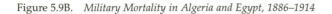
Figure 5.9B. *Military Mortality in Algeria and Egypt, 1886–1914*

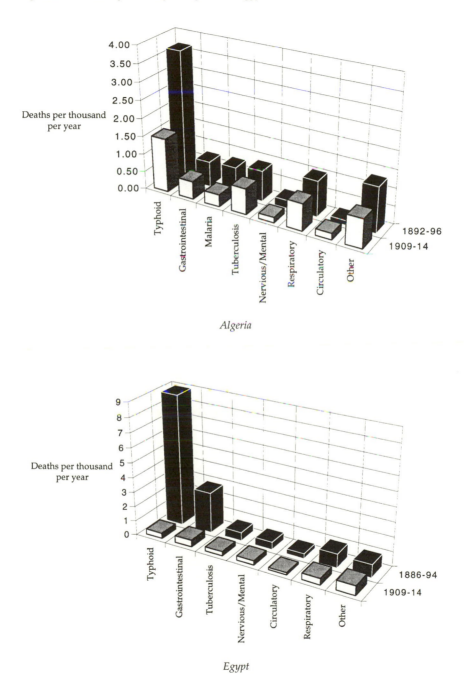

Algeria

Egypt

In short, European armies had made remarkable progress in preventive medicine for soldiers in barracks. For soldiers on campaign, serious problems continued. Just as European armies on campaign in West Africa could not match the precedent of the famous march to Kumasi in 1874, those in northeastern Africa could not match the disease record of the march to Magdala or of the garrisons of Cairo and Alexandria. The chapters that follow seek to explain why that was the case.

CHAPTER 6

THE TYPHOID CAMPAIGNS: NORTHEASTERN AFRICA IN THE 1880s

"... the tidiest little war fought by the British army in its long history..."

The beginning of the European "scramble for Africa," is usually dated from the 1880s. Some events occurred earlier, of course, but, unlike the march to Magdala or Kumasi, where European troops advanced and then withdrew, this new phase often led to lasting territorial claims of genuine strategic value – or so it was thought at the time. It was clearly so for objectives like control of the Suez canal or control of the gold fields of South Africa, but even when the prize at stake was less consequential – as it was in the Anglo-French crisis over Fashoda in 1898 – strategic questions would never be far from the central issue of European international rivalries.

The earliest wars of the scramble in northeastern Africa were also the earliest where typhoid fever had become the most important killer of European troops, such as the French seizure of Tunisia in 1881 and the British capture of Cairo a year later. The typhoid problem continued with the later conquest of the Sudan, and on to the Anglo-Boer War, but by then the political and strategic settings had changed. The new wars of conquest of the 1880s were still small wars by twentieth-century standards, but they were bigger than the small African wars of the 1870s and earlier, no longer limited to a two-month operation with 2,000 men on the European side, but now calling for ten to fifteen thousand troops, and keeping them in the field for six months or more, rising to three years in extraordinary cases, such as the final British advance up the Nile, or the South African War. The peak came during the Anglo-Boer War, when half a million troops were deployed.

As the stakes grew larger, public reactions shifted. What might have been an unacceptable cost in death from disease for the sake of a tiny corner of West Africa, now appeared in a new light. Where in the 1840s critics like Charles Dickens openly claimed that the cost in disease of the Niger expedition was too high to make such expeditions worthwhile, in the 1880s and 1890s, some Europeans still opposed specific imperial adventures, but they rarely argued for withdrawal after a successful conquest. Critics often claimed that military health problems should have been handled better, but they almost never claimed that the death of soldiers was a sufficient cause for abandoning imperial expansion altogether.

Tunisia and Algeria, 1881–82

The Tunisian campaign of 1881 was the first in northern Africa where typhoid was to play an important role. Earlier in the century, typhoid fever was an irregular visitor. It was important in the American Civil War, in the South African and Afghan campaigns of the 1870s, but not in the British operations in Burma of the 1880s, nor in the French conquest of Tonkin.[1]

The French seizure of Tunisia had been long expected. At the Congress of Berlin in 1877, France was given permission to acquire Tunisia as compensation for the British seizure of Cyprus. The French government was at first slow to act, and French opinion was disgruntled by the failure of Napoleonic imperial adventures in Mexico and elsewhere, followed by the lost war with Prussia. The French Right tended to pin its hopes on revenge against Germany, while the Left often opposed imperial adventures of any kind.

By 1881, however, Italian influence seemed to be growing in Tunisia, which might lead to informal Italian empire if France held back from taking up its option. On the initiative of the French Foreign Office, the army assembled a force on the Algerian side of the frontier and waited for an appropriate border skirmish. It then marched on Tunis with 20,000 men, while a smaller naval force seized Bizerte. Within two weeks, on May 12, the Bey of Tunis signed a treaty making Tunisia a French protectorate, but the fighting was not over. In June, a revolt broke out in southern Tunisia, leading to a brief additional campaign to subdue that region. The losses from enemy action were only about 50 wounded, of whom 14 died – but 4,200 soldiers came down with typhoid fever, and more than a thousand died.[2]

Typhoid hit French forces elsewhere in North Africa with a similar timing. In Algeria, the high plateau of southern Oran province had only recently come under a semblance of French control. It was three to six thousand feet above sea level, with an annual rainfall in the range of 300 to 400 centimeters – not unlike southern Tunisia. It was sparsely inhabited, suitable only for nomadic and semi-nomadic occupation. The French

---

[1] A.M. Davies, "Enteric Fever on Campaigns – Its Prevalence and Causation," TSICHD, 8:84–96 (1891), pp. 84–86.

[2] Jean Ganiage, *Les origines du Protectorat français en Tunisie (1861–1881)* (Paris: Presses universitaires de France, 1959), pp. 669–75; Ganiage has also treated the matter in Prosser Gifford and William Roger Louis, *France and Britain in Africa: Imperial Rivalry and Colonial Rule* (New Haven, Yale University Press, 1971), pp. 64–67.

paid it little attention until, in April 1881, dissidents assassinated a French military officer and rose in revolt. At the end of May, they ambushed a French mobile column and killed more than 50 French soldiers.[3]

That early success encouraged other tribes to join in a series of raids all across the high plateau country and against French settlements in the agriculturally productive *tel* region to the north.[4] The province of Oran normally had a garrison of about 13,000 men. With the war in the south, an additional 10,000 were deployed through the second half of 1881 and through 1882, until peace came early in 1883. Because so much of the army normally active in Algeria was tied up in the Tunisian campaigns, reinforcements for southern Oran came mainly from France itself.

The Algerian strategy was to launch hit-and-run raids against French posts and outlying settlements, retreating when the French advanced, in the way of guerrilla armies before and since. The French counter-strategy was to try to occupy known sources of water and send out mobile columns from their main base at Mecheria to find and destroy the enemy.

These campaigns in the Tunisian and Oranese south were similar in their operations, terrain, and tactics. Though about 20,000 men engaged in Tunisia was larger, so were the enemy forces. The smaller contingent in southern Oran, however, had a more elusive enemy and higher casualties from enemy action (refer to Table 6.1). Both campaigns also experienced typhoid fever at rates of infection and death ten to fifteen times higher than those in recent French experience with the Army in Algeria. Before the campaign was over, the morbidity from typhoid in the Tunisian expeditionary force reached 210 per thousand – nearly a quarter of the total force.[5] The annual disease death rates, at 43 per thousand in south Oran and 63 per thousand in Tunisia (refer to Table 6.1) was not notably higher than similar losses at Magdala or Kumasi, but they caused more alarm because they were unexpected, and because they came from an emerging pathogen.

Typhoid fever had been a growing cause of death in both France and Algeria over the previous twenty years, reaching a peak for the army in France in 1880 and in Algeria and Tunisia in 1881, but medical authorities were not especially alarmed before the two North African campaigns that year.[6]

Typhoid fever first arrived at Bône (now Anaba) in Algeria in April 1881. It was to be a principal port of disembarkation for reinforcement

[3] For the local background of this revolt see Ross E. Dunn, *Resistance in the Desert: Moroccan Responses to French Imperialism, 1881–1912* (Madison: University of Wisconsin Press, 1977), pp. 141–43.

[4] L. Delmas, "Relation medico-chirurgicale de la campagne du Sud-Oranais en 1881–1882," AMPM, 10;81–111,187–204 (1887), pp. 84–86.

[5] France, Ministère de la Guerre, *Statistiques médicale de l'armée metropolitaine et de l'armée coloniale* (Paris, 1862+), 1881, pp. 24–25.

[6] France, Ministère de Guerre,*Statistiques médicales*, for 1900, p. 31; Marvaud, "La fièvre typhoïde au corps d'occupation en Tunisie," AMPM, 3:273–83 (1884), p. 274; Philip D. Curtin, *Death by Migration: Europe's Encounter with the Tropics in the Nineteenth Century* (New York: Cambridge University Press, 1989), pp. 88–89.

Table 6.1. *Cause of Death among French Troops Stationed in France and Algeria 1872–76,
Compared with Deaths in the Tunisian Campaign of 1881 and the South Oran
Campaign of 1881–82*

Disease group	Annual Deaths per Thousand			
	France 1872–76	Algeria 1872–76	Tunisia 1881	South Oran 1881–82
Typhoid Fever	3.40	3.50	54.20	31.44
Malaria	0.10	2.33	2.35	4.53
Smallpox	0.13	0.31	0.05	0.07
Heart disease	0.14	0.26	0.10	0.00
Respiratory diseases	1.43	1.35	0.60	1.53
Tuberculosis	1.25	1.57	0.30	0.20
Diseases of the digestive system	0.66	1.38	4.60	3.73
Cholera	0.09	0.02	0.00	0.00
Diseases of the urinary system	0.13	0.23	0.00	0.00
Diseases of the nervous system	0.43	0.50	0.80	0.00
Heat stroke	0.00	0.00	0.00	0.40
Other disease	1.38	1.22	0.30	0.93
Total from disease	9.13	12.65	63.30	42.83
Accidents and suicides	0.28	0.49	no data	no data
Suicide			0.10	2.33
Enemy action			3.65	8.13
Total deaths	9.41	13.14	67.05	53.29

Notes:
South Oran data count missing as dead.
Tunisian and South Oran figures include accidents with enemy action, but list suicides separately.

Sources:
For the South of Oran: Delmas, "Campagne du Sud-Oranais," AMPM, 10: 95, 99, 188, 190, 193.
For Tunisia: France, Ministère de la Guerre, *Statistiques médicale*, Tables VIIA for 1881.
For France and Algeria, Curtin, *Death by Migration*, Appendix Table 26, p. 189.

from France, and it had been free of typhoid fever for some time. The typhoid appeared among soldiers of the 142nd line regiment previously stationed in Perpignan, which had recently been seat of a typhoid epidemic. The disease then spread to other elements of the 3rd brigade, to which the 142nd was attached, and it passed forward along with men and supplies massing near the Tunisian frontier.[7]

In the Oran division, typhoid had been increasing in recent years in the city of Oran, among the military and civilians alike. The spread to the south might have come from the city or, as in Tunisia, with troops arriving

[7] Marvaud, "La fièvre typhoïde," pp. 275–78.

from France. It appeared in late June among soldiers of a column advancing southward toward the fortified post of Kreider, a principal military hub for the high plateau region. Kreider was to be a principal locus of typhoid through the rest of the campaign and the center from which the disease spread to the outlying posts and then back up the line of advance to most towns and bodies of troops in the Oran division.[8]

French medical authorities dealt with the epidemics along existing lines of division between contagionists and anti-contagionists. The anonymous author (or authors) of the official medical report on the Tunisian campaign conceded that the disease was undoubtedly introduced into North Africa by the 142nd Infantry from Perpignan, but they refused to identify that source as the only one, or to concede that the disease spread from one man to the next. They pointed out two other occurrences in Tunisia where no clear link to the 142nd or to the 3rd Divisions seemed possible. After the revolt in the south, they identified another French source of infection from the barracks at Toulon giving a total of four presumed sources of infection, two from France and two in North Africa.[9]

According to these authorities, the multiplicity of sources tended to reduce the possibility of contagion through water supply, or through any other channel, and opened the possibility that the infection had a local origin each place it appeared. Field reports of medical officers suggested several different causes of the epidemic. One was lack of acclimatization; troops from the north of France suffered more than those that had already served in Algeria. Another was the infection of the soil originating from the bad sanitary condition of the African towns and the presence of pack animals. Still another was the consequence of heat and fatigue for troops on campaign, coupled with the youth of the soldiers, following the common belief that typhoid was especially prevalent among the young.[10]

For the campaign in southern Oran, Dr. Czernicki published the official report with similar analysis; and he may well have been the author of the official report on Tunisia as well. He conceded that the 9th Chasseurs came from France with typhoid already epidemic in their ranks, but he again put most faith in the medical reports from the field which showed local conditions – such as existing infection, heat, privation, and lack of acclimatization – as the true cause.

To this four-point analysis, Czernicki added a new twist to the current ideas about acclimatization. If typhoid really came from France, those most likely to die would be the oldest Algerians, because they would be least "acclimatized" to the French source; whereas, in Algeria and Tunisia, it was the soldiers fresh from France that suffered most, suggesting a local source to which they were unaccustomed. Most French military doctors were ill-informed about typhoid among African civilians, but

[8] Delmas, "Sud Oranais," pp. 100, 102–04.
[9] *Statistiques médicales*, 1881, p. 24.
[10] *Statistiques médicales*, 1881, p. 26; 1882, pp. 20–21.

Czernicki supported his argument by pointing out that the lowest rates of typhoid morbidity and mortality in the French army were those of the Algerian tiralleurs – partly the result of acclimatization, partly "le privilège de la race."[11]

Some contagionists also entered their opinions. Dr. Delmas, who wrote a medical report on the Oran campaign, suggested that if spontaneous generation caused the disease, why did it wait until fresh troops arrived from France? Dr. Marvaud was even more firmly contagionist, though conceding that his was a minority view. He argued that the disease was not only contagious, but the epidemic came from France and was spread in Tunisia by French troops, specifically by fecal contamination.[12]

Other critics pursuing the same line of argument blamed the French military doctors, whether the disease was contagious or not, for not carrying out the commonly understood measures of empirical hygiene. It was a mistake, for example, to lodge troops in a barracks that was already a recognized site of typhoid infection; it was safer to move to a fresh site under canvas. They supported the point with evidence that typhoid was more serious among immobile troops guarding strongpoints than among those of flying columns that broke camp every day.[13]

Some foreign criticism blamed the whole of the French sanitary administration, from the War Minister downwards – not so much for its failure to prevent disease as for its failure to treat disease adequately when it did occur. In their view, the case-fatality rate in Tunisia was inordinately high, though the officially reported rate there was 25.7 percent, about the same level as that for British troops, stationed in India or Egypt in the 1880s.[14]

Critics of these two French campaigns seemed to be ignorant of comparable disease death rates in other circumstances. The disease death rate on the campaigns for Magdala and Kumasi was of the same order of magnitude, and they were held up as medical triumphs; yet, losses from disease at 43 per thousand per year in southern Oran and 63 per thousand in Tunisia were taken to be disastrous.

Though medical opinion was critical, the main line of advice was to "do better next time," rather than don't "take such a risk again."[15] Only an

---

[11] Czernicki, "La fièvre typhoïde au corps d'occupation de Tunisie en 1881," AMPM, 2:397–416 (1882), p. 402, 414–15.

[12] "En résumé, la propagation de la fièvre typhoïde, en 1881, en Tunisie, démontre d'une façon rigoureuse et indéniable la contagion de cette maladie et l'influence exercée par les campements souillés par le matières fécales provenant des typhoïdiques, sur l'extension et la généralisation de cette affection parmi les troupes d'occupation de la Régence." Marvaud, "La fièvre typhoïde," pp. 279–81.

[13] Luc Guillot, La fièvre typhoïde pendant l'expédition de Tunisie (Paris, thesis no. 49, 1882), 68–70.

[14] A. Torres, "Algo sobre el servicio de sanidad militar en el ejército de la Argelia y expedicionario de Tunez," Gacetta de sanidad militar, 7:545–52 (1881); Appendix Table A5.7; Curtin, Death by Migration, pp. 184–85.

[15] Guillot, Typhoïde, p. 72, had these final words "cette expédition au point de vue sanitaire serve d'enseignement pour l'avenir. L'opinion publique est instruite, chacun est soldat, que tous exigent que les guerres nécessaires n'entraînent que le minimum de victimes!"

occasional critic suggested that these campaigns were not worth fighting, as Delmas did in his report on the campaign in south Oran:

[A]lways fatigue, the desperate steppes, the fiery sun, continual privation, every-where sickness and in the most fearful forms: in a word, a thoroughly worthless campaign and as murderous as many triumphant expeditions.[16]

In May of 1882, a year after the attack on Tunisia, the British and French agreed to new action in North Africa, this time as a joint expedition in Egypt to overthrow the military rebellion of 'Urabi Pasha. The French Chamber des Deputies, however, refused to vote funds for the expedition, and the government fell.

Given the outcry over the typhoid losses in Tunisia and southern Oran, it was possible these losses affected the Chamber's decision, though no such concern shows in the parliamentary debates, and only one deputy mentioned the danger of disease.[17] The Chamber's main concern was that overextension in North Africa would weaken France in Europe, specifically against Germany. There was additional resentment at the government's apparent deception in using a border skirmish as an excuse for the conquest of Tunisia. When the vote was called, the Egyptian project failed by a vote of 416 to 75.

From the retrospect of 1886 – when patriots could look back on the successful acquisition of Tunisia – Edouard Rochefort echoed Laffont's view on the Western Sudan, that the price of empire was high, but worth it:

Everyone recognizes the value of that attractive colony, submitted to our rule in two short campaigns at a price that is still high for the generation that had to pay it, but without which nothing of value can be gained. Nobody, for that matter, can be ungrateful to the soldiers who gave it to us.[18]

Egypt 1882

A mixed bag of motives led to the British decision to invade Egypt, and historians have been quarreling ever since about why that decision was taken. Egypt was on the way to India, and the Suez canal was now in full operation. Even more, Egypt had now become economically important to

[16] Delmas, "Sud-Oranais," p. 18. It was a campaign of "fatigues, toujours des fatigues, des steppes désolé, un soleil de feu, des privations continues, la maladie partout, sous ses formes les plus redoutable: en un mot, campagne ingrate entre toutes et aussi meutrière que bien des expéditions triomphantes."

[17] M. Laisant: "Ces hommes, ces soldats, ces Français, rencontreront, dans tous les cas, des ennemis que l'on peut méconnaître, que s'appellent la fièvre, le paludisme et la soif!" France, *Journal Officiel, Debats parlementaire*, 1882, 2:1494–1500.

[18] E. Rochefort, "Tunisie," DESM, 18(3rd ser.):597–408. On p. 408. "Tout le monde reconnaît la valeur de cette belle colonie soumise en deux courtes campagnes au prix de sacrifices toujours trop lourds à la génération qui les supporte, mais sans lesqueles rien au monde ne peut être obtenu. Personne, du reste, n'a jamais été ingrat pour les soldats qui nous l'ont donnée."

Britain. As of the early 1880s, Britain took 80 percent of Egyptian exports and supplied 44 percent of its imports.

Britain had a political interest in the Ottoman Empire as well as in Egypt. Egypt was still theoretically a province of the Ottoman empire, though independent for all practical purposes since 1805, when a military revolt under Muhammad 'Ali had established his descendants as a new dynasty of de facto independent rulers with the title of Khedive. Early in 1881, Col. Ahmad 'Urabi led a military revolt against the Khedive's government, rendering Britain's position in Egypt uncertain.[19]

Until the 1870s, the Khedival government had maintained its authority against Istanbul, but it built up an increasing load of debt to European bankers. European governments applied informal pressure to assure repayment. In 1878, they forced Khedive Isma'il to appoint one British and one French official to his cabinet. Isma'il responded in turn by organizing support from anti-foreign Egyptian political groups across a broad front. Britain and France, unwilling to see their influence weakened, persuaded the Ottoman Sultan to replace Isma'il as Khedive with his son, Muhammad Tawfiq.

That act was a public and open sign that informal empire from Europe was no longer even partly disguised. In 1881, with Colonel 'Urabi's revolt against Khedive Tawfiq, the European powers had either to accept a truly independent Egyptian government, or use force to remove it. When Tawfiq asked France and Britain to intervene on his behalf, they agreed to do so – more on French than on British initiative.[20] The two powers planned a joint expedition, but, when the French assembly refused to back the government, Great Britain went ahead on its own.

The British navy first bombarded Alexandria and then landed a force there on July 17, 1882. The expected British strategy would have been to march directly up the Nile to Cairo. Sir Garnet Wolseley, again the general in command, decided to outflank the Egyptian army by shifting his main force to the Suez canal, in order to attack Cairo from the east. A canal called the Sweetwater canal at that time (now Tir'at Isma'iliya) led from the Nile to Isma'iliya, midway along the Suez canal, supplying fresh water to the Suez region. A railroad ran parallel to this canal, and the combination of railroad and canal simplified the supply problem for the invading force, making it possible to reach Cairo without having to cross a wide stretch of waterless desert. The move also had the advantage of surprise; the invading force moved so fast that it had to confront only a small part of

---

[19] That revolution had its own complex background in Egyptian history, which cannot be pursued here, but see Juan R. Cole, *Colonialism and Revolution in the Middle East: Social and Cultural Origins of Egypt's 'Urabi Movement* (Princeton: Princeton University Press, 1993)

[20] A.G. Hopkins, "The Victorians and Africa: A Reconsideration of the Occupation of Egypt, 1882," JAH, 27:363–91 (1986); John S. Galbraith and Afaf Lutfi el-Sayyid-Marsot, "The British Occupation of Egypt: Another View" *International Journal of Middle Eastern Studies*, 9:471–88 (1978); Alexander Schölch, *Egypt for the Egyptians: The Socio-Political Crisis in Egypt, 1878–1882* (London, 1981), pp. 306–15.

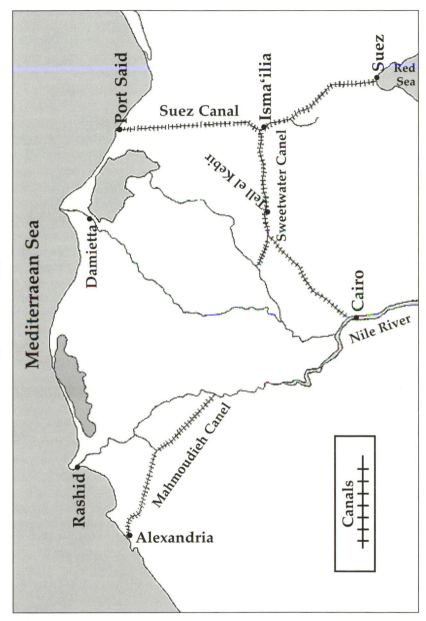

Map 6.1. Lower Egypt

Mediterraean Sea

Port Said

Suez Canal

Isma'ilia

Suez

Red Sea

Tell el Kebir

Sweetwater Canel

Damietta

Cairo

Nile River

Rashid

Mahmoudieh Canel

Alexandria

Canals

Table 6.2. *British Military Mortality in Egypt, 1882–83*

All rates are deaths per thousand mean strength per month

Disease	1882 Tel-El-Kebir Campaign	1882 Egypt Post-Campaign	1883 Egypt Per Month
Smallpox	0.00	0.00	0.03
Typhoid fever	0.78	3.00	0.53
Malaria	0.14	0.27	0.00
Cholera	0.00	0.00	1.47
Gastrointestinal infection	0.86	1.75	0.25
Tuberculosis	0.03	0.09	0.14
Diseases of the:			
Nervous system	0.08	0.12	0.14
Circulatory system	0.00	0.03	0.02
Respiratory system	0.03	0.13	0.11
Urinary system	0.00	0.01	0.02
Other disease	0.14	0.24	0.02
Total disease	2.06	5.65	2.72
Accidents	0.14	0.23	0.17
Enemy action	2.59	1.52	0.00
Poisons	0.00	0.01	0.01
Grand total	4.78	7.41	2.90

Notes:
The army recognized the campaign stretching from July 17 to October 9. (84 days). The official statistics for 1882, covered July 17 to the endof the year annualized. They are adjusted here to a monthly rate.

Source:
AMSR for 1881, p. 251; for1882, pp. 230–31; for 1883, pp. 230–31.

the Egyptian army at the decisive Battle of al-Tell el Kebir on September 13. With that, serious resistance collapsed; the British declared the end of the campaign on October 9.[21]

This campaign was different from most colonial campaigns of the period – and not only in its speed and quick conclusion. Man-for-man, the Egyptian army was far more formidable than any other African army at that time, being at least partly armed with Winchester rifles. The first

[21] For a review of Egyptian history at this period see G.N. Sanderson, "The Nile Basin and the Eastern Horn, 1870–1908," in Roland Oliver and G.N. Sanderson (eds.), *The Cambridge History of Africa* (Cambridge: Cambridge University Press, 1985), 6:592–631.

press reaction in Britain was simply to hail it as still another brilliant victory for Sir Garnet Wolseley. Neither the number killed by enemy action (7.5 per thousand) nor those who died of disease during the campaign itself was large enough to attract much attention.

Medical Aspects

From the medical point of view, the campaign was remarkable in other ways that escaped comment. It was, first of all, one of the few colonial wars in which more men were killed in action than died of disease – unusual for any war before the twentieth century (refer to Table 6.2). More important still, disease morbidity and mortality during the campaign itself were low. Sickness began to take its toll only after the army reached Cairo, reversing the usual expectation of a high disease death rate on campaign and a lower disease death rate in barracks. Finally, though typhoid fever became the principal cause of death once the troops reached Cairo, typhoid fever accounted for only 13 percent of all deaths before the proclaimed end of the campaign on October 9.

Before the end the year, however, typhoid fever would account for more than half the deaths from disease among the British troops stationed in Egypt. From the end of the campaign in October to the year's end, the monthly death rate from typhoid fever was 3 per thousand per month, the highest for any period in the British occupation of Egypt, as against a monthly rate on the campaign itself of 0.78 per thousand (refer to Table 6.2).

Aside from the typhoid danger, the monthly disease death rate during the advance up the Sweetwater canal was lower than the equivalent record for Magdala, Kumasi, or any of the campaigns on the upper Nile to the end of the century. Deputy Surgeon General Sir J.A. Hanbury, the medical officer throughout 1882, was either skilled or lucky in his medical advice during the campaign; later on, once the army advanced into the Nile valley, either his skill deserted him, or his luck changed. (Refer to Table 6.3.)

The medical preparations for the Egyptian expedition were thorough, though they took no special account of the typhoid problem nor of the French experience with typhoid in the previous year. The annual report of the Army Medical Department for 1881 listed the main diseases to be expected – along with their sources. It included typhus from crowding and dirt generally; enteric fever from bad latrines and drinking water; smallpox from direct infection; scurvy from lack of fresh fruits and vegetables; and ophthalmia from dirt, flies, and direct contagion. The author warned that filariasis was propagated by mosquitos, that cholera came from impure water, that plague was possible, and that venereal disease was to be expected; and he also mentioned the dangers of trichinosis, tape worm, and bilharzia. The survey was remarkably up-to-date scientifically and based on a broad knowledge of contemporaneous tropical medicine.[22]

Before the expedition sailed, T. Crawford, the new Director General of the Army Medical Department, issued a general order translating this survey of medical knowledge into warnings. He stressed the need to protect the water supply and the particular dangers of scurvy, ophthalmia, and dysentery. Hanbury followed up with his own numbered list of 39 "orders for the conduct of business" and 17 sanitary precautions, including the common hygienic rules and suggestions. Scurvy and ophthalmia were singled out for special attention. For personal protection, he emphasized the need always to wear a sun helmet and, for protection against gastrointestinal infection, a flannel cummerbund, worn day and night, to avoid the dangers of chill – "chills to the bowels being found to exceed all others in the production of disease." His only mention of possible problems of impure water was this: "8. The men should be cautioned against drinking stagnant or turbid water, from eating unripe fruit, uncooked vegetables, underdone meat, and the internal organs of animals, such as liver and brains."[23]

While the Army's stated appreciation of the disease danger was thoroughly up to date, the specific orders tended veer off toward the mass of hygiene rules current in past decades.

Medical administration in the field fell to Deputy Surgeon General J.A. Marston as Chief Sanitary Officer, seconded from the Indian army and rushed from Simla to arrive just as the advance from Isma'iliya was about to begin. A Sanitary Officer held a position unique to the British Army at the time. He was a public health officer with the responsibility to investigate and recommend, free of clinical responsibilities. The line officers might or might not accept his recommendations, and they accepted them less often on campaign than in barracks.

Marston's first concern was water supply. Many of the ships lying in the canal off Isma'iliya had distillation facilities, but not enough to supply such a large force, and no means to pass the water forward to the front. The only possible source of water in this desert region was the Sweetwater canal, and this in turn drew its water from the Nile, which was known to be polluted.

Many soldiers, including Marston himself, drank directly from the canal, but he tried to arrange alternate sources. One was to dig wells a short distance away from the canal, letting them fill with water by seepage, producing a degree of filtration, though its effect on bacteria was probably not nearly that of a slow sand filter. Another device was to drive Norton's tubes into the sand at intervals to tap ground water. Other filtration would have made the water more palatable, but not necessarily safer.

[22] AMSR for 1881, pp. 244–48.
[23] J.A. Hanbury, "Medical History of the War in Egypt," AMSR, 22:205–62 (1881), p. 212.

One impromptu filter was a meat tin with holes in the bottom and filled with sand, The Egyptians also used drip-stone filters made of porous clay, which allowed water to pass through and drip out the bottom; but these were not available till the army reached the Nile valley. The field hospitals boiled some water, and ships in the Suez canal supplied about 200 gallons a day of distilled water to the Isma'iliya hospital.[24]

The advance from Isma'iliya to Cairo took 25 days, with water from the Sweetwater canal alone until the battle of al-Tell el Kebir on September 13th, after which water was available from existing wells assumed to be safe; but they probably were not. The incubation time for typhoid fever is generally 7 to 14 days, though it can sometimes be shorter or much longer. The first hospital admission for typhoid among the advancing troops occurred on September 30, two weeks after the battle, and the disease became seriously prevalent among the Cairo garrison only in October and November.[25]

The outbreak seems to have been caused principally by the condition of the Cairene barracks and water sources at the moment of the British occupation. Sanitary officers described their shock in finding human wastes on the stairways and in the corridors of the barracks they took over from the Egyptian army. A certain cultural chauvinism colored British attitudes. They believed at times that the Egyptians were immune to typhoid fever, while simultaneously blaming their "filthy habits" for the spread of the disease. Marston remarked that:

It must always be borne in mind that Egypt is a subtropical country, and the Egyptian is an Oriental army with Oriental habits. Every place occupied or traversed by it is fouled, and from the beginning to the end of the campaign the British troops have consequently been exposed to unsanitary conditions.[26]

The other significant 1882 outbreak of typhoid occurred in and around Alexandria. At the outset, the barracks at Ramleh had been healthy at first, using water brought by canal from the Nile, but, when Egyptians cut the canal, the British were forced to use well water, and the typhoid epidemic began.[27]

Gastrointestinal infections were always an important cause of death on campaign, and this was no exception. On the march to Cairo, they caused more deaths than typhoid itself, suggesting that the Sweetwater canal may not have carried typhoid but it certainly carried other waterborne diseases. Heat stroke was a problem in India and a serious problem in the Magdala campaign. In Egypt in 1882 it was comparatively insignificant,

---

[24] AMSR for 1881, p. 246; Hanbury, "Medical History," pp. 242–43; J.A. Marston, "Sanitary Report, Egyptian Expeditionary Force," AMSR for 1882, pp. 269–71; *British Medical Journal*, 1882, 2, 648 (Sept. 30).
[25] Marston, "Sanitary Report," pp. 271, 280–81.
[26] Marston, "Sanitary Report," p. 271.
[27] J. Warren, "Notes on Enteric Fever at Ramleh," AMSR, 1881, pp. 287–8; Marston, "Sanitary Report," pp. 279–80.

causing only six deaths among the British forces, in spite of fighting in desert conditions at the hottest part of the year.[28]

Ophthalmia was another expected disease that turned out to be serious but controlable. The army had nearly 1,500 cases during the advance on Cairo, an admissions rate of 378 per thousand for all eye diseases. Ophthalmia then tapered off once the army was in barracks in the cities, and medical attention prevented any loss of sight – very different from the experience of earlier European armies in Egypt. In 1800–1801, the British army in Egypt had suffered 160 cases of total blindness and 1,260 cases with the loss of one eye.[29]

Public Reactions in Britain

As the campaign developed, it brought public acclaim for Wolseley and public notoriety for the Army Medical Department which had been fundamentally reorganized in the wake of the Cardwell reforms of the late 1860s. The principal director of the reorganization was Surgeon General Sir William Muir, who had headed the Department during the Kumasi campaign and continued in office until early 1882. Before the reforms, medical services had been attached to particular regiments. Only the hospitals at Netley and Woolwich were separate from the system of regimental command. The Cardwell reforms gave the Medical Department its own staff, organized as the Army Hospital Corps, which included enlisted personnel to act as stretcher bearers and nurses. The system began with mobile field hospitals, transferring sick and wounded to stationary field hospitals, on to base hospitals, and ultimately to the facilities at Netley and Woolwich.

The change was in some ways insignificant, because the front line of medical personnel were still attached to particular fighting units under the command of line officers; but some of the old tension between line and medical officers continued.[30] Many line officers resented the loss of the regimental hospitals, which they associated with the maintenance of regimental discipline and morale. They regarded the new base hospitals as professional but impersonal – men being treated by doctors they had never seen before. The principal complaints came from the pre-reform officer corps, but Wolseley and the military reformers also took part.

[28] AMSR for 1882, p. 111.
[29] Hanbury, "Medical History," p. 240; Marston, "Santiary Report", pp. 276–9; AMSR for 1882, p. 112; Albert A. Gore, ""Our First Campaign in Egypt," *Dublin Journal of Medical Science*, 84(3rd ser.):177–90 (1888).
[30] PP, 1883, xvi [C. 3607], "Report of Committee Appointed by the Secretary of State for War to Inquire into the Organisation of the Army Hospital Corps, Hospital Management and Nursing in the Field, and the Sea Transport of Sick and Wounded." pp. vii–xii; Edward M. Spiers, *The Late Victorian Army, 1868–1902* (Manchester: Manchester University Press, 1992), pp. 78–81; Neil Cantlie, *A History of the Army Medical Department*, 2 vols. (London and Edinburgh, 1974), 1:276–289.

As early as 1868, Wolseley had published the first edition of his *Soldier's Pocket Book for Field Service*. It was not just a service manual but contained his prescription for military reform. One of his central principles was that officers should be more than simply disciplinarians or leaders in combat. They should be responsible for their men, protecting them and seeing to their creature comforts.[31] To preserve this relationship, medical officers were merely to advise the unit commander, with no independent authority beyond the care of sick and wounded. Wolseley spelled out these prescriptions in greater detail in the 1886 edition of the *Pocketbook*. He believed that army regulation called for too many medical officers, and that many were useless impedimenta in the way of the main job of fighting.[32]

Wolseley was especially annoyed with military doctors' efforts at preventive medicine. A noteworthy passage from the *Soldier's Pocketbook* reads:

The *Sanitary Officer* is a creation of recent years, and as a general rule he is a very useless functionary. In the numerous campaigns where I have served with a sanitary officer, I can conscientiously state I have never known him to make any useful suggestions, whereas I have known him to make many silly ones. It is not his fault, for with an army moving it is impossible to drain a town, as I have known suggested, or carry out any other great sanitary measure. There is not time for any great sanitary works, and for the ordinary cleanliness of temporary camps or bivouacs, the P.M.O. [principal medical officer] with each division can do all that is necessary. In future, as long as this fad continues, my recommendation is to leave him at the base, where he may find some suitable occupation as a member of the Sanitary Board, which I think should have charge of all sanitary arrangements at the Base.[33]

Wolseley wanted the Sanitary Board to be under the command of a line officer, preferably from the Royal Engineers. It should include representatives of the local police and of the Royal Navy.[34] He was anxious, in short, to keep public health out of the hands of the doctors, an attitude that would emerge immediately after the campaign of 1882.

In the background was a long-standing social difference between the officer corps and doctors in British society at large, a difference that was magnified when it came to military doctors. The line officers were overwhelmingly "gentlemen of leisure," whose appointments came through political and social influence (and money to purchase a commission, before the Cardwell reforms). In the nineteenth century and far into the twentieth, an officer's pay was barely enough to live on, much less to meet the social and sporting obligations that went with regimental life.[35]

---

[31] Joseph H. Lehmann, *All Sir Garnet: A Life of Field-Marshal Lord Wolseley, 1833–1913* (London: Cape, 1964), pp. 156–165.

[32] Garnet Wolseley, *A Soldier's Pocket Book for Field Service*, 5th ed. (1886). p. 109. First published 1869.

[33] Wolseley, *Soldier's Pocketbook*, p. 110.

[34] Wolseley, *Soldier's Pocketbook*, p. 114.

[35] C.B. Otley, "The Social Origins of British Army Officers," *Sociological Review*, 8:213–39 (1970), esp. 216.

British physicians and surgeons were not as a rule independently wealthy, and military surgeons' pay was less than half the expected income of a doctor in civilian life. The military service was less attractive to English doctors than it was to those from poorer parts of the British Isles; a large proportion of military surgeons came from Ireland and Scotland. After the initial military-medical reforms of 1873, the condition of military doctors deteriorated and the voluntary recruitment of new surgeons began to dry up. By 1879, recruits were so few that the army had to raise the pay of new surgeons in order to fill the ranks.

The doctors' rank and status in the army nevertheless remained low and their resentment is obvious in the pages of the *Lancet* and the *British Medical Journal.* [36] Line officers' attitudes continued to reflect the financial and social difference. In the language of county cricket at the time, they regarded the surgeons as hired "players," not "gentlemen." The military surgeons were nevertheless a comparatively large part of the officer corps. In the Egyptian campaign of 1882, they made up 21 percent of all officers among the troops from Britain and 30 percent of those who came with the Indian contingent.[37]

Wolseley's analysis of military medicine in the 1886 edition of his *Field Guide* shows the prevailing attitude that, from a strictly military point of view, an army was a fighting unit where the prime objective was victory in the field. The sick and wounded were an inconvenient by-product whose care could hardly take a high priority. On the matter of invaliding, for example, he held that:

A commander should leave no stone unturned to get his sick and wounded removed from the theatre of war as quickly as possible. . . . On the other hand the commander will have to exercise a most careful watch over the medl. department, to prevent soldiers being sent away who are either malingerers, or whose state of health does not warrant their removal from the theatre of war. It is the natural tendency of all medl. offrs. to clear out their hospitals by sending home the sick with too little discrimination; unless this is checked the fighting strength of an army will soon fall off.[38]

Wolseley recognized that an officer was responsible for his men and that it was important to prevent sickness, if only for the sake of military efficiency.

The greater the care you can bestow upon the well-being of your men, the more attention you can pay to their food and clothing, the less you expose them to night duties, the fewer the straining demands you make upon their physical powers, and the more sanitary precautions you can take against diseases, the smaller will be the sick rate to be provided for.[39]

[36] Cantlie, *Army Medical Department*, p. 280; Spiers, *Late Victorian Army*, pp. 79–89.
[37] Hanbury, "Medical History," pp. 206–19; Wolesley, *Soldier's Pocketbook*, p. 119.
[38] Wolseley, *Soldier's Pocketbook*, pp. 117–18.
[39] Wolseley, *Soldier's Pocketbook*, p. 118.

Table 6.3. *Hospitalization Rates at British Military Stations, 1876–87*

Station	Non-effectives Per Thousand Mean Strength	Relocation Cost in Non-effectives Percent
United Kingdom	40.06	
Gibraltar	33.25	-17.00
Malta	41.15	2.72
Canada	31.17	-22.19
South Africa	49.63	23.89
Mauritius	56.58	41.24
Ceylon	50.76	26.71
China and Straits Settlements	56.19	40.26
Bengal	55.46	38.44
Madras	50.40	25.81
Bombay	49.12	22.62

Note:
Relocation cost is the percentage change between home and overseas service.

Source:
Garnet Wolesley, Soldier's Pocketbook (1886), p. 118.

In the light of the then-current debate in France between Czernicki and Marvaud, it is clear that Wolseley was firmly with Czernicki in underplaying the role of infection. If he and his field officers had taken the other side, they could have paid far more attention to water supply, and the death rate in Cairo and Alexandria toward the end of 1882 could have been far lower.

Another, and not very subtle, aspect of military priorities also appears in the *Soldier's Pocketbook*. Wolseley recognized that the disease environment, which he called "climate," was vastly different in different parts of the world. The Army Medical Department analyzed the health of the army with four different measurements – hospital admissions, deaths, "invaliding" or repatriation, and "constantly sick" – the average number per thousand mean strength that were non-effective from sickness or wounds at any time. Medical officers gave first attention to morbidity and mortality, but Wolseley's concern was fighting, not the health of the men. For him the important measure was the "constantly sick" – the number of men unfit for service, and the hospital space they would require.

To this end, Wolseley published the rates of hospitalized per thousand for various stations in the British empire over the decade ending in 1887, shown in tabular form in Table 6.3. (I have added a calculation of relocation costs to his figures.) Wolseley believed that, in preparing for war, it would be wise to double the rates of expected hospitalization. He also wrote:

"Troops in the field when well cared for should be quite as healthy as when in quarters in the same country."[40] This is a curious statement, given the conventional wisdom that morbidity and mortality from disease increased enormously on campaign. But Wolseley was not concerned with reducing the disease cost of warfare. His tacit assumption was that these costs were an inevitable part of warfare, and the higher cost for warfare overseas was a "given." In fact, the increase in death rate during service overseas was far higher throughout the empire than the increase in the rate of "constantly sick."

The Aftermath of the March on Cairo

Press criticism of the Army Medical Department began even before the official closing date of the Egyptian campaign of 1882. It began with the *Times* on September 29th, followed by despatches in the *Morning Post* and the *Daily Telegraph*, complaining that the Medical Department had simply broken down and failed to do its job of caring for the sick and wounded. The Government appointed an investigating committee under Lord Morley, the War Minister, consisting of five high military officers, the Director General of the Army Medical Department, and two civilians. The committee heard 140 witnesses and accumulated other evidence, producing a report of more than 800 pages.

In the course of the investigation it was clear that much of the problem came from the rapid and secret shift of the army from Alexandria to the canal, a move that succeeded strategically, but left the base hospitals in Cyprus and Malta a long way off, with only a field hospital in Isma'iliya itself. Wolseley himself was among the bitterest critics, often in ways that seem curious, coming from the commander of the expedition. He blamed the Medical Department for the bad bread given to the sick and wounded in Cairo and Isma'iliya, but supply was part of his responsibility, not theirs.

But underneath Wolseley's complaints was his conviction that medical officers were not gentlemen and had failed to take personal responsibility for their men. He contended that, if the bread supplied by the quartermaster was bad, medical officers at the hospitals should have gone to town and bought decent bread with their own money. He also blamed the officers of the hospital corps as poor disciplinarians, but most of all, he looked back to the good old days when hospitals were part of the regimental structure and under ordinary regimental control.[41]

Press reports from the field and other evidence provided to the committee made it clear that sanitary conditions were indeed unsatisfactory, especially the "filth" left by departing Egyptians in the Cairo hospitals and the barracks that were at first available; but the weight of the evidence was

[40] Wolseley, *Soldier's Pocketbook*, p. 118.
[41] Wolseley, evidence to the committee, PP, 1883, xvi [C. 3607], 269–79.

concerned with the adequacy of the treatment of the sick, not with preventive medicine.[42] This reflected the public view that doctors were supposed relieve the suffering of the sick and to cure them if possible.

The committee's report recognized that some of the deficiencies were unavoidable, but it generally defended the conduct of the Army Medical Department, placing the blame on the general administration of the army, not on the Medical Department alone. The committee's long list of recommendations called mainly for administrative change, though it recommended increased use of nursing sisters both at home and abroad. On preventive medicine, it called for more sanitary training for medical officers and for the organization of a "conservancy," or latrine unit, under the Quartermaster-General's department.[43]

In medical circles, opinion was less critical. Physicians recognized that enteric fever had been the main problem, and they recognized in retrospect the similarity to the French problem in Tunisia a year earlier, without solving issues raised at the time. R. Vacy Ash published a comparative study of the enteric fever on the Egyptian campaign, in the light of the Zulu war of 1879 and the first Anglo–Boer war of 1881–82. He went even further than Czernicki, denying that enteric could have been caused by a specific agent. He had seen three different columns of British troops in the Zulu war march through country supplied with "plenty of good water" and still come down with enteric fever. He had also been present on the advance toward Cairo in 1882, where the water was considered to be demonstrably bad, though it caused little enteric.[44]

His evidence may have seemed correct, though it was still not possible easily to test water for bacteria. Other medical officers who served in the Egyptian campaign followed the main lines of Czernicki's analysis, blaming the fever on the youthfulness of the troops, the climate, infection of the soil, and fatigue – though they, more than their French counterparts, also blamed water supply.

Military opinion was satisfied with the campaign in spite of disease. Both Wolseley and his most recent biographer believed that it was "the tidiest little war fought by the British army in its long history."[45] With the passage of time, even retrospective medical opinion saw the campaign in a more favorable light than it may have deserved, largely because it was over quickly, and because press reports of a victory made losses seem to fade away. In 1884, a writer for the *British Medical Journal* could use that campaign as the basis for an optimistic prognosis for the advance the Nile, then about to begin:

[42] BMJ, 1882, 2, 647–48 (Sept. 30)."Egyptian Expedition," BMJ, 1882, 2, p. 697 (Oct. 7); BMJ, 1882, 2, 1112–14 (Dec. 2); Hanbury, "Medical History," pp. 220–41; M.C. Zuber, "Histoire médicale de la campagne des Anglais en Egypte," AMPM, 5:227–, 275– (1884), pp. 276–7.
[43] PP, 1883, xvi [C. 3607], *passim.*
[44] R. Vacy Ash, "The Epidemic of Enteric Fever in the Transvaal, Zulu, and Egyptian Wars Compared," BMJ, 1883(1), pp. 2–4, (July 7).
[45] Lehmann, *All Sir Garnet*, p. 338.

The result of the searching inquiry by Lord Morley's Committee was to prove that the mortality in the last Egyptian campaign, notwithstanding some complaints which were made, was smaller than in any campaign of the kind known to history; and as the present expedition is undertaken at a favourable season of the year, there is every reason to anticipate that the mortality will be light, possibly not more than two per cent.[46]

This opinion was general. In the setting of the 1880s, it seems clear that, while people hoped for lower losses from disease, they were pleased enough with the medical record of this war to push on without any special concern on that account.

In fact, the disease deaths for the campaign itself were remarkably low at just over 2 per thousand per month, nearly the lowest of all the typhoid campaigns in northeast Africa in this decade (refer to Table 6.4). But if the deaths during the occupation of Cairo and Alexandria in the remaining months of 1882 are taken into account, then the disease death rate here was second only to that of the Tunisian campaign.

The Nilotic Sudan 1881–86

Simultaneous with 'Urabi Pasha's revolt in the north, another, separate revolt took place in the Sudan. Where 'Urabi opposed the growing informal European rule over Egypt, the Sudanese revolt struck back against the whole structure of Egyptian secondary empire in the south. The Sudanese problem came to a head in 1881, when Muhammad Ahmad b. 'Abdallah, a religious leader of reputed piety and asceticism, declared himself Mahdi, or savior, sent by God to establish justice on earth in preparation for the end of the world. The movement soon fell into the hands of men who were less pious and more political – especially 'Abdallahi b. Muhammad, who was to be Madhi's successor and the main opponent of the Anglo-Egyptian reconquest in the 1890s.

At first, the Mahdist movement appealed to the broad demand for religious reform that was common in nineteenth-century Africa all across the Sudan from the Atlantic to the Red Sea. In the Nilotic Sudan, however, it drew its main strength from an informal alliance of those who were especially disturbed by the increase in European influence. In the longer run, and perhaps only in retrospect, it has been seen as an incipient nationalist movement that led in time to Sudanese independence.[47] Some recent writers have seen 'Urabi Pasha's military revolt in the north in similar terms, but both movements (at that stage at least) were more nearly a form of opposition to European power and influence than a positive effort to create a independent nation on the European model.

---

[46] BMJ, 1884, 2, p. 434 (August 30).
[47] The most convenient summary is P.M. Holt and M.W. Daly, *A History of the Sudan from the Coming of Islam to the Present Day*, 4th ed. (London: Longman, 1988), pp. 85–98.

Table 6.4. *Mortality in Northeast African Campaigns, 1881–86*

All rates are mortality per thousand mean strength per month

	1881 Tunisia	1881–82 South Oran	1882 Egypt Campaign	1882 Egypt Post-Campaign	1884–85 Nile Expedition	1885 Suakin Expedition	1885–86 Sudan Frontier
Size of force	20,000	10,000	13,400	13,931	10,771	7,235	5,873
Disease:							
Smallpox	0.01	0.01	0.00	0.00	0.03	0.00	0.00
Typhoid fever	9.03	2.62	0.78	3.00	1.83	0.62	1.55
Malaria	0.39	0.38	0.14	0.27	0.00	0.06	0.00
Gastro-intestinal infection	0.77	0.31	0.86	1.75	0.47	0.00	0.45
Tuberculosis	0.05	0.02	0.03	0.09	0.03	0.00	0.00
Rheumatism	0.00	0.00	0.00	0.00	0.00	0.00	0.00
Diseases of the:							
Nervous System	0.13	0.00	0.08	0.12	0.10	0.12	0.00
Circulatory System	0.02	0.00	0.00	0.03	0.01	0.00	0.09
Respiratory System	0.10	0.13	0.03	0.13	0.06	0.00	0.18
Urinary System	0.00	0.00	0.00	0.01	0.00	0.12	0.00
Other disease	0.05	0.03	0.14	0.24	0.01	0.00	0.00
Total Disease	10.55	3.57	2.06	5.65	2.53	0.91	2.27
Accidents	0.02	0.19	0.14	0.24	0.26	0.06	0.27
Enemy Action	0.61	0.68	2.59	1.52	0.81	4.94	0.82
Grand Total	11.18	4.44	4.78	7.41	3.60	5.91	3.27

Notes:
All data are for enlisted men only, unless otherwise indicated.
1. For Tunisia, accidents are included under enemy action. The invasion began in April, but the most serious campaigning came only after July, estimated length of campaign is six months.
2. For southern Oran, counts missing as dead.
3. Egypt, 1882 – monthly rates for Tel-el-Kebir campaign only, July 17 to October 9.
4. Egypt, 1882 – monthly rates for the occupying force, October 10 to the end of the year.
5. Nile Expedition, March 1, 1884–July 31, 1885 (487 days).
6. Suakin Expeditonary Force, March 1 to May 14, 1885.
7. Sudan Frontier Force, November 27,1885 to January 27, 1886.

Sources:
For Tunisia: France, Ministère de la Guerre, *Statistiques médicales*, tables VIIA for 1881.
For the South of Oran: Delmas, "Campagne du Sud-Oranais," AMPM, 10: 95, 99, 188, 190, 19.
For Egypt, 1882, AMSR for 1881, p. 251, AMSR for 1882, pp. 230–31.
For Nile Expeditionary Force, 1884–85, AMSR for 1884, p. 297.
For Suakin Expeditionary Force, AMSR for 1884, p. 306.
For Sudan Frontier Force, 1885–86, AMSR for 1885, p. 315.

The Sudanese movement began in a small way in 1881, when Muhammad Ahmad shifted his residence from the White Nile above Khartoum westward to the province of Kordofan. Although 'Urabi's brief government of lower Egypt tried unsuccessfully to suppress the movement, Egyptian forces were necessarily called on to defend Cairo against the British. By the fall of 1882, when the British successfully occupied Cairo, the Mahdi's forces had seized almost all of the province of Kordofan. In January 1883, they occupied El Obeid, the provincial capital.

At first, the British in Cairo were unwilling to intervene, expecting that they would soon depart, leaving the Khedive to manage Egyptian affairs in the British interest – and to handle his own problems in the Sudan. British authorities did, however, allow the Egyptian government to send one expedition on its own, under the command of a British officer, Hicks Pasha. In November 1883, the Mahdi's forces surrounded that expedition south of El Obeid, destroyed it and killed most of the officers, including Hicks. Ever since the fall of El Obeid, the Mahdi's victories had brought new recruits to his banner, and his victory over Hicks and the Egyptian force added momentum.

One important group of new supporters came from the Beja-speaking nomads of the Red Sea hills. Under the leadership of 'Uthman Diqna, originally a merchant from the port of Suakin, they joined the Mahdi's forces and cut the desert route from Suakin to the Nile; only the British reinforcement of Suakin itself early in 1884 saved it from capture.

Suakin was a seaport and hence had some strategic importance in British eyes. It had long been important in the commercial strategy of the Sudan, since it could be reached easily by caravans from a number of points on the Nubian Nile below Khartoum, principally from the region of Berber, where the Nile begins its southwesterly bend toward Dongola, before resuming its northerly course. In the past, Suakin had been occupied at various times by the Ottomans, more recently by Egyptian forces. Even before the British occupation of Egypt, a railroad had been proposed, linking Suakin to the Nile; a later railroad reached from Suakin to the Nile at Atbara, and another south to the agricultural regions along the Ethiopian border. (Refer to Map 7.3.)

Although the British reinforced the garrison at Suakin, they ordered the evacuation of the remaining Egyptian troops from Khartoum and from the Nile valley down to the Egyptian frontier. To supervise the evacuation, the British sent out General George William Gordon, "Chinese Gordon," who had first made his reputation in China and had already served as Governor-General of the Sudan under Egyptian authority. In 1884, he arrived in Khartoum just as the Mahdi's forces cut the route to Suakin, and evacuation down the Nile would also have been difficult. His orders called for a speedy withdrawal, but he failed to move. By April 1884, the Mahdi had surrounded the garrison in Khartoum and an unaided evacuation was impossible. In the fall of 1884, the British government decided to intervene, rather than see still another British commander of Egyptian troops killed by the Mahdi's forces. It sent a relief expedition up the Nile under the command of Wolseley, whose advance steamboats arrived at Khartoum on January 28, 1885, just two days after the Mahdi's forces had captured the city and killed Gordon.

Wolseley's Nile expedition was to have important repercussions on British politics. In the late 1870s and into the 1880s, the major political parties had taken different attitudes toward imperial adventures. The Liberal governments under Gladstone had opposed them on principle, whatever they might do in practice, while the Disraeli government of 1874–1880 had celebrated the overseas empire with political fanfare, such as bestowing the title, Empress of India on Queen Victoria. When a Gladstone government *did* become involved in empire building, as it did with the Egyptian invasion of 1882, it did so with some reluctance, and the Tories were quick to blame it for not acting forcefully enough. In the election of 1885, just after Wolseley's army failed to "rescue" Gordon, the Tories won easily – more from Gordon's failure to obey orders than Gladstone's failure to act quickly enough. When events in Egypt and the Sudan could bring about the rise and fall of Governments, the mortality cost of the two Egyptian adventures of 1882 and 1884–85 was not a useful political issue for either party.

In military circles, the Nile Expedition had a different meaning. It helped to focus once more on a longstanding conflict between Wolseley and his supporters on one hand and the India-centered strategy advocated by Roberts, Kitchener, and Napier, on the other. Part of the quarrel went back to a service rivalry between officers of the Indian army and others based in Britain, a conflict that went back at least as far as the Magdala campaign and Wolseley's effort to show the superiority of British over "native" troops in Asante.

By the 1880s, it reemerged in an Asia-centered strategy, advocated by Roberts and his group, that saw the center of British interests in India, and the threat of a Russian advance toward India as its main concern. The strategic view of Wolseley and his followers, sometimes called Wolseley's "ring," was a naval-centered strategy based on the primacy of home defense, with colonial militias reinforced as needed by British units detached from home duty for service overseas. This concept lay behind the Cardwell reforms, and it was an important influence on moves like the annexation of Cyprus and the invasion of Egypt in 1882 – moves many of the Asia-centered group considered to be a weakening of the main effort farther east.[48]

In the light of this internal conflict, the Nile campaign of 1884–85 was Wolseley's first major defeat: he failed as a commander to rescue Gordon,

---

[48] Adrian Preston, "Wolseley, the Khartoum Relief Expedition and the Defence of India, 1885–1900," *Journal of Imperial and Commonwealth History*, 6:254–80 (1979), pp. 254–60.

but Asia-centered strategists gained even more from events in Asia. On March 30, 1885, a Russian force attacked an Afghan position at Panjeh on the central Asian frontier, nearly setting off a war between Britain and Russia. The incident's importance had waned by the summer of 1885; but it helped to turn Britain away from further thoughts of reconquering the Sudan, just as the continued German threat in 1882 helped to turn France away from conquest of Egypt

In a year of such major political and diplomatic events, the military medical record on the Nile got little attention. The death rate of the troops on the Nile campaign was taken to be normal – within the expected range of the Indian army on campaign – higher, but acceptably higher, than the mortality of soldiers stationed at home or in barracks overseas. The most serious recent fighting in India had been the Afghan War of 1878–80, fought by the Bengal Army, which lost 74.6 per thousand from disease alone in 1879.[49] Death rates from disease for the Indian army, mostly in garrison in 1884–85, came to 14.12 per thousand,[50] while the garrison in lower Egypt in those two years lost 16.17 per thousand. Losses from disease on the Nile expedition of 1884–85 were 36.29 per thousand (refer to Table 6.4), a bit more than those of the Tell el Kebir campaign, but much less than the death rate in Cairo later in 1882.

Dr. G.B. Mouat, the official medical reporter for the Nile expedition, was not especially concerned about the losses from disease, though typhoid caused nearly half of all deaths. He still followed the line of explanation that emphasized "predisposing causes" like heat and fatigue, taken along with "exciting causes" like infected milk, water, and fresh fruit. The special correspondent for the *British Medical Journal* initially gave much the same explanation; his early dispatches regarded typhoid as merely an expected risk, but the rising death rate led him in January 1885 to take it more seriously:

[W]e must, I fear, look for a high death rate; and, in cases of recovery, a tardy and difficult convalescence. At all events, be the cause what it may, climate, field-service, or an unusually severe type of disease, from one or all combined, enteric fever will claim far more victims than the Mahdi's bullets or spears.[51]

The *Lancet* continued optimistic somewhat longer. In a leader on April 4, 1885, it proclaimed:

We have not the least doubt that everything will be done by the heads of the medical service which practical experience and scientific knowledge can suggest, but we cannot help feeling anxious about the health of the troops during the coming hot season.[52]

[49] Cantlie, *Army Medical Department*, 2:306.
[50] Curtin, *Death by Migration*, p. 195.
[51] BMJ, 1885, p. 248, (January 31).
[52] *Lancet*, 1885, 1, 632, (April 4).

In spite of this guarded optimism, water for the expedition necessarily came from the Nile and was passed through the same ineffective filters that had been used in 1882. Other means of purification had been recommended for decades, but water was seldom boiled for lack of local fuel along the Nubian Nile and unwillingness to strain supply lines to bring it from a distance.[53]

At first, the comparative optimism about military mortality on the Nile gained support from Suakin. In February 1884, the British had sent 4,500 European troops, plus 300 Indians, to the Suakin hinterland. The expeditionary force fought two sharp actions, but then withdrew to the port and was mainly redeployed to Egypt. Medically, this brief period from February to April appears as one of unaccountable success, unless there were errors in the reporting. The force had only 127 hospital admissions and no deaths at all from disease, though it suffered 31.36 deaths per thousand from enemy action.[54]

The health record of subsequent expeditions from Suakin was also usually good. On the desert coast, there was little or no malaria, and the water supply came in large part from the ships. Typhoid and gastrointestinal illness were therefore rarer than usual. The largest available sample is from the new expeditionary force from March into May of 1885 (refer to Table 6.4). Later in 1885, when the occupying force was reduced to 465 men, it developed one of the worst medical records in the region. Annual deaths from typhoid were reported at 43 per thousand; all deaths from disease at 88.17 per thousand; and admissions at 2,346 per thousand.[55]

As early as the spring of 1885, the tone of the medical press began to shift from the guarded optimism of the recent past, coincidentally with the Panjeh alarm of April and Wolseley's withdrawal down the Nile. The Lancet's anonymous "special correspondent" in Suakin had, in any case, unusual attitudes for a correspondent to the medical press. He expressed sympathy, for example, for the 2,000 "misguided fanatics" mowed down by British fire in an engagement on March 22nd, calling them "patriots defending . . . their own country."[56] By May, he pointed out that the Red Sea in the hot season to come would be the worst climate on earth, bar the Persian Gulf, and recommended evacuation before the threat of disease and heat stroke became still worse. With Gordon dead, he saw no more need to "sacrifice men and treasure in this sickly sun-scorched earth."[57]

[53] G.B. Mouat, "Medical History of the Nile Expeditionary Force, from 18th March to 31st July 1885," AMSR, 26:279–97 (1884), esp. 280–18; "Medical Notes from the Nile Expeditionary Force," BMJ, 1884, 2, p. 1157 (December 6); 1884, 2, p. 1209 (December 13); 1885, 1, p. 44–45 (January 3); AMSR for 1885, p. 149.

[54] E.G. M'Dowell, "Medical Report of the Eastern Sudan Expeditionary Force, 1884," AMSR, 24:261–71.

[55] AMSR for 1885, pp. 141, 143.

[56] Lancet, 1885, 1, 774–75, (April 25).

[57] Lancet, 1885, 1, 818, (May 2), 886 (May 9).

By mid-May, the *Lancet* itself wrote an editorial recommending evacuation in the face of heat and disease:

The thousands of lives which have been sacrificed, the millions of money which have been thrown into the Nile, or wasted in the desert, have produced nothing but sorrow and shame. The events of the last twelve months in the Soudan must ever form a subject of bitter regret and lamentation to every right-thinking Englishman.[58]

This was, admittedly, a response to military failure as well as disease, but it remains one of the few instances where the medical press weighed the mortality cost of imperialism and found it too heavy. Political factors must have greatly influenced this change of attitude. The worst of the reported monthly disease death rates per thousand in Suakin were not very different from those of the Egypt campaign – 7.34 for Suakin in 1885, 5.65 for the Tell el Kebir campaign plus the occupation of Cairo in 1882. Nor were the death rates from typhoid very different – 3.58 per thousand for Suakin in 1884, 3 per thousand for Egypt in 1882. The difference was in the fact that the Tell el Kebir campaign gained control over Egypt, while Suakin was associated with the military failure of Gordon's death on the Nile.

In spite of the tone of discouragement in the medical reports from Suakin, the decade of the 1880s had witnessed general progress against typhoid in northeast African campaigns (see Table 6.4). Typhoid deaths in the Tunisian campaign had been 54 per thousand. On the Nile expedition they were down to 26 per thousand, but the improvement drew no prominent commentary in the press. In retrospect, the clear lesson could have been that, in that the region, European armies could move with half the typhoid deaths of 1881 and with a substantial decrease in all death from disease. With proper control over water supply, they could have done better still, but the possibility received little notice in the medical press. But this time, there was no crowing over victory, as there had been at the victory over tropical fevers on the Gold Coast. What attracted publicity was Wolseley's failure to rescue Gordon.

[58] *Lancet*, 1885, 1, p. 906 (May 16).

PICTURE GALLERY

Evacuation of the sick, Madagascar, 1895 (from *L'illustration*, October 1895)

French cannonière on the Niger (from Joseph Galliéni, *Deux campagnes au Soudan français, 1886–1888*)

Mounted marine infantry, Soudan 1890 (from Joseph Galliéni, *Deux campagnes au Soudan français, 1886–1888*)

Attack on Andrea Peak, Madagascar, 1895 (Painting by Louis Tinayre, Musée des Arts Africains et Océaniens)

Asante, 1874 – Sir Garnet Wolseley receiving news from the front (from *Illustrated London News*, September 1882)

Egypt, 1882 .– Evacuation of the wounded by the Sweetwater Canal (from *Illustrated London News*, September 1882)

Asante, 1874 – Scouts storming a village (from *Illustrated London News*, March 1874)

Magdala expedition, 1868 – Loading artillery elephants (from *Illustrated London News*, August 1868)

Asante, 1874 – Withdrawal of sick and wounded from Kumasi (from *Illustrated London News*, April 1874)

Tirailleurs choosing among the captives (from Joseph Galliéni, *Deux campagnes au Soudan français, 1886–1888*)

Western Sudan, 1868 – Marine artillery on campaign (from Joseph Galliéni, *Deux campagnes au Soudan français, 1886–1888*)

Western Sudan, 1888 – A Saphis camp (from Joseph Galliéni, *Deux campagnes au Soudan français, 1886–1888*)

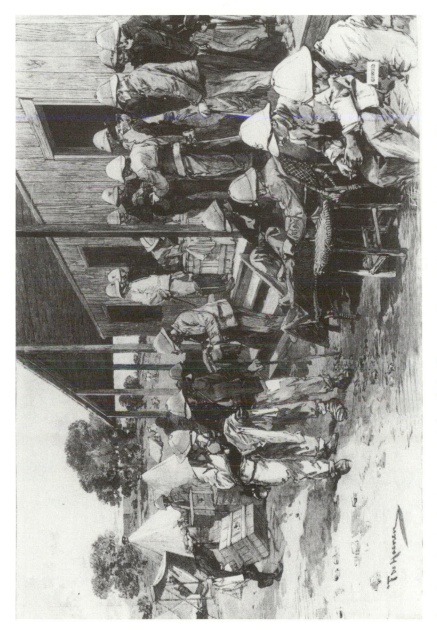

Red Cross distribution to invalids in hospital at Majunga (from *L'illustration*, September 1895)

CHAPTER 7

MADAGASCAR AND OMDURMAN: THE LAST CAMPAIGNS IN EASTERN AFRICA

"Somebody ought to have been disgraced or shot. . ."

The fullest territorial extent of European empire was not reached until the 1930s, but the decade before 1900 was the period of most intense rivalry among European powers; and it was also the zenith of secondary-empire building.

Three African kingdoms in eastern and southern Africa had consolidated their apparent power enough to make some Europeans believe that a substantial force was required to defeat them. They were the Merina kingdom that dominated highland Madagascar, the Christian and Amharic empire of Ethiopia, and the Mahdi's successor dominating the rainfall agricultural lands of the Nilotic Sudan. In addition, in the far south, the two Boer republics – the South African Republic (Transvaal) and the Orange Free State – had established their dominance as secondary empires on the high veld from the 1840s onward, and, in the 1880s, had successfully defended their claim to independence from Britain. All five of these states, whether Boer or African, were larger than typical African kingdoms of the early century. All five had gone some way toward acquiring for themselves the kind of European arms that had made African warfare so one-sided when rifles and Maxim guns were available only to one side.

Two of the many European military incursions of the late 1890 are noteworthy examples of a new scale of military operations in Africa and the undiminished the role of disease: the French invasion of Madagascar in 1895; and the British advance up the Nile from 1896 to 1898.

In spite of European advances in tropical medicine, these were among the most lethal campaigns in the conquest of Africa. The Nile campaign of 1898 had the highest death rate from typhoid of all the campaigns where that disease was the major killer, and the Malagasy campaign had the highest death rate from malaria of all those where malaria was the leading cause of death. One inevitable question is: Why a spectacular increase in death rates from disease after a half-century of progress in the science

175

of tropical medicine? The answer tells a good deal about the relationships between disease, medicine, and empire in the last decade of the nineteenth century.

Encroachment on Madagascar

French involvement with the island of Madagascar had begun in the seventeenth century, when the Compagnie des Indes and occasional private individuals seized coastal points to further their interests in Indian-Ocean trade. At that time, they had no interest in the interior of the island or in neighboring parts of Africa. But, in the 1780s, a local ruler named Andrianampoinimerina began to consolidate neighboring territories in the high plateau country. His gradual rise to power led to the formation of the kingdom of Imerina. By the first decade of the nineteenth century, the new kingdom had expanded beyond its own ethnic base. Its success was based partly on the comparative wealth of paddy-rice agriculture, partly on trade, and partly on the importation of European guns. Imerina was thus one of the earliest secondary empires on the African scene.

From the early 1800s, French and British missionaries and commercial agents began to arrive in Imerina, setting up a complex process of cultural and economic interaction that continued until the French conquest in 1895. The process included intricate political sparring between the two Western powers, between their resident nationals (whose interests were not always identical with those of their home governments), and between competing factions in Merina political life. The Merina ruling class sought to copy fashions, architecture, and other aspects of Western culture in the Victorian age, including Christianity and military modernization. In this, Imerina resembled the contemporaneous kingdoms of Siam and Hawaii, though the final outcome was to be quite different.[1]

In court politics, British Protestant missionaries were more successful than their French Catholic competitors; the French were ahead in local strategic advantage through their control of Malagasy port towns, notably Fort Dauphin (now Tôlanaro) and Diégo Suarez (now Antisranana) at either end of the island. French pressure on Imerina was largely diplomatic until 1882, when France claimed a protectorate over the northwestern corner of the island. In 1883–84, this claim led to a desultory Franco–Imerina war, marked principally by coastal bombardments and a brief occupation of the Malagasy ports of Majunga (now Mahajanga) and Tamatave (now Toamasina).[2] The concluding treaty gave France a claim

---

[1] Gerald Berg, "Sacred Acquisitions: Andrianampoinimerina at Ambohimanga, 1777–1790," JAH, 29:191–211 (1988). Françoise Raison-Jourde, *Bible et pouvoir à Madagascar aux XIXe siècle: invention d'une identité chrétienne et construction de l'état* (Paris, Editions Karthala, 1991) is the principal authority for the complex interaction between Western and Malagasy culture over the century.

[2] Many place names were changed officially after independence, but most Malagasy writing or speaking in French use colonial version of these and other place names.

to control Imerina's foreign affairs and the right to send a Resident to Antananarivo, though the Resident had no authority over Imerina's internal affairs.

In 1890, an Anglo-French exchange of favors cleared the way for more forceful action. Great Britain recognized the French protectorate over the entire island; France, in return, permitted a British protectorate over Zanzibar. From then on, French conquest was only a matter of timing and tactics, as it was in Dahomey at the same period, and, in 1894, the French government began planning an expedition to conquer Imerina.

The year 1895, when the expedition actually sailed, introduced a crucial period in the European conquest of Africa. The Italian attempt to conquer Ethiopia led to their defeat at Adwa in the 1896, and their subsequent withdrawal to Eritrea. In 1895 as well, Cecil Rhodes and the British South African Company launched the Jameson raid, designed to overthrow the Transvaal government. That too failed, but it set off the prolonged crisis that ended in the Anglo–Boer War in 1899–1902. In 1896, the British and Egyptian forces began their advance up the Nile against the successor of the Mahdi, ending with their victory at Omdurman in 1898 and the extinction of a major African state in the Nilotic Sudan.

Malaria and Madagascar

The Madagascar expedition of 1895 has the worst reputation for medical failure of any military campaign in the European conquest of Africa. The actual death rate was not so high as that of some yellow fever epidemics, but the absolute number of dead from disease counted heavily – more than 6,000 in a ten-month campaign, and less than 20 dead from enemy action. The number of French deaths in those ten months was probably greater than their losses in the conquest of all the territory that was to become French West and French Equatorial Africa, and the vast majority of these deaths were from malaria.

The French had long experience with Malagasy malaria. As early as 1652, they were forced to evacuate one island post on that account. In 1875, Alfonse Laveran, the French army doctor who discovered the protozoa that causes malaria, rated the malaria danger of overseas posts – from the best, fever-free New Caledonia, to the worst, Madagascar and Mayotte.[3] According to European lore, the rulers of Imerina on the high plateau believed their country was unassailable, protected by Generals *hazo* and *tazo* – forest and fever.

The fever was the same falciparum malaria found in West Africa, and the principal vectors were also the same – *Anopheles funestus, An. gambiae, strictu sensu*, its close relative *An. arabiensis* – but the Malagasy epidemiology of

---

[3] M. Vincent and F. Burot, "Paludisme à Madagascar," *Revue scientifique*, 18 juillet 1896, pp. 75–81, p. 75; Alphonse Laveran, *Traité des maladies et épidémies des armées*, 2 vols. (Paris, 1875), 1:144–49.

Map 7.1.   Madagascar Malaria, c. 1890

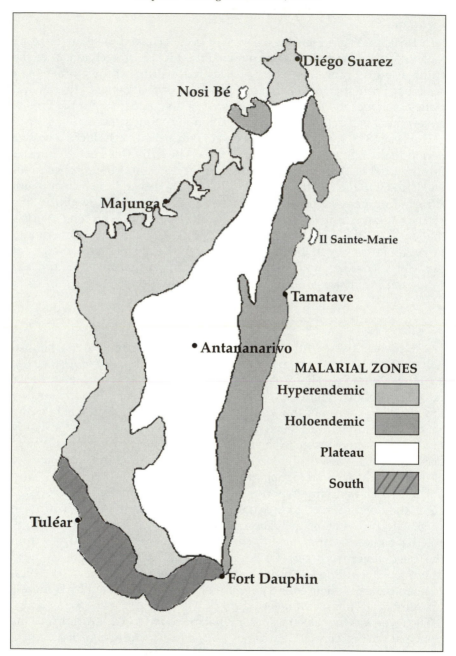

MALARIAL ZONES

Hyperendemic

Holoendemic

Plateau

South

malaria is different from that of the African mainland. Malariologists today distinguish four different epidemiological zones on the islands. Though these zones have changed through time, the recent situation provides a point of departure for understanding the probable pattern a century earlier.[4]

Most of the east coast is holoendemic for the local population, with extensive apparent immunity among people over the age of ten; clinical symptoms and death from malaria are mainly confined to those under five, a pattern similar to that of the forest regions of West Africa. The principal vectors are *An. gambiae, s. s.* and *An. funestus.*

The northern three-quarters of the west coast, the region where the expedition of 1895 was to operate, is similar to the West Africa savanna country. It is classified today as hyperendemic for malaria, and characterized by a stable period of malaria transmission longer than six months. *An. arabiensis* is present here, along with the other two vectors. The intensity of mosquito activity toward the end of the wet season means that malaria was probably holoendemic in the 1890s, before the mosquito vector was known and mosquito control possible.

The third region of malarial epidemiology is the far south, mainly too dry to support the usual African vectors. Only *An. arabiensis* is now present there, though *An. funestus* has been known in the past. The rainy season varies from about four months in the north of this region to two months or less in the south, some years with no rain at all. This aridity suggests that the region should be malaria-free, but this has not been the case recently; though the endemic level is so low that few develop protective immunity. If a year of comparatively heavy rainfall follows a sequence of dry years, a serious epidemic can break out with a heavy loss of life.

The epidemiology of malaria in the high plateau is historically similar in some respects to the south, with a pattern of periodic epidemics accompanied by high death rates among a non-immune population. The elevation varies between about 800 meters and 2,000 meters above sea level, with a sharp drop-off toward the coast on the east and a more gradual slope to the west. Malaria is endemic today to quite high altitudes, some places as high as 900 meters. In the plateau zone, the recent incidence of malaria varies greatly from rural to urban environments, depending on elevation and rainfall, and the way individual farmers manage paddy rice, the dominant crop.

This variability has meant that much of the plateau region was sometimes malaria-free, while at other times epidemics killed tens of thousands of people among a population that was effectively non-immune, like the population of the far south after a series of dry years. In the nineteenth century, the same Merina people who counted on fever as an ally

[4] J. Mouchet, S. Blanchy, A. Rakotonjanabelo, G. Raivoson, E. Rajaonarivelo, S. Laventure, M. Rossella, and F. Aknouche, "Stratification épidémiologique du paludisme à Madagascar," *Archives de l'institute Pasteur à Madagascar*, 60:50–59 (1993).

against invasion died themselves in great numbers when they left the plateau and moved toward either coast.

In the plateau region, a malaria epidemic is reported for 1878, another for 1896. A new outbreak occurred in 1902 followed by far more serious epidemics through much of the highlands in 1906 and again in 1987. Next to nothing is known about the causes of the earlier outbreaks, but the epidemic that began in 1987 was caused by the reintroduction of *An. funestus* into the highlands after a period of intense mosquito-control activity. An estimated 100,000 people died of malaria in the Malagasy highlands in 1988.[5]

In the 1890s, some advocates of French colonial expansion saw Madagascar as a future colony of settlement on the model of Algeria. A minority believed that even the coastal regions would be available for permanent settlement by French merchants and planters. French medical opinion at the time was convinced that the highlands had always been malaria-free, while the west coast was relatively safe in the dry season. The east coast had no dry season and was therefore dangerous all year long.

The French image of Madagascar was largely based on the Mascarene Islands, Mauritius and Réunion, about 500 miles to the east. Both those islands had been mainly malaria-free until the late 1860s, when a serious epidemic followed the introduction of *An. gambiae*. In 1870, the crude death rate on Réunion rose to 510 per thousand, falling again to 90 per thousand in 1872 and declining gradually in the decades that followed.[6] In spite of the high death rate during the epidemic, malaria in later decades was far less dangerous than it was in Madagascar or the Comoro islands. British military medical statistics for Mauritius can serve as a proxy for the Mascarenes as a whole. In the period 1886-1890, the annual death rate for British soldiers on Mauritius was 15.61 per thousand, of which 2.66 per thousand was from malaria. The most dangerous disease on the island in that decade was typhoid fever.[7]

Réunion was already the home of substantial French merchants and planters, represented in the National Assembly in Paris. The Réunionnais judged the disease dangers on Madagascar by the situation of their own

[5] Salanoue-Ipin, "Notes sur les causes d'insalubrité des casernements et établissements militaires de Tananarive," AHMC, 14:27–39 (1911), pp. 26–28; C. Severini, D. Fontenille, and M.R. Ramiakajato, "Importance d'Anopheles funestus dans la transmission du paludisme au hameau de Mahitsy, à Tananarive, Madagascar," *Bulletin de la sociétéede pathologie exotique*, 83:114–16 (1990); J.P. Lepers, P. Deloron, M.D. Andriamagatiana, J.A. Ramanamirija, "Newly Transmitted Plasmodiuum falciparum Malaria in Central Highland Plateaux of Madagascar: Assessment of Clinical Impact in a Rural Community," *Bulletin of the World Health Organization*, 68:217–11 (1990); "Winged Killer," *The Economist*, October 15, 1988, pp. 54–56.

[6] A. Le Roy de Méricourt and A. Layet, "Réunion et ile Maurice," DESM, 4(3rd ser.): 258–507 (1877), p. 302.

[7] AMSR for 1891, pp. 242–43. The enumerators listed 2.21 deaths from enteric fever per thousand mean strength, but they also listed 1.77 deaths per thousand from continued fever, which must have been mostly typhoid as well.

island, and their aggressive enthusiasm for the conquest of Madagascar was an important political force behind the expedition of 1895. Their assurances about the "climate" carried important weight with French opinion.[8] More attention to the evidence for disease on Madagascar itself would have been less encouraging.

In 1880, the peacetime garrison at the French post at Nossi-Bé had an annual death rate of about 75 per thousand, slightly higher than the common rate for troops on garrison duty in West Africa.[9] In 1884–85, the French war with Imerina was not so much a campaign as the simple occupation of coastal points, rather like the occupation of Cotonou in French Bénin in 1890, yet the morbidity in Madagascar in 1884–85 hovered around 800 per thousand, and those who went ashore for the occupation of Tamatave died at 95 per thousand. The equivalent rate for the occupation of Cotonou in 1890 had been about 53 per thousand (refer to Table 4.4). On the eve of the 1895 expedition, different French publically stated estimates of the probable death rate from disease ranged from 18 per thousand, based on the British Asante expedition of 1874, to 59 per thousand for the Malagasy expedition of 1884–85.[10] In the event, staff planning for the 1895 expedition was based on a much lower figure.

Evidence from the expedition of 1884–85 also led to some theoretical speculations about malaria prevention. As early as 1870, Léon Colin of Val-de-Grâce hospital in Paris had popularized a telluric theory of malaria, associating the disease with a particular miasma from the soil. Evidence from the expedition of 1884–85 tended to support the telluric theory: soldiers who spent the night ashore came down with malaria about fifteen days later; those who slept on board ship avoided the fever, even when a ship was anchored within 300 meters of the shore. It seemed to follow that the soil, not the climate, was at fault, though heat, humidity, and turning up the soil all added to the virulence of the poison.[11] This was, of course, a variant of the older beliefs about safety from fever on board ship that had governed the Royal Navy's anti-malaria precautions in West Africa.

Planning the March to Antananarivo

Those who actually planned the 1895 expedition paid far more attention to the sanguine hopes of the Réunionnais than to actual evidence from

---

[8] For assurances of the the the healthfulness of the island see Paul Leroy-Beaulieu, "La colonisation française: A propos de Madagascar," *Revue des deux mondes*, 132: 356–57 (Nov. 1895); Christian Schefer, "La question de Madagascar," *Nouvelle Revue*, 92: 660–78 (1895), p. 668 ff.

[9] Vincent and Burot, *Paludisme à Madagascar*, p. 75.

[10] François Amelineau, "Désastre sanitaire," *Revue historique des armées*, 41–51 (1992); Jean Lémure, "Morbidité et mortalité pendant l'expédition de Madagascar," AHPML, 34(3rd ser.):497–507 (1895).

[11] Léon Colin, *Traité des fièvres intermittentes* (Paris, 1870); Vincent and Burot, *Paludisme à Madagascar*, pp. 75–77.

Madagascar, and service rivalries also entered the picture. The Ministry of the Navy would have been the logical ministry to command the operation, and General Gustave Borgnis-Desbordes was its principal candidate to head it. The War Ministry, however, saw the Malagasy operation as a opportunity to gain a brilliant victory and recover some of the prestige captured by the navy's generals like Galliéni and Borgnis-Desbordes in the Western Sudan.[12]

Some influential generals in the War Ministry also wanted a chance to exercise the troops in real combat, especially troops that might have to stand once more against Germany.[13] In the end, the National Assembly gave the command of the expedition to the War Ministry, though the precise political maneuvering is obscure. The overt explanation was that the War Ministry rather than the navy had experience in planning and organizing such a large expedition. The War Ministry therefore carried out the detailed planning and the command went to General Duchesne, who had no experience in tropical warfare.

The troops assigned to the expedition were mainly those of the War Ministry, and many were short-term national-service draftees – contrary to the navy's view that long-term veterans of tropical service were preferred and the navy's preference for a majority of non-European troops in any case. As worries about disease emerged early in the planning, a Senatorial commission of inquiry made a special point of recommending that all, or almost all, of the force be made up of troops with experience in Algeria or elsewhere in Africa, and recommended budgetary shifts that would have more than doubled the appropriation for health services.[14]

General Mercier, the War Minister, paid no attention to these recommendations. He believed that French troops under his ministry were fit to fight "wherever our flag is engaged." For the coming expedition, he created two new units, the 200th line infantry and the 40th battalion of *chasseurs à pied*, both drawn from different parts of the army so as to spread the coming glory as widely as possible. A smaller part of the force was made up of marine infantry, and of soldiers recruited in Senegal,

---

[12] A great deal has been written about this expedition and the planning behind it, and I will not attempt to give a full account here. See especially the recent Yvan G. Paillard, "The French Expedition to Madagascar in 1895: Program and Results," in J.A. de Moor and H. L. Wesseling, *Imperialism and War* (Leiden: Brill, 1989), pp. 168–88; Marcel Coat, "La préparation de l'expedition," *Revue historique des armées*, 24–27 (1992); G. Chaulliac, "Contribution à l'étude médico-militaire de l'expédition de Madagascar en 1895," *Bulletin de Madagascar*, 240:411–41, 241:507–51, 242:624–40, 243:722–40 (1966), as well as the contemporary accounts of M. Ranchot, "L'expédition de Madagascar: Journal de M. Ranchot, 11 avril – 8 octobre, 1895," *Revue de l'histoire des colonies*, 18:337–506 (1930); Charles Duchesne, "Rapport au Ministre de la Guerre 25 avril 1896 . . . sur l'expédition de Madagascar (1895–96)," *Journal officiel*, 1896:4099–5114, 5130–40, 5158–69 (September 1896); J. Lémure, *Madagascar: l'expédition au point de vue médicale et hygiènique* (Paris, 1896).
[13] Paillard, "French Expedition," p. 186; Coat, "Préparation," pp. 25–26; Amelineau, "Désastre sanitaire," p. 45.
[14] *Journal officiel*, Sénat, December 1894, pp, 950–51.

Dahomey, or Algeria.[15] As it turned out, these and the troops of the Foreign Legion, also from Algeria, were those that actually reached Antananarivo after disease had wiped out the 200th as a viable fighting force. Health services were assigned to the War Ministry, which had little or no experience in regions more tropical than Algeria.[16]

The Government objective was to march on the capital and to confront the Merina army on its home ground. Some of the opposition argued that a coastal blockade was a cheaper form of pressure, one that would sooner or later compel the Malagasy government to accept a French protectorate. Others pointed out the logistic problems of advancing such a large force over narrow pathways. Still others criticized the use of national service troops and warned of the disease danger. But there was no vocal objection to France seizing Madagascar, only to the strategy for doing so.[17]

Given the decision to storm the highlands, the second problem was how best to get there. Two obvious routes presented themselves, the shortest and most common being the trail from the east coast. In order to discourage foreign armies, Imerina had left this a trail, rather than building a road. The other possibility was to march due south from Majunga on the west coast. That route was the one chosen because the countryside was more open – no *hazo* here – and the first 125 miles could use the navigable sections of the Bétsiboka river, leaving only 155 additional miles for the climb into the highlands. The overland part of this route had been surveyed in 1894, by the small evacuating force that had guarded the French Residence in Antananrivo. The navy had also conducted a six-month survey of the navigable section of the river and recommended small steamers for use on that part of the route.

The War Ministry, instead, ordered a dozen gunboats intended to pull steel barges up the river. These gunboats turned out to be underpowered for the current, and some of the barges were too long for the sharp curves in the meandering river. In the end, some supplies moved forward by water, but most of the troops marched overland, and the army had to build a road and four new bridges over tributaries to the Bétsiboka to make a passage for the supply carts.[18]

The 1894 evacuation from Antananarivo, 277 people in all, had marched down to Majunga in less than a month, using the Bétsiboka for the last stage and losing only one man to malaria. D'Anthouard, who came out with that group, recommended the route for the invasion as well, but only

---

[15] Amelineau, "Désastre sanitaire," 45.
[16] It is also possible that French military medical medical education for the army was slow in its consciousness of bacteriological discoveries. See Robert Osborne, "French Military Epidemiology and the Limits of the Laboratory: The Case of Louis-Félix Felsch," in Andrew Cunningham and Perry Williams, *The Laboratory Revolution in Medicine* (Cambridge: Cambridge University Press, 1992), pp. 189–208.
[17] See, for example, Henry Boucher, *Journal officiel*, Chambre, 24 Nov. 1894, pp. 2001–04.
[18] J. Lémure, "Les services sanitaires pendant l'expédition de Madagascar," AHPML, 35:97–111 (1896), pp. 97–100.

Map 7.2.   Madagascar – The French Invasion of 1895

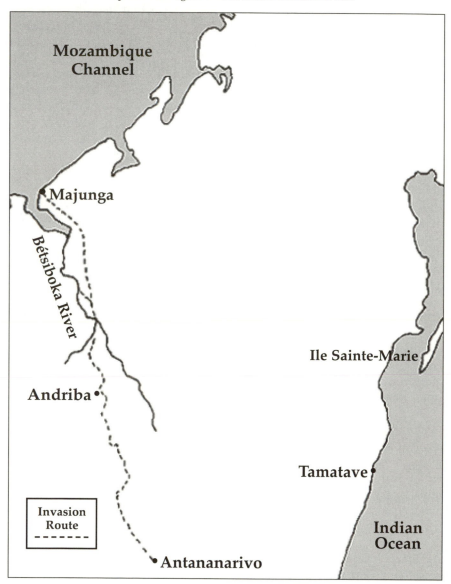

on certain conditions. The existing trails could accommodate only a limited force; D'Anthouard's recommendation was to mount a lighting raid with a small force on mule-back. From what he had seen of the Merina army, it was not a significant force, so the French expedition would not have to be large. Otherwise, with a larger force, he recommended the construction of a railroad from the head of navigation to the highlands – or at least that a cart track be built by non-European labor before the French troops arrived.[19]

The strength of the Merina army was a major concern in many of the decisions that followed. The War Ministry trusted its own intelligence reports, that the Merina army could field 25,000 to 35,000 men armed with rifles, trained by European officers, and supported by 40 to 50 modern pieces of artillery – a force that might well have been a serious opponent. The French planners therefore projected a requirement for a minimum of 12,000 fighting men, plus support staff, drivers, laborers, and the like.[20]

This was a transitional period in African warfare. In Dahomey in 1892, France had faced its first opponent using modern arms. At Adwa in 1896, too late for the experience to be useful to the French planners for Madagascar, an Italian army of 14,500 faced an Ethiopian force of more than 100,000, of whom at least 20,000 were armed with breech-loading rifles. The European force might well have won, even at these odds, but the Italian commander made a number of blunders and saw more than half of his force either killed or taken prisoner.[21] In 1899, the British were equally surprised at the initial offensive of the tiny Boer armies with their modern weapons. The French command was probably accurate enough in its assessment of the Merina army's weapons; they were only wrong about the Merina willingness to use them.

The War Ministry's assumptions about the size, equipment, and readiness of the enemy army dictated the size of the force to put in the field. That, in turn, required some kind of road to move supplies forward, which led the War Ministry to choose the two-wheeled mule-drawn carts called *voitures Lefebvre*, which were widely used in North Africa, the War Ministry's corner on the overseas world.

The War Ministry planned for the sanitary services based on experience in Europe and North Africa. The initial directives called for 70 doctors, 8 pharmacists, plus 22 administrative officers and chaplains. If the medical

---

[19] D'Anthouard, "L'Expédition de Madagascar: Journal de M. D'Anthouard, 26 octobre-26 novemebre 1894" *Revue de l'histoire des colonies françaises*, 18:225–78 (1930), pp. 225–26, 275–76.

[20] Duchesne, *Rapport*, p. 5105.

[21] John Lonsdale, "The European Scramble and Conquest in African History," in J.D. Fage and Roland Oliver, *The Cambridge History of Africa* (Cambridge: Cambridge University Press, 1985), 6:680–766, p. 702; Roman H. Rainero, "The Battle of Adowa on 1st March 1896: A Reappraisal," in J.A. de Moor and H.L. Wesseling (eds.), *Imperialism and War: Essays on Colonial Wars in Asia and Africa* (Leiden: Brill, 1989), pp. 189–200.

officers had been assigned in the same proportion as they were for the march on Kumasi in 1874, 300 would have been needed. Field hospitals and base hospitals together were to have a total of 2,500 beds, enough for 17 percent of the force to be sick or wounded at one time, whereas the British march on Kumasi in 1874 had prepared hospital space for 45 percent of the force at a time.[22] As it turned out in Madagascar, even that would have been far too little.

The Campaign

The expedition began with the naval bombardment and occupation of the two principal Merina ports: Tamatave in December 1894 and Majunga in January of 1895. A preparatory force arrived in January, though the main expeditionary force was not landed until May. Few laborers were available locally, and too few had been recruited elsewhere, yet a road was required for the passage of the Lefebvre carts. In 1896, when the British advanced on Kumasi, they had 13,000 carriers to support less than 1,400 fighting men. For the advance on Antananarivo, the French had ten times the number of fighting men and half the number of carriers. The French soldiers had to build the road as they went along. Even in the Magdala campaign, where little road-building was required, the British and Indian fighting force – also roughly 15,000 men – was supported by 25,000 "followers" and 40,000 mules.

By mid-August the French advance had only reached Andriba at the base of the highlands, where the Malagasy had a substantial and well-fortified base, roughly half-way between Majunga and Antananarivo. The defenders fled after a brief skirmish, but so many of the French soldiers had died of malaria, or had been invalided toward the coast, that the prospect of keeping on with the Lefebvre carts had to be abandoned.

Duchesne then reorganized the force into a "flying column" that could advance up the paths – a total of about 4,000 men, mainly African and Algerian soldiers and marine infantry, supplied by pack mules. It left Andriba on September 14 and arrived in front of Antananarivo by the end of the month. The Malagasy queen promptly surrendered, and Imerina became a French protectorate. Through the whole advance, the Merina army fought only a few skirmishes, and the loss of life on the French side from enemy action was only 25 men.[23]

What happened in the Imerina kingdom was something few French had even suspected. Though some French observers recognized that the Imerina army was no real threat, few, if any, realized that the kingdom itself was on the verge of collapse. The founder, Andrianampoinimerina,

[22] Duchesne, *Rapport*, p. 5108; Lémure, *Services sanitaires*, pp. 105–07.
[23] In addition to French works on the campaign, Manassé Esoavelomandroso, "Le mythe d'Andriba," *Omaly sy Anio* (Antananarivo), 1–2:43–73 (1975) used both French and Malagasy sources.

had slowly built a power base in the central highlands, and his successors had used it to dominate the rest of the island. He began in the era of spears and shields but soon turned to imported firearms. Missionaries came in force by the 1820s, and Protestant success seemed assured in 1860, when the Queen became a convert. [24]

Western observers were generally impressed by the overt signs of modernization, but Christianity had failed to penetrate far beyond the elite of Merina society. The regime rested on an economic base of wide-spread slavery and even wider use of forced labor for government and for some private purposes. The mass of the population deeply resented the enforced Christianity, forced labor, and oppression by central Imerina.

Anti-royal agitation came into the open even as the French invasions began. Overt revolt broke out here and there, some anti-European, some anti-Christian, some simply practicing banditry. The most prominent and best studied of these revolts was the *menalamba,* the rising of the red shawls, but it was only one among many different expressions of discontent. By the early months of 1896, the Merina state no longer existed. The French, in effect, accepted the surrender of power that the Queen and her Prime Minister no longer held.

After a brief protectorate, France annexed the island and exiled the Queen and some of her family to Réunion. Toward the end of 1896, Galliéni arrived as Governor and military commander for the suppression of the "rebellions"; the actual conquest of the island that took place over the next eight years.

Medical Aspects

Reports of a high disease death rate of the Malagasy expedition reached Paris by the mid-summer of 1895. It was clear as early as August that the expedition was becoming a medical disaster. One authority on the expedition called it "the most deadly of our epoch."[25] About a third of the force died of disease before the end of the year. Jean Lémure, who was present with the expedition, reported on medical aspects and published a book-length study in 1896.[26] Seventy years later, G. Chauliac, a doctor in the *troupes de marine*, went back to Lémure's findings and other evidence

[24] Raison-Jourde, *Bible et pouvoir à Madagascar*; Stephen Ellis, *The Rising of the Red Shawls: A Revolt in Madagascar, 1895–1899* (Cambridge: Cambridge University Press, 1985); Gwyn Campbell, "Slavery and Fanompoana: The Structure of Forced Labour in Imerina (Madagascar), 1790–1861," JAH, 29:463–86 (1988).

[25] J. Lemure, "Morbidité et mortalité pendant l'expédition de Madagascar," AHPML, 34(3rd ser.):497–507 (1895), p. 506.

[26] Ranchot, *Journal*, p. 453; Jean Lémure, "Morbidité et mortalité" pp. 497–507; "Nos pertes à Madagascar," AHPML, 34(3rd ser.):533–37 (1896); "Les causes de la mortalité pendant l'expédition de Madagascar," AHPML, 35:5–17 (1896); "Les services sanitaires pendant l'expédition de Madagascar," AHPML, 35:97–111 (1896). "Les measures hygiénique pendant l'expédition de Madagascar," AHPML, 35:223–42 (1896); *Madagascar: l'expédition au point de vue médicale et hygiènique* (Paris: 1896).

Table 7.1. *Disease Mortality for the Madagascar Expedition, 1895*

Morality per thousand per month

Disease	Deaths per month	Percent of all disease deaths
Malaria	32.16	72.00
Dysentery	3.57	8.00
Typhoid fever	5.36	12.00
Tuberculosis	1.79	4.00
Heat stroke	1.34	3.00
Tetanus	0.11	0.25
Ulcers and accidents	0.34	0.75
All Diseases	44.67	100.00

Notes:
Campaign dates March 1 to December 31, 1895.
Average monthly strength 15,000.

Source:
Chauliac, "Etude médico-militaire de l'expédition de Madagascar," pp. 546-57.

to produce still another detailed study of the expedition as failed military medicine.[27]

Table 7.1 summarizes Chauliac's reworking of Lémure's quantitative conclusions. Malaria was far and away the most important cause of death, and, since the expedition marched in the cool season, most of the deaths attributed to heat stroke were more likely cerebral malaria. If so, three-quarters of all deaths were from malaria. Though the troops were overwhelmed by malaria, waterborne diseases like dysentery and typhoid fever were also serious. Together they accounted for 20 percent of all deaths, a monthly mortality rate of almost 9 per thousand, even worse than the record of the marines in the western Sudan of 1880–83, when the monthly mortality of the two waterborne disease groups combined was just over 7 per thousand (refer to Table 4.3). The typhoid death rate alone was 5.36 per thousand per month, higher than any of the campaigns in northeastern Africa, except the British Nile campaign of 1898. French marine doctors in Haut-Sénégal-Niger apparently made no effort to boil drinking water. In Madagascar, orders called for both boiling and filtering all water for the troops, though the orders could seldom have been carried out.[28]

[27] G. Chauliac, "Contribution à l'étude médico-militaire de l'expédition de Madagascar en 1895," *Bulletin de Madagascar*, 240:411–41, 241:507–51, 242:624–40, 243:722–40 (1966).
[28] Chauliac, "Étude médico-militaire," 241:526–28.

The official precautions against malaria were the usual for the period. The expedition was planned for what was understood to be the off-season for malaria, the relatively cool and dry months from July into October. Prophylactic quinine was ordered from the beginning for laborers and soldiers alike, the compulsory dosage to be given under the orders of the company commander or equivalent official. The quinine was ordered with morning coffee at the rate of 10 to 20 centigrams on each of the first four days of the week – twice that in the wet months of March and April, and in the vicinity of swamps.[29] The total dosage of only 40 to 80 centigrams per man/week was surely too low. The British in Asante in 1874 had used 136 centigrams per man/week. By the 1890s, the recommended dosage in the British military, 5 grains per man/day, would have come to 227 centigrams per week.

It was not that French tropical medicine was inferior to British tropical medicine, as the British sometimes claimed. The error was that of the medical service under the Ministry of War, not of French malariologists who were severely critical at the time both of the dosage and lack of enforcement. Some criticized the army for failure to have enough quinine available. Enough was probably available somewhere in Madagascar, but not everywhere and all of the time. Nevertheless, the men only took it irregularly in any case, and the officers made no serious effort to enforce its use.[30]

Even the suggestions of the telluric theory of malaria would have made a difference, if they had been enforced. They would have kept the troops on board ships until the cart road was ready for a rapid advance. They would have assigned road building with its up-turning of earth to non-Europeans, assumed to have a degree of immunity to malaria. The telluric theory, in short, was empirically sound in trying to keep people away from the source of infection, even though it was wrong about what that source was; but it was not followed.

General Duchesne was sometimes blamed for the disaster, but those who placed him in command were more at fault. Duchesne was chosen for his reputation as an aggressive field commander, an "officier de troupe," but he also had a pronounced disdain for the auxiliary services like transport, engineers, administration, and health. In spite of the medical failure, the Government proclaimed victory and the Assembly voted a medal to all the men who had taken part; Duchesne was made a Grand-officier de la Légion d'Honneur.[31]

In one respect, the officers with the expeditionary force were outstanding—the protection of their own health. Where the overall campaign

[29] Lémure, Mésures hygienique, p. 239; Chauliac, "Etude médico-militaire," 241:526–28.

[30] Duchesne, *Rapport*, 5108; Ranchot, *Journal*, p. 358.

[31] Coat, "Préparation," pp. 25–26; G. Grandidier, *Le Myre de Vilers, Duchesne, et Galliéni: quarante années de l'histoire de Madagascar, 1880–1920* (Paris: Société d'éditions géographique, maritimes, et coloniales, 1923), pp. 91–92, 105–06; Ranchot, *Journal*, p. 422.

mortality of the enlisted men was 330 per thousand, that of the officers was only 58 per thousand.[32] A difference of this kind was unusual. In other campaigns of the period, the mortality of the officers was at least as high as that of enlisted men, often higher. During the Asante Campaign of 1874, for example, enlisted men died of all causes at the rate of 2.8 per thousand per month, while officers died at 3.8 per thousand per month.[33] No available evidence indicates how officers on the Malagasy campaign protected themselves. They no doubt had better food and less fatigue than enlisted men; they may have had more opportunity to stay away from swampy areas; or they may have been conscientious about their own use of quinine and filtered water.

The death rate also varied among other categories of troops. For all naval personnel, including marine infantry, it was 229 per thousand, compared to 373 per thousand for troops from the War Department. Contemporaries thought that the death rate of the *troupes de marine* was lower because they were older than the draftees and had developed a certain degree of immunity through tropical service. That is possible, and the troops of the *Régiment d'Algérie* – made up partly of *Tirailleurs algériens* and partly of foreign legionaries based in Algeria – also had a comparatively low death rate of 246 per thousand. It is also possible that naval doctors and those of the Régiment d'Algérie had more experience with preventive medicine on tropical service.

After the Campaign

After the expedition withdrew, disease mortality of the French forces in Madagascar dropped decisively, a fact that helps distinguish the price of mismanagement from the inevitable cost of moving into the Malagasy disease environment (refer to Table 7.2). From 1896 to 1903, the French were no longer fighting a single campaign, but many small campaigns. The death rate of French troops over these later years is partly a campaign death rate – not just a barracks rate – but by 1897, the *annual* mortality had dropped to less than the monthly mortality of during the campaign of 1895. Even during the period of military operations through 1903, general troop mortality had dropped by about 60 percent, and it leveled off at the new low rate of about 8.4 per thousand over the next decade.

By the final pre-war quinquennium, 1909–13, malaria was still the principal cause of death in the colonial army on Madagascar, but at a much lower rate per thousand (refer to Table 7.3). Mosquito control no doubt played some role, but the French quinine prescriptions had changed drastically by this period, to the higher dosage used earlier by the British. Alexandre Kermorgant, prominent hygienist in the colonial army, held

[32] Lémure, "Nos pertes à Madagascar," pp. 534–37.
[33] Anthony D. Home, "Medical History of the War in the Gold Coast Protectorate in 1873," AMSR for 1873, p. 258.

Table 7.2. *Mortality of European Troops in Madagascar, 1897–1913*

Year	Annual Deaths Per Thousand
1897	30.00
1898	28.00
1899	25.00
1900	29.00
1901	18.00
1902	10.00
1903	14.75
1904	7.69
1905	9.39
1906	10.29
1907	7.07
1908	12.76
1909	6.20
1910	9.66
1911	8.85
1912	5.92
1913	5.96

Source:
1897–1902: Service de Santé, Madagascar, published in Chauliac, Étude micro-militaire,"
24:722.
1903–13: France. Ministère des colonies.
Statistiques médicales des troupes coloniales en France et aux colonies pendant l'année . . . (annual
series).

that secure prophylaxis required a dose of 25 to 30 centigrams daily at breakfast, to be repeated in the evening in cases where the individual had walked in the sun, had done fatiguing work, or had been soaked by a shower – that is, a weekly dosage of 175 to more than 400 centigrams, depending on circumstances.[34]

Because of the variety of local conditions, the epidemiological geography of malaria on Madagascar was and remains different from that found elsewhere in Africa. Parts of the plateau were sometimes completely malaria-free, but otherwise important changes occurred over quite short distances.

Table 7.4 shows the mortality pattern for Malagasy, as well as for French troops in 1901. The fact that mortality for the two forces was not very different is a striking contrast to circumstances elsewhere in tropical Africa. We have no evidence about where Malagasy soldiers were

[34] Vincent and Burot, *Paludisme à Madagascar*, 79; Lémure, *Services sanitaires*, p. 239; V. Laborde, "L'expédition de Madagascar au point de vue de la mortalité des troupes et ses causes," *Tribune médicale de Paris*, 28(2nd ser.):61–64 (1896); A. Kermorgant, "Prophylaxie du paludisme," AHMC, 9:18–46 (1906), p. 28.

Table 7.3. *Disease Death Rate of European Troops Stationed in Madagascar, 1909–13*

Annual Deaths per Thousand Mean Strengh

Disease group	Deaths per Thousand	Percentage of all deaths from disease
Typhoid fever	0.40	5.32
Influenza	0.00	0.00
Malaria	3.81	51.06
Gastrointestinal	0.71	9.57
Tuberculosis	0.24	3.19
Cancer	0.08	1.06
Diseases of the nervous system	0.08	1.06
Diseases of the lungs	0.24	3.19
Diseases of the circulatory system	0.24	3.19
Diseases of the liver	0.95	12.77
Diseases of the urinary system	0.08	1.06
Other disease	0.64	8.51
Total Disease	7.46	100.00
Accidents	0.71	
Suicides	0.64	
Enemy action	0.00	
Total deaths	8.81	

N= 2,519
Source:
Statistiques médicales, 1909–13, annual series, Table VII. *Statistiques médicales coloniales*, 1909–13, Table VI A.

recruited, but life in the army certainly carried them to places where their home immunities no longer gave much protection. As of 1901, the high-land region was already in one of its periodic malaria epidemics, the death rates were therefore higher there (for French and Malagasy alike) than they were on the westcoast route the expedition used in 1895; the east coast route through Tamatave would have been notably more lethal – which makes the medical failings of the 1895 expedition all the more tragic.

Reactions in France

The French imperialists and their opponents both drew lessons from the Malagasy experience, but in diametrically different ways. Leroy-Beaulieu, the noted imperialist, could continue to celebrate the healthful climate,

Table 7.4. *Mortality of Malagasy and French Troops by Region in Madagascar, 1901*

Annual mortality per thouand mean strength

Region	Garrison site	Europeans	Malagasy
North and Northeast			
Territory of Diego Suarez		15	19
Northeast	Mandritsara	18	17
	Ambatondrazaka	141	0
East	Tamatave	38	15
West and Northwest			
Northwest	Ambato	12	12
	Analava	14	13
West	Mevetanana	19	15
	Majunga	12	12
	Sakalava Territory	16	13
Plateau Region			
East Uplands	Moramanga	20	14
Imerina	Tananarive	24	6
	Ankazohé	15	13
	Majakandriana	15	18
Betsiléo	Fianarantsoa	21	10
South			
Southwest	Tuléar	12	5
South	Fort Dauphin	9	15
	Mean	17	13

Source:
Vaysse, "Morbidité des troupes," AHMC, 17:336 (1903).

even as the death toll was reported in the press.[35] Most non-medical opinion in France was saddened at the unnecessary loss, but amazingly tolerant of the army. Jean Darricarrère, who had been present on the campaign as a medical officer, later published a journal of his experience with the ominous title of *Au pays de la fièvre*. He was something of an anti-imperialist, holding that war is a terrible thing and the Malagasy had a right to their island. But the main lesson he drew was that, while the

[35] Leroy-Beaulieu, "A propos de Madagascar," pp. 356–57 wrote "Les côtes, ils est vrai, de la grande île sont insalubres; mais presque tout le littoral français de la Méditerrenée l'est également, or le fut autrefois avant que des soins intelligens et le progrès des cultures n'aient atténué cet inconvénient."

French army had committed disastrous errors, those errors should be taken as lessons for the future, to insure a better performance next time.[36]

Several French governments had already fallen because of public displeasure over imperial adventures, but no such thing happened this time. Most considered Madagascar a plum ripe for the picking, though it was not crucial to the French view of their position in the world. By the mid-1890s, anti-imperialism was vastly weaker than it had been, and such incidents as the Fashoda crisis nearly provoked a European war before the end of the decade. Foreign commentators, potentially more free to criticize French blunders, sometimes praised the expedition as an imperial triumph. Bennett Burleigh, a correspondent who reported on the war from the Malagasy side, said he would have preferred English to French rule over the island, but he was pleased with the French success. It was good for "white man's prestige," and it avoided the danger of having to invade again in another year.[37]

The only spokesmen genuinely angered by the mismanagement were those who made a special study of the medical aspects, like Lémure in France, or an anonymous reporter for the *British Medical Journal* who wrote:

Anything more scandalous and culpable than the conduct of the Madagascar campaign of 1895 it were hard to conceive or parallel in modern times; it was so shameful as to cause dire heart-searching among thoughtful and humane Frenchmen.

Somebody ought to have been disgraced or shot.[38]

The British Advance up the Nile

Just as the Madagascar expedition was the last and most deadly of campaigns where malaria was the main killer, the resumed British advance up the Nile was the last and most deadly of the typhoid campaigns. By 1896, when that advance began, typhoid fever was far better understood than it had been in the early 1880s. Chemical purity was no longer the only test for pure water; it was now possible to test water for bacteria. The typhoid bacillus had been identified in the early 1880s and was now widely known in medical circles. Widal's serological test had been known since 1896. By 1896, typhoid deaths in the British garrison in lower Egypt were only 2.64 per thousand *annually* (refer to Appendix Table A5.3), down from 6.33 in 1883. Yet the *monthly* British losses from typhoid in the upper Nile in 1898 were to be more than 5.5 per thousand (refer to Table 7.6).

The new advance, which began in 1896, ended in 1898 with the destruction of the Mahdiyya and the foundation of the Anglo–Egyptian Sudan.

---

[36] Jean Darricarrère, *Au pays de la fièvre* (Paris, 1904), p. viii–xiii, 386.
[37] Burleigh, *Two Campaigns*, pp. 355–57. See, for example, A. Hilliard Atteridge, *The Wars of the Nineties* (London: Cassel, 1899), pp. 757–58.
[38] BMJ, 1898, 2, 992 (October 1).

In the beginning, it was not intended to reconquer Egypt's old Sudanese empire. The campaign originated as a limited British response in the complex pattern of competitive annexation in Africa, then entering its most frenzied phase.

The British government's decision to withdraw Egyptian Sudanese garrisons to the north of Wadi Halfa dated from January 1884, and neither the advance and withdrawal of the Gordon rescue expedition of 1884–85, Gordon's death in January in 1885, nor that of the Mahdi in June made a fundamental difference. 'Abdallahi, the Mahdi's successor, took the title of Khalifa and prepared to invade Egypt, as the Madhi had intended. In 1889, the Anglo-Egyptian frontier army decisively defeated the Khalifa's invading army, and, just as the capture of Khartoum in 1885 had increased the Mahdi's following in the Sudan, the military failure in 1889 weakened the Khalifa's support. For the next decade, the Mahdiyya still controlled Egypt's old secondary empire south of the desert, but it was no longer a threat to Egypt – or to other neighbors. The Italian defeat at Adwa in March 1896, however, raised the prospect of political and military disequilibrium. With Italy in retreat, the headwaters of the Nile might be tempting to others, notably either the Congo Independent State or France. A timely British move up the Nile could be a step toward protecting future Egyptian and British interests.

The advance was played out in a series of three annual campaigns. In 1896, the Anglo–Egyptian force conquered the province of Dongola and its capital city. In 1897, the invading army moved upriver beyond Dongola and simultaneously advanced across the desert directly from Wadi Halfa to Abu Hamad and Berber on the northern bend of the river below Khartoum. Abu Hamad fell in July 1897, and Berber followed at the end of August. The British then built a railroad across the desert from Wadi Halfa to the Nile bend, making it possible to launch the final campaign in force the following year. In July 1898, the first major battle of the new advance was fought where the Atbara River enters the Nile, and the campaign ended with the decisive Anglo–Egyptian victory at Omdurman in September.

The new advance was not simply a replay of the 1884 campaign. The Khalifa's government was more fully established than the Mahdi had ever been. The attacking force also included Egyptians and Sudanese in Egyptian service. These fresh troops were no longer the remnants of the Khedival army, defeated along with Hicks Pasha back in 1882. They were reformed, reorganized, and commanded by British as well as Egyptian officers. By 1897, the Egyptian army had more than 18,000 men, including infantry armed with Martini magazine rifles and Maxim machine guns, cavalry, camel corps, and artillery with some of the best guns available in Europe. Most of the Egyptian soldiers were conscripts, though a third of the infantry units were Sudanese.[39] The final advance on Omdurman in

---

[39] G.W, Steevens, *With Kitchener to Khartoum* (Edinburgh: Blackwell, 1898), pp. 11–21.

Map 7.3. British Nile Campaigns, 1883–98

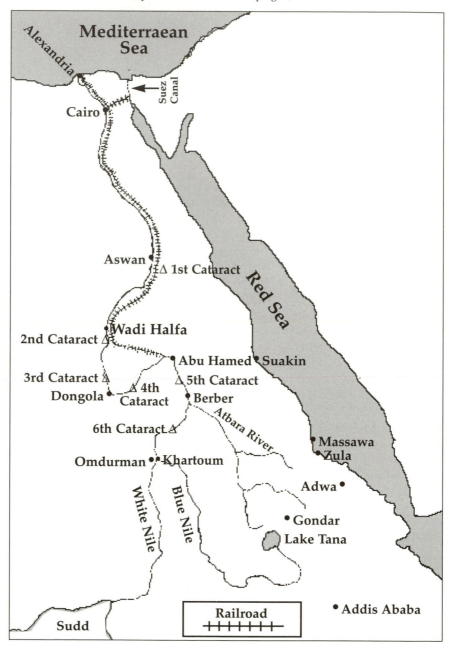

1898 was thus more Egyptian than British, with 17,200 Egyptians to 8,200 British troops. It was not a far different size from the French force that invaded Madagascar in 1895.

The new advance was technologically far ahead of the Gordon rescue expedition of 1884–85, and not simply in terms of its arms. Wolseley had a used few Nile steamers dragged around the cataracts above Aswan, and he also fell back on his North American experience and supplemented the steamers with whaleboats, manned by *voyageurs* recruited in Canada. Kitchener, the new commander, had the benefit of specially designed armored river steamers that could be broken down for shipment by rail. They were 140 feet long, with a speed of 12 knots, carrying one 12-pounder quick-firing gun forward, two six-pounders amidships, and four Maxim guns. Soldiers on deck were protected by steel plates, holed for rifle fire.[40] In 1896, they were assembled at the end of the rail line. At each higher cataract, the army built a railroad around the rapids, so the steamers could be taken apart and reassembled on each higher reach of the Nile. These vessels were especially important during the 1897 advance up the Dongola reach.

By 1896, the Army Medical Department's knowledge of preventive medicine was also far better than it had been in the mid-1880s, but it was still hard to apply that knowledge. In 1895–96, for example, a cholera epidemic killed more than 15,000 people in lower Egypt, but the army there reacted quickly, among other measures confining the troops in Alexandria to barracks. As a result, it suffered only five deaths in lower Egypt. It had some success upriver as well, where the cholera arrived in July 1896. Flight to desert camps protected some of the troops, and the army ordered the river bank patrolled to prevent men from drinking directly from the Nile. It nevertheless lost more men from cholera in the 1896 campaign than from any other cause, including enemy action and typhoid fever.[41] During the final campaign up the Nile in 1898, typhoid fever caused 64 percent of all deaths, and waterborne diseases as a whole caused 71 percent – a heavy cost in largely preventable deaths.

The medical department tried to ensure that all water was filtered and boiled, and Dr. Taylor, who wrote the medical report for the final expedition recognized that: "There is no doubt that if boiling were strictly carried out it would prevent water being a source of enteric fever and dysentery."[42] But it was not strictly carried out, partly for lack of time, fuel, or the simple fact that the men would not willingly wait for water to be boiled and cooled when it was instantly available from the Nile, and many officers were unwilling to enforce the prohibition. Water discipline

[40] Winston Churchill, *The River War; an Historical Account of the Reconquest of the Soudan* (London: Longmans, Green, 1899), p. 141.

[41] Churchill, *River War*, 140–61, esp. 161; BMJ, 1896, 2, pp. 779–800, Sept. 19.

[42] W. Taylor, "Report on the Medical Transactions of the British Troops of the Nile Expeditionary Force, from 4th January 1898 to 10th October, 1898," AMSR, 30:436–61, p. 443.

Table 7.5. *Comparative Mortality of British Troops in Barracks in Lower Egypt with Those on Campaign on the Upper Nile in 1898*

All rates are deaths per thousand per month

Disease	Lower Egypt 1895–1904	Upper Nile 1898	Percentage Increase on Campaign
Smallpox	0.004	0.000	
Diphtheria	0.003	0.000	
Enteric fever	0.440	5.525	1,156
Other continued fevers	0.010	0.000	
Gastrointestinal infections	0.128	0.591	360
Cholera	0.018	0.000	
Malaria	0.000	0.062	
Septic diseases	0.002	0.000	
Tuberculosis	0.085	0.000	
Gonorrhea	0.000	0.000	
Alcoholism	0.018	0.000	
Rheumatism/rheumatic fever	0.000	0.031	
Local diseases of the:			
Nervous system	0.022	0.000	
Circulatory system	0.051	0.031	
Respiratory system	0.064	0.156	143
Urinary System	0.008	0.000	
Other	0.027	0.000	
Total disease	0.880	6.396	627
Accidents and poisons	0.160	0.496	210
Enemy action	0.008	1.707	
Grand Total	1.048	8.599	721

Note:
The category "accidents" includes heat-stroke.
Data for the upper Nile cover the period January 4 to October 10, 1989, 279 days.

Source:
AMSR for 1905, pp. 274–5, 335, 358–9.
Taylor, "Report of the Medical Transactions," AMSR for 1898, pp. 441–3."

is hard to enforce, but not impossible; on the British Asante expedition of 1895, out of 1000 European officers and other ranks on the march to Kumasi only one died of dysentery, and none of typhoid.[43]

Effective porcelain filters were of course available, but the number of Pasteur-Chamberland or Birkeland filters was insufficient, and they

[43] BMJ, 1896, 1, p. 138, (January 25); Bennett Burleigh, *Two Campaigns: Madagascar and Ashantee* (London, 1897), p. 551.

tended to clog with Nile sediment. Water purification was most efficient at the beginning of the march, but it deteriorated as the expedition approached Khartoum, still more as the main force withdrew northward after its victory.[44]

Barracks and Campaign

Few noticed at the time, but, while the barracks death rates dropped steadily in all parts of the world in the second half of the nineteenth century, the disease death rates on campaign failed to drop as rapidly – or at all, if this campaign and the French invasion of Madagascar are taken as examples. Data to compare disease deaths in barracks and campaign are not always available, but they are for lower Senegal in 1852–73 and the columns in the Haut-Sénégal-Niger in 1883–88. At that time, the death rate on campaign was 178 percent higher than the rate for men in barracks (refer to Table 5.3). On the Nile in 1898, the campaign death rate was much lower than it had been in the Western Sudan, but barracks rate in Egypt was lower still. The disease death rate on the upper Nile that year was 627 percent the death rate for troops in lower Egypt. (Refer to Table 6.7).

This time, malaria, so continuously hard to control in most of tropical Africa, was not a factor. The men upriver died from typhoid fever eleven times more frequently than those in lower Egypt, and nearly four times more frequently from other gastrointestinal infections. Thus, while the risk of death from disease on this campaign was six times the risk of death in Cairo and Alexandria, the excess deaths on campaign were, for all practical purposes, caused solely by defective water supply, with a small assist from malaria and heat stroke.

Public Reactions

Perhaps the most remarkable aspect of the death rate "up Nile" in 1898 was the way the British press received it. The press began with some under-reporting that might not have been intentional. Dr. Taylor's official medical report listed 23.65 per thousand as victims of typhoid fever, but the rapid evacuation of the sick down the new railroad meant that many typhoid cases died in lower Egypt, or even in Britain. The monthly typhoid death rate of 5.43 per thousand in table 7.6 is based on upriver deaths, plus those of men whose death was reported in lower Egypt as a result of typhoid contracted in the Sudan.[45] Taylor's official report for that disease was therefore only about a third of actuality, but the probable source of complacency lay elsewhere.

[44] Taylor, "Nile Expeditionary Force," pp. 441, 443;. *The Lancet*, 1898, 2, p. 578, (August 27) ; p. 1234, (November 5); p. 1372, (Nov. 19).
[45] Taylor, "Nile Expeditionary Force," pp. 440–41; AMSR for 1898, p. 441.

This campaign took place at the height of British public interest in empire-building overseas. So many correspondents were present, including Winston Churchill, and they were so anxious to report the victory, that their casualty rate was greater than that of the force as a whole. One reporter was killed by enemy action; two were wounded; and one died of typhoid fever – this in a campaign where the Anglo-Egyptian force at Omdurman killed 11,000 Sudanese while suffering only 48 fatalities of its own from enemy action.[46]

As for the correspondents' coverage of disease, Churchill's *River War* paid serious attention only to the spectacular cholera epidemic of 1896. G.W. Steevens's book-length treatment of the campaign said nothing at all about a disease problem.[47] The British medical press and the foreign press as well were only congratulatory. In September 1898, when the main campaign had ended, the *Lancet* quoted *Le Temps* as saying that, "All had been foreseen, calculated, and regulated by the simplest means and according to a general plan so scientific that the march may be likened to the solution of a mathematical equation."[48] The *Lancet* followed up with praise for British superiority in the conduct of overseas military expeditions. One editorial claimed that casualties from disease in the march to Omdurman were "surprisingly light," and contrasted British superiority in military medicine to the mediocre performance of the Americans in Cuba or the French in Madagascar and Tonkin. For the *Lancet*, indeed, the only remaining problem was that soldiers could not easily be prevented from drinking impure water.[49] That belief probably had some truth to it, but the tendency to blame the individual for his failure to follow the appropriate rule of hygiene was as old as the humoral theory. This misconception lingered in the popular mind and among some members of the medical profession as well.

The *Lancet's* favorable reaction was not based on careful attention to the disease record of other campaigns; that rate for British troops at Suakin, which caused such distress in the medical press in 1885, had been 1.53 per month, as against 6.4 for the river war of 1898. The monthly death rate for typhoid had been 1.05 per thousand at Suakin, as against 5.53 per thousand in 1898.

Part of the error may have been caused by the fact that the medical press was no longer allowed to employ serving medical officers as correspondents, but there were political factors as well. The victory in the Sudan was not presented to the public as an expensive campaign to create a greater Egypt. It had to do instead with a triumph for "Christian civilization" over a "dervish empire," as it was called in the press and in many official dispatches. By 1898, control of the Nile watershed was associated with the

[46] G.W. Steevens, *With Kitchener to Khartum*, pp. 288–89.
[47] Churchill, *River War*; Steevens, *With Kitchener to Khartoum*.
[48] *Lancet*, 1898, 2, p. 698 (Sept. 10).
[49] *Lancet*, 1898, 2, pp. 1144–5 (Oct. 29).

stability of Egypt, and Egypt in turn was now seen to hold the key to Suez and the passage to India, the center of British imperial power. By this time, the scramble for Africa was nearing its climax; so was imperialist frenzy in the British press; and so too was the Franco–British rivalry overseas.

Nor was the decisive victory at Omdurman on September 4, 1898 the final victory. While the British had been advancing up the Nile, a small French force had left the Atlantic coast to march across Africa toward Ethiopia. By August of 1898, it had fortified a small island in the Nile at Fashoda, just below the sudd barrier and some 700 miles upstream from Khartoum. When news of the French action reached Khartoum, Kitchener set off full-speed with a small force loaded onto the steamers, which reached Fashoda on September 18. The ensuing diplomatic crisis nearly led to an Anglo–French war in Europe; but Britain succeeded in facing down France, and the crisis passed.

In British eyes, the Omdurman campaign therefore not only gained the Sudan; it was also a major victory over a European rival. In the light of that triumph, the disease cost could hardly count in the official or the popular mind. It was, in one sense, a chance reversal of the realignment created by the Panjeh incident of 1884. At that time, the apparent threat of war with Russia showed that British forces on the Nile or at Suakin were in the wrong place at the wrong time. In 1898, the British forces on the Nile, after the victory at Omdurman, appeared to be in the right place at the right time.

CHAPTER 8

THE ANGLO–BOER WAR:
THE LAST OF THE TYPHOID CAMPAIGNS

"... bad water costs more than all the bullets of the enemy..."

The Anglo–Boer War of 1899–1902 was unlike any other in the European conquest of African empire. It grew out of a set of circumstances unique in the history of Africa. The two Boer republics were secondary empires, in the sense that their power was ultimately based on European technology, but they were different from most other secondary empires in having a racially defined ruling class whose ancestors had come from Europe. Furthermore, the largest gold deposits yet discovered anywhere in the world lay under the Witwatersrand in central Transvaal. That wealth was a temptation to others, but it also allowed the Boers to buy the best weapons Europe produced in order to defend it.

In southern Africa, the principal campaigns for the conquest of African kingdoms took place between 1870 and 1890, in the parallel advance of the British and the Boer republics. The friction between Boer and Britain was mainly resolved by a series of shifting compromises. By the mid-1890s, it was apparent that the gold of the Witwatersrand was a major prize – *the* major prize, indeed, in all of Africa. With that realization, peaceful compromise became more difficult, if not impossible.

Perhaps it was inevitable that all the secondary empires would sooner or later fall to one European power or another. Only Ethiopia held out for long, but Madagascar and the Mahdist Sudan fell to expeditions at small cost, compared to that of conquering the Boer republics. Over the whole war period from 1899 to 1902, the British fielded nearly a half-million men against a Boer force that began the war with 60 to 65 thousand – roughly eight to one. Elsewhere in the European conquest of Africa, the proportions were often reversed, even then bringing easy victories to armies where one soldier in European service sometimes faced eight of the enemy.

In retrospect, the force required to conquer the Boer republics is not surprising; the Italians in the 1930s had to use an army of about the same size to conquer Ethiopia, but the military effort required in South Africa was a

202

surprise and a shock to the British at the time. Though the republics had little available manpower, their weapons were the best available, and their morale and support for their leadership were superb.

The Anglo–Boer encounter passed through a series of well-marked phases. A brief war in 1881 turned back an earlier British threat to annex the two republics; but British pressure increased, especially after the mid-1890s, and it was clear that Britain would sooner or later organize some form of takeover. Rhodes had already tried and failed with the Jameson Raid in 1895, but other British pressures continued. In 1899, the Boer republics decided on a preemptive strike. They invaded the two British colonies, taking advantage of the fact that the British garrison was not yet on a full war-time footing. In mid-October 1899, they laid siege to Ladysmith in northern Natal; to Kimberly, the diamond center just across the border from the Orange Free State; and to Mafeking just west of the Transvaal on the Cape-to-Rhodesia railway. The first British counter-offensives failed, but the military build-up continued, and a second phase began in mid-February of 1900 with a British advance on all fronts. Within four months, the British had relieved the besieged towns, overrun both republics, and captured their capitals of Bloemfontein and Pretoria. By September 1900, Britain formally annexed both republics.

The period of conventional warfare was over by July 1900, but the guerrilla phase was only beginning. Boer commandos attacked British posts, telegraph and railway lines, harassing the enemy in any way they could. The British response was to set up a lines of blockhouses joined by barbed wire, so that their forces could sweep one part of the country at a time, burning Boer farms and bringing women and other non-combatants into concentration camps. The tactics worked, though at a heavy price for Britain and an even heavier price for the Boers – and for the African population, which was involved in all phases of the war.

The war brought sharp swings in British opinion. It began at the height of imperialist fervor, only a year after British arms had faced down the French at Fashoda, but the flush of over-optimism ended quickly in the "black week" of mid-December 1899, when the first British attempt to relieve the besieged towns failed. The intensity of the patriotic fervor in Britain picked up with the victories of 1900, only to be followed by revulsion in the period of guerrilla warfare and concentration camps.

The British press reported the war in intense detail. Leo Amery began editing *The Times History of the War in South Africa* even before the war was over; his project finally reached seven volumes.[1] Those volumes have been central to much of the controversy which has continued down to the recent past, and the literature on this war is enormous.[2] This is not the

[1] *The Times History of the War in South Africa*, 7 vols. (London: Sampson Low, 1900–1909).
[2] Thomas Packenham, *The Boer War* (London: Weidenfeld and Nicholson, 1979) is a large-scale revisionist work dealing with military aspects of the war. S. B. Spies, *Methods of Barbarism? Roberts and Kitchener and Civilians in the Boer Republics: January 1900–May 1902*

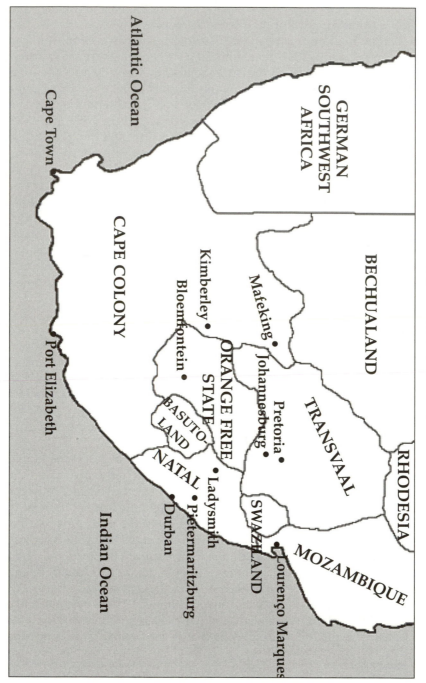

Map 8.1.   The South African War

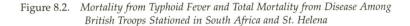

Figure 8.2. *Mortality from Typhoid Fever and Total Mortality from Disease Among British Troops Stationed in South Africa and St. Helena*

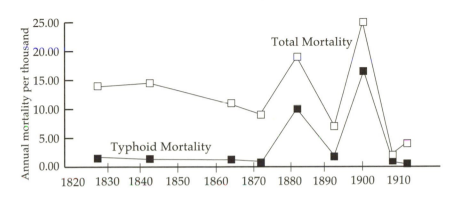

place to review these controversies, only to examine the interaction of disease and British imperialism.

The Emergence of Typhoid Fever in South Africa

South Africa is usually credited with Mediterranean climate, marked by moderate temperatures and winter rains, like coastal Algeria, Morocco, or central California. The former Cape Province does indeed, have a Mediterranean climate, in the sense that Mediterranean wine and wheat could flourish at the Cape. Outside that province, the similarity to the Mediterranean region no longer holds. Natal is subtropical, with summer rains, approaching fully tropical conditions toward the frontier with Mozambique. The high veld of the Orange Free State and southern Transvaal also has summer rains, though the climate and natural vegetation shift along a natural gradient of decreasing rainfall from east to west. The former northern Transvaal has another transitional zone toward the north, where tropical savanna (called bush-veld in South Africa) is more prevalent as one approaches the Limpopo and the boundary of present-day Zimbabwe.

Early in the nineteenth century, the South African health record for British troops had been excellent (refer to Figure 8.2 and Table 8.1). The initial surveys of 1816–37 showed the overall death rate in Cape Colony at about the same level as that for troops in Britain itself. Nor was the Cape

(Cape Town: Human & Rousseau, 1977) looks again at anti-guerrilla methods, and P. Warwick, *Black People and the South Africa War 1899–1902* (Cambridge: Cambridge University Press, 1983) returns to the neglected role of African participants and civilian onlookers. Edward M. Spiers, *The Late Victorian Army, 1868–1902* (Manchester: Manchester University Press, 1992), pp. 306–33 summarizes some of the controversies that have touched on army performance.

Table 8.1. *Typhoid Deaths Among British Soldiers in South Africa, 1818–1913*

| Dates | Deaths per Thousand | | Percentage of Deaths from Typhoid and other Continued Fevers |
	Typhoid and other Continued fevers	All Disease	
1818–36	1.80	13.44	13.39
1837–46	1.60	13.54	11.82
1859–68	1.13	9.88	11.44
1869–77	0.45	8.46	5.32
1879–84	9.61	18.52	51.89
1886–97	1.87	6.56	28.51
1899–1902	18.11	24.53	73.83
1905–09	0.80	2.58	31.01
1909–13	0.33	3.84	8.59

Note:
Enteric fever was not distinguished from other continued fevers until 1885, and misdiagnosis of continued fevers was so common that it was regarded as more accurate to count the small number of deaths from continued fevers as typhoid in years where they were reported separately.

Sources:
1818-36	PP, 1840, xxx [C. 228], p. 7b.
1837–46	PP, 1861, xxxvii, p. 97
1859–68	AMSR for 1869, p. 109–10.
1869–77	AMSR for 1878, pp. 76, 79.
1879–84	AMSR for 1885, p. 106–7.
1886–97	AMSR for 1898, pp. 280–1.
1899–1902	Simpson, Medical History of the War in South Africa, p. 52.
1905–09	AMSR for 1910, pp. 228–9.
1909–13	AMSR for 1914, pp. 144–57.

notable for typhoid fever. Over the period 1818–37, the South African death rate from all continued fevers (which would have included typhoid deaths) was only 13 percent of all deaths from disease in Cape Town and vicinity – as against 12 percent for soldiers stationed in Britain.

The eastern Cape was even healthier. In 1822–34 the garrisons around Grahamstown and the frontier forts had an overall mortality from disease of only 9.8 per thousand, the lowest death rate for British soldiers anywhere in the world at that time. For all forms of fever, the military death rate in the eastern Cape was only 1.2 per thousand. For the Khoikhoi troops serving there, it was only 0.7 per thousand – half the death rate for undifferentiated fevers in Britain itself.[3] Nothing in the military record from the first half of the nineteenth century, in short, indicated that typhoid fever was a particular problem in South Africa, for either Africans or Europeans.

[3] PP, xxx [C. 228], pp. 16b–19b; Curtin, *Death by Migration*, p. 165.

South Africa kept that reputation to the very eve of the Anglo–Boer War. A. Fuller's *Guide to South Africa*, the fifth edition of which appeared in January 1898, contained a section discussing the advantages of South Africa for people troubled with illness in Britain, and an unsigned article in the *British Medical Journal* as late as 1896 especially favored Grahamstown as a resort for consumptives.[4]

As in Europe and North Africa, typhoid fever in South Africa rose a to a peak in the early 1880s and then declined – or seemed to do so until the outbreak of the war.

Some disquieting evidence was available, however, in the Royal Army Medical Corps's own data on the health of the army over the years. Typhoid deaths had fallen consistently from the early century to the 1870s. After that, the rise in typhoid deaths per annum was not so notable as the fact that most other causes of death were dropping. The common typhoid death rates for soldiers in periods of relative peace in South Africa, moreover, were markedly lower than those in Algeria, and sometimes lower than those in France.[5] In 1878–84, the Zulu War, the first Anglo–Boer War, and associated clean-up campaigns against independent African states brought about a peak in military deaths from typhoid, like that of the three North African campaigns in those same years; but the typhoid death rates in the south were far lower. The British army typhoid losses in South Africa came to less than 20 per thousand annually, compared to the rates three to five times higher in the three North African campaigns of 1881–83 (refer to Table 6.4). Even leaving aside the two periods of campaigning, 1879–84 and 1899–1902, the importance of typhoid as a cause of death rose from 5 percent in the 1870s to 32.1 percent in the period 1905–07 (refer to Table 8.1).

Gastrointestinal infections, which are also carried by water, frequently move together with typhoid deaths, reflecting the quality of the water supply – but not always so. In the advance along the Sweetwater canal toward Cairo in 1882, typhoid deaths were low and gastrointestinal deaths were high. The South African garrisons, in the second half of the nineteenth century had fewer deaths from gastrointestinal infections, even when typhoid deaths were shooting up. In 1859–73, gastrointestinal infections had killed about one soldier per thousand per year in the British garrison. By 1884–98, that rate had dropped to 0.3 per thousand.[6]

Within South Africa, typhoid fever was most serious in regions of summer rain, and the pre-war garrisons that suffered most were at Pietermaritzburg and Ladysmith in central Natal.[7] The two Boer republics,

[4] BMJ, 1896, 1, 478.
[5] Philip D. Curtin, *Death by Migration: Europe's Encounter with the Tropics in the Nineteenth Century* (New York: Cambridge University Press, 1989), p. 151.
[6] R.J.S. Simpson, *The Medical History of the War in South Africa: An Epidemiological Essay* (London, HMSO, 1911), p. 9.
[7] Simpson, *Medical History*, p. 9–16.

where the war was to be fought, were also summer-rain country. The usual explanation at the time seems accurate enough: during the comparatively dry period, human fecal material was left in the open fields and along river banks. With the rains, the water rose and washed this matter into the rivers which were the main source of drinking water, hence, a marked increase in typhoid fever.

South African sanitary facilities were primitive at best. Only Cape Town had an adequate and safe water supply, drawn from the rain that fell on Table Mountain. Elsewhere, some water for civilian or military use came from shallow wells, but most came from running streams. Over the second half of the nineteenth century, the safety of the water supply diminished with the rise of urban concentrations, mining camps, railway construction, and commercial activity based on the extraction of gold and diamonds.

Sewage disposal systems were suited to a much sparser population. In towns, cesspits were common, but many had regular nightsoil collection in tubs, removed periodically. Done efficiently, this waste could be buried or used for agriculture, and all might have been well; but, as elsewhere, it was often done carelessly, dumping the refuse into gullies or other depressions away from the town, where the rains simply washed much of it into the water supply.[8]

Since neither the two British colonies nor the Boer republics had a regular system of death registration, it is impossible to know what the wartime toll of civilian disease might have been on either side. What few data do exist suggest that, as of 1902, European civilians in the Cape and Natal died of typhoid fever at a little more than twice the rate then current in England and Wales, while the Cape Coloured population died at a rate 77 percent higher than that of the whites.[9] Had this been known in 1899 or earlier, the unnecessary losses from typhoid in the South African War might have been avoided, though other warning signs were also neglected. The concomitant rise of typhoid among British troops in South Africa was barely noticed, as it went unnoticed during the Nile campaign only a year earlier.

The most prominent warning appeared as a leader in the *British Medical Journal* for January 20, 1900 – three months before the most spectacular epidemic began at Bloemfontein in March. Among other things, the editors wrote: "The conditions in South Africa are such that typhoid fever may break out in epidemic form at any time, especially where troops have to be concentrated."[10] The editorial was partly a commentary on an article by Almroth Wright and William B. Leishman, published as part of Wright and Leishman's campaign to make vaccination mandatory for all troops leaving for South Africa.

[8] Simpson, *Medical History*, pp. 18–25.
[9] Simpson, *Medical History*, pp, 25–31.
[10] BMJ, 1900, 1, 151–52 (January 20).

The army refused compulsory vaccination, but it allowed Wright to vaccinate those who chose to volunteer. The total number vaccinated is uncertain, but it is unlikely to have been more than 15,000 men, or less than 4 percent of the whole force; and some of the vaccine may have become ineffective through overheating. The typhoid mortality was 2.04 per thousand even among the vaccinated. The vaccine may not yet have been perfect, or perfectly administered, but the typhoid death rate of the whole South African expeditionary force was 21.08 – more than ten times higher.[11]

The Epidemics

Two serious epidemics struck British troops at Ladysmith and Bloem-fontein. Though typhoid fever was to be a problem throughout the war and its aftermath, these outbreaks attracted a level of public attention beyond any of the earlier typhoid campaigns. The epidemiology of these outbreak – indeed, that of the whole war – was carefully studied by Robert J.S. Simpson, Staff Officer to the Principal Medical Officer of the South African Field Force and later Professor of Tropical Medicine at the Royal Army Medical College. His *Medical History of the War in South Africa* appeared in 1911.

The first of these epidemics occurred among the British troops besieged in Ladysmith between November 2, 1899 and March 2, 1900. Ladysmith had been the scene of epidemic typhoid and gastrointestinal infections during previous warm seasons, and this siege took place at the height of the southern summer. The water supply from the Klip River had long been suspect; new Berkeland and Pasteur-Chamberland filters had been ordered but failed to arrive before the siege. The isolated garrison tried to distill water by using a dismounted railway engine, and they attempted to boil all drinking water; but it was not possible to deliver enough boiled or distilled water to all the troops all of the time. For the European troops (no record was kept of the African and Indian troops who were also present) the result over the 121 days of the siege was 177 cases per thousand of typhoid or simple continued fever, and 186 cases per thousand of gastroin-testinal infection. The monthly death rate was 7.11 per thousand from typhoid and continued fevers (which were almost certainly typhoid if death was the result), and 2.0 per thousand from gastrointestinal infection – considerably higher than the death rate from these diseases in the Omdurman campaign of 1898. The total was 465 deaths, almost all theo-retically preventable with the knowledge of public health then available.[12]

---

[11] Frederick F. Russell, "Anti-Typhoid Vaccination," *American Journal of Medical Science*, 146:803–33 (1913), p. 804; Almroth Wright, BMJ, 1901, 1, 647 (March 16); Leonard Colebrook, *Almroth Wright: Provocative Doctor and Thinker* (London: Henemann, 1954), p. 37–38.

[12] Simpson, *Medical History* , pp. 66–70.

Deaths during the siege were not widely publicized; the first sharp British reaction came after reports from Bloemfontein where a large body of British troops occupied the town in March and paused until the advance was resumed in July. The occupation began near the peak of the rainy season. A new water pipe had been laid from the Modder River to Bloemfontein, but its source remained in Boer hands, and water for the garrison had to come from shallow wells or from the river itself closer to the town. Wartime troop movement made it impossible to establish a monthly rate, but the medical authorities in Bloemfontein during the twenty weeks reported 8,568 cases of typhoid and simple continued fevers, leading to 964 deaths. During the same period, they reported 2,121 cases of gastrointestinal infection, leading to 81 deaths; in all, something like a thousand preventable deaths. Many others died after their evacuation to other hospitals.[13]

British Reaction to the Epidemics

Sir William Burdet-Coutts, a well-known philanthropist and member of Parliament, visited South Africa during the first half of 1900. His interest in hospital administration went back to the Russo–Turkish War of 1878, where he had served as Special Commissioner of the Turkish Compassionate Fund and had come down with enteric fever. The experience led him to some firm beliefs about the importance of nursing care in reducing case fatalities. His most famous dispatch to the *Times of London* from Bloemfontein was dated June 27, 1900, at the height of the epidemic. He followed up in Parliament, and with a book-length attack on the operations of British military hospitals in South Africa. These protests led ultimately to the appointment of a Royal Commission to look into the scandal.[14]

These complaints echoed those of Sir Garnet Wolseley and others after the Egyptian campaign of 1882, and, like those of Wolseley, had nothing to do with the prevention of typhoid and everything to do with the care of soldiers after they had contracted the disease. Burdett-Coutts demanded more and better doctors, more female nurses, and more and better-trained hospital orderlies. He also thought, as Wolseley had, that medical officers should buy whatever was needed on the spot, rather than depending on army supply; but he was silent about the possible role of preventive medicine.[15]

Others tended to blame the War Office and the army command in general, rather than the Royal Army Medical Corps, echoing the investigation into hospital scandals of 1882. This was another case where the

---

[13] Simpson, *Medical History*, p. 95.
[14] W. Burdett-Coutts, *The Sick and Wounded in South Africa: What I Saw and Said of Them and of the Army Medical System* (London: Cassell, 1900) esp. pp. 3–5, 18–31.
[15] Bourdett-Coutts, *Sick and Wounded*, pp. 46–47, 230–49.

decisions appropriate to the military situation were not those appropriate to civilian medicine. It seems clear in retrospect that army commanders, forced with a choice between medical supplies and artillery, sometimes left behind ambulances, water filters, and hospital equipment.[16] Medical men who had warned of the typhoid danger were shocked, but the military had been trained to fight wars, not to prevent sickness.

A Royal Commission under the Chairmanship of Lord Justice Romer reported in 1901, after gathering voluminous evidence both in Britain and in South Africa, and recommended a more thorough review of the Royal Army Medical Crops after the war. It conceded that wartime medical care is likely to be less than perfect, but it cleared the RAMC of the charge that hospital administration had broken down. In the end, indeed, it concluded that:

all witnesses of experience in other wars are practically unanimous in the view that, taking all in all, in no campaign have the sick and wounded been so well looked after as they have been in this.[17]

The *Lancet* and the *British Medical Journal* applauded the Commission's findings, while Burdett-Coutts attacked the Commission for its failure to recognize how correct he had been.

Part of the hospital controversy turned on the matter of case-fatality rates, as it had done in Tunisia, with the allegation that they were higher than they should have been. But the case-fatality rate during the Bloemfontein epidemic was 21 percent, as against 28 percent for the Nile Campaign of 1898. A typhoid case-fatality rate was, in any case, peculiarly susceptible to error. Many men were admitted to hospital with a simple continued fever, but their cause of death might be recorded typhoid as without a change in the admission record. Simpson, in his statistical work on the South Africa War, found that he had to correct for this error by counting all deaths recorded as simple continued fever as deaths from typhoid.

Preventive Medicine

The Royal Commission on Military Hospitals considered only the care of sick and wounded after they arrived in hospital – again, with no recommendation at all as to water supply, vaccination, or other aspects of preventive medicine. Only an undercurrent in the medical press called for preventive measures against typhoid. The *British Medical Journal* had already advocated compulsory inoculation of all troops sent to South

[16] Walter Foster, "The Hospital Scandal in South Africa," *Contemporary Review*, August 1900, pp. 290–304.
[17] "Report of the Royal Commission Appointed to Consider and Report On the Care and Treatment of the Sick and Wounded in the Military Hospitals During the South African Campaign," PP, 1901, xxix [C.453 and 455], xxix:70.

Africa and warned that a typhoid epidemic might be expected. The *Lancet* joined in, based on the experience following the Egyptian campaign of 1882, that of the American troops gathered for the invasion of Cuba, and the rising typhoid deaths in the Indian army.[18]

Up to April 7, 1900, the South African experience seemed exemplary: 1,960 enlisted men had been killed in action, and 465 had died from wounds, while only 1,485 so far had died from disease. In March, the *Lancet* could still comment that the disease record so far was better than that of recent wars.[19]

The medical press at first devoted more space to political and military news of the war than it did to medical problems, and it gave more space to surgical repair of wounds than to all diseases taken together. In this, it seemed to reflect the common lay attitude that the war was a national contest, in which sickness and death from disease were less important, and perhaps less honorable, than wounds or death in combat.

After the Bloemfontein epidemic, some correspondents gave the typhoid problem – and preventive medicine – more attention, especially Arthur Conan Doyle, who served in South Africa as a physician and filed stories with both the *Lancet* and the *British Medical Journal*. In one dispatch to the *BMJ*, he suggested that the Bloemfontein epidemic might well be the worst in modern warfare, with ten to twelve thousand in hospital at once and as many as six hundred dead in Bloemfontein alone. He nevertheless took the side of the Royal Army Medical Corps in the hospital controversy, defending the doctors, orderlies, and nurses who had carried out their duties at considerable risk to their own lives.[20]

He argued that the true culprit was elsewhere, that inoculation against typhoid should have been compulsory from the beginning, and preventive medicine had been terribly neglected. And he added:

All through the campaign, while the machinery for curing disease was excellent, that for preventing it was elementary or absent. If bad water can cost us more than all the bullets of the enemy, then surely it is worth our while to make the drinking of unboiled water a stringent military offense, and to attach to every company and squadron the most rapid and efficient means for boiling it – for filtering alone is useless.[21]

Others recognized that water was the crucial factor, but they also recognized that what was ordered was seldom done. Officially, all drinking water was supposed to be boiled and filtered through porcelain filters. More elaborate central filtration was also available in some places. The Maiche automatic water sterilizer, designed for permanent installation,

---

[18] BMJ, 1900, 1, 151–2 (January 20); *Lancet*, 1900, 1, p. 1218, (April 12).
[19] *Lancet*, 1900, 1, p 1152, (April 21); and 1, p. 794, (March 17).
[20] Arthur Conan Doyle, "The Epidemic of Enteric Fever at Bloemfontein," BMJ, 1900, 2, 49–50 (July 7).
[21] Arthur Conan Doyle, *The Great Boer War* (London, 1901), p. 371.

was set up late in the war in the barracks at Pietermaritzburg; it was capable of sterilizing about a thousand gallons of water a day, storing it automatically in a special tank and requiring no human intervention other than periodic maintenance.[22]

Chemical purification was also a known possibility. In 1898, a bromide process had been used experimentally in the Sudan, adding 0.06 grains of free bromide to each liter of water, then removing the excess bromide with ammonia. Other methods were based on chlorine, and potassium permanganate had been used occasionally for decades. Sodium bisulfate was especially effective against the typhoid bacillus and could be made up into pills weighing one gram, to purify one pint each. A box weighing a quarter of a pound would have served to purify more than twelve imperial gallons of water.[23]

None of these chemical methods was extensively used. In fact, little was done as systematically as it was done in the barracks of Cairo or Alexandria at the time At Bloemfontein, the medical officers made some effort to filter water from the Modder River with Berkeland filters, but within ten minutes the sediment in the river water clogged the filters. They also tried to clear the water with alum and then boil it, but the men disliked the taste, and their officers made no serious effort to stop them from drinking directly from the river. The latrines at Bloemfontein were simply open trenches, though the hospitals made an effort to segregate the waste of typhoid and dysentery victims, sterilizing it with a solution of "mercuric perchloride" before removing it to a separate shed where it was mixed with sawdust and burned.[24]

In effect, "science" knew the answer, but too few believed it had the solution. Leading medical authorities at the time were still unconvinced that water was the key source of infection. Even Professor Notter, the authority on typhoid fever at Netley, thought that water was only a minor source. For him, clothing and blankets of the typhoid victims were also important, as were flies from the latrines, or fecal matter that might be carried by the winds as dust.[25] It was hard for the most conscientious medical officer to concentrate on all these possibilities at once, and beyond the medical officers were the line officers, with their different class background and their lack of confidence in what the medical men had to say.

Leigh Canney, who had served with the army in Egypt, suggested that the problem of pure water could not be solved as long as only line

[22] W.J. Simpson, "Water Supplies," JTM, 6:132–38, 1723–74, 192–94 (1903), p. 192.

[23] BMJ, 1901, 1, 229–30, 242–43.

[24] Howard Tooth, "The Recent Epidemic of Typhoid Fever in South Africa," BMJ, 1901, 1, 642–47 (March 16)., BMJ, 1901, 1, 644 (March 16).

[25] J. Lane Notter, *Spread and Distribution of Infectious Diseases; Spread of Typhoid Fever, Dysentery, and Allied Diseases among Large Communities, with Special Reference to Military Life in Tropical and Sub-Tropical Countries* (London and Manchester, 1904), pp. 17–38.

officers made the decisions about what supplies went to the front. He suggested that the Royal Corp of Engineers and the RAMC should join forces to create a separate water corps whose sole task would be to make certain that boiled and filtered water was available throughout the army. He pointed out, as others had, that the lack of equipment to ensure pure water at Bloemfontein was no accident – it was an army decision to send forward something else. Canney believed that 500 mules devoted to carrying fuel and filters could have ensured pure water to the whole of Roberts' advancing army. The transport so allocated would have been a small price to pay for the men lost to fever in Bloemfontein.[26]

In 1901, an editorial writer in the *British Medical Journal* argued that one mule could carry a filter big enough to supply pure water to a hundred men. If only half the typhoid deaths were caused by impure water, if this minimal amount of transport had been provided, "and if officers and men had been intelligently convinced of the importance of avoiding unfiltered and unboiled water, probably half the sickness of the campaign might have been averted."[27]

The replies to Canney's suggestion were to be expected. The *Lancet* remarked that his idea was interesting but that field officers in a position to know believed it was impractical in wartime. The *BMJ* conceded that some agreed with Canney, but a significant body of authoritative opinion still held that dust and flies would have carried the typhoid, even if the water had been pure.[28]

The final, fallback position was, again, to blame the victim. Looking back on the South African campaign of 1900, James Jameson, the Surgeon-General, concluded that the fundamental problem was that, "Tommie Atkins was a peculiar man," who would simply refuse to obey orders about drinking water, and he backed this opinion with anecdotes from his Indian service.[29]

The weight of medical opinion, however, drifted slowly toward more concern about water supply. In January 1901, the subject was raised at a meeting of the Epidemiological Society in London, where the indiscipline of the men, the ignorance of the officers, and the practical problems of filtration were all considered. The BMJ's report of the meeting concluded that these problems could be solved if tough regulations were enforced, and if boiling and filtration were put under the command of intelligent and conscientious people.[30]

[26] H.E. Leigh Canney, "The Theory of Airborne Typhoid in Armies," BMJ, 1901, 2, 463–8 (August 24).
[27] BMJ, 1901, 1, 165–66 (January 19).
[28] Leigh Canney, letter to Lancet, 24 Sept. 1900, Lancet, 1900, 2, pp. 969–70 (Sept. 29); BMJ, 1901, 2, p. 742 (September 24); Canney, "Enteric Fever in Armies," BMJ, 1901, 2.; BMJ, 1901, 2, 1478–80 (Nov. 16).
[29] Jameson, BMJ, 1901, 1, 647 (March 16).
[30] BMJ, 1901, 1, 221–22 (January 26).

The Concentration Camps and Differential Immunities

The Anglo–Boer War had a second medical scandal. The typhoid epidemics in British barracks were followed by the more massive deaths of the Boer women and children in the concentration camps. These camps were originally set up to provide a haven for the many refugees escaping from the war zones. Civilians sought safety in towns, especially in the British-held towns, though the British often captured Boer-held towns and found them already overcrowded with refugee civilians. Once the war moved into the guerrilla phase late in 1900, however, the situation changed drastically.

Under Herbert Kitchener's command, the British anti-guerrilla response was typical of earlier wars; since guerrillas emerged from the civilian population, the civilian population itself had to be dealt with. At the time, the press referred to this tactic as "Weyler's method," after General Valeriano Weyler, the Spanish commander in Cuba who had cordoned off the country with lines of fortifications and collected all civilians into fortified towns, burning their homes. The concentrated civilian population then died of disease, as the concentrated civilians were to do in South Africa, though in fact, far more died in Cuba than were to die in South Africa. Nor was the method Weyler's discovery. "Punitive expeditions" were a normal part of the small wars of conquest in Africa and elsewhere. British forces had destroyed Magdala in 1868 and Kumasi in 1874 for the same reasons they burned the Transvaal farms in 1901.

Just as the Asante in 1873 and 1874 had suffered far more from disease than the British expeditionary force did, the civilian population of the Boer republics suffered more in this instance, especially in segregated refugee camps for black and white civilians.

The earliest camps for Africans were for genuine refugees from the fighting, but later on Africans were "cleared" involuntarily from rural areas where their presence or their cattle could attract Boer raids. By mid-1901, African refugee camps were mainly along the rail lines, where their cattle could be requisitioned for the British forces, and where the inmates could be assigned to work for the military or nearby civilian employers. By the end of the war, 115,700 Africans had been held in 66 camps, though the figure is imprecise.[31] Twelve percent of the inmates were recorded as having died, though that figure may be low on account of careless record keeping. In particular camps, annualized death rates reached 329 and 446 per thousand. The cause of death, where recorded, was 60 percent from pneumonia and 17 percent from gastrointestinal infections.[32]

It was Boer civilian deaths in the white camps that attracted British public attention, then and later. The total of white civilians in the concentration

---

[31] Warwick, *Black People and the South Africa War 1899–1902* (Cambridge: Cambridge University Press, 1983), pp. 145–46.

[32] Warwick, *Blacks in the War*, p. 152.

camps was more than 116,000, out of white population estimated at 200,000 in the two Boer republics at the beginning of the war; as many as half the total white population was imprisoned at some time during the war.[33] More than 27,900 died of disease in the camps, nearly 10 percent of the white population of the two republics. Only 4,000 Boer soldiers died in battle, and only 12,496 British soldiers died of all causes.[34] Of the dead in camps, 81 percent were children under 16, and 68 percent of the adult dead were women.

Cause-of-death data for the concentration camps are neither full nor very accurate, but they show marked differences from the pattern of disease death among British troops in South Africa at the time. Reasonably careful records exist for two of the Boer camps, Barberton and Nylstroom – records made by British officials, supplemented by the contemporaneous investigations by an amateur historian in the Orange Free State.[35]

Some diseases appear to have been almost equally dangerous for all. Gastrointestinal infections accounted for 17 percent of all deaths among adult African men in concentration camps, 11 and 15 percent respectively of deaths of Boer civilians in Barberton and Nylstroom, and 12.5 percent of deaths among British soldiers. These figures suggest that the water supply was none too good anywhere, while the level of immunity, or lack of it, was about the same for everyone.

For other diseases, the differences among the three groups were greater. Respiratory infections accounted for 70 percent of deaths in African refugee camps, against only 11.5 percent and 4.8 percent, respectively, in Barberton and Nylstroom, and 4.3 percent for British soldiers. In this case, differences among the whites were not significant, and the high rate for the Africans fits the recognized pattern of relatively weak African immunity to respiratory infections and tuberculosis.

The typhoid death rates were notably higher among British troops than in the concentration camps – 73 percent of all deaths from disease with the British, 46 percent of adult deaths at Nylstroom, and 31 percent at Barberton. These differences suggest that the white South African immune levels were higher than the British, probably because typhoid was more prevalent in South Africa than in Britain.[36] Dr. A. John Gregory, the Medical Officer for Health of Cape Colony, worked with sample data to estimate civilian death rates from typhoid for the year 1902 and came up with 6.5

[33] S.B. Spies, *Methods of Barbarism? Roberts and Kitchener and Civilians in the Boer Repbubics: January 1900–May 1902* (Cape Town: Human & Rousseau, 1977), pp. 215, n. 29, 378, n. 117. Emily Hobhouse, *The Brunt of the War and Where it Fell* (London: Methuen, 1902), pp. 327–47.

[34] S.B. Spies, "Women and the War," in Peter Warwick and S.B. Spies, *The South African War: The Anglo–Boer War 1899–1902* (London: Longman, 1980), p. 170.

[35] Bruce Fetter and Stowell Kessler, "Death by Concentration: The Burgher Camps at Barberton and Nylstroom," (Unpublished paper, presented at the African Studies Association, Toronto, November 1994).

[36] Fetter and Kessler, "Death by Concentration," pp. 2–3; Simpson, *Medical History*, p. 226.

per 10,000 for people of European descent, 11.52 per 10,000 for Africans. This compares to only 1.96 per 10,000 for civilians in England and Wales.[37]

Measles was another anomalous disease in wartime South Africa. It accounted for 11 percent of all deaths among adults at Barberton and Nylstroom, and for much higher figures among the children in the concentration camps – 42 percent of infant deaths at Nylstroom, for example. It was, indeed, an important reason for the high child-mortality rates in the other Boer camps as well. Yet the British army in South Africa lost only five men to measles during the entire period of the war; they must have been largely immune from childhood infection.

Measles is, of course, a "childhood disease" which seldom kills, but immunizes for life. Like many other childhood diseases, it requires a human community of a certain minimum size to maintain itself year in and year out. In small communities, the infection soon immunizes such a large portion of the available victims that it dies out for lack of hosts. Recent estimates suggest that measles will die out in an isolated community if the numbers drop much below a half million, only to return on contact with the outside world after a new generation of non-immunes has been born.[38] Measles is also one of the most infectious of diseases. As many as 90 percent of non-immunes who have close contact with a victim will be infected by airborne droplets.[39]

The South African population was, of course, larger than the normal minimum for continuous measles, but farmers on the high veld were relatively isolated, and the women and children brought into the concentration camps were overwhelmingly from rural areas. The fact that so many got measles in the camps is clear evidence that they had escaped infection in childhood. The case-fatality rate in the developed world today is about one per thousand cases, but it varies with nutritional status of the victim and the severity of the infection. Case-fatality rates in the tropical world are higher, in the range of 1 to 5 percent, and rates as high as 25 percent have been reported. The nutritional status of women and children from the veld was probably poor to begin with, and food supply to the camps was hardly adequate. Nor was the measles epidemic of these years confined to the camps. The wartime movement of people brought people together who had escaped childhood infection, not just the women in the camps, but Boer prisoners-of-war as well.

---

[37] Simpson, *Medical History*, p. 29.

[38] Cockburn, "Infectious Disease in Ancient Populations," *Current Anthropology*, 12:45–62 (1971), pp. 47–48; Francis L. Black, "Measles Endemicity in Insular Populations: Critical Community Size and its Evolutiary Implications," *Journal of Theoretical Biology*, 11 (1966) 207–11. The authoritative recent historical geography of measles is Andy Cliff, Peter Haggett, and Mathew Smallman-Rayor, *Measles: An Historical Geography of a Major Human Viral Disease From Global Expansion to Local Retreat, 1840–1990* (London: Blackwell, 1993), but it says next to nothing about measles in Africa.

[39] Joel G. Breman, "Viral Infections with Cutaneous Lesions," in G. Thomas Strickland (ed.), *Hunter's Tropical Medicine*, 6th ed. (Philadelphia: Saunders, 1984), pp. 110–20.

Table 8.2. *Comparative Military Mortality of the Nile Campaign of 1898
and the Anglo–Boer War, 1899–1902*

Deaths per thousand per month, average mean strength:

	1898 Upper Nile	1899–1902 Anglo–Boer War
Size of force	3,510	548,237
Disease		
Smallpox	0.00	0.00
Typhoid fever	5.53	1.51
Malaria	0.06	0.02
Gastrointestinal infection	0.59	0.26
Tuberculosis	0.00	0.00
Rheumatism	0.03	0.00
Diseases of the:		
Nervous System	0.00	0.00
Circulatory system	0.03	0.00
Respiratory system	0.16	0.00
Urinary system	0.00	0.00
Other disease	0.00	0.27
Total Disease	6.40	2.05
Accidents and Poisons	0.50	0.08
Enemy Action	1.71	1.04
Grand Total	8.60	3.17

Notes:
1. The data for the upper Nile are those published at the time and reported in Table 6.3.
2. Data for the South African War are for major diseases during the whole period of hostilities for all British troops, annualized. Blank spaces are not necessarily zero, but diseases the compiler chose to leave out.

Sources:
Nile campaign AMSR for 1898, p. 447.
South Africa, Simpson, *Medical History,* pp. 50–52.

The War in British Opinion

While the press and the public in Britain viewed the Omdurman campaign as a triumph of British military achievement in the age of empire building, the Anglo–Boer War was reported more fully, and much less favorably. The British press and public expected a short and victorious war. They got a long and expensive one, and the debate over the quality of military leadership still continues. British opinion had favored the war in the beginning, but it became more critical with the Boer seige of

Ladysmith and Mafeking in the early weeks of the war – still more so when these cities were not quickly relieved – and again during the final period of guerrilla warfare and "sweeping the veld" into the concentration camps.

Bitter complaints from the medical community about deaths from disease began with the early typhoid epidemics and continued through to the reports of death in the concentration camps. Yet the record of the Royal Army Medical Corps was far better in the South African war than it had been on the Nile a few years earlier. It was a point lost at the time on the British public, which was fully informed about the absolute losses in the typhoid epidemics in Ladysmith and Bloemfontein, but not about the proportionately greater losses to the smaller force on the Nile.

Part of the discrepancy between statistical fact and public recognition was the public's disappointment with the way the war was going. The correspondents on the Nile were too busy reporting the victories to pay attention to death from disease, but the more numerous correspondents in South Africa could turn aside from the action to report on typhoid epidemics and hospital care for the sick and wounded.

But then again, correspondents, like the public, thought in terms of total deaths, not death rates. They were appalled when 20,000 died in the Anglo–Boer War, 14,000 from disease alone. On the Nile, the disease death *rate* had been three times the South African level, but the actual number – 277 dead from all causes – was unimpressive; a mere 60 killed by the enemy on the Nile seemed insignificant, though, in fact, it was nearly double the number per thousand killed by the Boers (refer to Table 8.2).

What most surprised the public and the military leadership was the sheer size of the South African War. In the beginning, the expeditionary force was expected to be no more than 50,000 men, against a Boer force less than half that size. The ultimate force of more than 500,000 was completely off the scale of colonial campaigns. Some in Britain came, in the end, to think that the war should not have been fought at all, and many thought that it should have been fought differently; but the disease cost of the war was only one factor among many.

Once the scandals over hospitals and concentration camps had settled down, military medical opinion, most clearly represented by R.J.S. Simpson's medical history, held that the medical record was better than that of most recent wars.[40] The military medical establishment sought, however, to use the South African experience as a series of useful lessons for the future. The value of the lessons was to appear in such things as the way the Royal Army Medical Corps handled the threat of typhoid on the western front in the early months of the First World War.

---

[40] Simpson, *Medical History*, p. 46

Figure 8.3.   *Reynaud's Retrospect on French and British Colonial Campaigns*

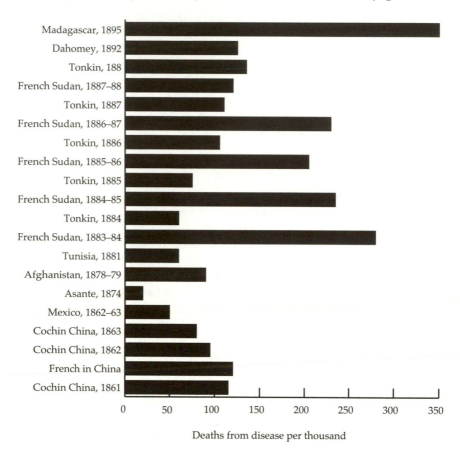

Deaths from disease per thousand

Evaluations of Disease in Colonial Warfare

In the last years of the century, a number of writers on military medicine looked back over the disease record of colonial warfare and began a kind of summing up of the experience. Gustave Reynaud, a French authority on tropical hygiene, published a comparative volume centered on the Malagasy expedition.[41] He dealt with a total of twenty expeditions – all French except for the British Asante campaign of 1874 and the British Afghanistan expedition of 1878–79 (refer to Figure 8.3 and Appendix Table A8.2). He was concerned with death rates by campaign – the cost of reaching a particular objective, not death rates over time – but all campaigns in his sample were shorter than a year, so that the comparisons had

[41] Gustave A. Reynaud, *Considerations sanitaires sur l'expédition de Madagascar et quelques autres expéditions coloniales, françaises et anglaises* (Paris, 1898).

Figure 8.4. British Medical Journal's *Appreciation of Past Campaign Mortality Rates, 1860–1898*

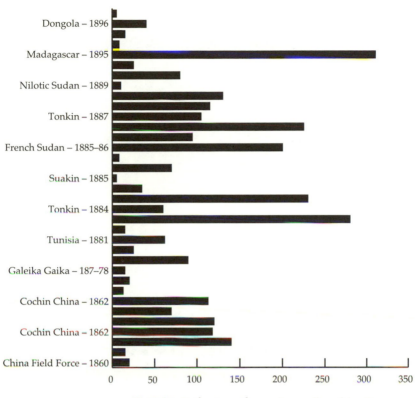

Campaign death rate per thousand, regardless of duration

some meaning. The implied criticism of French military medicine is clear, seen in Figure 8.3. Since the Asante expedition of 1874, campaign mortality had been rising until it reached its worst level ever, with Madagascar.

A second and similar survey was part of an unsigned article in the *British Medical Journal* in October 1898. The basic data were similar – death rates per thousand per campaign – but the purpose was different. This author was interested in the comparative record of the French and British medical authorities in tropical and subtropical campaigns back to 1860 (refer to Appendix Table A8.3). As published, the author arranged the data on eighteen British and eighteen French expeditions in order of rising death rates for each country, to show, among other things, that, except for the Afghanistan campaign of 1878–80, all British campaigns had lower mortality than the French. The data can be rearranged, however, as a single chart, showing campaign mortality through time (refer to Figure 8.4). The result is not identical with Reynaud's survey, but the

Figure 8.5.   *Trends in Monthly Mortality of European Troops on Campaign in Africa, 1823–1902*

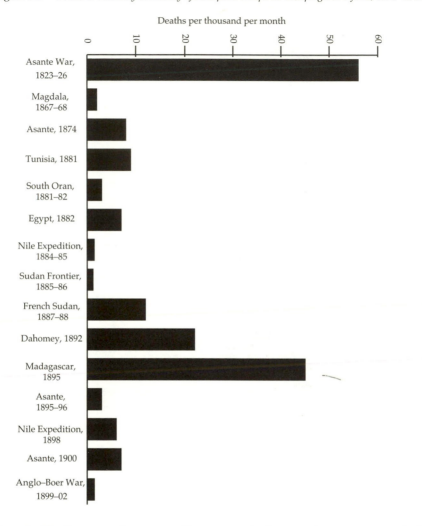

Deaths per thousand per month

clear indication was that mortality on tropical campaigns was not obviously falling with the passage of time.

These two surveys are important for what they show about contemporaneous opinion about the health of soldiers on campaign. Military victories attracted attention; the achievements of preventive medicine for
tropical garrisons did not. Even the medical press paid little attention to
the improvement in the heath of overseas garrisons in peacetime,
reflected decade after decade in reports on the health of troops in such
places as India or the Dutch East Indies. The popular press at large, however, noted the notorious losses to malaria in Madagascar or typhoid
fever in South Africa. One reason, therefore, that declining garrison death

Table 8.3. *Mortality from Disease in South Africa, Comparing Pre-war Peacetime with Campaign Death Rates, by Disease*

Mortality per thousand mean strength per year:

Disease	South Africa Annual Average 1884–98	Wartime Annual Average 1899–1902	Percent Increase in Wartime
Malaria	0.07	0.2	186
Enteric fever	2.37	18.06	662
Gastrointestinal	0.41	3.07	649
Liver Disease	0.38		
Tuberculosis	0.58		
Diseases of the:			
Nervous system	0.36		
Circulatory system	0.44		
Respiratory system	0.56		
Other	0.8	3.25	306
All Diseases	5.97	24.58	312
Accidents	1.33	0.98	-26
Enemy Action	0.07	12.53	17,800
Grand Total	7.37	38.09	417

Source:
Simpson, *Medical History*, pp. 8, 50–52.

rates were little encouragement for imperial adventures, was that the European public was not informed that they *were* declining.

While contemporary observers were more interested in disease deaths rates *by campaign*, another measure of the success of military medicine on tropical campaigns is to measure disease death rates per month. Figure 8.5 shows the comparative death rates for disease per month for the campaigns represented in this volume. Disease death rates measured in this way show no clear trend over time, though some particular distinctive campaigns stand out as much higher. Disease mortality on campaign in the late nineteenth century was highly variable but not notably diminishing. Even the Anglo–Boer War, which was a clear statistical improvement in retrospect, was seen as a medical disaster at the time.

Barracks and Campaign

Another measure of the efficiency of military medicine on campaign is to compare the peacetime disease death rates with those in wartime. Simpson

Table 8.4. *Mortality in Barracks and on Campaign in the Typhoid Campaigns*

Percentage Increase in Mortality on Campaign, Compared to Barracks Conditions

Major Causes of Death	Magdala 1867–68	Oran 1881–82	Tunisia 1881	French Sudan 1883–88	Dahomey 1892–93	Madagascar 1895	Upper Nile 1898	Gold Coast 1900	Anglo–Boer War 1899–1902
Typhoid fever		798	1,222	2,400	-	-	-	-	662
Malaria		95	147	443	-	-	1,156	-	186
Gastrointestinal		171	274	220	-	-	-	360	649
All Diseases	66	239	558	178	200	1,961	627	320	312

Sources:
Magdala, Table 3.1
French Sudan, Table 4.2
Oran and Tunisia: Peacetime control, death rate of all French troops stationed in Algeria, 1882–86.
Curtin, *Death by Migration*, Table A.27, p. 190.
Dahomey: Legrand, *L'hygiène des troupes*, pp. 412-13.
Madagascar, 1895. Comparison of campaign with disease deaths, 1897-1901 (Tables 7.1 and 7.2).
Upper Nile, Table 7.6.
Gold Coast, 1900, Tables 4.4 and 4.8.
South Africa, Table 8.1.

did this for South Africa by publishing the death data for British soldiers there for the fifteen years before the war broke out (refer to Table 8.3). South Africa is something of a special case, because the peacetime death rates were far lower than they were in tropical Africa, or even Algeria. In South Africa, nevertheless, the death rate from all disease approximately tripled in wartime, while the increase in deaths from the typhoid and gastrointestinal infections increased more than six-fold.

Similar data are not always available, but it is useful to look comparatively at the cases where data do exist, especially when it is possible to identify the disease groups that are responsible for the increased disease deaths on campaign (see Table 8.4). The examples are too few and too scattered to be more than suggestive, but a pattern of an increasing spread in the difference between barracks and campaign mortality rates is apparent up to the Nile expedition of 1898. This is, in short, an African manifestation of a continuing high disease mortality on campaign compared to the worldwide pattern of falling death rates in barracks.

The continuing high mortality on campaign outside of Africa is evident from Reynaud's survey and that of the BMJ. The real achievement in protecting troops in barracks in the tropical world was buried in the annual reports on the health of the armies. Between the 1860s and the 1890s, the annual disease death rate of British troops in India had dropped from 27 per thousand to 16 per thousand. That of French troops in peacetime Algeria had dropped from 16 per thousand to 11 per thousand. That of Dutch troops in the Dutch East Indies was down from 92 per thousand to 35 per thousand, and the conquest of Sumatra was still in progress in the 1890s.[42] These three armies were the largest European forces overseas in the second half of the nineteenth century.

Table 8.4 provides some explanation of the gap. The principal killers were malaria, typhoid fever, and gastrointestinal infections. In all cases, it was typhoid that increased most on campaign, followed by other waterborne infections. Malaria was a lesser problem, but in the long run much harder to control. A wealth of other evidence scattered through this book underlines a general proposition: that, although the importance of waterborne infection began to be recognized in Europe in the 1850s, practical applications were slow to come, even in barracks like those of lower Egypt. They were neglected even more on campaign until the early twentieth century, partly because the constraints of military action prevented their full application, but partly also because military authorities failed to realize that preventive medicine could be cost-effective in military terms.

Statistical evidence about disease and the conquest of Africa ends with the Anglo–Boer War. The data in Table 8.5 are indicative, though

[42] Curtin, *Death by Migration*, pp. 195, 200, 201.

Table 8.5. *Mortality of Europeans Garrisons in Africa, 1884–1913*

Death from Disease per thousand mean strength annually

Years	Egypt	Years	French West Africa	Madagascar
1886–1894	15.02	1897–1901		26.00
1895–1904	10.56	1903–1908	22.99	9.26
1909–1913	2.64	1909–1913	15.52	7.82

Years	South Africa	Years	British West Africa
1884–1898	7.37	1897–1904	21.94
1904–1908	3.73	1903–1908	12.42
1909–1913	2.77	1909–1913	4.87

Source:
Table A4.2, table 5.2, table 7.2, AMSR (annual series).

the changes they indicate were not tested in campaign conditions that left a record. In British West Africa between 1897–1904 and 1909–13, the death rate from disease fell by 76 percent over only two decades. The victory over typhoid fever in Egypt was even more impressive, with a reduction of typhoid deaths from 6.36 per thousand in 1883 to none at all in 1913, and the decline in barracks death rates in South Africa was similar. On Madagascar as well, the French military doctors, who had experienced in 1895 the worst death rates of any campaign in Africa, had achieved by 1903–13 an annual disease death rate of less than 8 per thousand.[43]

Just as the South African War was not typical of other wars for the conquest of Africa, its influence on policy was not typical of the earlier campaigns. The contrast between the public reaction to disease losses on the Nile and in South Africa was indicative. In spite of a higher rate of loss, the Nile expedition provoked no shadow of negative public reaction to the conduct of military medicine, and no shadow of a brake on enthusiasm for imperial expansion. The South African war ended British enthusiasm for imperial expansion in Britain, for a variety of reasons, of which the typhoid epidemics and the concentration camps were two among many.

More important for military medicine, the South African War provoked a flare of publicity that gave medical reformers a hearing. The epidemics at Bloemfontein and Ladysmith, plus the deaths in the concentration camps –

---

[43] Curtin, "The End of the 'White Man's Grave'? Nineteenth-Century Mortality in West Africa," *Journal of Interdisciplinary History*, 21:63–88 (1990), p. 80.

together with the spread of information about the progress of scientific medicine generally – brought home the lesson that the lack of pure water and proper sanitation cost lives. The publicity was among the influences that enabled RAMC to reform the practice of military medicine as never before. This is, in short, another variant of the proposition that the conquest of Africa did far more to bring about the improvement of tropical medicine than that the improvements in tropical medicine caused the conquest of Africa.

RETROSPECT

Before the 1850s, disease set limits on European activity in tropical Africa. Many informed Europeans understood that "fevers" took about 25 percent of the visitors from Europe in any year. At this price, it is a wonder that any Europeans at all could be persuaded to go to tropical Africa, in spite of the potential wealth flowing first from the gold trade and then from the slave trade. The explanation is that, then and later, the statistical risk of death from disease was rarely fully known to those who risked their lives. For that matter, life expectancy in Europe itself was less than half what it is today. Those who knew the risk made their own evaluation of costs and benefits, and those evaluations rarely accord with what we see looking back from the end of the twentieth century.

As the slave trade declined, the value of what trade remained could justify only limited European activity. In time, the Dutch and Danes withdrew from their trading posts. The British and French governments tried occasionally to limit official activity in West Africa, but strategic withdrawal, when attempted, was brief and half-hearted. This pattern was remarkable; while individuals seeking wealth might well gamble against long odds, European governments knew better the cost measured in the death rate of officials and soldiers; and they should have been able to calculate the risks to their own political life. Yet they kept on. Looking back from the late twentieth century, when a few deaths of UN peacekeepers could be a significant political issue, it is amazing that European leaders could sacrifice so many lives for such an insignificant national advantage, or, having done so, that the public protest was no more significant. The most general explanation is that politicians and the European ruling class as a whole, placed a low value on the life of their own working class, and a lower value still on the lives of foreigners and colonial subjects. The incidence of death from disease was also far higher than it is today, and death in the prime of life was more expected.

Between the 1840s and 1860s, the sharp drop in disease death rates of soldiers overseas introduced a new phase in the history of European military disease in the overseas world generally, but there is little evidence that military planners of the 1860s and 1870s paid serious attention to the change. Those who planned the Magdala and Kumasi expeditions seem to have had a general impression of improving disease mortality; but they knew nothing about the disease environment of the Ethiopian highlands, and they planned the attack on Asante in the face of abundant recent evidence that disease mortality on the Gold Coast was very high indeed. They launched the expedition knowing the danger, but with careful planning to prevent disease in the light of current medical knowledge; and they achieved a lower death rate than anyone had a right to expect.

In retrospect, it is hard to avoid the conclusion that the military medical success of these two expeditions depended more on luck than on medical skill or on foresight. The planners were mainly impelled by their own professional and political concerns, such as a wish to demonstrate the value of recent military reforms – the post-rebellion reform of the Indian Army and the Cardwell reforms of the army at home. Both reforms had medical aspects, but these were not central to the reformers' concerns.

Yet the medical achievements of these two expeditions were accepted by the public as revolutionary changes in the ability to deal with tropical disease. The Ethiopian success was made possible by an uniquely benign topical disease environment, combined with official disregard for the very high death rate of the Indian followers. In the Asante case, the measure of success was officially exaggerated, but, through a combination of good luck and good planning, it marked a record for disease deaths in tropical Africa that was to stand for the rest of the century.

These expeditions on the eve of the scramble for Africa clearly had *some* permissive influence on the drive for empire. As late as the 1890s, advocates of imperial advance still cited them as examples of the low disease cost of empire building, though abundant evidence of other recent and high-cost expeditions was also available. The press, however, rarely drew attention to the military's medical failings, in the way it praised the achievements on the march to Kumasi or Magadala.

Elsewhere, the death rate of soldiers overseas in barracks continued to decline, even after the sharp drop in mid-century, but the decline was more gradual. From the 1860s to the 1890s, the peacetime disease death rate dropped only at an annual rate of 0.9 to 1.6 percent, compared to 3 to 4 percent in mid-century. This modest gain, spread over several decades, attracted little attention in France or Britain, even from the medical press. The general press during these decades of the conquest of Africa wrote about campaigns, not barracks life, and the disease record of on campaign showed no notable improvement.

Then, between the 1890s and 1909–13, the germ theory of disease became an effective tool, and the mortality record for garrisons overseas improved more rapidly than ever, at 3.88 to 5.5 percent per year.[1] These

---

[1] Curtin, *Death by Migration*, p. 80.

rates of improvements included troops stationed in Africa (refer to Table 8.4). But by that time, the conquest of Africa was essentially finished; the triumphs of tropical medicine made Africa cheaper to administer, not cheaper to conquer.

The more significant question is not whether tropical medicine caused imperialism, but why European expeditionary armies profited so little from the new medical knowledge? In 1874, after all, orders for the march on Kumasi called for compulsory prophylactic quinine and for all drinking water to be boiled and filtered. It wasn't done perfectly, of course, but most later expeditions did it still less perfectly.

Part of the explanation is ordinary inefficiency combined with an unawareness of hygiene at all levels of European society. Even today, otherwise intelligent and responsible people can be careless about routine health precautions. A century ago, several sets of elaborate rules for tropical hygiene were available, but even trained physicians took them less seriously than they do today. The public seems to have regarded them no more seriously than the danger of walking under a ladder or planning activities on Friday the thirteenth.

For that matter, medical education underemphasized hygiene in favor of the clinical treatment of the patients who applied for help. Public health was just beginning to enter medical thinking. Curiously enough, the beginning of public health education on any scale was in the training of army doctors at Netley or Val-de-Grâce, or equivalent institutions elsewhere in Europe, America, and Japan, even through the ultimate objective of military medicine had to be tuned to the achivement of military victory. Many of the most significant advances in preventive medicine, and not only for the tropics, were made by army doctors or others on overseas assignments whose work involved research as well as clinical practice.

Military officers had another kind of training. They were selected for qualities such as dash, bravery, and the willingness to take risks that would win battles. Military reformers in the late nineteenth century, like Sir Garnet Wolseley, were concerned that new technology required new attitudes and a new kinds of military education, and this included preventive medicine, though still subbordinate to the main task of victory in the field. Other military leaders simply neglected the measures contemporaneous military medicine could provide, with a peak of irresponsibility in the French campaign in Madagascar in 1895.

Politicians were schooled in still another set of attitudes – to respond to the weight of public opinion within the ruling class of their respective countries, and to win elections. If their generals won battles, politicians were anxious to get the credit. If generals lost wars, politicians sometime lost office, as Gladstone did after Wolseley failed to "rescue" Gordon in 1885. If the soldiers suffered from disease, it rarely came to public notice; and, if it did, it was easy to blame the Medical Department, not the commanding general.

Even in the British hospital scandals of 1882 and 1900, critics came down on failure to care adequately for sick soldiers, not on the failure to prevent them from getting sick in the first place.

In the half-century before the First World War, furthermore, the European public forum was concerned with other issues. The 1880s and 1890s was the period of frenzied international competition for empire overseas, in which the conquest of Africa was only one theater of operations. The technological stars were the new weapons that brought cheap victory against those who still had no access to them – until the Anglo-Boer War showed what would happen if others were armed in the same way.

Even more, these campaigns took place in a European mood of increasingly emotional nationalism. This political mood was part of the European social pathology that was to permit the slaughter of 1914–18 in the European war. Given the tolerance for the destructiveness of modern warfare, it is small wonder that the European public or European politicians only a generation earlier cared so little about the death from disease of a few thousand soldiers on campaign in distant Africa.

APPENDIX TABLES

Table A1.1. *Monthly Malaria Morbidity, Tivaouane Senegal, 1961–62*

Month	Cases
January	94
February	48
March	18
April	5
May	49
June	1
July	574
August	641
September	1175
October	769
November	335
December	138

Source:
Delmont, "Paludisme et variations climatique," p. 125.

Table A5.1. *The Rise of Typhoid in Great Britain, France, Algeria, and India, 1860–1913*

	Typhoid Deaths per Thousand Mean Strength per Year					
Period of Averaging	1860–67	1869–77	1879–84	1886–94	1895–1904	1909–13
Central Year	1863	1872.5	1881	1889.5	1899	1911
Great Britain	0.25	0.20	0.18	0.27	0.21	0.06
India	1.11	1.44	1.51	5.11	5.62	0.62
Period of Averaging	1862–66	1872–76	1882–86	1892–96	1902–06	1909–13
Central Year	1864	1874	1884	1894	1904	1911
France	1.93	3.40	4.34	0.98	0.59	0.27
Algeria	2.60	3.50	4.10	3.66	2.74	1.50

Note:
Indian data before 1879–84 are for all Madras Presidency only.
Data for Great Britain and India before 1879–84 are estimated by subdividing the category "continued fevers" according to the proportion of typhoid to other continued fevers in 1879–84.

Source:
Curtin, *Death by Migration*, Appendix Tables.

Table A5.2. *The Health of British Troops in Egypt, by Station, 1883–1905*

Rates per thousand, mean strength

Year	Alexiandria						Cairo					
	Typhoid Case Fatality	Percent Typhoid Deaths	Total Admissions	Typhoid Admissions	Total Deaths	Typhoid Deaths	Typhoid Case Fatality	Percent Typhoid Deaths	Total Admissions	Typhoid Admissions	Total Deaths	Typhoid Deaths
1888	19.96	60.1	1027	28.30	9.4	5.65	20.57	37.38	1090	29.80	16.4	6.13
1889	7.71	33.39	834	24.00	5.54	1.85	11.01	36.38	1020	47.70	14.43	5.25
1890	14.64	57.96	1186	105.00	26.52	15.37	10.74	19.97	913	12.10	6.51	1.30
1891	11.18	33.43	1182	10.20	3.41	1.14	17.56	30.19	917	13.50	7.85	2.37
1892	28.56	84.64	1200	84.10	28.38	24.02	17.33	30.74	944	14.60	8.23	2.53
1893	21.93	21.17	1358	10.90	11.29	2.39	25.90	39.64	1356	21.20	13.85	5.49
1894	8.42	22.14	1141	20.20	7.68	1.70	21.44	55.01	1028	21.50	8.38	4.61
1895	10.00	33.45	917	9.30	2.78	0.93	18.13	36.34	931	19.30	9.63	3.50
1896	11.69	14.52	903	7.70	6.20	0.90	21.51	33.22	803	13.25	8.58	2.85
1897	14.26	9.04	889	6.10	9.62	0.87	30.56	29.22	674	7.20	7.53	2.20
1898	24.43	15.99	869	8.60	13.14	2.10	24.66	21.29	663	6.61	7.66	1.63
1899	30.03	20.00	848	11.09	16.65	3.33	17.61	13.62	651	6.02	7.78	1.06
1900	11.86	58.33	881	62.30	12.67	7.39	28.52	22.25	747	2.70	3.46	0.77
1901	36.05	56.25	1078	25.60	16.41	9.23	22.00	26.46	747	14.00	11.64	3.08
1902	14.29	27.30	809	22.60	11.83	3.23	22.89	34.40	624	15.90	10.58	3.64
1903	22.26	25.00	634	8.40	7.48	1.87	22.07	14.22	710	2.90	4.5	0.64
1904	44.46	49.94	520	9.20	8.19	4.09	19.89	28.55	699	9.00	6.27	1.79
1905	0.00	0.00	657	5.50	6.57	0.00	10.56	18.23	581	9.00	5.21	0.95

Notes: The reported statistics for morbidity and mortality in 1896 and 1898 are set aside in favor of interpolation to avoid the results of disease contracted in the Sudan campaign.

Source: AMSR (Annual series, volumes for 1883 through 1905)

Table A5.3. *Admissions and Death from Typhoid Fever among British Troops*
Stationed in Lower Egypt, 1883–1913

Rates per thousand, mean strength

Year	Deaths	Admissions	Case Fatalities Percent	Trend in Case Fatality	Tyhoid Death Percent of All Deaths
1883	6.33	32.70	19.36	22.18	18.18
1884	4.95	24.90	19.88	22.25	42.71
1885	10.86	45.05	24.10	22.32	52.40
1886	9.39	34.02	27.60	22.38	47.59
1887	6.63	28.38	23.36	22.45	43.76
1888	6.17	29.28	21.05	22.51	42.11
1889	4.16	40.08	10.37	22.58	35.90
1890	7.17	38.30	18.72	22.65	57.50
1891	2.84	12.60	22.54	22.71	39.17
1892	10.31	35.10	29.37	22.78	72.71
1893	5.32	20.50	25.95	22.84	39.12
1894	4.02	21.20	18.96	22.91	44.69
1895	7.99	16.87	47.35	22.98	36.12
1896	2.64	13.20	20.00	23.04	32.37
1897	1.85	6.90	26.81	23.11	22.24
1898	3.97	21.50	18.47	23.17	43.04
1899	1.61	7.25	22.21	23.24	15.89
1900	2.53	18.60	13.60	23.30	35.58
1901	4.62	16.90	27.34	23.37	36.01
1902	3.54	17.40	20.34	23.44	30.97
1903	0.96	4.30	22.33	23.50	18.64
1904	2.00	8.20	24.39	16.37	32.21
1905	0.54	6.70	8.06	15.17	9.52
1906	0.62	7.30	8.49	13.97	9.98
1907	0.19	5.30	3.58	12.76	3.99
1908	0.57	3.60	15.83	11.56	15.04
1909	0.73	3.80	19.21	10.36	17.34
1910	0.36	2.10	17.14	9.15	7.74
1911	0.18	2.53	7.13	7.95	4.34
1912	0.54	9.40	5.74	6.75	17.48
1913	0.00	1.07	0.00	5.55	0.00

Note:
Typhoid deaths are reported for cases acquired in lower Egypt only. Total deaths officially
reported for 1898 and 1899 include campaign deaths from the Omdurman campaign. They
are set aside in favor of interpolation from adjacent years.
Trend in Case-Fatality Rates is discontinuous, 1883–1903 and 1904–1913

Source:
AMSR reports (annual series).

Table A5.4. *British Troops Serving in Lower Egypt: Acclimization by Length of Service, 1891–95 and 1901–05*

	Admission rates per hundred mean strength Other rates per thousand mean strength				
Length of Service in Egyptian Command	Admissions	Deaths	Repatriated	D + I Index	Total Number in Category Over The Five Years
1891–95					
Under 1 year	124.18	9.73	11.57	21.30	10,891
From 1 to 2 years	107.62	12.32	21.29	33.61	5,683
From 2 to 3 years	84.08	6.03	21.70	27.73	2,488
From 3 to 4 years	71.25	12.67	16.57	29.24	1,026
From 4 to 5 years	40.29	7.19	16.79	23.98	417
Over 5 years	26.00	7.09	7.09	14.18	846
Total	109.01	10.62	14.44	25.05	18,081
1901–05					
Under 1 year	91.03	7.82	22.60	30.42	9,335
From 1 to 2 years	61.33	7.06	18.37	25.43	7,512
From 2 to 3 years	62.80	9.72	21.71	31.43	3,086
From 3 to 4 years	40.29	13.61	11.80	25.41	1,102
From 4 to 5 years	39.47	13.16	20.68	33.83	532
Over 5 years	30.83	3.95	21.74	25.69	506
Total	71.82	8.15	20.43	28.59	22,073

Source:
AMSR for 1891, p. 201; 1892, p.149; 1893, p. 157; 1894, p. 173; 1895, p.156.
AMSR for 1901, p. 225; 1892, p. 149; 1893, p. 157; 1894, p. 173; 1895, p. 156.

Table A5.5. *British Troops in Egypt, 1898–1905: Typhoid Admissions and Deaths by Age*

Admission rates per hundred mean strength
death rates per thousand mean strength

Age	Admissions	Deaths	Total Number in Category Over The Eight Years
Under 20 years	61	13	4,030
From 20 to 25 years	256	51	16,575
From 25 to 30 years	96	18	9,785
From 30 to 35 years	20	7	2,872
From 35 to 40 years	5	1	876
Over 40 years	1	0	207
Total	439	90	34,345

Source: AMSR for 1898, p. 265; for 1899, p. 228; for 1900, p. 246; for 1901, p. 226; for 1902, p. 262; for 1903, p. 296; for 1904, p. 38; for 1905, p. 263.

Table A5.6. *French Troops in France and North Africa: Mortality and Relocation Cost from Typhoid Fever, 1862–1912*

Mortality rates per thousand mean strength

| Year of Period of Averaging | Mortality | | Relocation Cost Percent |
	France	Algeria/Tunisia	
1862–66	1.93	2.60	135
1872–74	2.33	1.78	76
1875–79	3.13	4.00	128
1880–84	3.10	4.13	133
1885–89	1.98	4.25	215
1890–94	1.08	4.50	417
1895–99	1.03	4.10	398
1900	0.81	4.95	611
1901	0.63	3.56	565
1902	0.52	2.88	554
1903	0.72	4.03	560
1904	0.69	2.43	352
1905	0.41	1.88	459
1906	0.57	1.82	319
1907	0.53	1.35	255
1908	0.41	1.85	451
1909	0.47	1.08	230
1910	0.31	1.42	458
1911	0.46	1.57	341
1912	0.28	1.51	539

Source: For 1864, Curtin, *Death by Migration*, Appendix Table A.25, p. 188.
For 1873–1912, M. de Guerre, *Stastiques médicale*, volume for 1913, facing p. 128.

Table A8.1. *Reynauld's Retrospect on Mortality Rates of British and*
French Campaigns in the Tropics

Death rate from disease only, in deaths per thousand for the campaign

Campaign	Death Rate
Cochinchina, 1861	115.6
French in China, 1861	118.0
Cochinchina, 1862	93.3
Cochinchina, 1863	82.1
Mexico, 1862–63	53.0
Asante, 1874	18.0
Afghanistan, 1878–79	89.0
Tunisia,1881	61.0
French Soudan, 1883–84	280.0
Tonkin, 1884	60.0
French Soudan, 1884–85	225.0
Tonkin, 1885	75.0
French Soudan, 1885–86	200.0
Tonkin, 1886	99.0
French Soudan, 1886–87	221.0
Tonkin, 1887	106.0
French Soudan, 1887–88	116.0
Tonkin, 1888	133.0
Dahomey, 1892	121.0
Madagascar, 1895	334.0

Source:
Reynaud, *Madagascar*, pp. 471–73

Note:
Some data are annual. Others are for periods as short as two months, in the case of the Asante campaign of 1874.

Table A8.2. *British Medical Journal Comparison of England and French Campaigns, 1860–1897*

	British Army			French Army	
Date	Campaign	Deaths from Disease per Thousand	Date	Campaign	Deaths from Disease per Thousand
1860	China Field Force	14.9	1861	Cochin China	140.0
1860	China (Talienwan)	5.4	1862	Cochin China	117.0
1867–68	Ethiopian	12.1	1862	China (French)	118.0
1874	Asante	17.4	1862–63	Mexico	71.0
1870	Zululand	24.8	1863	Cochin China	107.0
1878–79	Afganistan	93.7	1881	Tunisia	61.0
1882	Egypt	5.7	1883–84	French Sudan	280.0
1877–78	Galeika Gaika	14.0	1884	Tonkin	60.0
1884	Suakin	nil	1884–85	French Sudan	225.0
1884–85	Nilotic Sudan	36.4	1885	Tonkin	75.0
1885–86	Nilotic Sudan	4.1	1885–86	French Sudan	200.0
1885	Suakin	2.2	1886	Tonkin	99.0
1889	Nilotic Sudan	6.0	1886–87	French Sudan	220.0
1895	Chitral	25.1	1887	Tonkin	106.0
1895–96	Asante	5.6	1887–88	French Sudan	116.0
1896	Matabeleland	16.5	1888	Tonkin	133.0
1896	Dongola	46.6	1892	Dahomey	87.0
1896–97	Mashonaland	2.0	1895	Madagascar	302.0

Source:
The British Medical Journal, 1898, 2, p. 691 (October 1).

Table A8.3. *Monthly Disease Rates in Conquest of Africa*

Deaths from disease per month per thousand mean strength

Campaign	Deaths
Asante War, 1823–26	55.69
Magdala,1867–68	3.01
Asante 1874	8.70
Tunisia, 1881	10.55
South Oran, 1881–82	3.57
Egypt 1882	7.41
Nile Expedition, 1884–85	2.53
Sudan Frontier, 1885–86	2.27
French Sudan 1887–88	13.22
Dahomey, 1892	22.21
Madagascar, 1895	44.67
Asante 1895–96	3.88
Nile Expedition, 1898	6.40
Asante 1900	7.68
Anglo–Boer War, 1899–02	2.05

Sources:
Asante War, 1824–26, PP. 1840 [228], p. 19.
Others, preceding tables.

BIBLIOGRAPHY

Abir, Mordechai, *Ethiopia in the Era of the Princes: The Challenge of Islam and the Re-unification of the Christian Empire 1769–1855* (London: Longmans, 1968).

Ackerknecht, Erwin H., "Broussais and a Forgotten Medical Revolution," *Bulletin of the History of Medicine*, 27:320–43 (1957).

Amelineau, François, "Désastre sanitaire," *Revue historique des armées*, 41–51 (1992).

Anon., "Reminiscences of the Gold Coast, Being Extracts from Notes Taken during a Tour of Service in 1847–48," *Colburn's United Service Magazine*, 3:587 (1850).

Anon., "Army Medical Efficiency: Mortality of French and British Military Expeditions," *British Medical Journal*, 1898, ii, 991–92.

Anon., "Statistiques coloniale. Mortalité des troupes," *Revue coloniale*, 10(2nd ser.):473–81 (1853).

Archinard, Louis, *Soudan français en 1888–89* (Paris, 1889).

Armitage, C.H., and A.F. Montaro, *The Ashanti Campaign of 1900* (London, 1902).

Ash, R. Vacy, "The Epidemic of Enteric Fever in the Transvaal, Zulu, and Egyptian Wars Compared," BMJ, 1883(1), pp. 2–4, (July 7).

Atteridge, A. Hilliard. *The Wars of the Nineties* (London: Cassel, 1899).

Baden-Powell, R.S.S., *The Downfall of Prempeh: A Diary of Life with the Native Levy in Ashanti, 1895–96* (London, 1900).

Baker, T. H., "Yellow-Jack. The Yellow Fever Epidemic of 1878 in Memphis, Tennessee," *Bulletin of the History of Medicine*, 42:241–64 (1968).

Balfour, Andrew, and H.H. Scott, *Health Problems of the Empire* (London, Collins, 1924).

Baril, Claude, *Souvenirs d'une expédition au Sénégal, pendant l'épidémie de la fièvre jaune, en 1878* (Paris, 1883, thesis no. 200).

"Une page d'histoire médicale. Rapport sur l'éxpedition militaire au Logo (Soudan, 1878) et l'épidemie de fièvre jaune qui la termina," *Archives de Médicine et de Pharmacie Coloniale*, 33:241–301 (1935)

Barry, Boubacar, *Le royaume du Waalo: le Senegal avant la conquête*, new ed. (Paris: Karthala, 1985).

Barthélemy, P., "La guerre de Dahomey: histoire médicale du 1re groupe de la colonne expéditionaire de Dahomey, 1892," AMN, 609:161–206 (1893).

Bates, Darrell,*The Abyssinian Difficulty: The Emperor Theodorus and the Magdala Campaign 1867–68* (Oxford: Oxford Univerisy Press, 1979).

Berg, Gerald, "Sacred Acquisitions: Andrianampoinimerina at Ambohimanga, 1777–1790," JAH, 29:191–211 (1988.

Biss, Harold C.J., *The Relief of Kumasi* (London, 1904).

Bonnafy, "Statistique Médicale de la Cochinchine (1861–1888)," AMN, 67:161–96 (1897)

"L'armée coloniale," *Bulletin de la société de géographie commericale du Havre*, 1900–01:13–26, 91–110 (1900–01).

Borius, Alfred, "Topographie médicale du Sénégal," AMN, 33:114– ,270– , 321– , 416– ; 34:1278– ,330–, 340– ; 35:114– ,280– , 473– ; 36:117– ,321– ; 37:140– ,230– , 297– ,367– , 456– , 33: 438 (1879–82).

Black, W.T., "Medical Notes and Statistics of the British Expedition to Egypt in 1801," TMCSE, 2(2nd ser.) :11–23 (1882–83).

Blerzy, H.,"La guerre d'Abyssinie," *Revue des deux mondes*, 74:449 (1868).

Boyle, Frederick,*Through Fanteeland to Coomassie* (London, 1874).

Boyle, James, *A Practical Medico-Historical Account of the Western Coast of Africa* (London: 1831).

Brackenbury, Henry,*The Ashanti War: A Narrative Prepared from the Official Documents by Permission of Major-General Sir Garnet Wolsely. . .*, 2 vols. (London, 1874).

Bruce, David, "Analysis of the Results of Professor Wright's Method of Anti-Typhoid Inoculation," JRAMC, 4:244–55 (1905).

Bruce-Chwatt, Leonard Jan, *Essential Malariology* (London, 1980).

Bryson, Alexander, *Report on the Climate and Principal Diseases of the African Station* (London, 1847).

"On the Prophylactic Influence of Quinine," *Medical Times and Gazette*, 8(n.s.):6–7 (January 7, 1854).

Buckley, Roger Norman, *Slaves in Red Coast: The British West India Regiments, 1795–1815* (New Haven, 1979).

Burleigh, Bennett, *Two Campaigns: Madagascar and Ashantee* (London, 1897)

Buxton, Thomas Fowell, *The African Slave Trade* (London, 1839).

The Remedy, Being a Sequel to The African Slave Trade (London: 1840).

Burot, Fernand, and Maximilien Albert Legrand, *Les troupes colonialiaux. Statistiques de la mortalité. Maladies du soldat aux pays chauds. Hygiène du soldat sous les tropiques*, 3 vols. (Paris, 1897–89).

Bynum, Wiliam F., and Roy Porter, *Companion Encyclopedia of the History of Medicine*, 2 vols. (London: Routledge, 1993).

Cabasse, Albert Numa, *Notes sur une campagne au Gabon, à bord de l'hôpital flottant, La Cordeliere, en 1873 et 1874* (Commercy, 1876).

Cain, P.J., and A.G. Hopkins, *British Imperialism: Innovation and Expansion 1688–1919* (London: Longman, 1993).

Campbell, Gwyn, "Slavery and Fanompoana: The Structure of Forced Labour in Imerina (Madagascar), 1790–1861," JAH, 29:463–86 (1988).

Cantlie, Neil, *A History of the Army Medical Department*, 2 vols. (London and Edinburgh, 1974).

Carbonnel, P.F.A.T., *De la mortalité actuelle au Sénégal et particulièrement à Saint-Louis* (Paris, thesis no. 10, 1873).

Chaudoye, "La fièvre typhoïde dans la garnison et dans la ville de Tébessa de 1890 à 1906." AMPM, 50:169–97 (1909).

Chaulliac, G.,"Contribution à l'étude médico-militaire de l'expédition de Madagascar en 1895," *Bulletin de Madagascar*, 240:411–41, 241:507–51, 242:624–40, 243:722–40 (1966).

Churchill, Winston, *The River War; an Historical Account of the Reconquest of the Soudan* (London: Longmans, Green, 1899).

Claridge, W. Walton, *A History of the Gold Coast and Ashanti*, 2 vols. (London, 1915).

Coat, Marcel, "La préparation de l'expedition," *Revue historique des armées*, 24–27 (1992).

Colbourne, M.J. and F.N. Wright, "Malaria in the Gold Coast," *West African Medical Journal*, 4:3–17, 161–174 (1955).

Cole, Juan R., *Colonialism and Revolution in the Middle East: Socila and Cultural Origins of Egypt's 'Urabi Movement* (Princeton: Princeton University Press, 1993).

Colin, Léon, *Traité des fièvres intermittentes* (Paris, 1870)

"L'expédition anglaise de la côte d'or: étude d'hygiène militaire et de géographie médicale," GHMC, 11(2nd ser.):37–40, 52–54 (1894).

Coluzzi, Mario, "Advances in the Study of Afrotropical Malaria Vectors," *Parassitologia*, 35(Suppl.):23–29 (1993).

"Malaria and the Afrotropical Ecosystems: Impact of Man-Made Environmental Changes," *Parassitologia* 36:1223–27 (1994).

Colebrook, Leonard, *Almroth Wright: Provocative Doctor and Thinker* (London: Heinemann, 1954).

Coleman, William, *Yellow Fever in the North: The Methods of Early Epidemiology* (Madison: University of Wisconsin Press, 1987).

Cope, Zachary, *Almroth Wright: Founder of Modern Vaccine-therapy* (London: Nelson, 1966).

Claridge, W. Walton, *A History of the Gold Coast and Ashanti*, 2 vols. (London, 1964).

Crummey, Donald, "Tewodros as Reformer and Modernizer," *Journal of African History*, 10:457–469 (1968).

Currie, C.B., "Medical History of the Abyssinian Expedition," AMSR, 9:277–99 (1867).

Curtin, Philip D., "The White Man's Grave: Image and Reality, 1780–1850," *Journal of British Studies*, 1:94–110 (1961).

The Image of Africa (Madison: University of Wisconsin Press, 1964).

Economic Change in Precolonial Africa: Senegambia in the Era of the Slave Trade, 2 vols. (Madison: University of Wisconsin Press, 1975).

Death by Migration: Europe's Encounter with the Tropical World in the Nineteenth Century (New York: Cambridge University Press, 1989).

The End of the 'White Man's Grave'? Nineteenth-Century Mortality in West Africa," *Journal of Int erdisciplinary History*, 21:63–88 (1990).

"Malarial Immunities in Nineteenth-Century West Africa and the Caribbean," *Parassitologia*, 36:69–82 (1994).

Czernicki, "La fièvre typhoïde au corps d'occupation de Tunisie en 1881," AMPM, 2:397–416 (1882).

D'Anthouard, "L'Expédition de Madagascar: Journal de M. D'Anthouard, 26 octobre-26 novemebre 1894," *Revue de l'histoire des colonies françaises*, 18:225–78 (1930).

Darricarrère, Jean, *Au pays de la fièvre* (Paris, 1904).

Davies, A.M. "Enteric Fever on Campaigns – Its Prevalence and Causation," TSICHD, 8:84–96 (1891), pp. 84–86.

Davies, K.G., "The Living and the Dead: White Mortality in West Africa, 1684–1732," in Stanley L. Engerman and Eugene D. Genovese, *Race and Slavery in the Western Hemisphere: Quantitative Studies* (Princeton, 1975), pp. 83–98.

Delmas, L., "Relation médico-chirurgicale de la campagne du Sud-Oranais en 1881–1882," AMPM, 10;81–111,187–204 (1887)

Delmont, Jean, "Paludisme et variations climatiques saisonnière en savanne soudanienne d'Afrique de l'Ouest," *Cahiers d'études africaines*, 22:11–34 (1983).

De Singly, Charles, *L'infantrie de marine* (Paris, 1890).

Deschamps, Hubert, *Quinze ans de Gabon: les débuts de l'établissement français,1839–1853,* (Paris, Société française d'histoire d'outre-mer, 1965).

Dickinson, Nodes, *Observations on the Inflamatory Endemic . . . Commonly called Yellow Fever* (London, 1819).

Doughty, E., *Observations and Inquiries into the Nature of Yellow Fever* (London, 1816).

Dowling, Harry F., *Fighting Infection: Conquests of the Twentieth Century* (Cambridge: Harvard University Press, 1977).

Duchesne, Charles, "Rapport au Ministre de la Guerre 25 avril 1896...sur l'expédition de Madagascar (1895–96)," *Journal officiel*, 1896:4099–5114, 5130–5140, 5158–5169 (September 1896).

Dunn, Ross E., *Resistance in the Desert: Moroccan Responses to French Imperialism, 1881–1912* (Madison: Uniersity of Wisconsin Press, 1977).

Duval, Pierre-Emmanuel, *Gorée considéré comme foyer de fièvre jaune au Sénégal; imminence de l'importation en France* (Bordeaux: Imprimerie nouvelle A. Bellier, 1883, thesis no. 24).

Earle, Carville V., "Environment, Disease, and Mortality in Early Virginia," in Thad W. Tate and David L. Ammerman, *The Chesapeake in the Seventeenth Century* (Chapel Hill: University of North Carolina Press, 1979), pp. 96–125.

Ellis, Stephen, *The Rising of the Red Shawls: A Revolt in Madagascar, 1895–1899* (Cambridge, 1985).

Esoavelomandroso, Manassé, "Le myhe d'Andriba," *Omaly sy Anio* (Antananarivo), 1–2:43–73 (1975).

Fabre, Albert (ed.), *Histoire de la médicine aux armées*. 2 vols. (Paris: Lavauzelle, 1984)

Farley, John, *Bilharzia: A History of Imperial Tropical Medicine* (Cambridge: Cambridge University Press, 1991).

Fage, John D. *Ghana: A Historical Interpretation* (Madison: University of Wisconsin Press, 1959).

Faure, Claude, "La garnison européene du Sénégal et la recrutement des primières troupes noires," *Revue de l'histoire des colonies*, 5:5–108 (1920).

Findlay, G.M. and T.H. Davey, "Yellow Fever in the Gambia," *Transactions of the Royal Society of Tropical Medicine and Hygiene*, 29:667–678 (1936).

Firth, R.H., "Report of the Progress of Hygiene from the year 1900–01," AMSR, 42:369–98 (1900).

Feinberg, H.M., "New Data On European Mortality in West Africa; The Dutch On The Gold Coast, 1719–1760," *Journal of African History*, 15: 362–67 (1974).

Fortescue, John William, *A History of the British Army* 12 vols. (London: Macmillan, 1930).

France, *Journal Officiel, Debats parlementaire*.

France. Ministère de Guerre. *Statistiques médicale de l'armée metropolitaine et de l'armée coloniale* (Paris, 1862+).

France. Ministère de la Marine et des Colonies, *Sénégal et Niger. La France dans l'Afrique occidentale 1879–83*, 2 vols. (Paris, 1884).

Galliéni, Joseph, *Voyage au Soudan français (Haut-Sénégal et pays de Ségou), 1879–1881* (Paris: Hachette, 1883)

Deux campagnes au Soudan français, 1886–1888 (Paris: Hachette, 1891).

Gallagher, John, and Ronald Robinson, "The Imperialism of Free Trade," *Economic History Review*, 6(2nd ser):1–15 (1953).

Galbraith, John S., and Afaf Lutfi el-Sayyid-Marsot, "The British Occupation of Egypt: Another View" *International Journal of Middle Eastern Studies*, 9:471–88 (1978).

Ganiage, Jean, *Les origines du Protectorat français en Tunisie (1861–1881)* (Paris: Presses universitaires de France, 1959)

Gardiner, W.A., "Sanitary Report of the Gold Coast, Including Likewise a Short Account of the Expedition against Ashanti," AMSR, 5:323–38 (1863).

Genebrias de Boisse, Jean. *Étude sur une épidémie de fièvre jaune à bord des bâtiments de l'état (Sénégal 1881)* (Paris, Ollier-Henry, 1884, thesis no. 52).

Gifford, Prosser, and William Roger Louis, *France and Britain in Africa: Imperial Rivalry and Colonial Rule* (New Haven, Yale University Press, 1971).

Giraud, T., "Le pays du Bénin," AMN, 55:376–89, 401–23 (1891).

Gore, Albert A., "Leaves from my Diary During the Ashantee War," BMJ, 1, 1874, pp. 377, 572.

A Contribution to the Medical History of Our West African Campaigns (London, 1876).

"Our First Campaign in Egypt," *Dublin Journal of Medical Science*, 84(3rd ser.):177–90 (1888).

Grandidier, *Le Myre de Vilers, Duchesne, et Gallieni: quarante années de l'histoire de Madagascar, 1880–1920* (Paris: Société d'éditions géographique, maritimes, et coloniales, 1923).

Great Britain, Admiralty, *Instruction for Surgeons of the Royal Navy* ([London], 1814).

Great Britain, Admiralty, *Statistical Reports of the Health of the Navy* (annual series).

Great Britain, Parliamentary Sessional Papers, *Statistical Reports on the Sickness, Mortality, & Invaliding, Among the Troops in Western Africa, St. Helena, The Cape of Good Hope, and Mauritius* (London, 1840).

Griffon du Bellay, "Rapport médical sur le service de l'hopital flottant la *Caravane* mouillé au rade du Gabon, comprenant une period de deux années (du 1er novembre 1861 au 1er novembre 1863), AMN, 1:14–80 (1864).

Guillot, Luc, *La fièvre typhoïde pendant l'expédition de Tunisie* (Paris, thesis no. 49, 1882).

Hamon, J. and J. Cos, "Épidémiologie générale du paludisme humain en Afrique occidentale. Répartition et fréquence des parasites et des vecteurs," *Bulletin de la société de pathologie éxotique*, 59:466–83 (1966).

Hanbury, J.A., "Medical History of the War in Egypt," AMSR, 22:205–62 (1881).

Hardy, Anne, "Water and the Search for Public Health in London in the Eighteenth and Nineteenth Centuries," MH, 28:250–82 (1984).

Epidemic Streets: Infectious Disease and the Rise of Preventive Medicine, 1856–1900 (Oxford: Clarendon Press, 1993).

Hargreaves, John, *West Africa Partitioned*, 2 vols. (Madison: University of Wisconsin Press, 1985).

Hart, Ernest, "Letters from the East," BMJ, 1885, 1, 619–, 672–, 754–, 810–, 857–.

Headrick, Daniel R., *The Tools of Empire: Technology and European Imperialism in the Nineteenth Century* (New York: Oxford University Press, 1981).

Hobson, William, *World Health and History* (Bristol, 1963). p. 95.

Hoffman, Stephen L., "Typhoid Fever," in G. Thomas Strickland, *Hunter's Tropical Medicine*, 6th ed. (Philadelphia, 1984), pp. 282–297.

Holland, T.J., and H.M. Hozier, *Records of the Expedition to Abysinia Compiled by Order of the Secretary of State for War* (London, HMSO, 1870).

Holt, P. M., and M.W. Daly, *A History of the Sudan from the Coming of Islam to the Present Day*, 4th ed. (London: Longman, 1988).

Home, Anthony D., "Medical History of the War in the Gold Coast Protectorate in 1873," AMSR, 15:217–59 (1873).

Hooker, J.R., "The Foreign Office and the Abyssinian Captives," *Journal of African History*, 2:259–71 (1961).

Hopkins, A.G., "The Victorians and Africa: A Reconsideration of the Occupation of Egypt, 1882," JAH, 27:363–91 (1986).

Hopkins, Donald R., *Princes and Peasants: Smallpox in History* (Chicago: Chicago University Press, 1983).

Horton, James Africanus Beale, *Letters on the Political Condition of the Gold Coast* (London, 1870).

Howard, L.O., "A Contribution to the Study of the Insect Fauna of Human Excrement," *Proceedings of the Washington Academy of Science*, 2:51–604 (1900).

Huas, P.C.V., *Considerations sur l'hygiène des troupes en campagne dans les pays intertropicaux* (Bordeaux, thesis no. 17, 1886).

Humphreys, Margaret, *Yellow Fever in the South* (New Brunswick: Rutgers University Press, 1992).

Kanya-Forstner, Alexander Sydney, *The Conquest of the Western Sudan: A Study in French Military Imperialism* (Cambridge, 1969).

"The French Marines and the Conquest of the Western Sudan, 1880–1899," in J. H. De Moor and H. L. Weselling, *Imperialism and War* (Leiden: Brill, 1989).

Keisser, Prosper Léonard,*Souvenirs médicaux de quatre campagnes du transport a la côte occidentale d'Afrique (Sénégal et Gabon)*, (Bordeaux, Seudre et Arièges, thesis no. 31, 1885).

Kermorgant, A., "Prophylaxie du paudisme," AHMC, 9:18–46 (1906), p. 28.

Kimble, David, *A Political History of Ghana, 1850–1928* (Oxford: Clarendon Press, 1963).

Kuczynski, Robert R., *Demographic Survey of the British Colonial Empire*, 5 vols. (London, 1948–).

Kuhnke, LaVerne, *Lives at Risk: Public Health in Nineteenth-Century Egypt* (Berkeley: University of California Press, 1990).

Laborde, V., "L'expédition de Madagascar au point de vue de la mortalité des troupes et ses causes," *Tribune médicale de Paris*, 28(2nd ser.):61–64 (1896).

Lacroix, Jean Bernard, *Les français au Sénégal au temps de la Compagnie des Indes de 1719 à 1758* (Vincennes: Service historique de la marine, 1986).

Laffont, "Rapport médical sur la campagne de 1887–1888 dans le Soudan français," AMN, 51:164–74, 259–93, 338–354, 426–(1889); AMN, 52:35–54, 122–143, 225–237 (1890).

Lémure, Jean, "Morbidité et moralité pendant l'expédition de Madagascar," AHPML, 34(3rd ser.):497–507 (1895).

"Les services sanitaires pendant l'expédition de Madagascar," AHPML, 35:97–111 (1896).

Madagascar: l'expédition au point de vue médicale et hygiènique (Paris, 1896).

"Les causes de la mortalité pendant l'expédition de Madagascar," AHPML, 35:5–17 (1896).

"Les measures hygiénique pendant l'expédition de Madagascar," AHPML, 35:223–42 (1896).

Lepers, J.P., P. Deloron, M.D. Andriamagatiana, J.A. Ramanamirija, "Newly Transmitted Plasmodiuum falciparum Malaria in Central Highland Plateaux of Madagascar: Assessment of Clinical Impact in a Rural Community," *Bulletin of the World Health Organization*, 68:217–11 (1990).

Laughlin, Larry W., "Schistosomiasis," in G. Thomas Strickland, *Hunter's Tropical Medicine*, 6th ed. (Philadelphia: Saunders, 1984), pp. 708–40.

Alphonse Laveran, *Traité des maladies et épidémies des armées*, 2 vols. (Paris, 1875).

Legrand, A.,*L'hygiène des troupes européenes aux colonies et dans les expéditions coloniales* (Paris, 1895).

Le Jemble, Alexandre, *Epidémiologie de la fièvre jaune au Sénégal pendant l'année 1878* (Paris: Alphonse Derenne, 1882, thesis no. 91).

Lehmann, Joseph H., *All Sir Garnet* (London, 1964).

Leishman, William B., "The Progress of Anti-Typhoid Inoculation in the Army," JRAMC, 8:463–71 (1907).

"Enteric Fevers in the British Expeditionary Force," JRAMC, 37:1–22 (1921).

Le Roy de Méricourt, A., and A. Layet, "Réunion et ile Maurice," DESM, 4(3rd ser.):258–507 (1877).

Lewin, Thomas J., *Asante Before the British: The Prempean Years, 1875–1900* (Lawrence: The Regents Press of Kansas, 1978).

Lloyd, Alan, *The Drums of Kumasi* (London, Longmans, 1948).

Lloyd, Christopher, and Jack L.S. Coulter, *Medicine and the Navy, 1200–1900*, 4 vols. (Edinburgh: Livingstone, 1957–1963).

Lonsdale, John, "The European Scramble and Conquest in African History," in J.D. Fage and Roland Oliver, *The Cambridge History of Africa* (Cambridge: Cambridge University Press, 1985), 6:680–766.

Luckin, Bill, "Evaluating the Sanitary Revolution: Typhus and Typhoid in London, 1851–1900," in Robert Woods and John Woodward, *Urban Disease and Mortality in Nineteenth-Century England* (London and New York, 1984), pp. 103–05.

Luxmoore, Percy P., "Ashantee: Extracts from the Journal of a Naval Officer Addressed to His Wife," *Blackwood's Edinburgh Magazine*, 115:518–524 (April 1874).

Mackenzie, A.G., "War Mortality in Recent Campaigns with Special Reference to the German Experience in the War of 1870–71, *Transactions of the Actuarial Society of Edinburgh*, pp. 137–54 (1881).

Manson, Patrick, *Tropical Diseases: A Manual of the Diseases of Warm Climates* (London, 1898).

Tropical Diseases: A Manual of the Diseases of Warm Climates, 2nd ed. (London, 1900).

Mbaeyi, Paul Mmenga, *British Military and Naval Forces in West African History, 1807–1874* (New York, Nok, 1978).

Markham, Clements R., *A History of the Abyssinian Expedition* (London: Prideux, 1869).

Marston, J.A., "Sanitary Report, Egyptian Expeditionary Force," AMSR for 1882, pp. 269–71.

Martin, Eveline C., *The British West African Settlements 1750–1821* (London: Longmans, Green and Co., 1927).

Marvaud, "La fièvre typhoïde au corps d'occupation en Tunisie," AMPM, 3:273–83 (1884).

Matthews, J. Rossen, "Major Greenwood versus Almroth Wright: Contrasting Visions of Scientific Medicine in Edwardian Britain," BHM, 69:30–43 (1995).

Maurice, J.F.,*The Ashantee War: A Popular Narrative* (London, 1874).

Metcalfe, George E., *Maclean of the Gold Coast: The Life and Times of George Maclean, 1801–47* (London: Oxford University Press, 1962).

Molinier, M., "Quelques remarques sur les filtres Chamberland en usage dans la colonne expéditionaire du Dahomey (1892)," AMN, 62:460–66 (1894).

Monath, Thomas P., "Yellow Fever, " in G. Thomas Strickland (ed.), *Hunter's Tropical Medicine,* 6th ed. (Philadelphia: Saunders, 1984) pp. 176–81.

Mouat, G. B., "Medical History of the Nile Expeditionary Force, from 18th March to 31st July 1885," AMSR, 26:279–97 (1884).

"Medical Notes from the Nile Expeditionary Force," BMJ, 1884, 2, p. 1157 (December 6).

Mouchet, J., S. Blanchy, A. Rakotonjanabelo, G. Raivoson, E. Rajaonarivelo, S. Laventure, M. Rossella, and F. Aknouche, "Stratification épidemiologique du paludisme à Madagscar," *Archives de l'institue Pasteur à Madagascar,* 60:50–59 (1993).

M'Dowell, E.G., "Medical Report of the Eastern Sudan Expeditionary Force, 1884," AMSR, 24:261–71.

M'William, J.O., *Medical History of the Expedition to the Niger River in 1841* (London, 1843).

Murchison, Charles, *A Treatise on the Continued Fevers of Great Britain,* 2nd ed. (London, 1871).

Myatt, Frederick, *The March to Magdala* (London, 1970).

Netter, Arnold, "Les inoculations préventives contre la fièvre typhoïde," *Bulletin de l'Institut Pasteur,* 4:873–83, 921–27, 969–80, 1024–34 (1906).

Newbury, Colin W., *The Western Slave Coast and its Rulers* (Oxford: Clarnedon Press, 1961).

Notter, J. Lane, *Spread and Distribution of Infectious Diseases; Spread of Typhoid Fever, Dysentery, and Allied Diseases among Large Communities, with Special Reference to Military Life in Tropical and Sub-Tropical Countries* (London and Manchester, 1904).

Osborne, Michael, "French Military Epidemiology and the Limits of the Laboratory: The Case of Louis-Félix Felsch," in Andrew Cunningham and Perry Williams, *The Laboratory Revolution in Medicine* (Cambridge: Cambridge University Press, 1992), pp. 189–208.

Otley, C.B., "The Social Origins of British Army Officers," *Sociological Review,* 8:213–39 (1970).

Pakenham, Thomas, *The scramble for Africa : the White man's Conquest of the Dark Continent from 1876 to 1912* (New York : Random House, 1991).

Paillard, Yvan G., "The French Expedition to Madagascar in 1895: Program and Results," in J. A. de Moor and H.L. Wesseling , *Imperialism and War* (Leiden: Brill, 1989), pp, 168–88.

Pankhurst, Richard, "Ethiopia and Somalia," UNESCO, *General History of Africa: Africa in the Nineteenth Century until the 1880s* (London, Heinemann, 1989), 6:376–411.

Parish, Henry James, *A History of Immunization* (London, 1965).

Park, Mungo, *Travels in the Interior Districts of Africa* (London, 1799).

Parkes, Edmund Alexander, "Review of the Progress of Hygiene During the Year 1861," AMSR for 1860, 2:343–367.

Person, Yves, *Samori: une révolution Dyula,* 3 vols. (Dakar: Ifan-Dakar, 1968–)

Piot Bey, J.B., "L'eau d'alimentation dans les villes du Caire et d'Alexandre," AMPM, 33(3rd ser):487–96 (1895)

Pluchon, Pierre, *Histoire des médecins et pharmaciens de marine et des colonies* (Paris: Privat, 1985).

Plouzané, Edouard François, *Contribution à l'étude d'hygiène pratique des troupes européenes dans les pays intertropicaux: Haut Sénégal et Haut Niger* (Bordeaux, Thesis no., 89, 1887).

Poirier, Jules, *Campagne du Dahomey, 1892–1894* (Paris, 1895).

Preston, Adrian, "Wolseley, the Khartoum Relief Expeditiohn and the Defence of India, 1885–1900," *Journal of Imperial and Commonwealth History,* 6:254–80 (1979).

Priestley, Margaret, *West African Trade and Coast Society; a Family Study* (London, Oxford University Press, 1969).

Primet, "Rapport sur l'épidémie de fièvre jaune au Soudan," AMN, 59:241–56, 357–77, 443–67; 60:16–42 (1893).

Pulvenis, Claude, "Une épidemie de fièvre jaune (Saint-Louis du Sénégal, 1881)" Bulletin de l'IFAN, 30 B:1353–73 (1968).

Rainero, Roman H., "The Battle of Adowa on 1st March 1896: A Reappraisal," in J.A. de Moor and H. L. Wesseling (eds.), Imperialism and War: Essays on Colonial Wars in Asia and Africa (Leiden: Brill, 1989), pp. 189–200.

Raison-Jourde, Françoise, Bible et pouvoir à Madagascar aux XIXe siècle: invention d'une identité chretienne et construction de l'état (Paris, Editions Karthala, 1991).

Ranchot, M., "L'expédition de Madagascar: journal de M. Ranchot, 11 avril – 8 octobre, 1895," Revue de l'histoire des colonies, 18:337–506 (1930).

Rangé, M.L.C., "Rapport médical sur le service de santé du corps expéditionnaire d'occupation du Bénin," AMN, 61:26–62, 90–109, 174–92, 262–84 (1894).

Reade, Winwood, The Story of the Ashantee Campaign (London, 1874).

Reynaud, Gustave A., Considerations sanitaires sur l'expédition de Madagascar et quelques autres expéditions coloniales, françaises et anglaises (Paris, 1898).

Rochefort, E., "Étude médicale sur l'expédition anglaise contre les ashantis," AMN, 21:321–46 (1874).

"Egypte," Dictionaire encyclopédique des sciences médicales, 33(lst ser.):1–33 (1886), pp. 23–50.

"Tunisie," DESM, 18(3rd ser.):597–408.

Rogers, E., Campaigning in West Africa: The Ashantee Invasion (London, 1874).

Ross, David, "Dahomey," in Michael Crowder (ed.), West African Resistance. The Military Response to Colonial Occupation (London: Hutchinson, 1971), pp. 144–69.

Rubensen, Sven, King of Kings: Tewodros of Ethiopia (Addis Ababa and Nairobi, Oxford University Press, 1966)

"Ethiopia and the Horn," in John E. Flint (ed.) Cambridge History of Africa. Volume 5 (Cambridge: Cambridge University Press, 1976), pp. 51–98.

Russel, Frederick F., "Anti-Typhoid Vaccination," American Journal of Medical Science, 146:803–33 (1913).

Salanoue-Ipin, "Notes sur les causes d'insalubrité des casernements et établissements militaires de Tananarive," AHMC, 14:27–39 (1911).

Sanderson, G.N., "The Nile Basin and the Eastern Horn, 1870–1908," in The Cambridge History of Africa (Cambridge: Cambridge University Press, 1985), 6:592–631.

Severini, C., D. Fontenille, and M.R. Ramiakajato, "Importance d'Anopheles funestus dans la transmission du paludisme au hameau de Mahitsy, à Tananarive, Madagascar," Bulletin de la sociéteéde pathologie exotique, 83:114–16 (1990).

Schefer, Christian, "La question de Madagascar," Nouvelle Revue, 92: 660–78 (1895).

Sheriff, Abdul, Slaves, Spices & Ivory in Zanzibar: Integration of an East African Commercial Empire into the World Economy, 1770–1873 (London: James Currey, 1987).

Shick, Tom W., "A Quantiative Analysis of Liberian Colonization from 1820 to 1843 with Special Reference to Mortality," JAH, 12:45–59 (1971).

Schnapper, Bernard, La politique et le commerce francais dans le golfe de Guinee, de 1838 a 1871 (Paris: Mouton, 1961).

Schölch, Alexander, Egypt for the Egyptians: The Socio-Political Crisis in Egypt, 1878–1882 (London, 1981).

Shaw, George Bernard, Bernard Shaw, "Preface on Doctors," The Doctor's Dilemma, Getting Married, and The Shewing-up of Blanco Posnet (New York: Brentano's, 1911).

Shepherd, A.F., The Campaign in Abyssinia (Bombay: Times of India Office, 1868)

Shryock, R.H., "Nineteenth-Century Medicine: Scientific Aspects," Journal of World History, 3:881–908 (1957).

Smith, Dale C., "The Rise and Fall of Typhomalarial Fever," Journal of the History of Medicine, 37:182–220, 287–321 (1982).

"Introduction," in William Budd, On the Causes of Fevers (1839) (Baltimore: Johns Hopkins University Press, 1984), pp. 1–39. Edited by Dale C. Smith

Spiers, Edward M., The Late Victorian Army 1868–1902 (Manchester: Manchester University Press, 1992).

Stanley, Henry Morton, Coomassie and Magdala: The Story of Two British Campaigns in Africa (London, 1874).

Steevens, G.W., With Kitchener to Khartoum (Edinburgh: Blackwell, 1898).

Stone, Mary, "The Plumbing Paradox," Winterthur Portfolia, 14:292, 284 (1979).

Strachan, Hew, European Armies and the Conduct of War (London, Allen and Unwin, 1983).

Tarr, Joel A., James McCurley, and Terry F. Yosie, "The Development and Impact of Urban

Waste Technology: Changing Concepts of Water Quality Control, 1850–1930, in Marton V. Melosi (ed.), *Population and Reform in American Cities, 1870–1930* (Austin: University of Texas Press, 1980), pp. 74–78

Tarr, Joel A., James McCurley III, Francis C. McMichael, and Terry Yosie, "Water and Wastes: A Retrospective Assessmenmt of Wastewater Technology in the United States, 1800–1932," *Technology and Culture*, 25:226–63 (1984).

Taverna, E., "Un detail des expéditions coloniales: le service du train dans la campagne des Anglais en Abyssinie (1867–68)," *Journal des sciences militaries*, 63 (9th series):185–210 (1896).

Taylor, W., "Report of the Medical Transactions of the Ashanti Expeditionary Force During the Period from 14th December 1895 to 7th February 1896," AMSR, 38:300–15 (1896).

"Report on the Medical Transactions of the British Troops of the Nile Expeditionary Force, from 4th January 1898 to 10th October, 1898," AMSR, 30:436–461.

Temperley, Howard, *White Dreams, Black Africa: The Antislavery Expedition to the River Niger 1841–1842* (New Haven: Yale University Press, 1991).

Thévenot, Jean Pierre Ferdinand, *Traité des maladies des Européens dans les pays chaud, et specialement au Sénégal, ou essai statistique, médicale et hygiènique sur le sol, le climat et les maladies de cette partie de l'Afrique* (Paris, 1840).

Thompson, J. Malcolm, "Dissemination Camps and Disease Foyers: Military Quarantine and the 'Contaminated' African in Colonial Senegal, 1878–1883," (Unpublished paper presented. African Studies Association, Toronto, 1994).

Thomson, T.R.H., "On the Value of Quinine in African Remittant Fever," *Lancet*, 1846, 1, pp. 244–45 (28 February).

Torres, A., "Algo sobre el servicio de sanidad militar en el ejército de la Argelia y expedicionario de Tunez," *Gacetta de sandidad militar*, 7:545–552 (1881).

Ukpabi, S.C. "West Indian Troops and the Defense of British West Africa in the Nineteenth Century," *African Studies Review*, 18:33–50 (1974).

Ubaeyi, Paul Mmegna, *British Military and Naval Forces in West African History, 1807–1874* (New York: Nok, 1978)

Vidal, "Contribution à l'étude de l'immunité de la race arabe à l'égard de la fièvre typhoïde,"AMPM, 42:438–443 (1903).

Vincent, H., "Sur l'immunité de la race arabe à l'égard de la fièvre typhoïde," AMPM, 37:145–52 (1901).

Vincent, Henri, and Louis Muratet, *Typhoid Fever and Paratyphoid Fevers (Symptomatology, Etiology and Phophylaxis)* (London: University of London Press, 1917).

Vincent, Jacques, *La fièvre jaune (épidémies de 1878 et de 1881 au Sénégal)* (Montpellier, Grollier et Fios, 1883, thesis no. 47).

Vincent, M., and F. Burot, "Paludisme à Madagascar," *Revue scientifique*, 18 juillet 1896, pp. 75–81.

V.F., "Médecine coloniale. Le service de santé de Madagascar," *Médecine moderne*, 6:27–28 (12 January 1895).

Ward, E.W.D., "To Kumassi and Back with the Ashanti Expeditionary Force 1895–96," *Journal of the Royal Service Institution*, 40:1021–1030 (August 1896).

Ward, W.E.F., *A History of the Gold Coast* (London: Allen and Unwin, 1948).

Warren, J., "Notes on Enteric Fever at Ramleh," AMSR, 1881,pp. 287–88

Wesselling, Henri L., "Les guerres coloniales et la paix armée, 1871–1914: esquisse pour une étude comparative, " in *Etudes en l'honneur de Jean-Louis Miège* (Aix-en-Provence: Publications de l'universitée de Provence, 1992), 1:105–126.

Wilks, Ivor, *Asante in the Nineteenth Century* (Cambridge: Cambridge University Press, 1975).

Willcocks, James, *From Kabul to Kumasi* (London, 1904).

Williams, C. Theodore, "The Winter Climate of Egypt," BMJ, 1896, 1, pp. 669–70.

Wolseley, Garnet, *A Soldier's Pocket Book for Field Service*, 5th ed. (1886).

Wright, A.E., "Note on the Results Obtained by the Anti-Typhoid Inoculations in Egypt and Cyprus during the Year 1900," *Lancet*, 1, 1272 (May 4).

Wright, A.E., and W.B. Leishman, "Remarks on the Results which Have Been Obtained by the Antityphoid Inoculations . . ." BMJ, 1900, 1, , p. 122–29 (January 20)

Zuber, M. C., "Histoire médicale de la campagne des Anglais en Egypte," AMPM, 5:227–, 275– (1884).

INDEX

Abakrampa, 58
Abbasiyeh barracks, 133
'Abdallahi bin Muhammad, Khalifa, 167, 195
Aboasa, battle of, 100
Abomey, 105
Abu Hamad, 195
Abyssinia, *see* Ethiopia
Accra, 50, 96
Aden, 34, 106
Adwa, 185, 195
Aëdes aegypti, 9–11, 18–19, 79–82
Afghanistan, 150, 171, 210
African Association, see Association for Promoting the Discovery of the Interior Parts of Africa
African soldiers in European service: morality rates of, 101, 109, 191–93; recruitment of, 16–18; reputation of, 56–57; *see also* tirailleurs sénégalais, tirailleurs algérien, West India Regiments
Afro-Americans, 3, 15; disease immunities in Africa, 53
Afro-Arabs, 34–35
Afro-Brazilians, 94
Afro-Europeans, 2
Agyeman Prempeh, 96, 99–100
Ahmad 'Urabi, see 'Urabi Pasha
Ajuda, see Ouidah,
Akan ethnic group, 50
Akyem, 55
Alexandria, 139, 148, 156, 166, 199, 213; cholera 130, 197; typhoid deaths, 130–34
Alexandria water company, 130–34
Algeria, 22, 23, 74, 75, 89, 98, 105, 118 , 180, 183, 204, 225; disease profiles of troops, 142; malaria, 26; mortality of troops,140–47; racial immunities considered, 138–40; *see also* Oran campaign of 1881–82
Algiers, 139
Amadu Seku, 83
amebic dysentery, 11
American Civil War, 31, 37, 88, 150

Amery, Leo, 203
Amhara ethnic group, 175
Amharic language, 29n
Anaba, 151
Andes mountains, 23
Andrianampoinimerina, 186
Andriba,186
Anglo-Asante Wars, 50, 52–53; *see also* Asante Campaigns of 1874, 1895, 1900
Anglo-Boer War of 1899–1902, 124, 149, 185; concentration camps in, 203, 215–17; military events, 201–05; public reaction to, 210–04, 218–26; typhoid fever in, 205–10
Anglo-Boer War of 1881–82, 167, 203, 207
Annesley Bay, *see* Zula
Anopheles arabiensis, 6, 87, 177–81
Anopheles funestus, 6, 20–21, 177–81
Anopheles gambiae, 20–21, 87, 177–81
Anopheles melas, 21
Antananarivo, 183, 186
Antsiranana, see Diego-Suarez
Arabia, 34
Arabian Sea, 34–5
Archinard, Louis, 76, 86
Armitage, C.H., 110
Asante campaign of 1824–26, 49, 52
Asante campaign of 1874, 27, 29, 30, 89. 98, 171, 181, 220–21, 229–30; British background of, 54–55; comparisons with other campaigns, 78, 92, 186; military operations, 55–60; public understanding of, 30
Asante campaign of 1896, 75, 99–100, 105–09; public reaction to, 110–12
Asante campaign of 1900, 75, 99–100, 108–10
Asante kingdom: armament, 31; disease problems, 51; political affairs 1872–1890s, 96
Ash, R. Vacy, 167
Assin, 56
Assinie, 22; French evacuation of, 50
Association for Promoting the Discovery of the Interior Parts of Africa, 13
Aswan, 130